Places of
Encounter
VOLUME II

Places of Encounter in Global Perspective

Places of
Encounter

Time, Place, and Connectivity in World History

VOLUME II

ARAN MACKINNON

ELAINE MACKINNON

EDITORS

Westview
PRESS

A Member of the Perseus Books Group

WESTVIEW PRESS was founded in 1975 in Boulder, Colorado, by notable publisher and intellectual Fred Praeger. WESTVIEW PRESS continues to publish scholarly titles and high-quality undergraduate- and graduate-level textbooks in core social science disciplines. With books developed, written, and edited with the needs of serious nonfiction readers, professors, and students in mind, WESTVIEW PRESS honors its long history of publishing books that matter.

Published by WESTVIEW PRESS,
A Member of the Perseus Books Group

Find us on the World Wide Web at *www.westviewpress.com.*

Every effort has been made to secure required permissions for all text, images, maps, and other art reprinted in this volume.

WESTVIEW PRESS books are available at special discounts for bulk purchases in the United States by corporations, institutions, and other organizations. For more information, please contact the Special Markets Department at the Perseus Books Group, 2300 Chestnut Street, Suite 200, Philadelphia, PA 19103, or call (800) 810-4145, ext. 5000, or e-mail special.markets@perseusbooks.com.

Editorial production by Lori Hobkirk at the Book Factory.
Typeset in 9.5 Plantin by Cynthia Young at Sagecraft.

Places of encounter : time, place and connectivity in world history / Aran MacKinnon, Elaine MacKinnon, editors.
    v. cm.
  Includes bibliographical references and index.
    ISBN 978-0-8133-4737-0 (v. 1)—ISBN 978-0-8133-4738-7 (v. 1 : ebook)—
    ISBN 978-0-8133-4739-4 (v. 2)—ISBN 978-0-8133-4740-0 (v. 2 : ebook)
    1. World history. 2. World history—Sources. 3. Cities and towns—History. 4. Cities and towns—History—Sources. 5. Social change—History. 6. Social change—History—Sources. 7. Cultural relations—History. 8. Cultural relations—History—Sources.
  I. MacKinnon, Aran S. II. McClarnand MacKinnon, Elaine.
  D21.3.P56 2012
  909—dc23

                                   2012000612

All maps have been created by International Mapping.

10 9 8 7 6 5 4 3 2 1

Aran MacKinnon dedicates Places of Encounter
to his co-editor/author and wife, Elaine,
whose shared love for South Africa inspired this project,
and to their fellow traveler, Kieran.

Contents

VOLUME II

List of Features

Maps

Primary Documents' Credits

Chapter 1

Thom, H. B., ed. *Journal of Jan Van Riebeeck*, Vol. III, 1659–1662. A. A. Balkema for Van Riebeeck Society: Cape Town, Amsterdam, 1954. Used with permission by the Van Riebeeck Society.

Chapter 3

Kaempfer's Japan is excerpted from Engelbert Kaempfer, *Kaempfer's Japan: Tokugawa Culture Observed*, ed. and trans. Beatrice M. Bodart-Bailey (Honolulu: University of Hawai'i Press, 1999), 362, 409, 413. Copyright ©1999 University of Hawaii Press. Reprinted with permission.

Japan: The Dutch Experience is excerpted from Grant K. Goodman, *Japan: The Dutch Experience* (London and Dover, NH: The Athlone Press, 1986), 50, 112–113, 134. Originally published by Continuum.

Chapter 8

"Memorial: Xu Naizhao, Governor of Jiangsu, Reports on British, Americans, and Frenchmen at Shanghai during the Small Swords Uprising," is excerpted from Earl Swisher, *China's Management of the American Barbarians: A Study of Sino-American Relations, 1841–1861, with Documents* (New Haven: Yale University for the Far Eastern Association and Far Eastern Publications, 1953), 203–204.

Chapter 9

The Wretched of the Earth is excerpted from Frantz Fanon, *The Wretched Earth* (New York: Grove/Atlantic), copyright © 1963 by *Présence Africaine*. Used by permission of Grove/Atlantic, Inc.

Chapter 11

"Resolution on the Crisis of Authority and the Current Moment" is excerpted from Mark D. Steinbert, *Voices of Revolution*, 1917 (New Haven: Yale University Press, 2001), 189–190. Documents translated by Marian Schwartz. Copyright © 2001 Yale University Press. Reprinted with permission.

Chapter 13

"East Germans Lost Much in 1989" is excerpted from Bruni de la Motte, "East Germans Lost Much in 1989," *The Guardian*, November 8, 2009, www.guardian.co.uk/commentisfree/2009/nov/08/1989-berlin-wall. Copyright © Guardian News & Media LTD 2009.

Chapter 15

"Human Rights Watch Letter to UAE Minister of Labor" is excerpted from
    "Building Towers, Cheating Workers: Appendix 1: Human Rights Watch Letter to
    UAE Minister of Labor," July 14, 2006, www.hrw.org/en/node/11123/section/10.
    Copyright © 2006 by Human Rights Watch.

About the Contributors

Eliza Ablovatski
Eliza Ablovatski is an associate professor of history at Kenyon College. After earning her PhD in East Central European History from Columbia University, she spent two years in Berlin as a fellow at the Center for Comparative European History and the Wissenschaftszentrum Berlin.

Jonathan E. Brooke
Jonathan Brooke is an assistant professor of history at William Carey University, where he teaches courses on world history, imperialism, and social studies education, and is currently researching missionary printing presses in India. He has made numerous trips to Calcutta and other parts of India, studying the British presence there as well as local missionary and church history.

Julia Clancy-Smith
Julia Clancy-Smith is a professor of history at the University of Arizona, where she teaches courses on North Africa, the Middle East, and Islam, as well as women's and world history. She has just published a monograph, *Mediterraneans: North Africa and Europe in an Age of Migration, c. 1800–1900* (University of California Press). Clancy-Smith is currently finishing a book on the history of French colonial education. Her first encounters with North Africa were in 1971 as a student, and then in 1973 and 1974 as a Peace Corps volunteer. She has been returning to the region regularly for research ever since.

Lane Earns
Dr. Lane Earns is a provost and vice chancellor, as well as a professor of history, at the University of Wisconsin Oshkosh. He earned his MA in Asian Studies and PhD in history from the University of Hawaii at Manoa. Between 1974 and 1986, he spent a year as a researcher at the University of Tokyo and lived and worked in Nagasaki for five years, a place to which he has returned annually since his arrival in Oshkosh in 1987. In addition to his responsibilities as provost and numerous publications on Nagasaki's historical and cultural relations with the outside world, he teaches classes on traditional and modern Japan.

Christopher Ebert
Christopher Ebert is an associate professor of history at Brooklyn College/CUNY, where he teaches courses in Latin American and Atlantic history. He has traveled to many archives in Brazil and Europe researching his latest book, a social and economic history of Salvador da Bahia, colonial Brazil's first capital.

Edward J. Erickson

Dr. Edward J. Erickson is an associate professor of military history at the Marine Corps Command and Staff College in Quantico, Virginia, where he teaches the Operational Art course. He served in Turkey for many years while in the US Army, and he is the author of numerous books about the Gallipoli campaign and the First World War.

Trevor R. Getz

Trevor R. Getz is a professor of history at San Francisco State University, where he teaches classes on the ethics, methods, and philosophy of African history. He has taught and studied at three African universities and used to take study breaks from the National Archives of Senegal by taking the ferry to Gorée to watch the sunset with a calico cat who made its home on the island.

Didier Gondola

Didier Gondola is a professor of history and Africana Studies at Indiana University-Purdue University in Indianapolis and the author of several books and articles on popular cultures and the African diaspora in France. He is currently based at the Institute for Advanced Studies in Nantes (France), where he is completing a manuscript on cowboy films, colonial violence, and masculinity in Kinshasa, Congo.

Charles Lipp

Charles Lipp is an assistant professor of history at the University of West Georgia, where he teaches classes on issues ranging from world history to early modern Europe to French America. His research focuses upon the connections between society and political formation in Europe during the seventeenth and eighteenth centuries. He recently coedited a collection of essays entitled *Contested Spaces of Nobility in Early Modern Europe* (Ashgate), and completed a monograph entitled *Noble Strategies in an Early Modern Small State: The Mahuet of Lorraine* (University of Rochester Press).

Aran S. MacKinnon

Dr. Aran S. MacKinnon is a professor of history and director of the Center for Interdisciplinary Studies at the University of West Georgia. He is the author of *The Making of South Africa* (Prentice Hall) and coauthor of an *Introduction to Global Studies* (Wiley-Blackwell), as well as numerous scholarly articles on South African history. He earned a PhD from the University of London and an MA in history from the University of KwaZulu-Natal in South Africa, where he lived and taught for over four years. He currently teaches courses on South African, African, and world history, as well as global studies.

Elaine McClarnand MacKinnon

Elaine MacKinnon is a professor of Russian and Soviet History at the University of West Georgia. She is the translator and editor of *Mass Uprisings in the USSR* (ME Sharpe), and has written an array of journal articles, book chapters, and review essays on Russian and Soviet history. She earned her MA and PhD in modern European history at Emory University, and she currently teaches courses on world history, Russian and Soviet history, and the Cold War.

Neema Noori

Neema Noori is an assistant professor of sociology at the University of West Georgia, where he teaches courses on globalization, political sociology, state and society in the Middle East, social theory, and urban sociology. He is currently involved in research on the social and political implications of the proliferation of American-style universities in the Middle East. He spent three years teaching at the American University of Sharjah, located in the United Arab Emirates.

Dana Rabin

Dana Rabin is an associate professor of history at the University of Illinois, Urbana-Champaign, where she teaches courses in British history, global history, and the history of crime. Her current project examines themes of empire, race, and gender as they played out in legal events throughout the eighteenth century. She lived in London for two years and has spent many summers there.

Christopher A. Reed

Christopher A. Reed is an associate professor of Chinese history at The Ohio State University, where he teaches Qing, Republican, and People's Republic history, including courses on treaty-port Shanghai (1842–1949). His book *Gutenberg in Shanghai: Chinese Print Capitalism, 1876–1937* (University of British Columbia Press, 2004) examines China's modern printing and publishing media industries and was awarded the 2003–2005 ICAS (Humanities) Book Prize. He has lived in China and Taiwan for a total of five years, including two years in Shanghai from 1991 to 1993. He is married to the artist Leah Lihua Wong.

Gregory Smithsimon

Gregory Smithsimon is an assistant professor of sociology at Brooklyn College, City University of New York. He is the author of *September 12: Community and Neighborhood Recovery at Ground Zero* (New York University Press), about Lower Manhattan after September 11, 2001. He is also author, with Benjamin Shepard, of *The Beach Beneath the Streets: Contesting New York City's Public Spaces* (State University of New York Press), which examines privatization and resistance in the city's parks, streets, and plazas.

Preface

Note to the Student

Welcome to *Places of Encounter*. This text offers a new approach to learning about world history by taking you to the places where major developments in our past have occurred. Each chapter is designed to send you on a journey to a specific location associated with momentous historical events and epochs. Both volumes of this text are inspired by our desire to share with you the passion we have for the places we study and conduct our research as historians. We want to convey the excitement we feel in the places where major changes in human history occurred. Like you, we started learning the stories of our past as readers. We too discovered that we are connected to many places in the world through our common human ancestry and through the interactions of people and societies over time and across the globe. We wondered what it would be like to travel back in time to the places we read about but could only imagine. We realized that being in a historical place unlocks a portal to the past and allows us to see the intersections of land, environments, and human structures that lie at the heart of historical processes.

Themes

Places is organized around three main principles: change over time, connectivity, and the recurrence of certain themes throughout human history.

- To show change over time, the text offers a basic chronological sequence of history that begins in Volume I with the emergence of hominids (early humans) in Ethiopia and ends in Volume II with the emergence of the global, postindustrial city of Dubai in the United Arab Emirates. The volumes cover important turning points in human history, from the formation of the earliest human communities and towns through the foundation of cities, states, and empires and the development of industrialization, to the emergence of postindustrial globalization.

- To demonstrate the second principle, connectivity, both volumes present individual locations as part of a global nexus of historical and geographic connections. Each chapter identifies key regional and global connections among societies, places, peoples, and eras, demonstrating that world history is very much about connections and interactions across time and space. Each place in these volumes developed through linkages to previous historical eras and in turn shaped future historical actors and movements. Geography and environment also shaped the links people forged. In some cases, these links were regional—connecting people along a coastline with others in the interior, as in Cape Town, South Africa, or within areas of oceanic trade in the Atlantic or Indian oceans. In other cases global connections spanned outward from major urban centers such as Carthage or London in search of resources, territory, and labor, building land- and sea-based empires in the process.

Similarly, technologies in the form of ships, airplanes, and even rocket-propelled weapons provided for global strands of connectivity.

- Third, the text emphasizes significant thematic elements that recur in human history. History is so vast that, in order to find some meaning in it, historians study it through different lenses or viewpoints that reflect what we deem important in our own lives. In *Places* we have emphasized themes that include migration (where and why people moved around the continent or globe); class, race, ethnicity, and gender (how humans form social and economic identities); urbanization and colonialism (how they organized themselves spatially and politically); and technology, trade, and commerce (what they built and the values they placed on those things). In the thematic table of contents you'll see all these major themes and which chapters emphasize which themes.

Overall, as you will see, the picture of our past that emerges from these volumes is like a satellite map of the world at night: as a particular place becomes important, it glows and then fades as another location takes preeminence. Like a mosaic with endless links connecting the different locations, *Places* spotlights individual pieces, inextricably linked to the others, together making up the picture of each epoch. *Places* will show you a picture of history not as a simple sequential process but rather a dynamic, multitextured combination of overlapping eras—like overlapping notes in a musical chord. We hope you will appreciate the chapters both individually and collectively, as they provide a broader landscape of the ways people and places interacted to shape our past.

Reading and Using Places of Encounter

Places is intended to allow you to engage with history in various locations around the world, even if you cannot actually be there. When you've studied history before, it was probably narrated like a story, with one event following another in a linear way. Instead of telling a linear story, this book uses place-based history to illustrate the past. If you have ever visited a historical site like an old house or a historic location like a battlefield, you're familiar with place-based history. The chapters are organized similarly:

- **A Personal Prologue** outlines the author's personal engagement with the place—how he or she came to be interested in that particular place and why. Consider how and why the authors found their passion in a particular place and time. Do you have a similar interest in a historical place or have you been inspired by a visit or tour to a historical monument marking an important political, religious, or cultural event that happened there? Perhaps you've visited a location where your ancestors lived or emigrated?

- **The main narrative of the chapter** introduces the place in a particular time. Understanding the historical context—including geographic and environmental features; available technologies and skills; and ethnicity, language, gender, nationalism, and religious beliefs—is essential to understanding the history of the place you are reading about. Imagine, for example, what your life would be like without cars or computers (technology), or how your life would be different if you lived in a society where some people were enslaved due to their race, gender, or ethnic background.

- **The Global Connections** section of the chapter shows the linkages of this place and time with other parts of the region or the world as well as how this chapter relates to the chapters that come before and after. Because human encounters are often the precursors to historic developments as a result of the exchange of ideas and goods or the clash of cultural and religious beliefs, these connections tell the story of this place's role in world history.

- **The Encounters as Told: Primary Sources** section gives you a chance to read firsthand accounts about those human encounters in the sources they left behind. These sources range from travelogues and diaries to government documents and treatises related to historical developments. Questions and notes at the beginning of each document will help you explore the relationship between the documents and the chapter narrative. You will also need to consider the context of the documents by asking questions such as, Who wrote the document and who was the intended audience? What was the writer's intent—to write a newspaper article, a government document, a propaganda piece, or something else? What sorts of things are left out or hidden in the document? Are women or indigenous people mentioned, and in what context? How do the writer's gender and socioeconomic class compare to those of the people mentioned in the document? What sorts of biases can you see in the source? How does the document help you better understand the chapter you just read? Does it refer to the physical place or perhaps to different people in the location? Does it depict people or place positively or not?

- **Maps** will show you the relationship of the place to the rest of the world and the region with which it is associated as well as the important spatial features that are referred to in the body of the chapter.

- Finally, each chapter provides a list of **additional resources** divided into two main categories. The first is further reading resources authors have recommended. Although these are not an exhaustive list of what other historians have written on the topic, they will enable you to get a deeper, more detailed understanding of some of the key developments that occurred in each location and to consider why these places are so important to world history. The second is a list of Internet URLs or web page references. These websites provide important visual materials and discussion of related ideas and analyses, and they are well worth exploring. Although you may not be able to travel to every place in the text, the chapters and secondary readings and recommended secondary resources may be the next best thing, providing you with significant insight into these places and the important roles they played. We hope that *Places of Encounter* will inspire you to ask questions of the past and the places in which it took shape as well as to undertake your own journeys of discovery to visit some of these locations—and others—that are part of the living history of our world.

Read on, and may you find the world to be as exciting a place as we and our fellow authors do!

Aran and *Elaine MacKinnon,* editors

To the Instructor

Welcome to *Places of Encounter*. This text provides a unique approach to world history. It is designed to allow students to experience the places where major developments took shape and to feel the excitement that comes from imagining historical events as and where they happened. It is inspired by the connections the authors have to the locations they have studied and visited as well as their belief that students share their excitement about world history as they are introduced to these places. It builds on well-established approaches to writing history by situating stories in a specific place to show how the local experience can be relevant to broader global experiences. It also goes beyond these studies by taking advantage of new approaches in environmental and place-based history. These approaches emphasize the importance of the historical and imagined relations between people and the land, and they show how these can be understood by considering the connections people make between place and the past. Additionally, *Places of Encounter* takes these place-based relationships and connects them to the wider currents of global history. Each chapter shows the reader how and where its place is connected temporally and spatially to other historically significant regions and developments. In these ways it seeks to provide students and instructors with both new perspectives and new tools for looking at major developments in world history.

The text is divided into two volumes, one for each of the major chronological blocks of time that are most often taught in two-term courses at college and universities. (For courses with different chronological breaks, each chapter is also available in digital form so that the book can be easily customized to fit every course.)

Places of Encounter can be assigned in at least two ways. First, by supplementing the content with lecture material, instructors can assign *Places* as a main text, guiding students along the overall arc of chronological history through the chapter progression. Volume I begins this progression with the emergence of modern humans in Hadar, Ethiopia, and South Africa, and then it takes the students through the development of early settled human communities and urban complexes in Mesopotamia, China, and the Mediterranean. It shows how and where trade-based societies and their cultures emerged and made connections in the Middle East, Africa, and Europe, and how these then connected to the emergence of imperial ventures and global commercial connections from Europe to the Americas and elsewhere on the globe.

The arc continues in Volume II and guides students through the early-modern period of burgeoning empires and the expansion of merchant-capitalism in the Atlantic world and Asia to the emergence of major industrial metropoles in Europe and East Asia. It then turns to the era of competition and conflict through the World Wars and into the global Cold War, ending with the era of intensified decolonization, globalization, and urbanization.

Alternatively, the volumes can be used to supplement a traditional survey text. The place-based approach allows for more detailed studies of the major developments and themes addressed in a survey textbook, providing a foundation for discussion and analysis of multiple topics and themes for each location. The primary source documents, called "Encounters as Told," can be the foundation for primary sources analyses in class.

Chapters have a consistent structure, including the following components (described in the Note to the Student, above):

- **Personal Prologue** discusses the author's personal connection to the place, often including the author's own physical and cultural encounters with the locality and its people.

- **The Chapter Narrative** explains how and why particular places became important. Additionally, they provide a compelling and focused case study of how the local environment intersects with major historical developments.

- **Global Connections** in each chapter show how broader regional and global developments are tied to various places that were central to specific historical eras and movements.

- **Maps** show the relationship of the place to the rest of the world and the region with which it is associated as well as the important spatial features that are referred to in the body of the chapter.

- **Encounters as Told: Primary Sources** provide opportunities for students to consider voice, biases, and agency in history.

- **Further Reading and Web Resources** provide more detail on select topics as well as ways to further explore the location in the context of the latest historiographical approaches to the field.

Places is organized to be flexible and can be used in a number of ways:

1. Most obviously, successive chapters can be assigned in the rough chronological order the book reflects. Each chapter then shows how broader regional and global connections and developments are tied to various nodes, places that were central to specific historical developments. Thus, the chapters help explain how and why particular places became important. Additionally, they provide a compelling and focused case study of how the local environment intersects with major historical movements.

2. Because the chapters are based around a series of major themes, an instructor might choose to cut across chronology and follow these categories of analysis across time and space. The thematic table of contents shows the thematic connections among chapters. Instructors can select one or more themes to revisit as they move through the world history sequence to see how these themes differed from place to place and over time. For example, students can compare and contrast how people interacted with their environments as early hominids in Ethiopia and as globalized investors developing real estate in Dubai. Alternatively, chapters can be selected to supplement the instructor's own lectures or a traditional text.

3. The regional table of contents shows which chapters touch on which global regions. A list of regional connections provides the possibility of showing students how various locations intersect and influence each other. As with many approaches to world history, we believe the links and contingencies among societies and regions are fundamental to understanding world history. Each chapter, therefore, makes explicit links to other chapters, regions, and time periods as well as to broader developments that relate to a given region.

4. *Places of Encounters* takes advantage of exciting new Internet-based technologies to enhance the ways students can see and engage with the chapter locations. Each chapter concludes with suggested websites. Using Google Earth, readers can see the geographical location in a global context and may use Google Earth tours to see more details about particular places.

We would like to thank the many reviewers whose careful reading of the chapters provided helpful insights to make this book a better fit for their classrooms:

Brett Berliner, Morgan State University

Gayle K. Brunelle, California State University, Fullerton

Samuel Brunk, University of Texas at El Paso

Alister Chapman, Westmont College

Arthur T. Coumbe, Troy State University

Eugene Cruz-Oribe, California State University, Monterey Bay

Edward Davies, University of Utah

Margaret Handke, Minnesota State University, Mankato

Paul Hatley, Rogers State University

Andrew J. Kirkendall, Texas A & M University

Ari Daniel Levine, University of Georgia

Senya Lubisich, Citrus College

Harold Marcuse, University of California, Santa Barbara

David Meier, Dickinson State University

Chad Ross, East Carolina University

Quinn Slobodian, Wellesley College

Evan R. Ward, Brigham Young University

Jeffrey Wilson, California State University, Sacramento

Special thanks to the students in Eugene Cruz-Uribe's world history class at Cal State Monterey Bay, who read and evaluated chapters from the book.

Read and enjoy, and hopefully together we can inspire students to follow in our footsteps!

Aran and *Elaine MacKinnon*, editors

Volume II.
Regional Table of Contents

	Africa	Atlantic Ocean World	Europe	Indian Ocean World	Latin America	Mediterranean	Middle East	Southeast Asia	Pacific Ocean World
CAPE TOWN	X	X		X					
SALVADOR DA BAHIA		X			X				
NAGASAKI								X	X
LONDON		X	X						
GORÉE	X	X							
PARIS			X						
CALCUTTA				X				X	
SHANGHAI			X				X	X	
ALGIERS	X		X			X			
GALLIPOLI			X			X			
ST. PETERSBURG			X						
KINSHASA	X	X	X						
BERLIN:			X						
NEW YORK:		X							
DUBA				X			X		

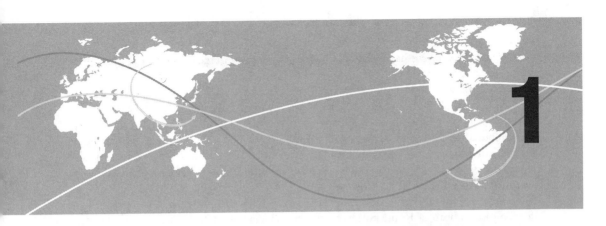

Cape Town

At the Cross-Currents of the
Atlantic and Indian Ocean Worlds

(1500–1800)

Aran S. MacKinnon

I FIRST BECAME FASCINATED WITH THE IMPORTANCE OF CAPE TOWN WHILE wandering the streets of the ancient port city of Melaka (Malacca), thousands of miles away in Malaysia. I was there en route to graduate school in South Africa. Meandering down a street, I came across the very rough and shabby-looking remains of an old fort. While scanning the sun-bleached bricks and stones that formed an archway, I spotted the unmistakable imprinted symbol of the *Vereenigde Oostindische Compagnie*, or VOC, the Dutch East India Company. Around the historic Dutch quarter of the town, I could visualize the entire grand design of the trading empire the VOC carved out in the seventeenth century. In that moment I realized the great significance of South Africa's Cape of Good Hope as the key stepping stone to the Indian Ocean world of spices, gems, timbers, teas, and other luxuries. Here lay the object of long-sought-after European commercial desires. But my passion for history remained focused on Africa, and I set off for Cape Town, where the VOC established an early foothold.

I am always struck by a profound sense of the convergence of historical and cultural forces in the Cape Town region. Like the Benguela ocean current pressing up from the Antarctic and the Agulhas current coursing down the Mozambican coast to meet it off

Cape Point, these forces have heaped a myriad of people and ideas together at the southern tip of the continent. People from around the world have long sought safe haven here, yet when I first arrived in South Africa in 1985, it was a country torn apart by racial and class conflict. P. W. Botha, state president of the whites-only government, had just extended a state of emergency in the Cape to further the clampdown on African, Indian, and Coloured (referring to people of mixed ethnic descent; collectively, all these groups were referred to as black) opposition to one of the world's most notorious racist regimes. Driving in from the airport, I could see township (the forcibly segregated areas designated for Africans) residents throwing rocks in protest at affluent whites as they passed by on their way into the whites-only city. As a white, I had the guilty privilege of staying in the beautiful suburb of Rondebosch, nestled in the shadow of Table Mountain. This was where Dutch East India company employees were first allowed to settle their own farms along the Liesbeek River. Rondebosch later served as a staging ground for the Boers (early white Dutch settlers, later known as Afrikaners) to penetrate African lands and displace the Khoe herders who had long lived in the region. A favorite weekend drive of mine, down to the Cape Point national wildlife refuge, took me past beautiful white-owned homes and vast shanty settlements where Africans struggled to eke out a living in fear of brutal police harassment. It also brought me near the infamous Pollsmoor prison where Nelson Mandela, then condemned by the white government as a terrorist but later celebrated as the country's first black president, was incarcerated. In my mind there was clearly much to be learned of this place and its history, where people from around the world had converged and clashed in their struggles with the land and each other. What continues to captivate me most about Cape Town is the way the place and the people invite you in to explore these convergences that are cast in such sharp relief in its history.

This chapter will highlight how Cape Town and its environs provided the setting for the bridging of the Atlantic and Indian Ocean worlds. It also shows how the powerful forces of white settlement and slavery had profound effects on African societies. The ensuing displacement and subordination of Africans and Asians set the stage for the later continent-wide intrusion of European colonialism. Other key themes in the chapter include the role of women in shaping society, the importance of the environment and how humans interacted with it, the construction of racial and ethnic identities, and the emergence of a cosmopolitan, globally connected society.

CAPE TOWN AND THE WORLD:
Cultural Blending in an Abundant Environment

Perhaps the best way to appreciate the global significance of Cape Town is to see its geographic location in relation to the region and the world. Cape Town is situated in a wide, sheltered bay on the western shore of the southernmost part of Africa. (See Map 1.1.) Some thirty-five miles further south is the famed Cape of Good Hope, so called by the Portuguese king John II (1455–1495) as an expression of his maritime country's aspirations to profit from trade in the Indian Ocean region beyond Africa. Just a mile or so to the east of that is Cape Point. Standing at the tip of Cape Point, one can look across False Bay and see the coastline of the great African continent stretching to the northeast. Although this point is not technically the southernmost tip of Africa, it is the symbolic geographic turning point for maritime travelers passing from the Atlantic world into the Indian Ocean circuit of trade. It is the same point ancient Phoenician mariners might have passed in a circumnavigation of the continent over 2,600 years ago. One cannot but be in awe of this historic geographic location.

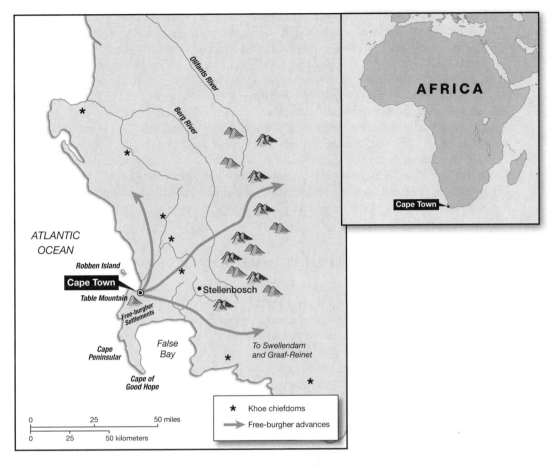

Map 1.1. Khoe Chiefdoms, ca. 1650

The Cape of Good Hope peninsula and environs have played host to a variety of people and societies. The local environment supported indigenous pastoral Khoe chiefdoms, which ranged over the coast and interior. The strategic location of the Cape later attracted Europeans seeking to connect to commercial opportunities in the Indian Ocean region. Thereafter, interdependence between whites and Africans gave way to conflict and the emergence of one of the world's most unequal societies.

The terrain surrounding Cape Town is among the most impressive and ruggedly beautiful in the world, boasting magnificent mountains and seaside cliffs; the pounding surf of the wild southern oceans; the arid, scrubby interior of the Karoo Desert; and the well-watered and fertile valleys where wine making and citrus growing abound. The weather alternates between warm, dry, Mediterranean summers and wind-lashing cool rains in the winter, justifying both of the region's nicknames: Cape of Storms and the Fairest Cape. Local lore speaks of healthful air to breathe, maintained by strong winds that blow away accumulated haze. On the top of majestic Table Mountain, which dominates Cape Town as a massive geological backdrop, a delicate ecosystem persists, with over nine thousand species of plants. It is one of the world's most diverse vegetation zones. At the base of the mountain, the shores of Table Bay provide a safe harbor, endless beaches, forested *kloofs* (valleys), and the setting for one of the world's most fascinating human stories. It was here, in Cape Town itself, where Africans gathered and held councils, passing ships left letters under a white-washed stone to be gathered by sailors for delivery as they returned to other ports of call, and a myriad of peoples, economic systems, cultures, and historical aspirations converged. It also became, for better and worse, the gateway for the intrusion of European imperialism and settlers into southern Africa.

This dynamic synthesis of nature is mirrored in the human landscape. The built city bears the unmistakable imprint of Dutch and British colonial architecture, and African styles are found everywhere, but there is also a powerful underlying Asian influence, with a blending of Malay and Islamic cultures. The cuisine also highlights the syncretism (the social blending of cultures and people) of African, Asian, and European influences. The classic Cape Malay dish, bobotie, is accented with curry powder and raisins. Everywhere I looked, the creolized fashions, people, landmarks, plants, and foods remind me that dynamic historical forces have made Cape Town one of the most fascinating cosmopolitan centers in the world.

Cape Town and the Emerging Global Trade, ca. 1500 CE

Cape Town is said to have had accidental foundations. Many of the people who, throughout time, have touched upon her shores—and even recent historians—have argued that it was intended to serve merely as a rest stop or replenishment way station for vessels making their way to the more important and highly prized trading regions of southeast Asia and China. This earned it the dubious title "Tavern of the Seas." Such characterizations, however, mistake the forces of history that early on bound people, both European travelers and indigenous Africans, to this place. Cape Town was central to the early emergence of globalization and interconnections that made possible the rise of merchant trading empires. Between the early 1500s and the early 1800s, all the major forces of the early modern world came together in the Cape. Europeans embarking on long-distance voyages for trade and exploration connected southern Africa to seafaring global trade networks for established and new exotic goods, emergent networks of finance and investment, new techniques for farming, and powerful technologies for war. Europeans in the Cape also negotiated ideas about how Africans were seen and understood both in Africa and around the world as the "other"—that is, as people set apart by these European observers as different culturally or ethnically. And together, Europeans and Africans forged new, if decidedly unequal, societies that were in turn connected to the Atlantic and Indian Ocean circuits and to the world beyond.

Beginning in the early 1400s, northwestern Europeans were on the move, transforming their productive capacities, using new technologies (especially military and maritime) to expand overseas, and developing the new economic system of merchant capitalism. Merchant capitalism entailed accumulating and reinvesting profits from global trading in further overseas ventures. The Portuguese were the first to use this system to build an empire in South America and parts of Africa; later the Dutch and English outpaced Portugal's commercial activity. These enterprises necessitated taking land and rendering indigenous peoples into compliant workers on this land, which they had formerly claimed as their own. Where this could not be done, as in both America and South Africa, local societies were pushed aside and new labor was introduced, most often in the form of slavery.

As a precursor to the era of industrial capitalism (c. 1800), the Dutch, like the English in North America, forged the most advanced system of merchant capitalism in the form of their East India Company. They ventured into the Atlantic world, seeking to reconnect to the spices and luxury products of China, Indonesia, and India. With the rise and expansion of Islam and the threat of infectious disease from Asia, maintaining regular trade traffic to the east from Europe was a challenge. Powerful Islamic states demanded higher tariffs and posed greater competition, so the Dutch sought alternative routes to Asia.

The People and the Environment: Local and Regional Connections

Of course, human history in the Cape did not begin with the arrival of the Portuguese or the later Dutch. KhoeKhoe or just Khoe ("men of men" or the "real people") and San (or Soaqua) people had been well established in the region long before the whites. They and other African states and societies in the interior had engaged in long-distance trade for many centuries across the southern part of the continent and with the Indian Ocean trade network. By about 1000 CE, Africans had established the towns of Toutswemogala and Mapugngubwe along the Limpopo River. Their legacy of glass beads, cowry shells, sophisticated ironwork, and fabulous gold statues are testament to their impressive advances. These efforts helped connect foragers and pastoralists in the south with farmers who planted crops and kept cattle in the north and along the coast, eventually leading to a vibrant regional trading network centered on the goldsmiths and ivory hunters of Great Zimbabwe and linked to the Indian Ocean.

San and Khoe people formed the earliest communities, making the Cape region their home. They shared a common heritage from what were probably the first modern humans in the world, and as they settled across southern Africa they adapted to the demands of an often unforgiving environment. They also shared interrelated strategies in the building of communities. San hunting and foraging communities lived in the interior, were decentralized, and were small in number. There were likely only about twenty thousand San when the first whites arrived in the Cape. San hunting strategies often included the practice of robbing stock from nearby herding communities—a practice that led to vilification and retributions from later European farmers. San relations with the Khoe were open and fluid, with a range of social and economic links that blurred the lines between them. Indeed, many Khoe who moved into the arid interior or lost stock due to wars or disease adopted a San lifestyle, making the two groups indistinguishable and creating a dynamic social formation sometimes referred to as KhoeSan.

The Khoe were herders of sheep and cattle. They emerged from earlier groups of Tshu-Khwe-speaking people who probably dispersed from an area of modern Botswana about fifteen hundred years ago. The Khoe had already started to acquire livestock—fat-tailed sheep and the "Africander" long-horned cattle—when they arrived in the Cape. Their chiefdoms were larger than San clans, comprising up to two thousand members, and the overall Khoe population grew to possibly over one hundred thousand by the mid-seventeenth century. Overall, the Khoe's herding and trading lifestyle made them more inclined to engage in trade and work relations with whites than the San hunter-gatherers, who could retreat to the Cape interior, and so the Khoe were the first in this region to face the impact of white settlement.

The KhoeSan were probably, and understandably, suspicious about the intrusion of white colonizers onto their lands. What began as simple forays by the Europeans to find meat and water developed into permanent white settlement and the displacement of indigenous peoples. As this pattern emerged, settlers began to develop ways of thinking that justified their desire to gain wealth and power, including ideas about ownership and cultivation of the land. They were convinced that their more intensive use of the soil was superior to indigenous practices, which to them seemed less productive. Many European perceptions of Africans demonstrated biased misunderstandings and a disdain for the indigenous societies. Early European maps of the Cape and interior showed vast expanses of vacant land—presumably open for white settlement—and only a sprinkling of indigenous peoples. Paintings of the KhoeSan portrayed them in misshapen or even bestial forms. Early Europeans also devalued KhoeSan culture, showing little appreciation for San rock paintings of their engagement with nature and spirituality. Europeans did not even acknowledge that the Khoe had an intelligible language, let alone make an effort to learn it. They referred to the Khoe as "hottentots" because their speech sounded like turkeys clucking, and they called the San "bushmen" because they lived in an "uncivilized and dangerous" wilderness. As the pace of imperial expansion intensified, Europeans established similar views and derogatory terms for indigenous people across the globe, including for Indians in the Americas and Asians in the Far East.

Portuguese Forays and KhoeSan Responses

The Portuguese were the first Europeans to arrive in the Cape. This small Iberian nation set the pace for exploration and early trade missions around the coast of Africa. Beginning in the 1420s, Prince Henry, known as "the Navigator," sought to connect with the mythical Christian king Prester John and the riches of Asia by marshaling a wealth of seafaring and cartographic knowledge about Africa and beyond. He coordinated and spurred a growing fleet to push south, past the fabled "end of the earth" at Cape Bojador on the West African coast, beyond which few if any Europeans had previously ventured. This set the stage for a vast Portuguese trading empire. By the 1460s, Portuguese ships were trading along the West African coast and laying the ominous foundations for the slave trade. The Portuguese cultivated a sense of cultural and technological superiority. By the later 1480s, they arrived in the Cape of Good Hope convinced both of the righteousness of their mission to spread Christianity and commerce in the Indian Ocean region and of their entitlement to the supplies and resources they needed.

The arrival of Portuguese mariners in the Cape illuminates the deeply ambiguous economic and cultural encounters between Europeans and Africans. While Europeans lionized as heroes Bartolomew Dias, the first-known European to round the Cape of Good Hope in 1488, and Vasco da Gama, who passed the point en route to India in 1497, indigenous people had a different perspective, seeing the Portuguese as ill-mannered savages, not "civilizers." Early Portuguese forays onto Khoe lands were often unfortunate engagements in which misunderstandings and prejudices led to tension and violence. Coastal Khoe often scattered at the sight of the Portuguese or were suspicious of their motives and disdainful of their manners. The Portuguese, no doubt anxious to obtain water and supplies, may have feared the Khoe, possibly in part because they knew the precious resources they sought were vital to the local pastoralists. When Bartholomew Dias's party came ashore for water in 1488, some Khoe threw stones at them, presumably to defend their watering hole. The Portuguese retaliated with a crossbow and killed one of the Khoe before retreating to their ship with filled water casks.

Engagement in sporadic skirmishes escalated as the increasingly determined Portuguese sought to enforce their own terms of trade. Moreover, they sought to inscribe their own values and culture on the land and people, erecting various *padrão* (Christian crosses) along the coast. Over the course of the next one hundred years, relations deteriorated as more Portuguese ships landed in the Cape and their passengers demanded ever greater numbers of cattle for meat. In 1510, when the high-ranking viceroy of Portuguese India, Francesco de Almeida, put in at Table Bay to replenish supplies, he sent his crew out to trade for meat. After an initially friendly exchange of goods, Almeida's shore party seized a Khoe hostage in order to induce his people to bring more cattle for trade. The outraged Khoe attacked, precipitating an aggressive Portuguese counterattack. The Khoe drove the Portuguese back to their ship and killed a number of them, including the viceroy. Thereafter, Portuguese and other merchant expeditions, fearing the Khoe, avoided the Cape and turned their attentions elsewhere in Africa, to Angola and Mozambique, leading to the expansion of their slaving empire. Then, in the 1650s, the Dutch opened a trading fort at Table Bay, establishing a new European presence in the Cape.

The VOC: Global Merchant Capital and the Cape

The *Vereenigde Oostindische Compagnie* (Dutch East India Company), or VOC, initially thought of the Cape only as a means to support its vast trading empire centered in Batavia, Indonesia, by providing a conveniently located way station for ships. The company chose Table Bay for its safe anchorage and especially for its potential sources of timber and water. It was, however, the production of meat, fruit, and cereals for the ships that were the key factor in transforming the resupply station into a costly colony. As VOC shipping grew in volume and the demands of its merchant base in Batavia expanded, the company called upon the station in Cape Town to provide ever-increasing amounts of timber, fresh meat, and vegetables. The small contingent of company employees at the fort could not meet the demand, and so they turned, as European colonizers around the world did, to making these demands of local people.

The VOC station never turned a profit in over 140 years of operation despite the imperatives of the Heeren XVII, the company board of directors. It did not need to. The rest of the company's holdings and enterprises from Sri Lanka to Indonesia, along with its privileged access to the shogun's Japanese markets, rendered a handsome profit. The strategic geographic location of Cape Town as a replenishment point, however, ensured that the Dutch kept a tight grasp on the Cape. Unlike their counterparts in the English East India Company (EIC) elsewhere, however, the VOC did not initially plan to establish a plantation economy in the Cape.

To provide for its passing ships, the VOC directed employees to establish a garden for fruits and vegetables and to engage in trade with the local Khoe herders. The establishment of a fort (later transformed into a full military castle) and the Company Gardens in the 1650s, however, was not just the implantation of what became a long-term European presence. This was also the beginning of a concerted effort to manipulate the environment and manage the people living in it. (See Map 1.2.) Like the wider project of European colonizers to consciously appropriate and order their empires, the Dutch sought to render the Cape Eden-like. The garden was planted with species from around the world and displayed a living catalogue of the considerable global botanical knowledge of the VOC for both commercial and medical purposes.

As part of this effort, Jan van Riebeeck, the first VOC commander in Cape Town, oversaw the planting of what became perhaps one of the most important export crops: grapes for wine making. The company imported vines from Germany, France, and Spain and experimented with a wide range of varietals. By the end of the century, company officials

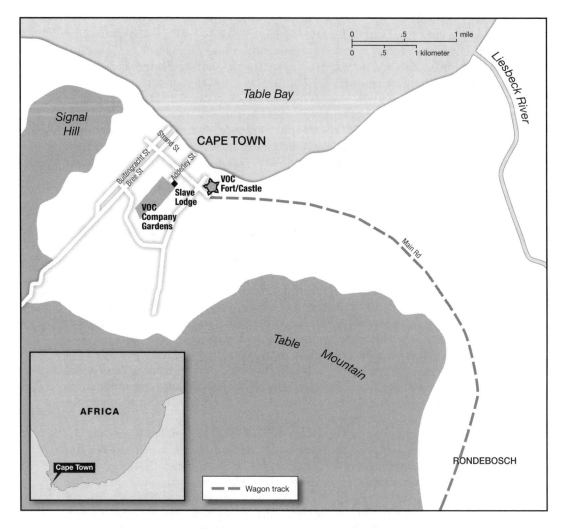

Map 1.2. Cape Town, ca. 1700

Table Bay provided an ideal sheltered harbor and way station for commercial maritime traffic between the Atlantic and Indian Oceans. By the mid-seventeenth century, the Dutch East India Company had established a formal presence with a fort and settlement at Cape Town. The Dutch then implanted themselves and their political economy in the Cape through expanding white settlement and the development of slavery, at the same time displacing and subordinating the indigenous Khoe.

in Batavia raved about imported Cape wines. African and Malay slaves then expanded various company officials' wine estates and built what would become a world-class export industry that still exists today. Thus, in many ways, the expansion of the Dutch colonial empire was driven by both a mercantile imperative and a desire to learn about and manage landscapes and plants to be useful and profitable to a global market. The Cape's gardens acted as a sort of nursery for acclimatizing tropical plants for use elsewhere, further contributing to the fermentation of ideas and practices shaping the wider world of European expansion.

VOC Relations with the KhoeSan

Beginning in the mid-seventeenth century, Africans and Europeans shaped Cape society through an interdependent relationship. It is important to note that, as with many areas of the world where European imperial expansion occurred, indigenous people made the essential developments of this globalizing economy possible. The Dutch, like many European trading states, had to forge new relations with indigenous people in order to extend trade and gain access to local resources. Initially, the Dutch established friendly trade relations with the Khoe, bartering copper, tobacco, and iron for cattle and sheep. Indeed, the VOC issued a strict policy that company employees must not harass or enslave the indigenous people so as to avoid potentially costly conflicts. There were, however, instances of mutual distrust, and the Dutch complained that shrewd Khoe herders refused to part with their best livestock, hiding them behind hills until a desired price was met or training their cattle to flee back to their former owners after being traded. The Dutch viewed the San with even greater contempt, condemning as theft their tradition of taking availalbe lifestock.

As with European merchant companies in Asia, the VOC relied on the San and Khoe to act as *compradores* (cultural and economic intermediaries) to facilitate their commercial enterprise and develop wider political relations among the chiefdoms in the region. Some Khoe leaders embraced this opportunity to bolster their status and to gain access to prized, if unessential, European manufactured goods. A Khoe named Dorha (called "Klass" by the VOC) of the Chainouqua chiefdom, for example, gained official status as a "captain" of the VOC by helping the company establish a lucrative cattle trade with other friendly clans. Dorha and 250 followers then allied with the Dutch in a war against a rival Khoe group, the Cochoqua, and Dorha was duly rewarded with looted cattle and sheep. As often occurred, however, the alliance turned sour when Dorha was attacked and arrested by VOC governor Simon van der Stel in 1693, in part because of Dutch concerns about Dorha's rising influence and wealth and in part because of the jealous accusations of other Khoe trading clans. Although Dorha was later released on company orders, he lost his wife, his status, and his livestock as a result of his arrest, and in 1701 he was killed by a rival Khoe chief. Other Khoe such as Doman and a young woman named Krotoa not only learned to speak Dutch and English but later developed a keen understanding of whites and their motives. This knowledge allowed them to capitalize on trade and enhanced their ability to lead resistance when the tide of cooperation turned to conflict.

Krotoa, called "Eva" by the Dutch, had important connections to various Khoe herding groups and was about ten years old when she was placed with VOC governor Jan van Riebeeck's family as a domestic servant and protégé. Her sister was the wife of Oedasoa, the chief of the important Cochoqua chiefdom. This royal connection enhanced Krotoa's prestige and usefulness to the Dutch because it afforded her special access to the Khoe leaders. She was formally educated and quickly learned to speak both Dutch and Portuguese. She also acquired a taste for European clothing and Dutch cuisine. Unlike most Khoe girls in her position, Krotoa was encouraged in the Christian religion and was eventually baptized. As Krotoa grew older she was torn between her life within VOC society and her links with the Khoe. The Dutch did not fully trust her, but nor was she completely accepted by the Khoe, who remained suspicious of white motives. After van Riebeeck left the Cape, Krotoa's fortunes improved for a time when she married Danish soldier and physician Pieter van Meerhoff in 1664. The stresses in her dual life, however, provoked her to abuse widely available European liquor. In her final years, the Dutch described her as an alcoholic, an adulteress, and a prostitute. At various times, Krotoa was arrested and imprisoned on Robben Island, where she died in July 1674 and was given a Christian burial.

White Settlers and Their Demands: Slavery

Cape Town is also the place where Europeans unleashed the two forces that would have the greatest impact on Africa: white settlement and slavery. In order to satisfy the increasing demand for supplies, both for the ships that called at Table Bay and the growing population of Cape Town, the first commander of the VOC operation, Jan van Riebeeck, instituted a policy that had profound effects. Despite the initial desire not to colonize the land, van Riebeeck allowed a few company employees (known as "free burghers" after they were released from company service and could acquire their own property) to settle and farm outside the confines of the fort. These "settlers" quickly set about transforming the land by staking out vast farms, building homes and towns, and obtaining the labor they needed to undertake intensive agriculture. At the same time, they still relied heavily on the Khoe for trade and the VOC for weapons, tools, and protection.

As the free burghers moved into the interior of the Cape, their demands grew and trade with the Khoe deteriorated from a voluntary commercial exchange to a barely compensated form of tribute. The free burghers' introduction of larger numbers of sheep and cattle—some obtained from the Khoe, but most imported from Europe—together with growing demands for lumber had a significant impact on the environment. Company officials tried to limit the environmental impact of indiscriminant timber cutting, but to no avail. The VOC's imprint on the land intensified when the wooden fort was transformed into the massive Castle of Good Hope beginning in 1666. In short order, Khoe grazing lands, San hunting grounds, water sources, and trade routes were brought under settler control and VOC authority with the establishment of European-style political districts in Stellenbosch (1685), Swellendam (1745), and Graaf-Reinet (1785). Even the imposition of these European names added a cultural and temporal dimension to Dutch control of the landscape. The Khoe sought to muster a spirited resistance. Leaders such as Doman marshaled alliances among chiefdoms, especially those disgruntled by the increasingly poor terms of trade, and led attacks on white farms. Doman had learned much about European weapons and led attacks on rainy days when the gunpowder in Dutch muskets got wet and often failed to fire. Quickly, however, settlers with guns and horses came to dominate the land well beyond the area of the fort and official colony.

More fateful for the course of Cape history was the VOC decision in 1658 to import slaves. As with other slave-based societies, notably in the Americas, this had significant and ominous implications for Cape and later South African society. Early VOC officials had debated the possibility of creating a white labor force, but European workers were considered too expensive and not malleable enough. Instead, enslaved people were brought from Asia and other parts of Africa. In the early years of Dutch settlement, Khoe women married white men and were accepted into VOC society. Perceived physical or racial characteristics did not determine social status. The use of enslaved Africans, however, began to change perceptions of race and class. Although it remained illegal to enslave the Khoe, the VOC enforced this policy largely only to encourage the Khoe to carry on essential trade and to avoid potential hostilities.

In 1658 the VOC imported its first shipment of enslaved people from Angola and West Africa. For the next 150 years, more were brought in from Madagascar, Mozambique, and VOC holdings in the Far East. They included a multiracial blend of mostly African, Indonesian, Malay, and some Indian and Chinese people who contributed to the vibrant religious and ethnic diversity of the Cape. Enslaved people with different African beliefs coexisted alongside those very few who were converted to Christianity and the substantial number of Muslim slaves with wider social and religious networks. Significantly, these

Muslims introduced Islam, a global faith which continued to influence South African society thereafter.

Slave labor in South Africa never approached the numbers exploited in the Americas—there were fewer than twenty thousand slaves by the 1770s and only about sixty thousand near the end of the slave period in the 1810s. In contrast, some three million slaves were exported to the Portuguese colony of Brazil, and the British slave trade resulted in close to seven hundred thousand slaves in the United States alone by the time of American independence. Slavery in South Africa was nevertheless a pernicious system. Enslaved people were often torn from their families, held in bondage, and used predominantly for arduous physical work. Through an established code of paternalism and the law, masters could beat and punish their slaves. If a slave failed to obey a master's orders or tried to escape, which was a real threat to the order of slave society, the slave could be branded or suffer the brutal amputation of a leg, ear, or nose.

Although slavery in South Africa was a minor affair when compared with the vast plantation systems of the Americas, it was a rigidly closed and controlled part of society. Initially the VOC managed most of the slaves in Cape Town in the company-owned slave lodge, and thus the same sorts of cultural blending and social interaction among slaves and free people did not occur in the Cape as they did in Brazil, where a more creolized society emerged. This separation had an enormous impact on South African society. In addition to the inhumanities of slavery, the company-sponsored immigration of significant numbers of European women in the late eighteenth century further contributed to the cultural chauvinism and hardening of racial attitudes in Cape Town. The newly arrived white women sought to establish their elite status by accentuating perceived race differences as part of the social hierarchy. They managed, increasingly, to assert that lighter skin, European-style clothing, and the Dutch language were signifiers of worth and status. In response to growing settler demand, the VOC officially excluded children of mixed marriages from full legal rights and, by 1765, official social and cultural distinctions were added to the informal classification of race and class groups. Similar to European sumptuary laws, which stipulated what sort of clothing certain classes in society could wear, the VOC prohibited even free black women from wearing lace and hoopskirts, which became the privileged domain of white women. Coloured (people of "mixed-race" born to white and Khoe or Bantu-speaking African parents) domestic servants were further denigrated and openly referred to as *skepsels,* or "living tools." Moreover, the patterns of labor coercion and control established by whites over black people through slavery and informal contracts with the Khoe in the early Cape persisted.

Settler Expansion

As with other places of European colonial settlement, Dutch, German, and later British settlers presented an overwhelming force of change in the Cape. Europeans, falsely claiming that the land was unused by its original inhabitants, felt justified in taking African lands to establish "legal" ownership. These were foreign concepts to most African societies across the continent, where land was held in common trust for all people in the society. Europeans viewed themselves as a superior civilization, not initially because of race but because of their culture. Over time, this air of cultural superiority was overlaid with a growing race consciousness reinforced by the association of servile labor and slavery with African and Asian people. Even more unfortunately for the Khoe and San, settlers combined these values with the powerful new technology of guns. These enabled them to shock and overwhelm many of the Khoe and to vent their anger at San theft of their livestock through the "sport" of exterminating these people as "vermin."

Settlers brought other things from the outside world that further eroded weakened Khoe chiefdoms. In 1713 a Dutch ship arrived in Cape Town with a very sick crew. They sent their soiled linens and clothes to the VOC slave lodge to be cleaned, which spread the deadly smallpox virus. Within months, the disease had spread like wildfire, sparking a widespread epidemic in the Cape peninsula. After it had burned itself out among the Dutch and slaves in the port city, it devastated the Khoe. As they fled the city, many Khoe carried the disease with them into communities that had no previous exposure to this new virus, and members of these communities succumbed at a frightening rate. While up to 20 percent of Europeans, slaves, and Asians in the city died from the epidemic, perhaps twice that percentage of Khoe died in the interior. In this way, as with other port cities such as Istanbul, Turkey; Venice, Italy; and Malacca, Malaysia, Cape Town was exposed to a global range of infections that were easily communicated to vulnerable peoples in the interior. Smallpox visited death and its disfiguring pustules at least twice more on Africans during the colonial era. Combined with a severe drought and the fragmentation of the Cape Khoe chiefdoms, the epidemic contributed to the complete dissolution of any cohesive Khoe society near Cape Town. The remaining families were either absorbed as menial laborers into the city or fled into the interior, where they often combined with San groups to form KhoeSan societies. There they hoped in vain to avoid the further expansion of white settlers.

In many regards Cape Town was the launching point for the sorts of settler penetration into the interior that was a familiar and unwelcome pattern elsewhere in Africa. The expansive force of armed settlers and their allies soon transformed the relatively fluid and interdependent relations among whites and Africans into sustained violent confrontation. Through the rest of the eighteenth century, settlers thrust into the interior, pushing aside or brutalizing Africans in their bid to wrest the land from them. Bolstered by a growing sense of self-reliance and regular supplies of weapons, settlers organized "commandos," or raiding parties, to force the KhoeSan off the land and to capture people who could be forced into indentured labor. The KhoeSan resisted as fiercely as they could, employing effective guerilla tactics and using what guns they had acquired. Many of the KhoeSan resisters were former servants and laborers from the colony and had learned well European battle strategies. In the end, however, the spirited KhoeSan could not fend off the overwhelming power of modern weapons and the subsequent takeover of their lands. By 1795, after over one hundred years of resistance and following a series of wars in which many Khoe who had settled in the colony fought alongside whites, the Cape interior fell to settler domination. After the British took the Cape in 1806 as a prize from the Napoleonic Wars, more disaffected settlers penetrated the interior to find fortune and escape the new colonial government, setting the stage for further tensions and ultimately the white domination of Africans under Apartheid.

GLOBAL ENCOUNTERS AND CONNECTIONS:
Cape Town as a Vital Point of Convergence

By this time, the pace of world history was changing, driven by new, more competitive imperial nations. Soon to be first among these was Britain, which developed a highly sophisticated imperial enterprise and a government bureaucracy that brought together the wealth of industry with the might of the world's most powerful navy. When Britain replaced the VOC in the Cape, they were reluctant to get too entangled in costly local tensions, but they recognized the need to manage the expansive forces of colonialism. For example, they developed a vast government bureaucracy to directly administer policies and to moderate the excesses of settler demands for land and labor. They also sought to harness elements of Christian missionary efforts to "civilize" Africans, and this connected Cape Town to the emerging evangelicalism of the Atlantic world. It was, however, the profound transformations of the industrial revolution the British brought to the region that marked the greatest departure from the era of VOC merchant capitalism. Global forces of change, including the connections that brought settlers, new labor relations, new economic systems, new diseases, and new ideas, demanded new, more cohesive, and more direct forms of administration, such as those that would sustain British interests in China and Malaysia. Cape Town played an equally important part in these developments precisely because it had been so well connected to global patterns of change that emanated from encounters among cultures; encounters among Europeans and Africans competing for trade, land, and labor; and encounters that transformed the environment.

In the end, it was its geographic location that made Cape Town both possible and indispensable for the particular way that new global connections were made among Europeans, Africans, and Asians. Cape Town thus represents a key focal point for the convergence of the major forces of change during the early modern period until the end of the age of merchant capitalism and beyond. The burgeoning economies of northwest Europe found the Cape to be the ideal strategic place—a keystone in the arch they would build between the Atlantic and Indian Ocean worlds. It was the place where the trade with Africa connected to both these worlds. It was the place where European ideas about science, botany, land use, property rights, and racial hierarchies were tested and used to forge a highly stratified and yet remarkably cosmopolitan society. Plants and animals from around the world found a place in the gardens and farms of the Cape, just as people from Europe, Asia, and Africa mingled and formed new families and communities in the city of Cape Town. Grapes brought from the "Old World" and cultivated in the Cape were fermented and bottled as wine to sustain the mariners who frequented the port of Cape Town.

New globalizing forces also converged in the Cape. The "crowd diseases" that had emerged from Asia and overwhelmed Europe arrived by ship to play out their devastating effects. Global diseases such as smallpox and tuberculosis brought epidemics that further eroded African societies. Sailors from around the world brought to and contracted in Cape Town various communicable diseases, such as syphilis. Slavery played its abhorrent role in bringing enslaved people to the Cape from Asia and elsewhere in Africa, and the Cape hosted ships moving slaves and slave-produced goods such as spices and sugar around the world. Ironically, Cape Town was later visited by African Americans—many descendants of slaves taken from Africa previously—working as sailors, whalers, and entertainers who travelled the Atlantic world in the eighteenth and nineteenth centuries. Cape Town was also the place where European technology, especially in the form of guns, played a decisive role in enforcing severe inequality among people throughout southern Africa. Yet, however unequal the relations among people were, society in Cape Town was a product of the many contributions of its global, cosmopolitan community. Whether these foundations were accidental or not, clearly Cape Town played a significant role in connecting the world as a place of encounter.

ENCOUNTERS AS TOLD: PRIMARY SOURCES

The following excerpts illustrate the complex connections between Cape Town's original inhabitants, the KhoeSan, and Dutch settlers. They reveal both opportunities and tensions surrounding the relations between the two cultures and two different economies. As you read them, consider to what extent the two societies cooperated and clashed and what factors led to changing relationships.

Dutch Trade with the Khoe, from the *Journal of Jan van Riebeeck*

Jan van Riebeeck distinguished himself as a VOC administrator and company surgeon in Batavia before arriving in the Cape to serve as the first VOC governor from 1652 to 1662. Viewed as a founding father of the country by many Afrikaners of Dutch descent, he initiated the developments that led to the building of a fort, the release of company employees to become settlers in the interior, and the deterioration of trade relations with the Khoe. His wife, Maria, first employed the Khoe servant girl Krotoa and took her into the van Riebeeck family to be educated and converted to Christianity. While governor of the Cape, van Riebeeck kept a detailed journal that is one of the earliest records of VOC life in the region, and one of the only sources that chronicles the voice, as understood through European ears, of Khoe people such as Krotoa and her colleagues.

- What does the following excerpt reveal about who initially controlled the terms of trade?

- What were the implications of the way trade worked for the unfolding relations between the Dutch and the Khoe?

22 MAY 1656

It is in any case impossible to obtain animals from the Kaapmans [a local Khoe chiefdom], because though they are rich in cattle, and are offered every inducement to sell, they only act as brokers between ourselves and other natives. Thus they manage to obtain copper and tobacco, etc. to satisfy them, to the considerable discouragement and detriment of the trade. In this Harry, just as if he were their overlord, plays his part, gradually enriching himself and making himself the chief Captain, as is evident from the number of his cattle, with which he is still encamped . . . under the protection of the Company.

Source: H. B. Thom, ed., *Journal of Jan van Riebeeck, Vol. III, 1656–1658* (Cape Town, Amsterdam: A. A. Balkema, 1954), 89.

On Political and Trade Relations, from the *Journal of Jan van Riebeeck*

Krotoa, called "Eva" by the van Riebeecks, played an important role in relations among the Khoe chiefdoms and Dutch as an interpreter and intermediary. She was originally brought into the VOC fort as a slave girl, but she soon came to the attention of the governor's family, and they took her in, taught her Dutch, and relied on her to translate and to explain Khoe history and politics. She was instrumental in helping the Khoe and the Dutch communicate and in navigating many complex political and trade relations. Krotoa was a remarkable woman—one of the very few indigenous women noted in primary sources and in history for having achieved so much in a world so dominated by white men. In the following excerpts we get a sense of the kinds of challenging negotiations she was involved in, the roles that she played, and how the VOC relied on her so much. We also get a sense of Krotoa's ambiguous position, as she was caught at times between loyalties to the VOC, her own chiefdom and people, and the KhoeSan in general.

- Take note of the role of Doman, who had travelled to the VOC headquarters in Batavia. What did he learn there?

- How did it affect his relations with the Dutch?

22 JUNE 1658

[After unsuccessful efforts to find the escaped slaves and the apparent lack of interest in the effort on the part of the local Khoe, The governor ordered that some Khoe be taken hostage to induce their compatriots to aid in the recapture] . . . they said that they would go at once and search energetically for the slaves. They did not want to acknowledge that they knew where the slaves were. But Doman, who had been to Batavia (VOC headquarters in Indonesia), was so angry that he could not restrain anger and said in the presence of all the Hottentots that the interpreter Eva had advised us to do this, and that he wished to destroy her at once. She immediately denied the charge and, though the charge was true, we confirmed the denial. We assured them that she had nothing to do with it. . . . Doman, however, would not cease accusing Eva, and he has proved in everything . . . that he is not to be trusted and that we should be on guard against him. We sincerely wish that he had never been to Batavia, or that he may be induced to go back by fair words; there he has learnt how to use firearms effectively, and we are now obliged to exercise great care to keep them out of his hands.

Source: H. B. Thom, ed., *Journal of Jan Van Riebeeck*, Vol. II, 1656-1658, (Cape Town, Amsterdam: A. A. Balkema, 1954), 289.

A Khoe Woman's Work as a Liaison, from the *Journal of Jan van Riebeeck*

Later, Eva explains more of her plight and experiences.

- What had she learned about Dutch culture and society?

- Do you think van Riebeeck is being honest about what they expected of Eva?

- Do you think she understood all the implications of what the VOC was doing in Cape Town?

- Who is van Riebeeck's audience?

- Is his journal, intended for the VOC, completely fair, or does it suggest he and Eva are perhaps saying things they want others to hear?

29 OCTOBER 1658

She [Eva] stated that when she left the fort the Kaapmans had robbed her of everything on the way, and that her mother, living with the Kaapmans, had not taken steps to have it restored. Therefore, Eve went to her sister living among the Cochoquas [a neighboring Khoe chiefdom]. She [the sister] is one of the wives of Oedasoa, one of the two greatest captains [chief], and had not seen Eva since she was a baby. Eva, who was received with great joy, told Oedasoa all about our nation and in particular explained to him our desire to live with them on friendly terms, and also that she had been educated by the Commander's wife in her house and learnt our language and also partly our religion, etc. Oedasoa was likewise well-disposed towards us and to prove this had now sent some of his men to bring sheep [Khoe Sheep as opposed to the variety that Europeans brought in] and cattle to us. He desired to enter into an alliance with us, but was prevented by the Kaapmans and the Gorachouquas [a third competing Khoe chiefdom], being afraid that we would help the latter. For that reason Oedasos did not dare visit the Commander, in spite of all of Eva's efforts to persuade him and the examples adduced by her of the forbearance displayed by is in the face of the serious wantonness and annoyance which we had to endure from time to time from the Kaapmans. On being asked whether it would not be advisable to send Commissioners [sic] with presents to Oedasoa, she agreed that it would, . . . and added that cinnamon . . . and also cloves, nutmegs, mace and pepper [all spices brought to the Cape by VOC and traded for in Batavia and India]. . . . She was told that the interpreter Doman was daily warning us against the Cochoquas, and that he stated they were very hostile towards us, and that he had requested 20 soldiers from us to make war on the Cochoquas and seize their cattle. . . . She replied: "Doman lies. He is a worthless fellow and speaks with a double tongue. He tries to incite the Dutch against the Cochoquas and the Cochoquas against the Dutch." . . . She added she would have returned sooner [from her visit to her sister] but she had been very ill, as also her sister. Oedasoa's wife, whom she had taught to pray to our Blessed Lord, to which (as she said and indicated by action) all the natives listened with tears in their eyes instead of laughing like Doman. . . . The Cochoquas, however, told her to learn everything carefully from us [the Dutch] so that she could teach them because, she said, she had prayed night and day, when she was not sleepy or asleep, until her sister had recovered. She thereupon instructed her sister how God was to be thanked for her recovery. This was very pleasing to the natives, who were desirous of further instruction.

Source: H. B. Thom, ed., *Journal of Jan van Riebeeck, Vol. II, 1656–1658* (Cape Town, Amsterdam: A. A. Balkema, 1954), 362–363.

Further Reading

Elphick, Richard. *Kraal and Castle: KhoiKhoi and the Founding of White South Africa*. New Haven and London: Yale University Press, 1977.

Elphick, Richard, and Hermann Giliomee, eds. *The Shaping of South African Society, 1652–1840*, 2nd ed. London: Longman, 1989.

Hall, Martin. *The Changing Past: Farmers, Kings, and Traders: The People of Southern Africa, 200–1860*. Chicago: University of Chicago Press, 1990.

Hamilton, Carolyn, Bernard Mbenga, and Robert Ross. *The Cambridge History of South Africa*. Vol. I. Cambridge: Cambridge University Press, 2010.

Keegan, Timothy. *Colonial South Africa and the Origins of the Racial Order*. Charlottesville: University of Virginia Press, 1996.

MacKinnon, Aran S. *The Making of South Africa. Culture and Politics*, 2nd ed. Upper Saddle River, NJ: Prentice Hall/Pearson, 2012 .

Ross, Robert. *Cape of Torments*. London: Routledge, 1983.

Thom, H. B., ed. *Journal of Jan van Riebeeck, Vol. III, 1659–1662*. Cape Town, Amsterdam: A. A. Balkema, 1958.

Ward, Kerry. *Networks of Empire: Forced Migration in the Dutch East India Company*. Cambridge: Cambridge University Press, 2008.

Worden, Nigel. *Slavery in Dutch South Africa*. Cambridge: Cambridge University Press, 1985.

Worden, Nigel, Elizabeth van Heyningen, and Vivian Bickford-Smith. *Cape Town*. Cape Town: David Philip, 1998.

Web Resources

Atlas of Mutual Heritage, http://www.nationaalarchief.nl/amh/main.aspx?lang=en.

Castle of Good Hope (the VOC Castle), www.castleofgoodhope.co.za/.

The KhoiSan, http://www.khoisan.org/.

South African History Online, http://www.sahistory.org.za.

Table Mountain National Park, http://www.sanparks.org/parks/table_mountain/.

Verenigde Oost-Indische Compagnie, Dutch East India Company, http://www.tanap.net/content/voc/organization/organization_intro.htm.

VOC Company Gardens, www.capetown.gov.za/en/parks/facilities/Pages/CapeTownGardens.aspx.

Women in World History, "Cultural Contact in Southern Africa," http://chnm.gmu.edu/wwh/modules/lesson7/lesson7.php?s=0.

2

Salvador da Bahia

A South-Atlantic Colonial Crossroads

(1549–1822)

CHRISTOPHER EBERT

THE BRAZILIAN CITY OF SÃO SALVADOR DA BAHIA DE TODOS OS SANTOS (Saint Savior of the Bay of All Saints), in the past usually just called Bahia, is a product of human mobility. In its colonial heyday it was the center of vast networks characterized by the mobility of people, products, and ideas. Salvador, founded in 1548, was a new place, an old place, and a hybrid place, containing great ethnic and cultural diversity. Other great colonial cities, such as Mexico City or Cuzco, Peru, arose from the ashes of just-conquered indigenous empires, often incorporating their neighborhoods, people, and even building stones into new European-style cities. The original inhabitants of the Bay of All Saints were not city builders, and so the Portuguese settlers there had to start from scratch. The city that they constructed over time had no rival for importance or magnificence on the entire eastern coast of South America for several centuries.

On my first visit to Salvador's historical center, I felt that I had somehow been transported back eastward across the Atlantic Ocean to Lisbon, Portugal, where I had previously lived and done research. Within the elite homes and churches crowded onto the steep streets and alleys of the Pelourinho historical district, floors and walls were finished with marble imported from southern Portugal that had come as ballast in the many ships that arrived in Salvador's harbor every year from the Portuguese metropolis. The profusion of ornate churches, the layout of streets and squares, and the structural embodiment of important Portuguese political and social institutions all spoke to a faithful recreation of an early-modern Portuguese city.

And yet, as a modern visitor, I was also struck by the city's differences and aware that these would have been obvious as well to someone newly arrived from Europe three hundred years ago. For while on its resplendent stone surfaces historical Salvador shows itself a European city, its soul has always been, and remains to a significant degree, African. Although in its modern period Salvador has embraced its African heritage, this was not always the case. In colonial times, the presence of Africans in the colony was strongly desired; their slave labor kept Salvador, and the productive agricultural countryside of Bahia, humming. However, the enslaved status of most Africans brought to Salvador, and that of their children, presented challenging problems. Many forms of slave production required a harsh regime of discipline, punishment, and control, and slave populations in Bahia were always considered, and frequently proved themselves to be, rebellious. The African drumming that often resounds through the streets of the historic center now draws huge crowds of tourists and locals. This drumming has been going on for centuries, but in the distant past, colonial officials heard in it the sounds of slave resistance and a threatening affirmation of African culture over that of the Europeans.

I went to Salvador to study the colonial city: its history, people, markets, and institutions, as well as its built environment, much of which has survived into the modern period. The countryside of Bahia, including its plantation system, has had its historians, but the city itself in the colonial era has rarely taken center stage in historical accounts. My work in studying and writing about this hugely important early Atlantic port city has led me to many archives on both sides of the Atlantic and is still ongoing. For me, one of the great charms of working on a historical project in Salvador has been that it really wears its past, especially compared to other large Brazilian cities. This gives me a lot of help when I try to exercise my historical imagination!

Salvador's history is one of global connections, from its early settlement to its role at the center of a sugar-producing plantation society, and the impact on the city of the discovery of gold in the Brazilian interior. Founded in the Americas by the Portuguese, Salvador's sugar trade was overseen by Portuguese landowners and merchants and fueled by enslaved people brought from Africa. The draw of the Brazilian colony, Salvador's busy port, and the vibrant economy brought explorers and opportunists from all over. The city absorbed all comers and the legacies of these connections can still be seen today in the city's religious and cultural life.

SALVADOR DA BAHIA AND THE WORLD: An Atlantic Trading Hub

The early history of Portuguese Brazil was easily overshadowed by the glittering success of Portugal's seaborne routes to the luxury commodities markets of South Asia and China, established in 1498. Brazil was discovered by accident by Portuguese mariners led by Pedro Álvares Cabral, who landed on the northeast coast of the South American continent in 1500 on his way to India. Cabral duly notified the Portuguese Crown of his discovery, and

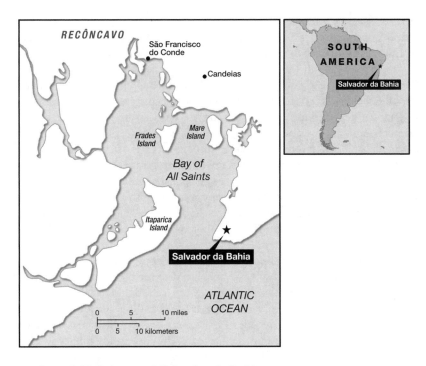

Map 2.1. Bay of All Saints and Salvador da Bahia

Salvador da Bahia guarded the entrance to the Bay of All Saints and served as the center of administration both for the Captaincy of Bahia and the whole colony of Brazil. Its large port was the point of embarkation for ships carrying sugar, tobacco, hides, and other exports produced in the rich agricultural regions around the bay. Here, too, came products and people from Europe, Asia, and Africa, including large numbers of African slaves.

Portugal subsequently claimed a new colony, but it had no clear idea of what to do with it. The Bay of All Saints was discovered in 1501 on a subsequent Portuguese voyage, and its potential as a harbor was immediately recognized—if not exploited—for many decades. (See Map 2.1.) The colony was eventually called Brazil, which was also the name of a useful dyewood tree that grew in the Atlantic rainforests on large stretches of the coast. Brazilwood logging formed the first European-controlled economy in Brazil; a profitable activity that nevertheless paled in comparison with the Asia trade.

Salvador before Sugar (to 1600)

The Brazilian coast was not empty at the time of the arrival of the Europeans, and it had excellent material conditions for human habitation. The northeast of the continent is tropical, and beyond the coastal region, inland roughly sixty-two miles (one hundred kilometers), the land turns arid. The coast, however, is fertile, the ocean fisheries are plentiful and, though now much decimated, the mangrove swamps along the coast were once teeming with crabs and shellfish. Palms, game, and a wide variety of native fruits contributed to Brazil's allure for human communities. Furthermore, while the region occasionally gets battered with intense storms, it is prone neither to hurricanes or earthquakes.

Brazil's coastal people were highly capable hunters, agriculturalists, and warriors. The first description of coastal peoples was provided by a chronicler accompanying Cabral in

1500, Pedro Vaz de Caminha, who, possessed of strong biases about what constituted proper dress, deemed the local people "naked" and seemed little convinced about their value to Europeans other than as objects of missionary activity. We know little about what these groups thought about Europeans, or even of themselves, since they did not possess the skill of writing, and early contacts were mediated through missionaries with strong religious agendas. Their language family has generally been called Tupí-Guaraní, but probably with a great deal of imprecision. They formed fairly strong population densities, but they did not root themselves permanently in towns or villages, preferring some degree of seasonal mobility. Their political units, constituted in various types of tribal identities, were small by European standards, and many different groups can be named. They were also capable of mounting serious and effective resistance to European interlopers who attempted to settle on the coast, although many were receptive to European initiatives to trade, finding value in European steel, copper, and iron implements, usually in exchange for brazilwood. The coastal group that was dominant in Bahia at the time of European arrival was called the Tupinambá.

The Portuguese monarchy did not initially take a strong interest in settling Brazil, especially since its promise seemed so weak compared to the burgeoning direct trades that Portugal was developing with China, India, and Africa during the sixteenth century. However, merchants' ships from many of Europe's trading communities visited the Brazilian coast in the first five decades of the century to collect the aforementioned brazilwood, which could be used to make a coveted red dye in the luxury woolen goods factories of northwestern Europe. Worries about imperial rivals eventually led the Portuguese to an official policy of settlement on the Brazilian coast. The first attempt to settle the Bahia region in 1536 failed due to the effective military resistance of local Indian groups.

Eventually, the Portuguese Crown recognized the potential of Bahia as both a port and as a potentially good location for sugar cultivation, and Salvador came fitfully into being. In 1549 the Crown sent Tomé de Sousa to serve as governor and head of a large expedition responsible for building the new colonial capital. By the close of the 1550s, Salvador was established, but, like the many European settlements springing up around the coasts of North and South America, it was an unimpressive place: small, unhealthy, violent, subject to attack by sea, materially primitive, and slow to attract investment from either the Portuguese Crown or private investors. At this juncture it seemed few Europeans were motivated to move to the Americas except for members of missionary orders who were willing to brave physical hardship, privation, and sometimes even martyrdom for the cause of their religion.

Salvador, Sugar, and Slaves (after 1600)

Within fifty years the situation in Salvador had changed dramatically, at least for its European settlers. Several historical and biological processes conspired to catapult Salvador to an Atlantic "center" and a place of encounter *par excellence*. Tomé de Sousa's successor, Mem de Sá, spent the decades before 1572 consolidating Portuguese gains and waging successful wars against local Indians. But the chief cause of Salvador's success was the transference of the sugar plantation system to Brazil. By the time Salvador was established, Portuguese investors and planters had become the leading European producers of sugar in their various Atlantic island possessions, notably Madeira and São Tomé. Successful sugar production depended upon a confluence of factors, including proper soil and temperature, major capital investment, and the securing of a large permanent labor force. In regards to the latter requirement, the Portuguese had resorted to the use of slave labor, and they increasingly purchased their slaves on the coasts of West and West-Central Africa for use in their island manufactories. Some of the more skilled jobs in sugar production were paid, but the majority of the tasks would not attract European or native wage workers and required some type of coerced labor. This was a situation that applied to many of the commercial enterprises in the Americas, including Spanish silver mining in colonial Potosí, which relied on coerced Indian workers. The suitability of many of the Brazilian coastal soils to sugar production had not gone unnoticed in the early decades of the colony, and Bahia was a particularly promising region, as it boasted a vast area suitable for sugar cultivation. In the second half of the sixteenth century, investment poured into Bahia, fueled by rising prices for sugar in Europe. People there were increasingly developing a taste for this sweetener, first introduced via the Middle East from Asia, where it was a native product.

The rise of the sugar industry transformed Salvador in several major ways, since the sugar was shipped from there. Salvador became an important port town with an attendant infrastructure of wharves, warehouses, packing houses, hospitals, provisioning facilities, residences, and churches. Even more investment came from the Portuguese Crown, which saw sugar as an excellent source of tax revenues. Along with taxes came the crown agencies to supervise their collection, and by 1600 Salvador contained most of the institutions of local and crown governance typical in an early-modern Portuguese town.

This left the issue of the labor supply to be resolved, and here biological factors played a decisive role. European planters did not have rigid views about who could work on a plantation, and throughout the history of sugar production in the Americas, Europeans, Africans, and Indians all worked in cane fields at various times. Sugar cultivation had long been associated with enslaved labor, and, as noted above, Portuguese planters relied on it to grow sugar in their other colonies. Usually the slaves were African, but in Brazil colonists initially enslaved Indians to supply their plantations with labor. There were various mechanisms that allowed them to do so; for example, some of these slaves were the captured enemies of allied tribes. Others were seized on expeditions specifically fitted out for slaving, usually under the legal pretext—though not always untrue—that the particular Indian group targeted practiced cannibalism and therefore might be legally reduced to an enslaved state. The success of Europeans in capturing and enslaving Brazil's coastal Indians after 1550 speaks to a balance of power slowly turning from indigenous groups to Europeans. As elsewhere in the Americas, the main reason for this shift was the accelerating mortality of Indians from the endemic diseases of the Eastern Hemisphere, such as smallpox, to which they had no immunity and which fell upon them in wave after devastating wave. The same biological forces that permitted Europeans to gain advantages over these Indians spent themselves so relentlessly that by 1600 Indian slavery was no longer a viable permanent solution to the burgeoning sugar industry of coastal Brazil, even though Indian slavery persisted at a reduced level for a long time.

At this juncture, Salvador began to become an "African" city, mainly because enslaved African workers were more available than European peasants to run the sugar economy. Amongst the European kingdoms, the Portuguese had achieved the most success in their trading relationship with various African political entities. With trading stations in West Africa, the Kongo Kingdom, and Angola, the Portuguese were in the best position to respond to opportunities in the African slave markets, and they took advantage, exporting enslaved Africans to Europe, to the Spanish Americas, and to the sugar plantations on their island holdings. By the end of the sixteenth century, the prices for African slaves were sufficiently low to warrant their large-scale importation to the Americas to work in the sugar industry of Brazil. Thus began the second and most intense phase in the transatlantic slave trade, which culminated in the transportation of over 10 million enslaved Africans to various American colonies, including probably at least 2.5 million to Brazil, between 1550 and 1800. Salvador was central to this process, both at its inception and for most of its duration. By 1600 Salvador was the most important slave market in the western Atlantic, and it remained so for several centuries before finally being eclipsed by Rio de Janeiro toward the middle of the eighteenth century. Closely related to the infrastructure of the sugar trade was the apparatus of the trade in human lives, which gave further impetus and rationale to Salvador's port facilities. However, not all slaves were destined merely to pass through Salvador en route to the interior. Many stayed in the city, and much of Salvador's workforce and population were wholly or partly of African descent.

Seventeenth-Century Hardship and Recovery: From the Dutch Invasion to the Gold Rush

Salvador underwent an abrupt reversal of fortune in 1624 when a large fleet of ships financed by the Dutch West India Company (WIC) sailed into the Bay of All Saints and captured the city after a few days of fighting. The date marked an extended period of challenge and decline for Salvador, one that was only overcome decisively by the end of the century. Approximately one year later, in 1625, the largest war fleet yet to sail across the Atlantic attacked Dutch-controlled Salvador and regained the city for the united Crown of Portugal and Spain. However, the WIC was not yet done with Brazil. Motivated by the possibility of gaining profits by monopolizing the trade in the lucrative Brazilian sugars, the WIC launched an attack in 1630 on the captaincy north of Bahia, Pernambuco, and this time managed to stay for a full twenty-four years, operating a Dutch colony in Brazil known as the "New Netherlands." During this period, Salvador became the headquarters of anti-Dutch war operations in Brazil and was saddled with permanent military garrisons, refugee populations, and special taxes. It also endured intermittent attacks from Dutch warships that especially targeted the rural sugar economy, the principal source of wealth in the colony.

Salvador survived this difficult period, but when it emerged triumphant in the decades-long war against the Dutch, it found itself in a different world. Its rural sugar industry had been devastated by war, especially since both sides in the conflict engaged in scorched-earth tactics of destroying each other's sugar plantations. Also, by the 1650s, American sugar was no longer a Brazilian monopoly. In particular, English colonists had developed viable sugar colonies in the Caribbean, and the French were not too far behind them. Now Brazil had successful competitors in its markets for sugar in Europe. Not only that, but colonial competitors, including Dutch, French, and English merchants, had successfully challenged Portuguese claims to exclusive trade on the African coast, and they had set up their own profitable trading centers in various places in West and South Africa to compete in the African commodities markets that offered slaves, gold, and other valuable products. Atlantic waters, always risky, had turned even more violent, as various trading nations preyed upon one another's shipping interests, and pirate activity increased.

One response of the Portuguese Crown to these issues was to organize by 1649 all of its merchants' shipping into a system of annual convoy sailing, in which all of the goods meant to sail between Portugal and Brazil left from the three principal ports—Salvador, Rio de Janeiro, and Recife—once a year and were accompanied by large warships. This was in imitation of the large Dutch joint-stock chartered trading companies such as the WIC. It was a type of capitalist innovation that pooled investment for large overseas trading ventures. At the same time, it reinforced merchant monopolies on most of the items traded between Brazil and Europe, including ordinary products such as soap and salt. This was disruptive to trade in Salvador and distorted markets terribly, because a year's worth of supplies from Portugal would arrive all at once, and natural prices—if not official prices—for all kinds of commodities could fluctuate dramatically as a result. Other than the richest of merchants who benefitted from the policies, citizens in Salvador complained bitterly about these practices, to no avail.

In the latter half of the seventeenth century, Bahia's economy was mostly stalled, but several historical events converged to give it new life. In the agricultural heartland of the colony, Indian settlements had all but disappeared. However, new conquests of Indian groups on the western margin of the region had opened up productive land for cattle and tobacco. Both of these products subsequently became important in Salvador's export markets and allowed it to diversify beyond its traditional sugar economy. Additionally, Salvador benefitted from the huge gold strikes starting in the 1690s in the southern part of Brazil in Minas Gerais (General Mines), previously a mountainous wilderness far into the interior, situated north and west of Rio de Janeiro. Much of the gold passed through Rio de Janeiro on its way to Europe, but plenty passed through Salvador as well, which was an authorized port of exit for gold and even received a Royal Mint in 1694.

To some extent, however, Salvador was becoming less dependent on trade with Europe in general over the course of the seventeenth century. During this time the town began to intensify its bilateral trade with Africa, and dozens of ships traveled back and forth between the two continents each year. By the latter part of the eighteenth century, Salvador engaged in constant, direct trade with various regions in West and West-Central Africa, including Upper and Lower Guinea, Angola, and São Jorge da Mina. (See Map 2.2.) To Africa it sent cane liquor and rolls of tobacco cured in molasses; these Bahian products were hugely popular with African consumers. In return, it received enslaved men and women to work (and usually die) in the cane fields and on the tobacco plantations and cattle ranches of its interior. Salvador's economy was further lubricated by the arrival of almost annual fleets from Portugal's trading posts in the Indian Ocean. These ships, laden with rich cargoes of Indian and Chinese goods, were not authorized to trade with Salvador, since they were meant to be unloaded only in Portugal. This prohibition was widely flouted, however, and there seems little doubt that there were few cities in the western Atlantic with greater access to Asian commodities than Salvador. These activities supplemented Salvador's European trade, which continued to be strong with Portugal and also indirectly with England, France, and Italy.

The City and Its Trade

As it emerged in the sixteenth century as the South Atlantic's premiere seaport, Salvador had distinctive characteristics. As a well-equipped port, it facilitated trade with Europe, Africa, the Indian Ocean region, and various Atlantic islands; additionally, it boasted a ship repair yard and served distressed shipping from all maritime nations. As the capital of the whole colony of Brazil, Salvador contained all the major institutions of Portuguese colonial governance, including the High Court and the Governor's Palace. It was an archbishopric and a major seat of all the missionary orders, including the Jesuits, the Franciscans, and the Dominicans, all of which built magnificent churches in the town center. Additionally, it served as the home of elite members of the colony. These included members of the sugar aristocracy, the *senhores de engenho* (planters), who owned large sugar-producing estates in Salvador's agricultural hinterland, known as the Recôncavo.

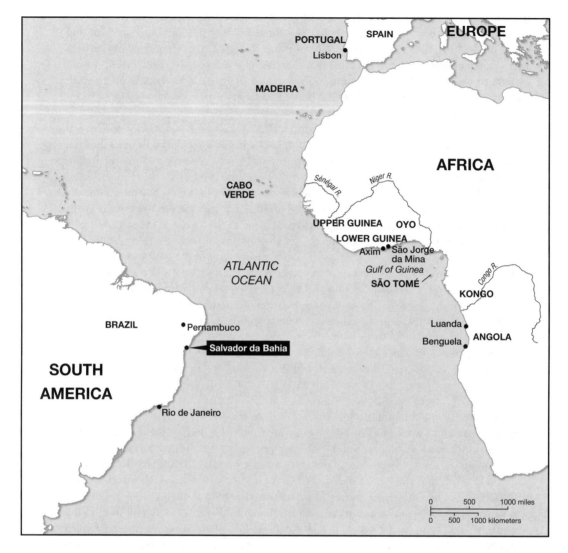

Map 2.2. Brazil and Africa in Portugal's Empire

Salvador da Bahia was situated in the heart of Portugal's Atlantic trading empire. It was the premier seaport in the South Atlantic and a linchpin in early-modern global trade in general. Every year it received ships from Europe, Portugal's Atlantic islands, and even Asia. Its proximity to West and West-Central Africa spawned a thriving bilateral trade in slaves and other products, and Salvador consequently became a highly Africanized place.

This latter group was not necessarily in residence full time, preferring to spend much of the year at their estates. This was in contrast to the Spanish colonial aristocracy, the members of which almost always preferred to reside full time in colonial towns and cities.

In fact, transience was a feature of Salvador's population at all social levels. The Portuguese Crown made efforts to prevent non-Portuguese immigrants—with the exception of African slaves—from coming to the colony, but it was not always successful. As was typical in port cities around the world, people moved in and out at a steady rhythm. Dozens of large ships visited Salvador each year from every part of the world, and some of them had cargoes of very sick sailors. These often landed in Salvador's hospital, the Santa Casa da Misericórdia, where they frequently died. No doubt some surviving sailors stayed in the colony, even without permission. Slaves moved through Salvador en route to plantations, but others stayed and took up urban occupations—usually hired out by their owners to do various kinds of work—and still others plied a steady traffic in small shipping between the town and outlying farms and plantations.

Throughout the colonial period, many of Salvador's most important residents were foreign-born. High royal officials, arriving with servants and family members, also set up residence for several years before they moved back to the metropolis or to an assignment elsewhere in the Portuguese Empire. Merchants high and low moved back and forth between Salvador and various parts of Europe, and most of Salvador's merchants were born in Portugal. These included members of most of Portugal's largest wholesale merchant houses who commanded large capital resources, acted as bankers, and moved commodities over vast distances around the globe. Other merchants traded on a small scale or simply opened retail shops. Some of them, through hard work and clever marriages, eventually entered into the planter aristocracy. This was the case with João Peixoto Viegas, who migrated from northern Portugal in 1640 at the age of twenty-four as a small-scale merchant, gained a fortune on African and Portuguese trade routes, married into the sugar aristocracy, and ended his life both as one of the largest landowners in Brazil and as an important local magistrate in Salvador. Immigration and the fluid nature of social relations undoubtedly irritated some of the planter aristocracy. These attitudes can be seen in the satirical works of colonial Salvador's most famous poet, Gregório de Mattos, who, in the latter half of the seventeenth century, railed against Portuguese upstarts. Nevertheless, social mobility was a well-established pattern.

What did someone arriving in Salvador's harbor at the end of the seventeenth century see? Shipping left the Atlantic and entered the Bay of All Saints from the south, between a triangular peninsula of the landmass to the east and the large island of Itaparica to the west. Along the western concave edge of the peninsula, protected by a series of forts and batteries, lay a ridge of hills running a distance of about six miles (ten kilometers). Midway along this ridge, which at its highest point rose above 260 feet (eighty meters), stood the town of Salvador on cliffs overlooking the harbor below. Hence the city is divided sharply between its upper and lower sections. Colonial visitors, such as William Dampier, whose impressions are conveyed in this chapter's primary sources section, laid anchor close to the harbor, a natural deepwater port. Crowded along the strip of land below the cliffs was the working port.

At the southern end of the port stood the Ribeira das Naus, by 1700 probably the most important shipbuilding and ship repair yard in the South Atlantic. Most days this would have been a hub of activity, with the sawing of logs, the making of pitch, and other activities being carried out by slaves, and large ships on dry dock receiving repairs. Further north was the harbor, where, when he arrived in 1700, Dampier saw thirty large ships at anchor. Small craft carried trade items back and forth to the wharf, and their cargoes usually passed in both directions through the *alfândega*, or custom's house, where royal revenues from trade were assessed. Alongside the wharfs, and right up to the bottom of the cliffs, stood the town's private warehouses, called *trapiches*. These were piled with goods as various as tobacco rolls; hides; Indian cottons; European woolen goods; brightly painted Italian ceramics; jugs of olive oil, wine, brandy and cane alcohol; salt; soap; whale oil; Indonesian spices; ships stores; ropes; lumber; marble; bars of metals; finished luxury goods; and the ubiquitous chests of sugar.

Many of these commodities were just passing through the town, but some were bound for the Cidade Alta, Salvador's "Upper City." This area contained most of the town's residences, urban markets, and principal institutions. By 1700 this area boasted three-story stone houses, convents, monasteries, and churches—formidable even by Portuguese standards—and paved roads. The Cidade Alta contained fountains, fixed marketplaces, groceries, bakeries, and butcher shops. The city straddled several hills, and so roads meandered up and down, and charming views beckoned at every turn. Much of this colonial built environment persists to this day, although a few landmarks, such as the cathedral, fell to ill-considered urban "development" projects early in the twentieth century. Beyond the town lay farms, the town's cattle corral, and even a few sugar plantations. Indian populations near the city had mostly disappeared by this point after being decimated by European diseases.

In 1700 Salvador was in the midst of a boom. Its population growth demonstrates its rising importance in the Atlantic economy and strong linkages to Africa. No records permit reasonable population estimates before the eighteenth century, but the town council said that Salvador's population had tripled between 1647 and 1717, and in 1724 the total population has been estimated at about twenty-five thousand, of which half were enslaved. In this year, Salvador was probably about twice as big as Boston, Massachusetts—British North America's largest city. Mexico City was undoubtedly far larger, but that owed partly to Indian populations. Construction boomed in Salvador, and the sound of hammers on stone and iron must have been common throughout the city. The expanding city grew due to the labor of slaves known as *escravos de ganho*, hired laborers sent out by their masters. Other slaves plied skilled trades in masonry.

The Impact of Slaves on Commerce and Society

The expanding city was becoming one of the largest on the entire western side of the Atlantic. Slave-run provisioning estates in the hinterland provided many of the commodities used to feed Salvador, although luxury foodstuffs such as wine, wheat flour, and olive oil, which could not be produced in the tropics, arrived from Portugal. For common residents, the daily bread was manioc flour made from rasped and toasted manioc tubers, beans, local fruits and vegetables, fish, and beef from cattle raised in Bahia's back countries and fattened in the city corral before they arrived in the town's slaughterhouses. The circulation of virtually all of the town's comestibles was taxed and regulated by the town council, which was staffed by local notables that were subject to local elections. Official shops rented out by the city, as well as designated market stalls, allowed officials to keep a watchful eye on the trade.

A chief feature of the system that circulated food through the city was the participation at most levels of African slaves—many of them women—who worked as confectioners, butchers, cooks, bakers, and vendors. These slaves gained opportunities that were much rarer on plantations. One observer in late-eighteenth-century Salvador described a veritable army of African slave women who poured out of elite homes every morning with trays and parcels of sweets and pastries to sell in the streets or from door to door. Other itinerate slave vendors sold cane liquor, ox heads, and cow's offal furtively in the streets. Urban slaves in Salvador—as elsewhere in the Atlantic world of urban slavery—were highly active participants in the marketplace, and, as a consequence, they could earn money, not just for their masters, but for themselves as well. This was the beginning of a process that could lead to eventual manumission, or freeing, of an individual slave, as many enterprising slaves eventually saved enough money to buy their freedom from their owners. While slavery is now long since gone in Salvador, a colonial echo remains in the profusion of street vendors in modern Salvador selling everything from pirated computer software to savory bean-flour fritters fried in pungent red palm oil.

Little else is known about these slaves as individuals, although work has been underway to uncover in greater detail the slave demography of Salvador. In 1724 nearly half the population of Salvador was composed of slaves, totaling around twelve thousand. All colonial areas in Brazil contained both newly arrived Africans and acculturated slaves who were born in the colony and spoke Portuguese. As indicated above, some Brazilian slaves also won their freedom, and Salvador contained a large population of free blacks and their descendants. Salvador's position as a primary destination of the transatlantic slave trade probably contributed to an intense cosmopolitanism among its slave populations, with numerous African languages being spoken in the streets.

While virtually all of Salvador's current residents are now chiefly Portuguese speakers, the African influence on Brazilian Portuguese is probably the most intense in Salvador, where African words abound in the local dialect. Colonial slaves are present in parish records, in wills, and in other legal documents, although usually few details are proffered about their lives and occupations. Alongside the African-descended slave populations stood substantial populations of mixed ethnicity that were the product of rampant miscegenation in the Portuguese colony; these individuals could sometimes achieve impressive levels of social mobility. This was a situation that priests and colonial officials sometimes railed against, but it appears to have been extremely common, and European men in the colony sometimes even married women of other or mixed ethnicities. Portuguese males usually preferred Portuguese wives, but, unlike in the English colonies, there was no stigma in sexual relations with women of African and/or Indian descent. These relations probably ranged along an uneasy spectrum between voluntary and coerced, but their results by the later colonial period made Salvador a place where there was no clear social delineation based on color, a situation that persists to the present day.

The Role of the Church

The mental world of Salvador's inhabitants was limited, but by no means impoverished. Literacy in the colony was rare in all social groups. Through the eighteenth century, Salvador boasted neither a university nor even a printing press (Portuguese monarchs feared the sedition it might bring). While it lacked a permanent base there, the Portuguese Inquisition made intermittent trips to investigate charges of heresy; the Crown was officially intolerant of religious diversity. The scientific investigations of flora, fauna, and geology that were exploding around the Atlantic world by the eighteenth century were largely absent in Brazil until the nineteenth century, due to the lengthy resistance of Catholic officialdom in Portugal to Enlightenment thought and practices. However, residents of all social stations found an outlet in the liturgical life of the Catholic Church, in religious brotherhoods, and especially in designated feast days, notably Corpus Christi, usually celebrated in the late fall (May or June) with lavish spending and ceremony. Carnival, which ended the summer with a more secular tone, was, and remains, another important holiday. In both cases, the celebrations involved members of every social class, including slaves. Elite members of society channeled their religious participation through Catholic lay orders, parish churches, or the Santa Casa de Misericórdia, Brazil's most prestigious charity.

Ordinary people and especially blacks often formed so-called *irmandades* or "lay brotherhoods" (though they involved women as well) that were associated with parish churches and devoted to the worship of a particular saint or aspect of Christ or the Virgin Mary. These organizations gathered money for festivals and charitable functions, such as paying for Catholic burials for indigent members. In the case of slaves, many of the records of their involvement in brotherhoods exist to the present day and remain a priceless avenue for understanding the lives of slaves and free blacks in the colonial period. In 1811 Josefa da Silva, a freed slave who had been born in Angola, left her last will and testament in Salvador. Along with noting her possessions (including two slaves from Mina, which is now the Ghana coast) she mentioned her membership in four different black lay brotherhoods. This was an indication of her relative high level of wealth and social standing in Salvador's black community.

Though channeled through Catholicism, the religious beliefs and practices of the inhabitants of Salvador were probably hybrid. In the present day, Salvador remains one of the most vital places in the world for religious syncretism, especially the blending of Christianity with polytheistic African and indigenous religions. The best example of this is the practice of a religious tradition known as Candomblé. One of the most important religious festivals in Salvador today is the huge procession every January that ends with the washing of the steps of the Church of Our Lord of Bonfim. This festival—as with Carnival—seems to involve nearly the whole population of the city. Many of the white-clad Bahian women who participate are also active in Candomblé houses, the members of which associate the Christ of Bonfim with the West-African creator deity Oxalá. It is difficult to know how far back into history to read such syncretic practices. As with all religious traditions, they have changed over time, and the practice of African religion in the Americas in particular has not always left much of a record. However, recent research indicates that syncretic religious practices and other forms of religious heterodoxy were common features of life in colonial Brazil, for slaves as well as other social groups.

This latter fact may at first seem to suggest that the church and state in Salvador were either tolerant or too weak to enforce the monopoly on religious expression claimed by Catholicism. People probably did get away with more in the colonies, where the institutions and social pressures that kept people in place in Europe were weaker and the populations far less homogenous. Nevertheless, the Portuguese Crown and the Catholic Church did make efforts to keep order.

At stake was not only religious orthodoxy but the stability of the entire economy and society. As we have seen, Bahia was a slave society, and its capital, Salvador, also ran on slave labor. This was a situation that, wherever present in the Atlantic world, was a recipe for violence and paranoia. Bahia may have conveyed the impression of a balmy tropical paradise, but it was seething with tensions that not infrequently burst into the open, sometimes resulting in urban rioting. Relations between masters and slaves were complex, often involving negotiation and both individual and collective resistance on the part of slaves. However, the final resort of the slave master to ensure the obedience of slaves was the exercise of violence, and this exercise received the full backing of local authorities, and, ultimately, the Portuguese Crown. In the center of Salvador stood the *pelourinho*, or public pillory. In modern Salvador, the old pillory has lent its name to the entire neighborhood comprising the old colonial city. In its day, however, the *pelourinho* represented the state-sanctioned exercise of violence against slaves. Here disobedient slaves were whipped, branded, and mutilated in public while their blood ran down upon the cobblestones.

GLOBAL ENCOUNTERS AND CONNECTIONS:
The Spread of Bahian Culture

In the present day, Salvador remains an important South Atlantic port city and the third-largest city in Brazil. However, in the post-colonial period Salvador continued to evolve, and in some ways not for the better. Until recently, Salvador had missed the industrialization that characterized the southern states of Brazil. Large landowners in the Bahian countryside persisted with extremely oppressive practices, even after the abolition of slavery in 1888. Salvador and the northeast part of Brazil in general have often been considered backward regions, although this impression has begun to change as Salvador and the area have been undergoing a significant economic revival in recent decades.

Nevertheless, as Salvador and the state of Bahia slid into relative economic obsolescence in Brazil's national period, their importance as a symbol of Brazil both at home and abroad could not be underestimated. In the twentieth century, Bahian emigrants spread to the south of Brazil, particularly to large cities such as São Paulo and Rio de Janeiro, and they carried Bahian culture across the whole country. Bahia's importance has been especially felt in cultural matters. Writer Jorge Amado popularized Salvador and Bahia abroad, and he has remained one of the world's best-known Brazilian novelists. Bahian music has also achieved iconic status both in Brazil and globally, with international stars such as Caetano Veloso popularizing Bahian genres. Bahia's cultural appeal undoubtedly owes to its African cultural legacy and the myriad forms of creativity unleashed from its status as a place of encounter in the past.

As noted, Salvador was a place where a large number of ethnicities mingled. This was a product of diffuse patterns of human migration, some of them forced. Indian and African slavery was a terrible tragedy linked intimately with the creation and development of the colony of Brazil—as elsewhere in the Americas—and Salvador was one of the chief recipients of enslaved Africans throughout the colonial period and beyond. At the same time, African cultural forms took deep root here, and the prevalence of unions of people of different ethnicities helped to foster cultural hybridism. While these historical phenomena did not contribute to make Brazil a "racial democracy" as some earlier generations of Brazilian scholars claimed, they did serve to soften the legacy of racism in the post-slavery period, especially when compared to places such as the United States and South Africa, where racial lines were—and continue to be—much more rigidly delimitated.

Racial discrimination is an ongoing problem in Bahia, as in the rest of Brazil, but most people in Salvador recognize and celebrate their African heritage, and Bahia ranks as one of the most Africanized places in all of the Americas and a magnet for "heritage" tourism. It is small wonder that hundreds of thousands of people from all over the world visit Salvador da Bahia every year. They are attracted not just by sunshine and beaches, but also by Salvador's cultural cosmopolitanism, a fortuitous modern outcome of its brutal colonial past.

ENCOUNTERS AS TOLD: PRIMARY SOURCES

"South of the Line to Brazil," by William Dampier

William Dampier (1651–1715) was a seasoned merchant, buccaneer, and sea captain who several times sailed around the globe. He was also a prolific observer of both nature and human society and set his observations of distant ports and peoples down in several books. The following excerpts record some of his observations of the town of Salvador in 1699.

- What does Dampier find worthwhile to record and why?

- What types of social and economic activities does he observe? How does he interpret them?

- What is his view about relations between different ethnicities in Salvador?

- How does he view slavery?

Bahia de todos los Santos lies in latitude 13 degrees south. It is the most considerable town in Brazil, whether in respect of the beauty of its buildings, its bulk, or its trade and revenue. It has the convenience of a good harbour that is capable of receiving ships of the greatest burden: the entrance of which is guarded with a strong fort standing without the harbour, called St. Antonio. . . .

The houses of the town are 2 or 3 stories high, the walls thick and strong, being built with stone . . . and many of them have balconies. The principal streets are large, and all of them paved or pitched with small stones. There are also parades in the most eminent places of the town, and many gardens, as well within the town as in the out parts of it, wherein are fruit trees, herbs, saladings and flowers in great variety, but ordered with no great care nor art. . . .

A great many merchants always reside at Bahia; for it is a place of great trade: I found here above 30 great ships from Europe, with 2 of the King of Portugal's ships of war for their convoy; beside 2 ships that traded to Africa only, either to Angola, Gambia, or other places on the coast of Guinea; and abundance of small craft that only run to and fro on this coast, carrying commodities from one part of Brazil to another.

The merchants that live here are said to be rich, and to have many negro slaves in their houses, both of men and women. Themselves are chiefly Portuguese, foreigners having but little commerce with them. . . . Here was also a Dane, and a French merchant or two; but all have their effects transported to and from Europe in Portuguese ships, none of any other nation being admitted to trade hither. There is a custom-house by the seaside, where all goods imported or exported are entered. And to prevent abuses there are 5 or 6 boats that take their turns to row about the harbour, searching any boats they suspect to be running [smuggling] of goods.

The chief commodities that the European ships bring hither are linen cloths, both coarse and fine; some woollens, also as bays, serges, perpetuanas, [different types of textiles] etc. Hats, stockings, both of silk and thread, biscuit-bread, wheat flour, wine (chiefly port) oil olive, butter, cheese, etc. and salt-beef and pork would there also be good commodities. They bring hither also iron, and all sorts of iron tools; pewter vessels of all sorts, as dishes, plates, spoons, etc. looking-glasses, beads, and other toys; and the ships that touch at St. Jago bring thence, as I said, cotton cloth, which is afterwards sent to Angola.

The European ships carry from hence sugar, tobacco, either in roll or snuff, never in leaf, that I know of: these are the staple commodities. Besides which, here are dye-woods, as fustick, etc. with woods for other uses, as speckled wood, Brazil, etc. They also carry home raw hides, tallow, train-oil of whales, etc. Here are also kept tame monkeys, parrots, parakeets, etc, which the seamen carry home. . . .

Besides merchants and others that trade by sea from this port here are other pretty wealthy men, and several artificers and tradesmen of most sorts, who by labour and industry maintain themselves very well; especially such as can arrive at the purchase of a negro slave or two. And indeed, excepting people of the lowest degree of all, here are scarce any but what keep slaves in their houses. The richer sort, besides the slaves of both sexes whom they keep for servile uses in their houses, have men slaves who wait on them abroad, for state; either running by their horse-sides when they ride out, or to carry them to and fro on their shoulders in the town when they make short visits near home. Every gentleman or merchant is provided with things necessary for this sort of carriage. The main thing is a pretty large cotton hammock of the West India fashion, but mostly died blue, with large fringes of the same, hanging down on each side. This is carried on the negroes' shoulders by the help of a bamboo about 12 or 14 foot long, to which the hammock is hung; and a covering comes over the pole, hanging down on each side like a curtain: so that the person so carried cannot be seen unless he pleases; but may either lie down, having pillows for his head; or may sit up by being a little supported with these pillows, and by letting both his legs hang out over one side of the hammock. When he hath a mind to be seen he puts by his curtain, and salutes everyone of his acquaintance whom he meets in the streets; for they take a piece of pride in greeting one another from their hammocks, and will hold long conferences thus in the street: but then their 2 slaves who carry the hammock have each a strong well made staff with a fine iron fork at the upper end, and a sharp iron below, like the rest for a musket, which they stick fast in the ground and let the pole or bamboo of the hammock rest upon them till their master's business or the complement is over. There is scarce a man of any fashion, especially a woman, will pass the streets but so carried in a hammock. . . . All these tradesmen buy negroes, and train them up to their several employments, which is a great help to them; and they having so frequent trade to Angola, and other parts of Guinea, they have a constant supply of blacks both for their plantations and town. . . . The negro slaves in this town are so numerous that they make up the greatest part or bulk of the inhabitants: every house, as I said, having some, both men and women, of them. Many of the Portuguese, who are bachelors, keep of these black women for misses, though they know the danger they are in of being poisoned by them, if ever they give them any occasion of jealousy. A gentleman of my acquaintance, who had been familiar with his cookmaid, lay under some apprehensions from her when I was there. These slaves also of either sex will easily be engaged to do any sort of mischief; even to murder, if they are hired to do it, especially in the night; for which reason I kept my men on board as much as I could; for one of the French king's ships being here had several men murdered by them in the night, as I was credibly informed.

Source: William Dampier, *A Voyage to New Holland*, 3rd ed. (London, England: John and James Knapton, 1729). Accessed online via Project Guttenberg.

Recopilação de Noticias Soterpolitanas e Brasilicas, by Luis dos Santos Vilhena

Luis dos Santos Vilhena was a well-educated Portuguese man who moved to Brazil at the end of the eighteenth century. He recorded detailed impressions of the city in the form of letters to a friend back in Portugal that were compiled in 1802. His descriptions of enslaved women who were active in urban marketing contribute to our knowledge that these individuals formed a vital part of Salvador's colonial economy.

- What does this source suggest about the level of control exercised over urban slaves?

- Why do you suppose that slave women dominated many of the marketplace functions in Salvador?

- Do you think that there were any economic advantages for them in these jobs?

There is not in this city only one market square, but rather several places that are called quitandas, at which many black women join together selling everything they can carry; this could be fish, half cooked meat—which they call moqueada—bacon, whale meat during the whaling season, vegetables, etc. There are three of these quitandas in the whole city; one on the coast, another that was at the town square—the Terreiro de Jesus—but which has now regrettably gone to what's called the New Street, where there are few houses. Here the town council had some cottages built for the market-women, but they are so terribly small that nobody wants to rent them. The third marketplace is at the São Bento gates.

It is worth seeing and remarking that from the very elite houses of the city—in which the most important business is conducted—eight to ten blacks move out into the streets every day to sell insignificant foods as if they were great delicacies. These include [a huge variety of sweets, savories and pastries] of infinite degrees of quality, many of which—owing to their level of cleanliness—are perfect for inducing vomiting.

Groups of black [slave] women go out with baskets full of small manufactures. This is mostly contraband that was either taken or purchased either from foreign ships that dock here and then leave with cargoes of cash, or other ships that [are Portuguese and] come from the trading stations in Guinea and Mina [in West Africa]. In this way they are depriving her Majesty's rights of custom and avoiding her good laws. And it only happens because of the greed of the guards [at the wharfs], both civilian and military; and many of these people consider it a lucky break to get such a post. However, there are plenty of very honest guards too. These same women also carry goods that have been cleared by the customs house, and nobody can harass them or call them to account out of the respect for the powerful merchant families they belong to. Those black women that don't come from elite houses get a license from the City Council to sell, free from the devices of the watchful tax collector.

Source: Luis dos Santos Vilhena, *Recopilação de Notícias Soterpolitanas e Brasílicas* (Bahia: Imprensa oficial do estado, 1921).

Further Reading

Klein, Herbert S., and Harold Vidal Luna. *Slavery in Brazil*. Cambridge: Cambridge University Press, 2009.

Russell-Wood, A. J. R. "Ports of Colonial Brazil." In *Atlantic Port Cities: Economy, Culture, and Society in the Atlantic World, 1650–1850*, edited by Franklin Knight and Peggy K. Liss. Knoxville: University of Tennessee Press, 1991.

Schwartz, Stuart B. *Sugar Plantations in the Formation of Brazilian Society: Bahia, 1550–1835*. Cambridge: Cambridge University Press, 1985.

Web Resources

Bahia-Online, http://www.bahia-online.net/.

UNESCO World Heritage Convention on Salvador, http://whc.unesco.org/en/list/309/.

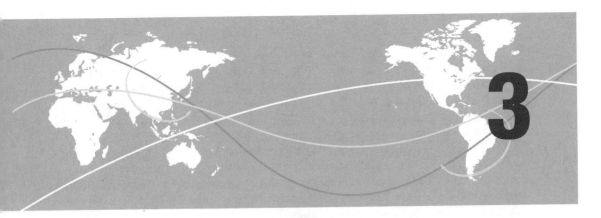

3

Nagasaki

Fusion Point for Commerce and Culture

(1571–1945)

LANE EARNS

NAGASAKI (MEANING "LONG CAPE") IS LOCATED IN SOUTHWESTERN JAPAN ON the island of Kyushu. Known today primarily as the second (and, at this point, last) city to suffer an atomic bombing, Nagasaki also has an extensive and fascinating history as a regional and international place of contact. For more than four centuries, its long, deep, narrow harbor has been renowned as one of the most beautiful in the world. The lush green hills that rise sharply from the harbor offer not only a striking first impression to incoming visitors who arrive by ship, but also provide protection from seasonal typhoons. Many travelers have noted how the view of the city's encircling hills from the water gives the appearance of entering a natural amphitheater. These same hills protected the downtown area of Nagasaki from suffering even more damage than it did during the atomic bombing of the city in 1945, and they have provided a final resting place for thousands of Japanese, Chinese, and Westerners buried in the myriad cemeteries there.

I first came to the study of Nagasaki's history when I was assigned to the city in 1974 as a Fulbright English Fellow to assist with the improvement of English-language speaking skills in the schools of Nagasaki Prefecture (an administrative district equivalent to a state in the United States). From my base in Nagasaki, I traveled to schools in every corner of the prefecture. As the only fellow in the area (there were only seven of us for the entire country), it was a perfect opportunity to learn about the people, traditions, and places of Nagasaki. Since that time, I have continued to teach, conduct research, and write about Nagasaki from its beginnings as a port city to the end of the American occupation after World War II.

My first exposure to the city coincided with the annual August 9 commemoration of the dropping of the atomic bomb by American pilots in 1945. More than seventy thousand people were killed in that bombing. Twenty-nine years later, at the commemorative ceremony at the Nagasaki Peace Park, I participated in a seminar with peace activists from around the world. I also witnessed immediately the commitment of the people of Nagasaki to openness and internationalization, which has long been at the core of their local culture. The commemoration of the bombing and celebration of peace have become part of an annual cycle of events that reflect the complex history of this port city. While today Nagasaki is almost exclusively associated with the devastation it suffered in World War II, I was able to experience the influence of a far longer history of encounter that has shaped one of Japan's—and Asia's—most enduring examples of cultural interaction and exchange. I was impressed by the extent to which the annual cycle of events reflected this long past, as the people of the city wove international influences together with local customs to create civic traditions that are unique to Nagasaki. This annual cycle includes events such as the late-summer, Chinese-influenced Buddhist Bon Festival (Festival of the Dead); the autumn Shinto festival called Okunchi, which dates from the 1620s and was begun to counteract early Christian influences in the city but which now incorporates a variety of Chinese, Portuguese, and Dutch influences; a spring kite festival reportedly brought to Nagasaki by seventeenth-century Indonesian traders in which individuals (primarily adults) battle each other in an attempt to sever the kite string of their opponent using kite strings covered with abrasive glass powder; and the midsummer *peiron* (dragon boat) races first brought to Nagasaki by Chinese traders in the mid-seventeenth century. It is impossible not to be swept up in the vibrancy and international flavor of these festivals.

The story of Nagasaki, from the founding of its port town in 1571 to its atomic bombing in 1945, is inextricably intertwined with its role as Japan's primary point of contact with the outside world. While foreign trade has always been the key to Nagasaki's importance, this trade also introduced many components of foreign culture to the city and to the rest of Japan.

NAGASAKI AND THE WORLD: Japan's Window to the Outside

In spite of its magnificent harbor, Nagasaki remained a small fishing village from its founding in the twelfth century until the mid-sixteenth century, when Jesuit missionaries and Portuguese traders dredged the reed-filled bay and helped create a thriving regional and international port town that served as a trading post for the silk and silver trade between China and Japan and as a sanctuary for Japanese Christians. From this point forward, Nagasaki's prominence, like its rich local traditions, depended on its regional and international role as the easternmost port in East Asian and world trading networks. (See Map 3.1.) It is important to remember that, geographically, the city is closer to Shanghai in China and Pusan in Korea than it is to Tokyo, the capital of Japan.

The founding of the city's port by Portuguese traders and Jesuit missionaries in 1571 was directly related to the initial wave of expansion of European trade networks into Asia.

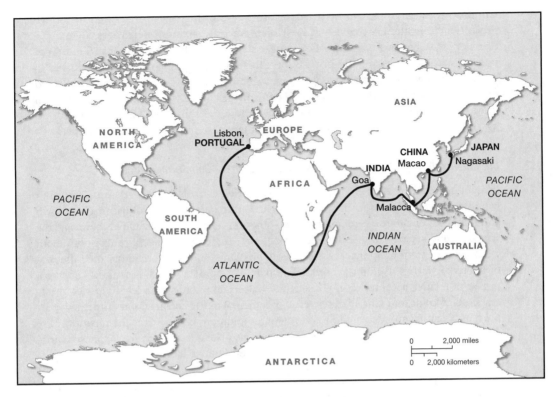

Map 3.1. Asian Trade Route of the Portuguese Empire, 1600

Portuguese traders founded Nagasaki's port in the mid-sixteenth century, soon after they had been allowed to establish a trading base in Macao in southeast China. The system of trade they created paved the way for later Dutch and English trade in Japan. Unlike the Dutch and English, however, the Portuguese also brought Christianity along with their commerce, and when the shogunate moved to eliminate the religion in the country in the late 1630s, it also banned Portuguese trade.

Portuguese explorers rounded the tip of Africa and sailed into Asia at the turn of the six-teenth century in search of opportunities to trade and proselytize. Using a system mod-eled after the Venetian and Genoese trading post arrangement in the Mediterranean, the Portuguese set the pattern for the creation of later Dutch and English overseas trade net-works in Asia. By 1511 the Portuguese had established fortified stations on the eastern coast of Africa in Mozambique, on the west coast of India in Goa, and in Malacca in present-day Malaysia. In the mid-1550s, after years of struggle, they were given permis-sion by Chinese authorities to build a trading base at Macao in southeastern China. While this base gave the Portuguese a small foothold in the vast Chinese market, it also led them to bump up against the traditional Chinese-dominated regional trade network of East Asia. Due to heightened piracy in the area, China's Ming government had banned foreign trade, allowing the Portuguese—with their foothold in Macao—to control the lucrative silk-for-silver trade between China and Japan as third-party intermediaries, provided they could find a permanent home for their ships in western Japan.

Like the vast majority of Japanese, the residents of Nagasaki held both Buddhist and Shinto beliefs. However, the top two Japanese officials of the area, the *daimyo* (territor-ial lord) Omura Sumitada and his vassal Nagasaki Jinzaemon, had both converted to

Christianity, in large part to help secure profits from the Macao trade and to receive protection from the Portuguese against their warring Japanese neighbors. In the autumn of 1570, the Jesuits and the Portuguese sounded the harbor at Nagasaki in preparation for the opening of the port. Soon afterward, Omura ordered construction to begin on a new town (which would soon become uniquely Christian) at an unsettled promontory at the head of Nagasaki Harbor in the hopes of attracting more foreign trade, and in the summer of 1571 the first Portuguese ship from China called at Nagasaki, thus ending the search for a permanent Japanese port for the Macao trade.

Christianity in Nagasaki: Early Successes and Japanese Countermeasures

When Portuguese traders and Jesuit missionaries first came to Japan in the mid-sixteenth century, the country was in the midst of civil warfare; central control had broken down and hundreds of *daimyo* were fighting each other for territorial gains. Oda Nobunaga, the strongest military ruler of the day, welcomed Portuguese trade, since it brought him both wealth and Western weapons, and tolerated Christianity in order to counter the influence of bands of warring Buddhist monks. The port of Nagasaki was thus founded during a period of relative acceptance of Christianity by certain national and local Japanese leaders. Foreign trade and Christianity were fundamental to the construction of the new port town at Nagasaki and its subsequent growth. In addition to serving as the Japanese base for the Portuguese ships from Macao, Nagasaki also became a haven for Japanese Christians, an increasingly persecuted minority. By 1580 Omura found he was unable to protect Nagasaki against attacks by neighboring Buddhist *daimyo*, and, desirous of maintaining the considerable benefits of the Portuguese trade, agreed to cede judicial authority over the port town to the Jesuits. Through this arrangement, the Portuguese ships from China came to Nagasaki on a regular basis, and the Jesuits were put into a position that allowed them to assure directly the security of the port.

Jesuit success during this period was symbolized by the dispatching of a Japanese embassy to Europe in 1582 that included the sons of prominent *daimyo* from the Nagasaki area. The embassy was organized by Jesuit Alessandro Valignano in an effort to show Christian Europe how prosperous Christianity had become in Japan in such a short time. The group visited various European capitals and the pope in Rome. Unfortunately for the Japanese envoys, by the time they returned home in 1590, Christian missionaries had been banned from Japan by Nobunaga's successor, Toyotomi Hideyoshi.

Although Nagasaki generally prospered during the period it was a church territory, hostilities in the area by non-Christian *daimyo* against Christians remained. In 1587 Hideyoshi was forced to intervene in the fighting during his final campaign to unify the country. He defeated the enemies of the Christian *daimyo* but took Nagasaki from the Jesuits and made it a public territory subject to his direct control. In addition, because Hideyoshi was angered by the forced conversion tactics of many Christian *daimyo*, he issued an edict calling for the expulsion of all Christian missionaries. He ordered one of his vassals to destroy all the castles and churches within Omura's domain, to confiscate the church territory of Nagasaki, and to collect a fine from the residents of Nagasaki. Some churches were torn down and fines extracted, but after receiving a substantial bribe from the Jesuits and local townspeople, the vassal chose not to enforce the expulsion order to its fullest, and the missionaries managed to go into hiding until the turmoil died down. Hideyoshi, although he condemned the missionaries, appreciated their role as interpreters and intermediaries in the Portuguese trade and did not want to jeopardize this profitable arrangement. After Nagasaki was ordered to become a public territory, Japanese officials came to town from time to time, but, in actuality, foreign missionaries and local Christian merchants continued to manage day-to-day administrative concerns and foreign trade.

In the latter half of the sixteenth century, Chinese traders and Spanish missionaries and traders from Manila in the Philippines also made their way to Nagasaki. The Portuguese and the Spanish were called "southern barbarians" by the Chinese and Japanese because they arrived in Asia from the south, but their tendencies to bathe infrequently and eat vast quantities of animal flesh with their hands also reinforced this characterization. This characterization did not, however, prevent the Portuguese and Spanish from feeling superior to their East Asian counterparts.

The Chinese traders, who had prior experience dealing with the Iberians in Manila and other parts of Southeast Asia, came to challenge the Jesuit role as intermediaries between the Portuguese traders and local Japanese merchants. Some of the Chinese not only had considerable trade experience in the region, but also spoke Portuguese, Spanish, and Japanese. Over time, a number of Japanese merchants also learned enough Portuguese, the *lingua franca* of the area, to communicate with Western traders. The Spanish missionary orders also challenged the Jesuits in terms of their approach to proselytizing. The Spanish missionaries were mendicants who concentrated on converting individual members of the poorer classes in Japan, while the Jesuits (employing the same strategy that proved successful for them in Europe) concentrated on converting local lords, who would then order the conversion of all residents within their domains. According to the papal bull of 1585 secured by the Jesuit Valignano, the Spanish were not supposed to have territorial jurisdiction in Japan, but they ignored the ruling and continued to trade, and later evangelize, there.

Matters became worse for all Christians in Japan after an episode in 1597, referred to as the *San Felipe* or 26 Martyrs Incident, occurred. In an attempt to regain his confiscated cargo, the captain of a Spanish ship that was shipwrecked off Japan threatened Hideyoshi with the boast that Spanish soldiers would soon follow Spanish missionaries to Japan. In reaction, Hideyoshi had six Franciscan missionaries and twenty Japanese Christians marched from Kyoto to Nagasaki in the dead of winter. In February 1597 they were all crucified at the Nishizaka execution grounds overlooking Nagasaki Harbor. Shortly thereafter, the Jesuits were forced to close both their college and their seminary in Nagasaki.

These events had little immediate effect on Portuguese trade, however, as Hideyoshi died the following year. With the onset of the Tokugawa period (1600–1868) and the rise to power of the shogun Tokugawa Ieyasu, new European players and new Japanese shogunate policies toward foreign trade and Christianity ushered in significant changes in Nagasaki's relationship with the outside world. The days of Nagasaki as a relatively open port filled with freewheeling traders from Portugal, Spain, China, and Japan, as well as European missionaries and Japanese Christians, soon ended, and a considerably more structured and restrictive atmosphere prevailed.

Initially, the shogun Ieyasu tolerated Christianity as a necessary evil as he attempted to maintain and expand foreign trade relations with the Catholic West, but by 1614 he was able to take a stronger stand against Christianity because by this time both Dutch (1609) and English (1613) Protestant traders, unaccompanied by proselytizing missionaries like the Portuguese and Spanish, had established trading posts at Hirado, just north of Nagasaki. These new European encounters diminished the need for Catholic missionaries to serve as foreign trade intermediaries between Japan and the West. Tokugawa government officials, in fact, soon prohibited Christianity throughout Japan and expelled all foreign missionaries. The edict effected the deportation of the last of the Christian *daimyo* and some foreign missionaries and the destruction of Christian churches, but it did not fully eradicate Christianity. Many foreign missionaries were able to escape depor-tation and carry on their work underground, and their numbers actually increased in the following decade as more missionaries were smuggled into Japan.

In what has come to be known as the Great Martyrdom of 1622, Japanese officials be-headed thirty Christian prisoners and put another twenty-five to death by fire. The exe-cutions took place at Nishizaka in Nagasaki, where twenty-five years earlier Japan's first martyrdom had occurred. Later in the decade, however, Tokugawa leaders changed their strategy in an attempt to eradicate Christianity in the Nagasaki area once and for all. Rather than killing Christians and, thus, making them instant martyrs, the local Nagasaki commissioner devised methods to force them to abandon their faith, including torturing them by pouring boiling sulfuric water into incisions on their bodies. By using measures such as this, and employing strict administrative controls, Tokugawa officials were able to drive Christianity even further underground. In time, Christianity all but died out in Na-gasaki and other large cities, but it remained strong in some rural areas and on small is-lands where strict application of the law was more difficult.

Trade in Nagasaki: Increased Japanese Control Through the Maritime Prohibition Policy

Nagasaki was Japan's largest foreign shipping port when Tokugawa Ieyasu reconfirmed its status as a public territory in 1600, but he was concerned about the degree of Por-tuguese control over the trade there. To rectify the situation, he established policies in which the Japanese came to control both *who* traded, by requiring the official sanctioning of all vessels that were allowed to trade abroad, and *how* goods were traded, by granting designated merchants of Nagasaki and other select Japanese cities the exclusive right to purchase, distribute, and negotiate the price of the silk brought into Japan by Portuguese ships.

For a brief period in the second decade of the seventeenth century, the Chinese, the Portuguese and Spanish, and the Dutch and English (whom the Japanese called "red-haired barbarians") traded side by side in Nagasaki and Hirado, but poor business deci-sions by the English led to their voluntary withdrawal from Japan in 1623. The following year Spain was ordered by Japanese officials to leave due to repeated violations of Japan's Christian-control measures. These departures left the Portuguese and Chinese in Na-gasaki and the Dutch in Hirado, and even this situation would soon change. Over the course of the 1630s, the Japanese shogunate enacted its maritime prohibition policy—one that, on pain of death, banned the dispatching of Japanese ships abroad and the return of those Japanese merchants already living overseas. Any Japanese trying to leave or return to Japan faced execution if caught by officials. The prohibition policy also deported the Japanese female companions and mixed-blood children of Westerners living in Nagasaki and Hirado. Finally, in 1639, in the aftermath of the Shimabara Rebellion (1637–1638), the Portuguese were expelled from Japan. Although viewed by Japanese officials of the day as a Christian rebellion, the Shimabara Rebellion was in fact a peasant-led protest against high taxes and the effects of famine. Many of the peasants of the region, however, were Catholics. In the end, thirty-seven thousand protesters were killed by government forces. (See Map 3.2.)

The ban came as a shock to many Nagasaki merchants who had invested heavily in building the man-made island of Dejima (Deshima) in Nagasaki Harbor from 1634 to 1636. However, after the Shimabara Rebellion, the shogunate was intent on stamping out Christianity in Japan, and it felt that Dutch and Chinese ships could take up the slack in

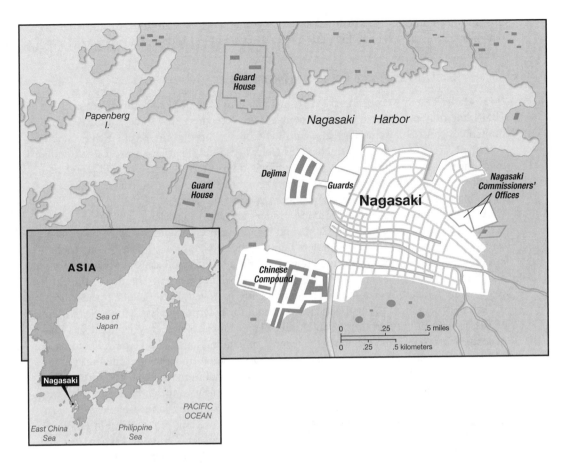

Map 3.2. Nagasaki Harbor

From the sixteenth century onward, Nagasaki served as East Asia's easternmost port. Beginning in the 1630s, first briefly the Portuguese, then for two centuries the Dutch, were forced to live on the man-made island of Dejima in Nagasaki Harbor, away from the local population. Later in the seventeenth century Chinese traders were also restricted to an isolated walled compound in the city near the harbor.

the absence of Portuguese trade. While the Portuguese stood to lose a fortune on the expulsion order, they gambled on the fact that other seemingly disastrous orders had been circumvented in the past. Their merchants in Macao made an attempt to reopen trade relations with Japan in 1640, sending seventy-four passengers and crew by ship to Nagasaki. They were immediately arrested pending the Japanese government decision on their petition to reopen trade; they later received word that not only was their petition rejected but they were to be executed for disobeying the expulsion order. Sixty-one were executed at Nishizaka, with thirteen Chinese crew members being spared in order to carry news of the event back to Macao. The Portuguese attempted one last time to reopen relations in 1647, but with the failure of that mission, they decided not to try again.

In their seven decades of activity in Nagasaki, the Portuguese made significant contributions to local culture. As the *lingua franca* of the day, the Portuguese language introduced a number of words to the Nagasaki dialect, such as those for spongecake, tobacco, cup, and raincoat. Furthermore, the Portuguese and their Jesuit partners introduced hospitals, schools, and the printing press to Nagasaki, to say nothing of Christianity, which fundamentally shaped the period of early encounters, as described above.

Chinese Merchants as Private Traders and Intermediaries

In 1641 the Dutch were transferred from Hirado to Dejima. From this time until the 1850s, the only permissible Japanese contact with foreigners was trade conducted with the Chinese and Dutch in Nagasaki, with the Chinese through the Ryukyu Islands, and with the Koreans via trade representatives from Tsushima. That Japan had established a maritime prohibition policy was not at all unique in East Asia. Both China and Korea had established at different times their own restrictive measures to control maritime relations, including relations with their Asian neighbors, not just the West.

As mentioned above, private Chinese traders came to Nagasaki in the late sixteenth century, as official trade between China and Japan had been prohibited by Ming officials due to high levels of piracy in the waters between the two countries. These private traders not only conducted their own trade, they also served as intermediaries between the various Westerners and the Japanese merchants in both Nagasaki and Hirado. In the early years, some Chinese merchants lived permanently in Nagasaki to facilitate trade there, while others continued to ply their trade back and forth across the East China Sea. In the 1630s, in light of the maritime prohibition policy of the Japanese government, the Chinese were forced to decide whether they would remain in Nagasaki on a permanent basis and become Japanese citizens or serve merely as seasonal traders with Chinese citizenship and not be allowed to live in the town. A substantial number chose the former and intermarried with local Japanese women. The others continued to sail back and forth between China and Japan and came under increased scrutiny by Japanese authorities. At first the Chinese traders were required to stay in certain sections of town, but in 1689, after the Chinese government reopened official trade between China and Japan and the number of ships coming to Nagasaki increased dramatically, they were confined to a seasonal residence within an enclosed Chinese compound near the harbor. By this time, the Tokugawa shogunate had established its own elaborate system of guards, interpreters (who were chosen from the Chinese that had earlier decided to reside in Nagasaki permanently), and officials to oversee the visiting Chinese traders.

Chinese influence on present-day Nagasaki from the Tokugawa period is considerable. Especially striking are the number and variety of Buddhist temples and stone arch bridges built by Chinese residents of the city. Important styles of Chinese art and music were also introduced into Nagasaki. In addition, many of the city's annual rituals are heavily influenced by China, including the *peiron* boat races, the Buddhist Bon Festival, and the dragon dance from Nagasaki Kunchi. Its cuisine also reflects Chinese influence. Nagasaki's *shippoku ryori*, a multicourse meal containing influences from Japanese and Western cuisine as well, clearly owes its origins to Chinese food eaten on round, rotating, Chinese-style tables that became popular in Japan during the early Tokugawa period.

Nagasaki: Japan's "Window on the World" (1641–1853)

In addition to the activity of the Chinese in Nagasaki, the seventeenth-century city was also profoundly shaped by the Dutch. The first Dutch arrived in Japan on the ship *Leifde*, which ran aground off the eastern coast of Kyushu in 1600. Most of the surviving crew members returned home in 1605 with a trading permit from Tokugawa Ieyasu inviting other Dutch merchants to come to Japan to trade. Two ships belonging to the newly created Dutch East India Company (VOC) arrived at Hirado in 1609 and, with the support of the local *daimyo*, established a trading post there. The Dutch remained headquartered at Hirado until 1641 when they were ordered by Japanese officials to relocate to the man-made island of Dejima in Nagasaki Harbor. This was their punishment for having used the phrase "in the year of the Lord" on a warehouse building they were dedicating.

The nature of the Japanese administration of the Dutch trade at Nagasaki varied over time, as did the goods allowed to be exported, the number of Dutch ships allowed to visit Nagasaki annually, and the value of goods allowed to be traded. However, the routine for the handful of Dutch living on Dejima when ships were not in port remained monotonously unwavering. Only a single small bridge connected the island to the Nagasaki mainland. The Dutch spent almost all of their time on the island except when they were allowed brief local excursions or made their annual visits to Edo (Tokyo) to pay homage to the shogun. The Dutch were not allowed to bring their wives to Nagasaki, and they were usually permitted visits from only the lowest class of Japanese prostitutes in town.

When ships were in port, however, life bustled with the activities of unloading, storing, and selling goods and making room for all the visitors. One of the most important duties of visiting Dutch traders was to provide information on what was happening in terms of political, military, and scientific developments in the outside world. Japanese officials kept meticulous records of these sessions and forwarded all reports to Edo. Dutch visitors and merchants also brought gifts and manufactured goods from around the world to share with the shogun and others in Japan. In this way, Nagasaki served as the port of entry for both Western ideas and Western products. Eventually, Nagasaki became a center of *rangaku* (literally "Dutch learning," but more accurately "Western learning"), which provided Japanese scholars the opportunity to learn about Western science, medicine, mathematics, military weapons and tactics, clocks, glassmaking, and, later, photography. The Dutch language became the new *lingua franca* for trade at Nagasaki from the mid-seventeenth to the mid-nineteenth centuries. Not only did hundreds of Dutch words enter the Japanese vocabulary (including words for coffee, beer, and glass), but some scholars argue that the Dutch language went so far as to influence Japanese grammar. Through the Dutch window at Nagasaki, the Japanese learned much about the outside world, and when Japan's maritime prohibition policy was successfully challenged by Western powers in the mid-nineteenth century, Japan was in a better position to protect itself from outside aggression than most other Asian nations.

Western Challenges to the Japanese Maritime Prohibition Policy

With the implementation of the Japanese shogunate's maritime trade prohibition, all Westerners (except the Dutch) who strayed into Japanese waters—no matter the reason—were taken to Nagasaki, where they were imprisoned until they could be deported on the next Dutch ship leaving the harbor. The British, Russians, and Americans all made attempts to challenge this policy. The foreign trade at Nagasaki was not particularly lucrative, but Western nations kept bumping into Japan's prohibition policy as they tried to expand trade opportunities in the Pacific and East Asia. The Dutch and the British, with their East India Trading companies, were firmly established in Batavia and Canton, respectively, while the Russians were trying to expand into contested waters to the north, and the United States had whaling ships and clippers involved in its China trade being constantly harassed by Japanese officials. The British, who had voluntarily severed trade with Japan in 1623, tried to reopen relations fifty years later by sending the ship *Return* to Nagasaki. The ship was allowed to resupply, but then Japanese officials promptly ordered it to leave. The most notorious incident involving the British occurred in 1808, when the *Phaeton* attempted to capture Dutch ships by entering Nagasaki Harbor flying a Dutch flag. (The two countries fought on opposite sides during the Napoleonic Wars of 1799–1815.) The incident proved the defenses at Nagasaki woefully inadequate, and the commissioner in charge of administering the town committed suicide to take responsibility for the debacle. In light of this and other failures, the British largely turned their attention to China. In reaction to the incidents provoked by the British in the early nineteenth century, Nagasaki government officials ordered the Dutch on Dejima to develop a Dutch-English dictionary and teach English-language classes to Japanese interpreters in order to prepare them for what was clearly becoming the next *lingua franca* of the region—English.

The Russians had also been trying, unsuccessfully, to challenge the prohibition policy. Russia had long been interested in Japanese territories in the north, and in 1792 its first formal attempt to establish trade relations with Japan occurred when a Russian ship sailed to Hokkaido to return castaway Japanese sailors. Per standard Japanese practice, the Russian envoy was instructed to go to Nagasaki, but he declined and returned to Russia instead. In 1804 the head of the Russian-American Company traveled to Nagasaki in another attempt to open trade relations. Treated poorly by local officials, however—black panels were erected around their quarters so that residents could not see the Russians— and given the fact that the envoy was forced to wait six months in Nagasaki for a denial to his trade request, the Russians did not come to Nagasaki again until after American commodore Matthew Perry opened the country.

Americans had traded in Nagasaki from the 1790s, when, for a decade, they substituted for Dutch sea captains during the Napoleonic Wars, but later interactions were confined primarily to American shipwrecks in Japanese waters. It was not until the arrival of Commodore Perry and his armed fleet in 1853 and 1854 that Japan's maritime prohibition policy was finally overturned. Perry's threat to use his fleet's guns to bombard Edo (an attack that Japanese leaders knew they could not repel) led to a change in policy by Japanese officials. Perry's use of armed force to open Japan, along with the British defeat of China in the Opium War a decade earlier, represented the beginning of the second major phase of Western imperialism in Asia. Various commercial treaties between Japan and the West followed in 1858; these opened Nagasaki and two other Japanese ports to foreign trade and residence. A foreign settlement was constructed, with landfill brought in from neighboring islands to fill the eastern side of Nagasaki Harbor. The Russians, who later used Nagasaki as a winter port for their Asiatic fleet, lived in a separate area across the harbor. Soon the settlements were crowded with Western missionaries, sailors, merchants, and government officials. The latter were necessary because the new so-called unequal treaties enabling foreigners to reside and trade in Nagasaki provided for "extraterritoriality"—the right to try Westerners according to Western law. Also included in the treaties were a "most-favored-nation clause" and the right of Western nations to determine tariff duties on most Japanese goods. Having seen how easily British military might had defeated outdated Chinese forces a decade earlier, some Japanese leaders decided that the better part of valor would be to meet Western demands, at least until Japan could strengthen its economy and its military defenses.

The Nagasaki Foreign Settlement, 1859 to 1899

The opening decade of the foreign settlement in Nagasaki held great promise for some Westerners, especially merchants and missionaries. Expectations ran high among Western merchants that trade in Nagasaki would immediately soar because of the city's experience with foreigners, its excellent harbor, its proximity to Shanghai and the China coast trade, and its ample supply of coal. People remarked that Nagasaki was destined to become the "Honolulu of Japan" or "another New York." Hope also prevailed among Western missionaries, who had been excluded from Japan since the early seventeenth century. Christianity had been virtually eliminated from Japan by 1638, with the last bloody campaign of suppression having been fought at Shimabara near Nagasaki. While still facing an official Japanese government ban of the religion, nineteenth-century missionaries, both Protestant and Catholic, recognized the symbolism of rekindling the fires of Christianity in the very place where two centuries earlier they had been extinguished.

Joining the agents of God and greed in Nagasaki were consular officials and Western employees of the Japanese government. Completing the foreign population was a short-term assortment of sailors, travelers, entertainers, and vagabonds. British merchants dominated trade in the early years of the Nagasaki foreign settlement because of their leadership in the China trade, in which they had been active in Canton since 1699, and then at various coastal treaty ports since the 1840s. The only large American trading firm during the settlement's first decade was aided by the fact that its head also served as US consul. While the British and American merchants boasted the largest numbers, the French, Dutch, and Prussians also actively traded in Nagasaki. Many of the merchants worked as provisioners, shipbuilders, harbor pilots, tavern owners, and hotel proprietors. Most of these merchant-adventurers were young men (there were very few women) who arrived in town with little money in their pockets, looking for whatever work they could get and advancing as far as their wits and skills would take them.

The decade of the 1860s was vibrant and exciting in Nagasaki, as hundreds of Western merchants (and their Chinese *compradores*, or intermediaries) moved in and out of the port town looking for easy money. A few made early fortunes on currency exchange and the sale of tea, ships, and weapons, but these were usually lost as quickly as they had been gained. Only a handful of merchants from the decade remained in Nagasaki into the 1870s. Almost from the beginning, the shrewder foreign merchants in Nagasaki realized that greater profits could be made in Yokohama and Kobe, the two foreign settlements near the large commercial and industrial centers of Tokyo and Osaka. Yokohama was not only close to Tokyo, but also had direct access to the rich silk trade of eastern Japan. Situated on the east coast, Yokohama was also much closer than Nagasaki for Americans coming from San Francisco, California. Kobe's opening in 1868 virtually sealed the fate of Nagasaki as a major trade center. Almost all of the major trading firms in Nagasaki had moved their headquarters to Yokohama or Kobe by the end of the 1860s. Even the first English-language newspaper in Japan, which had been founded in Nagasaki in 1861, lasted only a few months before the editor took his business to Yokohama.

The other important source of wealth for foreign merchants in Nagasaki in the 1860s also disappeared with the victory of the opposition domain forces over the Tokugawa government forces in the Meiji Restoration of 1867–1868. Having made considerable money selling arms and ships to both sides in the early and mid-1860s, individual foreign merchants saw the well go dry with the success of the restoration. The restoration eliminated the Tokugawa shogunate and replaced it with what would become a constitutional monarchy, a bicameral legislature, and political parties. The new government came to be headed by a small group of oligarchs from the former domains of Satsuma and Choshu who pushed the country toward rapid industrialization and militarization.

If trade waned after the opening decade of the foreign settlement in Nagasaki, these years did see renewed activity of Western missionaries. According to treaty provisions,

Westerners were allowed to practice their religion within the confines of the foreign settlement, but the propagation of Christianity among the Japanese population was still prohibited, due to the fact that, in the eyes of Japanese leaders, Christianity remained a threat to centralized government control. By 1869 the pioneer Protestant missionaries who had arrived in Nagasaki ten years earlier were gone, as was the dream of having American Protestant missionaries reestablish Christianity in the Japanese city where it had been virtually eliminated two hundred years earlier.

Nevertheless, other missionaries continued their efforts within the foreign settlement as they studied the Japanese language and waited for the ban against Christianity to be lifted. Joining the early American and British Protestants in Nagasaki was the Paris Foreign Missionary Society, which monopolized Catholic missionary work in town. These missionaries had even higher hopes for Nagasaki because of the Catholic successes at conversion in the area more than two centuries earlier and the prospect that some of the descendants of the original Catholics might have survived. In fact, despite intense persecution by Tokugawa officials in the early seventeenth century and continued government efforts throughout the period to enforce the anti-Christian ban, thousands of Japanese Catholics—almost all of whom lived in the vicinity of Nagasaki—retained their faith into the nineteenth century. These so-called *kakure kirishitan* (hidden Christians) survived by taking their religious beliefs underground and restricting membership to family and friends that they knew could be trusted. This meant secret ceremonies, Christian images disguised as Buddhist icons, oral transmission of beliefs, and, quite often, dangerous marriages within restricted gene pools, but through these measures they managed to keep their religion alive. What resulted was a crypto-Christian religious movement that was unique to Japan.

By the end of the first decade of the foreign settlement, the French Catholic missionaries had achieved mixed results. They had constructed an impressive church that had coaxed thousands of Japanese Christians out of hiding, but now these Christians faced persecution by the Japanese government. It would be 1873 before Western pressure and a change of heart by Japanese government officials, after witnessing firsthand the close relationship between Christianity, Western politics, and economic growth during a trip abroad would reverse the ban on Christianity and allow the return of Japanese Christians to Nagasaki. The French Catholics faced different problems from the American Protestants, but for both groups the opening decade of the foreign settlement in Nagasaki proved a frustrating experience.

Also playing an important function in the first decade of the foreign settlement were Westerners invited by the Japanese government to serve as technicians, doctors, and teachers to the Japanese community. This group was led by the Dutch, who had gained the confidence of the Tokugawa shogunate during their long residence on Dejima prior to Perry's opening of Japan. In 1857 Japanese officials employed roughly a dozen Dutch at their shipbuilding factories in Akunoura, across the bay near Inasa. The Nagasaki Government Hospital and the foreign language school also employed foreigners. At the latter, Japanese officials studied English (which came to replace Dutch as the language of trade), French, and sometimes Russian with foreign teachers, most of whom came from the ranks of British, American, and French consular officials and missionaries.

In addition to these long-term residents, a significant short-term population of sailors, travelers, entertainers, prostitutes, and vagrants also populated the foreign settlement. Of these, the sailors had arguably the greatest impact on Nagasaki—both in the foreign settlement and in the native town. The British, Americans, French, Dutch, Russians, and Prussians in particular sent large numbers of sailors, sometimes hundreds of them at a time, to the port. Tensions between the traders and the locals could run high, such as in the aftermath of the August 1867 death of two British seamen who were killed by a Japanese swordsman as they lay in a drunken stupor at the entrance to a Nagasaki "tea house." The incident almost led to war between Japan and Great Britain. Only victory by the opposition forces in 1868 brought an end to attacks on foreign sailors. The new Japanese government came to realize that attempts to drive away the heavily armed Western sailors with traditional swords were futile and that the only means of protecting the polity of Japan was to emulate the West by creating a strong country—both in terms of its industry and its military.

During the opening decade of the foreign settlement, the number of Westerners in Nagasaki increased almost threefold, from approximately seventy to two hundred. As the Western population expanded, the foreign residents took it upon themselves to develop various governing institutions and social organizations to regulate their activities. They adopted as models for most of these institutions and organizations those developed by the British at the foreign settlement in Shanghai, which, in turn, were modeled after those that they knew back home in London, England; Edinburgh, Scotland; Paris, France; New York City, New York; and Boston, Massachusetts. By the early 1860s, Westerners in the Nagasaki settlement had created a municipal council, a chamber of commerce, a fire brigade, a land renters' association, the Nagasaki Club, an amateur dramatic club, an annual regatta, and a church and cemetery society.

GLOBAL ENCOUNTERS AND CONNECTIONS:
Nagasaki's Nineteenth-Century Legacy

Nagasaki would never again reach the level of trade activity and cosmopolitan interaction of the 1860s. Frustration among Western merchants began to emerge as the great promise of the late 1850s diminished in the face of the harder realities of the last decades of the century. Foreign trade declined significantly when the major Western trading firms moved their headquarters to Kobe and Yokohama; the face of the Nagasaki foreign settlement during the 1870s and 1880s changed dramatically as the eclipsed town became primarily a coaling and supply site for passenger and military steamships. While there was a brief economic resurgence in Nagasaki in the decade bookended by the Sino-Japanese War (1894–1895) and the Russo-Japanese War (1904–1905), despite the increased ship traffic brought about by these two conflicts, as well as the Boxer Rebellion, the Spanish-American War, and the presence of the Russian Far Eastern Fleet and the Russian Volunteer Fleet, the port town never regained its earlier prominence.

For the missionaries of Nagasaki, conversely, the 1870s and 1880s brought better times. The persecution of Japanese Christians ended in 1873, and the Protestant and Catholic orders had some success building mission schools and churches for Japanese residents of Nagasaki. In spite of a conservative backlash by Japanese leaders in the 1890s, these schools and churches maintained a small, loyal following at the turn of the twentieth century.

During this period, Nagasaki also provided the evocative setting for one of the world's most popular operas, *Madama Butterfly*. First performed in 1904, Giacomo Puccini's work was based on a book written by John Luther Long, the brother of an American missionary stationed in Nagasaki in the 1890s. Long's book itself was inspired both by an earlier account of a French sailor's "marriage" to a Nagasaki prostitute and the anecdotes of Long's missionary sister. Together, these stories and the opera testify to the history of encounters in this important port city.

The "Window on the World" Today

Over the last century, as port cities nearer Tokyo have usurped Nagasaki's traditional trading role, Nagasaki has became increasingly isolated. Whereas the image of the city used to be that of Japan's "window on the world," the "Naples of the Orient," and the home to *Madama Butterfly*, today it exists in relative obscurity at the western extremity of Kyushu. This is not all bad, however, because the obscurity has enabled Nagasaki to retain much of the unique charm that distinguishes it from other similarly sized cities of Japan—especially those connected to the capital by the bullet train network—that have been overwhelmed by the creep of Tokyo's economic and cultural power.

Today, Nagasaki relies greatly upon historical tourism related to the atomic bombing of the city in 1945 and its long-time association with the outside world. While it has the Atomic Bomb Museum and the Peace Park to commemorate the bombing, the city has struggled to determine how best to showcase the richness of its international interactions. City officials have recently recreated Dejima's original fan shape and restored some of its structures, but many other Western-style buildings from the former foreign settlement were allowed to decay and have subsequently been torn down. The harbor coal mining islands of Takashima and Hashima, which helped make Nagasaki a vibrant recoaling stop for great passenger ships and naval vessels from around the world in the late nineteenth and early twentieth centuries, are now ghost towns and ecological disasters. Saddest of all, local officials have permitted Nagasaki's greatest treasure—its magnificent harbor—to be filled in little by little over the years until today it is a mere shadow of its former self. In spite of these setbacks, contemporary Nagasaki still weaves a wealth of Chinese temples and stone bridges, French and American churches and schools, British mansions, and reconstructed Dutch Tokugawa-period buildings across its historical cityscape.

ENCOUNTERS AS TOLD: PRIMARY SOURCES

The Dutch left a wide variety of written records documenting their more than two centuries of trade with the Japanese in Nagasaki. The following two sources speak to the interest of some Japanese officials and scholars in learning more about Western medicine, politics, customs, geography, astronomy, and other subjects.

Kaempfer's Japan: Tokugawa Culture Observed, by Engelbert Kaempfer

The most comprehensive chronicle of the Dutch experience on Dejima and of their journeys to Edo to pay homage to the shogun is Engelbert Kaempfer's *The History of Japan*, first published in London in 1727. Kaempfer, a German physician in the service of the Dutch, lived on Dejima from 1690 to 1692. Of the Japanese, he wrote: "[They] are brave, clever and imperious people. . . . In spite of their pride and military ethos, they are friendly, sociable, and as inquisitive a people as any that exists in the world. . . . I served them willingly and without charge in my profession, with medicines, and with a little instruction in astronomy and mathematics. . . . I questioned them about local matters, nature, and secular and spiritual topics with total freedom" (p. 28).

Kaempfer had the opportunity to accompany the Dutch chief factor (captain) on two processions to the shogun's court in Edo. His account of these audiences with the shogun, Tsunayoshi, reveals much about the Japanese curiosity of the Dutch and the outside world. After a formal ceremony in which they were presented to the shogun, the Dutch party was led to a large chamber in the shogun's castle. Tsunayoshi and several of his attendants sat behind blinds that shielded them from view and observed the Dutch, posing a number of questions to them.

- Why would the shogun be interested in the relative power of the political and military leaders within territories controlled by the Dutch?

- Why would he ask questions about Dutch religious practices compared to those of the Portuguese?

- What can we learn from the Japanese questions about Western medicine?

Our captain was asked: How far is Holland from Batavia? Batavia from Nagasaki? Who was mightier, the governor general of Batavia or the Prince of Holland? I was asked: Which internal and external illnesses I considered to be the most serious and most dangerous? How I treated damage caused by cancer and internal abscesses? Whether I had not searched for an elixir of long life like the Chinese doctors have done for many hundred years, and whether our European doctors had discovered anything? . . .

[Tsunayoshi asked] . . . whether I had ever cured any serious illness. . . . He asked after our funerals. . . . After our prince: What was his rank? Was the general of lesser rank and below him? Whether the latter governed by himself. . . . Whether we did not have prayers. . . . Whether we also had idols like the Portuguese? Whether there were thunder and earthquakes in Holland and elsewhere.

[The shogun had two of his physicians meet with Kaempfer.] I gave them the opportunity to take my pulse first. After that I, in turn, felt theirs and judged both to be healthy. The first was by nature cold and could do with an occasional nip of brandy to improve his circulation. The constitution of the other was a little too hot, his head was weak, and he suffered from ailments of the head, which was also obvious from his appearance. Thereupon the senior of the two asked me at what time an abscess became dangerous, and when, how, and in the treatment of which illness people were bled. He also indicated that he knew about our ointments and mentioned their names with awkward pronunciation, and I helped him with my awkward Japanese. And since the names I was saying were partly Latin and partly awkward Japanese, the shogun wanted to know in which language the Dutchman was speaking. The answer: Japanese, but badly.

Source: Engelbert Kaempfer, *Kaempfer's Japan: Tokugawa Culture Observed*, ed. and trans. Beatrice M. Bodart-Bailey (Honolulu: University of Hawai'i Press, 1999), 362, 409, 413.

Japan: The Dutch Experience, by Grant Goodman

An important study of *rangaku* (Western learning) is Grant Goodman's 1986 account *Japan: The Dutch Experience*. In the selections below, Goodman cites Japanese *rangaku* scholars of the Tokugawa period on their views of Western scientists and how these views clashed with traditional Chinese and Japanese interpretations of the world.

- What is the Japanese view of the role of reason in Western astronomy?

- Why do you imagine that it was difficult for the Japanese to accept certain scientific and medical ideas from the West?

People of the red-hair country customarily do things by mental reckoning and by reason; they only use implements they can see; if a fact is not certain, they do not say so, and they do not make use of it; having a high regard for the sun, they do not talk about the "upper regions"; they do not believe in Buddhism, and they do not accept mysterious things. . . .

Everyone in Europe knows about [the Copernican theory of heliocentricity] . . . but Chinese and Japanese do not even dream of such things. It is understandable that people think that the sun causes the day and night, but some are of the opinion that every day a new sun is created, travels from east to west, and then disappears. . . . In recent years, however, European astronomy has been introduced to Japan, and everyone has been astonished at the theory that the earth is actually whirling about. No one is prepared to accept it as the truth. Thus it is that in Japan great scholars astonished at the idea, have declared, "If the earth were spinning about, my rice bowl and water bottle would turn over, and my home would be broken into bits. How can such a theory be true?"

One day I was told of European medicine. I rejected those theories obstinately and spoke evil of it, without studying the good and the evil. Later I was introduced to [various *rangaku* scholars]. . . . I profited largely from this intercourse and regretted my former obstinacy. I sighed: "I have been mistaken. Medicine is an art that does a great deal of good and however studied does not matter, as long as it has the aim in view to cure."

Source: Grant K. Goodman, *Japan: The Dutch Experience* (London and Dover, NH: The Athlone Press, 1986), 50, 112–113, 134.

Further Reading

Burke-Gaffney, Brian. *Starcrossed: A Biography of Madame Butterfly*. Norwalk, CT: EastBridge, 2004.

Chaiklin, Martha. *Cultural Commerce and Dutch Commercial Culture: The Influence of European Material Culture on Japan, 1700–1850*. Leiden, the Netherlands: Research School CNWS, 2003.

Doeff, Hendrik. *Recollections of Japan*, translation and annotation by Annick M. Doeff. Victoria, Canada: Trafford, 2003. (Originally published in Dutch in Haarlem by Francois Bohn in 1833.)

Hellyer, Robert I. *Defining Engagement: Japan and Global Contexts, 1640–1868*. Cambridge: Harvard University Asia Center, 2010.

McKay, Alexander. *Scottish Samurai: Thomas Blake Glover, 1838–1911*. Edinburgh: Canongate Press, 1993.

Moran, J. F. *Japan and the Jesuits*. London and New York: Routledge, 1993.

Nakano, Michiko, ed. *Nagasaki under the Atomic Bomb: Experiences of Young College Girls*. Tokyo: Soeisha/Sanseido Bookstore, 2000.

Nobile, Philip, ed. *Judgment at the Smithsonian: The Bombing of Hiroshima and Nagasaki*. New York: Marlowe & Co., 1995.

Web Resources

Crossroads: A Journal of Nagasaki History and Culture, www/uwosh.edu/faculty_staff/earns/home.html.

"Dejima Comes Back to Life," www1.city.Nagasaki.Nagasaki.jp/dejima/en.

Japanese old photographs, http://oldphoto.lb.Nagasaki-u.ac.jp/en/.

Nagasaki Atomic Bomb Museum, www1.city.Nagasaki.Nagasaki.jp/peace/english/abm/.

Nagasaki: People, Places, and Scenes of the Nagasaki Foreign Settlement, http://www.nfs.nias.ac.jp/

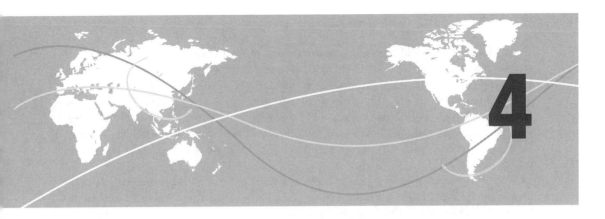

London

Emerging Global City of Empire

(1660–1851)

DANA RABIN

ONE ICY WALK ACROSS LONDON ON CHRISTMAS EVE 1992 ENCAPSULATES MY ambivalent relationship with this world city. I spent the academic year 1992–1993 in London researching my dissertation on crime and legal responsibility in eighteenth-century England. My fiancé and I had been invited to dinner at the home of a college friend and his family who lived in Richmond. After dinner they prepared to attend midnight mass while we made our way to the train station where we were assured a ride into the city, though on Christmas Eve we had been warned that service would stop at midnight. We weren't particularly worried, thinking naively that we'd be able to get a cab if no buses and trains were running in London. We caught the last train from Richmond that night, but it went only as far as Hammersmith—and we wanted to get back to my apartment in central London.

Snow and wind aside, we started walking steadily toward my apartment in central London, on Southampton Row. I was so proud of finding the place because the location allowed me to avoid the London transit system almost entirely. Most days I would walk through London's crowded streets passing a diversity of people speaking many different languages, their dress divulging their ties to places all over the world. On my way to the Public Record Office on Chancery Lane (now relocated to a new facility in Kew and re-named the National Archives) or to the British Library at its old location inside the

British Museum I would pass cafés whose menus offered curried salads and hummus sandwiches alongside the English standard of beans on toast. That night we enjoyed a wonderful walk through Earl's Court, Knightsbridge, and Hyde Park. When we got tired and decided to hail a cab, the prices were astronomical—even in terms of London's tremendously high cost of living. We would be travelling a distance of just over five miles with no traffic. We thought, how much could it be? Given our limited graduate student budget, we declined each cab, explaining to the driver that we only wanted to *ride* in the cab, not buy it.

What was memorable for me that night was walking through the streets of London, imagining the lives of the eighteenth-century men and women about whom I was reading every day. When we got to Piccadilly Circus (so quiet compared to its usual hustle and bustle) and Leicester Square, Covent Garden, and Soho, I was struck by how much activity was usually packed into this rather small area. In the stimulation of London's crowded streets, vitality and culture were on display alongside the snobbery of the capital, its fashion victims, and the homelessness and grinding poverty of many who flocked there seeking work that was scarce in the 1990s. While I had studied the city's contradictions for the four months that I had been there, when the ceaseless activity, noise, and pollution so typical of the place was still and quiet on that snowy night, I saw it from a new perspective that revealed the deep layers of the city's daily life.

This chapter seeks to demonstrate the interplay between London and Britain's growing empire in the eighteenth and nineteenth centuries. In addition to an overview of the city's physical growth and the trade, crafts, and manufacturing that grew up within and beyond its Roman walls, we will see the vitality of London's populace, its diversity, and its mobility. London was known as "the metropolis of the Empire," and indeed it was a center of government and finance, as well as the site of cultural production and change. Although some eighteenth-century contemporaries and current scholars might separate London from the British Empire, this chapter places them in the same frame in order to show how inseparable they were. To complicate our view, we must keep in mind that the idea of empire was more coherent than the empire itself. London functioned to bind together that set of far-flung places, each with their own distinctive cultures, histories, and ways of life all over the world. As a dynamic site of exchange, Britain's global empire came home to London in the form of people, goods, and ideas reshaping English food, music, language, literature, politics, and daily life.

LONDON AND THE WORLD: *Empire's Global Reach Made Local*

The Roman-British city of London was established as a market town in the first century of the Common Era. Indeed, trade remained the city's most important feature throughout its history. Set along the Thames River, a thoroughfare crowded with boats and barges, and spanned by many bridges, the city is forty miles from the sea, affording protected access to the English Channel. As the capital of England, London was the center of government along with administrative, legal, and economic activity. In 1660 England was emerging from a tumultuous period of civil war, which had included the beheading of the king, Charles I, and an experiment with republicanism. With the restoration of the monarchy in 1660, the land-owning gentry demanded more of a say in governance, and the role of their Parliament grew over the following century. The consolidation of political and economic power led to a period of tremendous growth in Britain's power and global reach. The "integration" of Wales in the sixteenth century, war and colonial occupation of Ireland, and a union with Scotland in 1707 expanded the English presence and influence

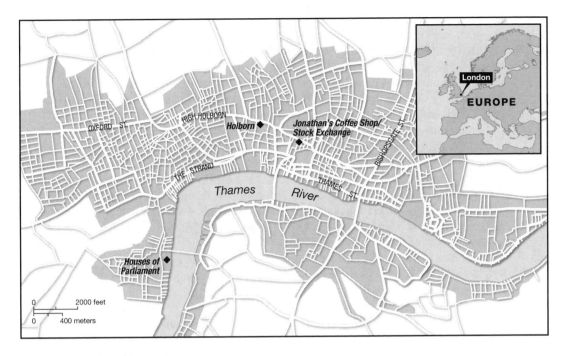

Map 4.1. London, ca. 1700s

The map of eighteenth-century London dramatically illustrates the city's dynamic force. Situated along the Thames, a thoroughfare that winds its way through the capital connecting the British Isles, the English Channel, the Atlantic Ocean, and Britain's imperial holdings, London was a site of exchange for exotic goods, ideas, and people.

throughout the British Isles. English men and women traveled and lived all over the world and established trading outposts and settlements from Ireland to Japan and from Virginia to Madagascar. Nonetheless, at the beginning of the seventeenth century Britain was lagging behind Europe's other empires—the Portuguese, Spanish, Dutch, and French—in its imperial expansion. Over the century and a half covered in this chapter, England forged a union with Scotland and consolidated its hold in North America, India, and Australia. During the "long eighteenth century," London became the world's greatest city and the capital of an expanding global empire—for a time the most powerful in the world. (See Map 4.1.)

English author Samuel Johnson (1709–1784) described London as a great city that provided an inexhaustible breadth of experiences and people such that "when a man is tired of London, he is tired of life; for there is in London all that life can afford." London in the eighteenth century was a city of perpetual activity, creativity, growth, and stimulation. A vibrant marketplace of ideas and a node of cultural exchange, London life offered—to those who could afford it—an infinite number of lectures, concerts, discussions, and debates. These activities often took place in new venues, most prominent among them the coffeehouse. Along with newspapers and plays, new genres like the novel emerged to convey opinions and commentary on the human condition and knowledge of the world. Nor was this endless conversation limited to the elite. A flourishing industry in images and cheap print circulated information and opinions about the latest religious controversies, political scandals, gender conflicts, economic crises, and news of the world.

And there was no shortage of things to buy. The Port of London handled 80 percent of the country's imports, with spices, tobacco, sugar, silk, and tea featured among the products that arrived from all over the world. London's booming market for luxury goods supported the skilled craftsmen who made china and earthenware, carvings of wood such as picture frames, coaches and carts, cabinets and upholstery, glass, jewelry, toys, clocks, watches, optical instruments, ironwork, coins and medals, buildings and ships, swords, snuff boxes, and belt buckles.

In the eighteenth century, Britain's global economic, political, and cultural reach connected the British Isles, including Wales, a colonized Ireland, and Scotland, by formal union. Gibraltar in the Mediterranean, the North American colonies, the islands of the West Indies in the Caribbean, and India formed a network of global connections in which the British exercised influence through military strength, commercial ties, or colonial settlement. Although Britain conceded its loss of the North American colonies along the eastern seaboard of what became the United States in 1783, the voyages of James Cook in the second half of the century extended British holdings into the antipodes, literally the opposite side of the world, in what is now Australia and New Zealand. (See Map 4.2.) The Napoleonic Wars brought even more holdings, including Cape Town in southern Africa and Singapore on the Malaya Peninsula. London proclaimed itself the center of this expansive empire, but the vast networks that produced the British Empire decentered and provincialized London. For example, when the British acquired Quebec in the Seven Years' War, the government in London, known for its fiercely Protestant rhetoric, extended religious toleration to these new Catholic subjects with the Quebec Act of 1774, which allowed the inclusion of Catholics in the British military throughout the world. The demands of maintaining a global empire, such as the facilitation of trade or the conduct of war, multiplied the points of encounter and exchange, so no one place was the uncontested dominant imperial center. Nevertheless, London was an important and influential administrative and commercial node through which ideas, people, and commodities traveled constantly. London during this period epitomized encounter. Much of the scholarship on the British Empire has shown that London's influences stretched across the globe. This chapter seeks to demonstrate that London's people, institutions, and culture were transformed by the experiences of empire, difference, and mobility.

The Empire Manifested in London

Our story begins with the end of the old City of London. From September 2 until September 5 in 1666 the Great Fire of London raged, destroying much of the city. Over 373 acres within the city itself and 63 acres beyond its walls were destroyed. At least one hundred thousand people lost their homes. Rebuilding the city coincided with a tremendous influx of people into the metropolis. The capital's population was nearly 630,000 in 1715, up from a half a million in 1674. By 1760 the city's population had grown to 740,000, and in 1815 it was estimated at 1.4 million. This number doubled by 1850. Of Europe's cities only Paris, France; Naples, Italy; and Istanbul, Turkey, came close to London in size. Despite these numbers, London's rate of growth was inconsistent: periods of demographic and economic stagnation alternated with booming expansion. Among the city's impoverished close quarters, poor hygiene and malnutrition contributed to high mortality rates. The city depended on constant in migration for growth. Those who flocked to London looking for work were overwhelmingly young, and a full 25 percent of the nation's residents spent at least part of their lives (mostly in their youth, employed as servants) in the city's environs. Women outnumbered men. Immigrants were drawn to the city: Huguenots from France

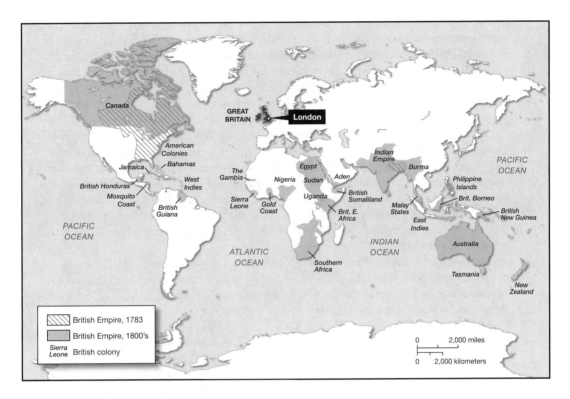

Map 4.2. Growth of the British Empire

Britain emerged as a world empire through the international wars of the mid-eighteenth century. Although the American colonies gained their independence in 1783, Britain retained its lucrative colonies in the Caribbean, and over the next century its holdings grew to include Canada, South Asia, and parts of Africa, earning it the title "the Empire on which the sun never sets."

and other Protestants came to escape religious persecution; South Asian seamen, the lascars, were lured to London's port by the insatiable demand for skilled mariners; Irish men and women and young people from all over England and Scotland came to the city seeking employment; and enslaved persons were imported by their masters.

As befits the metropole of a global empire, the city's population was ethnically, religiously, economically, and racially diverse. Over the period covered in this chapter (1660–1851), the city was peopled largely by those from Scotland, Ireland, Wales, and England. During the last half of the eighteenth century, refugees came to Britain after the Seven Years' War, the American Revolutionary War, the French Revolution, and the Napoleonic Wars. In the 1830s and 1840s, migration brought political refugees exiled from repressive regimes. The well-known among them included Guiseppe Mazzini, Karl Marx, and the future Napoleon III. (Marx spent most of his time in the reading room of the British Library, where he wrote *Das Kapital*.) Many of London's immigrants settled first in the city's East End. Although this area was best known for the density of its Jewish population, Chinese and Irish immigrants settled there as well. As they became more established, the communities spread elsewhere in the metropolis. These constant new additions to the city's population imprinted London with cultural, intellectual, economic, and political influences.

The most obvious evidence of the entanglement of colonial and metropolitan Britain was the presence of some ten thousand to fifteen thousand people of African descent in the capital in the eighteenth century and estimates that up to five thousand blacks lived in other parts of England, most of them concentrated in Bristol and Liverpool. Britain's visual culture provides a rich record of black presence in eighteenth-century England, especially in the portraits of wealthy absentee landlords surrounded by their families, servants, and slaves. Masters brought enslaved Africans to London from Africa, the Caribbean, or the North American colonies, and free Africans who had emancipated themselves arrived at London's busy port after serving as sailors on slave ships or other British vessels. England's black population was overwhelmingly young, male, and transient. While many black men worked as sailors and soldiers, they also appear in visual sources as footmen, coachmen, pageboys, street vendors, and musicians, and they are mentioned in some criminal records as pimps, prostitutes, highway robbers, and beggars. The city was not segregated, and blacks and whites lived in close proximity, socialized together, and intermarried.

Another significant minority came from Britain's South Asian colonial territories. British trade in South Asia dated back to the early seventeenth century, and the contacts of colonialism in India, Cape Town, and Malacca brought many thousands of Indians to Britain as servants, scholars, students, royalty, officials, merchants, tourists, and settlers. Indian seamen, known as lascars, were the largest group. "Lascar" comes from the word *lashkar* or *khalasi,* the name for a crew or maritime labor gang hired by captains to work on their ships, so the term refers to their employment status rather than their ethnicity. Although the name as used by the English implied coherence among these immigrants from South and East Asia, the lascars were far from homogenous in terms of their ethnicity, religion, and caste backgrounds. Their labor built the expanding empire, especially in light of the shortage of experienced sailors, a consequence of the tremendous expansion of the British navy and no lack of opportunities for employment in global maritime trade.

The city's religious groups were also diverse. Some of the lascars were Muslims, and Romani (gypsies) and Irish Catholics who came to Britain to work as summer seasonal laborers found a winter home in London. The majority in the Protestant Church of England were joined by London's Catholic communities, which flourished especially toward the end of the eighteenth century. French Protestant Huguenots, who had been protected by the 1598 Edict of Nantes that granted them certain privileges, including religious liberty, fled to England with the edict's revocation in 1685. Two hundred thousand Huguenots left France for non-Catholic Europe. Fifty thousand Huguenots, many of them skilled craftsmen, sought refuge in England and ten thousand in Ireland. The modern term "refugee" has its origins in these events. Jews had been exiled from England by Edward II in 1250. Although they were never formally invited back or officially readmitted, Jews began to immigrate to England in the middle of the seventeenth century and comprised a growing population.

Slavery in the British Empire

The first fledgling English colonies in the Americas were established in the early seventeenth century in Virginia and Bermuda. Residents of both places found that they could grow tobacco, and, by providing for the insatiable European appetite for this product, they secured their economic future. The West Indian colonies began as private initiatives. Bermuda and the Bahamas were settled by an enterprise that had separated from the Virginia Company, and other islands, including St. Kitts, Barbados, Jamaica, and Antigua, were colonized by small chartered companies. Many of these places were already claimed by Spain, and the first English colonists engaged in violent clashes to seize and defend their plantations. By the middle of the seventeenth century, the English had taken control of several of the Caribbean islands that had been Spanish colonies and established sugar plantations in Barbados and Jamaica. The monocrop plantations of the New World in the Caribbean and the Chesapeake eventually cultivated sugar, tobacco, indigo, and cotton, thereby increasing the demand for slave labor.

The West Indian islands attracted many settlers seeking cheap land and the promise of quick profits. In the early seventeenth century, the labor working these crops was provided by indentured servants. The companies promoting the settlements facilitated the immigration of hundreds and sometimes thousands of indentured servants each year. These servants from England and Ireland exchanged the cost of their passage, food, and clothing for work contracts with a four- to seven-year term, at the end of which was the promise of freedom and their own land. By the 1640s there were twenty-five thousand English and Scots in the West Indies. After the tobacco trade peaked in the middle of the seventeenth century, the plantation owners switched to growing sugar cane. This profitable crop made the West Indies the most valuable part of the British Empire in the early eighteenth century. Sugar was much more difficult to grow than tobacco, and it required a much larger workforce that was charged with arduous tasks. The supply of indentured servants no longer met the needs of the planters, who turned to importing black slaves from Africa. The slave population grew rapidly, and by the 1660s there were more black slaves than white settlers in the British West Indies.

Slaves for the West Indies and the southern colonies of North America were supplied by chartered companies, the Company of Royal Adventurers, and, later, the Royal African Company, which established forts and other contacts along the African coast. Private investors put up vast amounts of capital to finance the trading circuit that ran from Europe to Africa to the Americas and back to Europe. Factories in England and other parts of Europe produced guns. In the early period textiles from India were traded for slaves, rum, and tobacco from the Americas. By the end of the eighteenth century, the English were exporting an average of three hundred thousand guns to West Africa every year to trade for slaves. Although the first Europeans to dominate the slave trade were Portuguese, Spanish, and Dutch, by the eighteenth century Great Britain became the world leader. The trade was brutal, the conditions atrocious, and the treatment of Africans horrific and inhumane. Thousands of Africans died on the crowded slave ships and in their first months on the plantations. Bristol and Liverpool were the hubs of this extremely profitable trade. In the 1750s fifty-three slave ships a year carrying thirty thousand human beings across the Atlantic Ocean left from Liverpool on the triangle trade; by the end of the century it was eighty thousand to one hundred thousand young African men and women transported per year. By the 1780s more than 1.25 million Africans had been shipped to Jamaica, Barbados, and the smaller West Indian "sugar islands," and almost three hundred thousand had been sold in North America. Nine million enslaved persons were delivered between 1700 and 1850. Many more than that were captured.

Britain's dominance of the slave trade can be attributed to the convergence of several factors. The maritime resources and the strength of its navy certainly played a part. However, the fiscal resources and the sophisticated financial processes and institutions that developed in England in the seventeenth century provided the necessary infrastructure for the huge enterprise, from credit to insurance to the joint stock companies that raised capital and gathered investors. Certainly Britain's colonial expansion played a role, as did its manufacturing strength.

The first enslaved Africans were brought to England during the reign of Elizabeth I, and slavery was tolerated both at home and across the British Empire throughout the seventeenth and eighteenth centuries. Wealthy West Indian landlords and their families were more tied to Britain than the settlers in North America, and they always aspired to "go home." They established large communities in London, Bath, and Bristol, bought landed estates in the British countryside, and commissioned individual and family portraits that often featured their black slaves. An increasing number of West Indian planters became absentees after 1763 and returned to England with their slaves. In England enslaved persons were generally not used for labor; slaves were brought over as a mark of prestige and for convenience. Most slaves in England worked as domestic servants. The circumstances of urban slavery often allowed opportunities for escape, and many Africans self-emancipated while in Britain, though their owners hired slave catchers to discover and recapture them.

The presence in London of wealthy West Indian planters, their families, and their slaves drew attention to the moral, social, and legal contradictions between the English ideology of rule of law and equality before the law and the reality of slavery. The discomfort caused by these contradictions is evidenced in broadsides, newspapers, cartoons, novels, and plays in which returning planters were resented for their wealth and mocked for their social pretension. Although ridiculed in the press, the planters established strong organizations to lobby Parliament on their behalf. West Indian planters who returned to London served as concrete reminders of the realities of slave ownership and the wealth created by the slave plantations, all of which unsettled metropolitan sensibilities. They represented the inescapable fact that much of Britain's wealth was built on the slave trade and on slave labor and that the English (later British) government had sanctioned slavery in the colonies. In the eighteenth century the government accommodated and facilitated both slaveholding and the trading of slaves in ways that expanded the practices and maximized the profits garnered. It was the metropolitan demand for the products of the plantation—the same products on offer in London's markets and shops—that fueled the enterprise and its longevity.

London as a Center of Commerce

As the trade hub of a global empire, London also housed its financial center and what later became the London Stock Exchange. There was no stock exchange building in the seventeenth century, and shares were traded at two coffee shops in central London: Garraway's and Jonathan's, named after its owner Jonathan Miles, who opened it in 1680. Although trading in stocks was not new in the late seventeenth century, the level of trading intensified with the arrival in England of the Huguenots, who were experienced traders with strong connections to the markets in the Netherlands. They had liquidated their assets when they left France and were looking to invest. The business took off and London housed at least one hundred companies selling stocks by 1690. Although stock markets have medieval precedents in France and Italy, during the sixteenth and seventeenth centuries they developed around shipping and the spice trade in Europe's maritime empires, especially the Netherlands. Investors included wealthy British merchants, among them many Sephardic Jewish immigrants who came to England from Spain and Portugal via Amsterdam. The financial markets formed another imperial network of information, commerce, and confidence, and the value of stocks rose and fell according to the reports exchanged on these international webs of gossip, news, and speculation. Prices often fluctuated depending on hearsay about treasures lost, cargoes delayed, and weather predicted. Boys were paid to collect news at the docks or from the houses of wealthy merchants and to bring back whatever intelligence they could find.

The stock market was tremendously important to the growth of the British Empire as it provided the capital necessary for imperial expansion. The unregulated nature of the venture inevitably led to unscrupulous practices such as the rigging of markets and the use of insider information. Starting in 1697 brokers were required to be licensed and swear to act honorably in their stock trading. The South Sea Bubble of 1720 was the first stock market crash, prompted by the promise of profits from imperial trade with new markets, especially with Spain's South American colonies.

The crash and scandal of the South Sea Bubble was followed by financial crisis and ruin. This stock market crash encapsulated the political, economic, and cultural encounters so typical of London as a center of empire and a hub of financial and commercial activity. The bubble represents an irony of the eighteenth century: although the profits from trade with Europe and domestic markets far exceeded trade with Africa, Asia, or the Americas, commercial interaction with distant and seemingly exotic imperial partners lured many more investors who sought to participate in what would become the speculation and bribery at the heart of the scandal.

Through the wars of the last half of the seventeenth century, the British government had spent itself into debt that totaled over £10 million. Robert Harley (1661–1724), a Tory leader, founded the South Sea Company in 1711 to rival the Bank of England, which he saw as an arm of the politically dominant Whig party. An act of Parliament created the company and granted it a monopoly to conduct England's trade with Spain's South Sea colonies in the West Indies and South America, a source of extraordinary wealth. A large group of merchants joined together and bought some £9 million of the British government's debt, assured by the government of a 6 percent interest rate—about £540,000 annually. The company was organized as a joint-stock corporation that would raise working capital by borrowing on the security of the debt due from the government.

The stockholders were not promised any of this money as dividends. The promise of profits from trade in the New World, particularly South America, led eager investors to demand shares. Many envisioned the profits coming from the *asiento de negros*, which was the right to traffic in African slaves and to exchange them with the Spaniards in South America for payment in gold. Britain's occupation of Jamaica starting in 1655 provided a convenient stopover point in the long and arduous journey from Africa before crossing the Caribbean on the way to the final destination in the mines of Peru. In addition to transporting slaves, the *asiento* ships were used to smuggle profitable textiles and other manufactured goods. Slaving was the key to this prosperous trade with South America.

These trading opportunities envisioned by the company's founders never materialized. The Peace of Utrecht brokered in 1713, ending the War of Spanish Succession (1701–1714), contained very few Spanish concessions, but the company did secure a contract to transport and sell annually in Spanish America 4,800 "*piezas de Indias.*" The term did not refer to an individual slave; instead it was used as a unit of the slave trade, equivalent to an adult slave of a certain height with no visible physical defects. The same contract also allowed the company to send one ship a year to trade with the Spanish colonies. The British were allowed at seven ports: Buenos Aires, Caracas, Cartagena, Havana, Panama, Portobello, and Vera Cruz, at which they could sell, duty free, any merchandise that could fit on a single five-hundred-ton ship accompanying the annual Spanish treasure fleet from Europe. This was to be the wedge into the Spanish colonial market. The company contracted with the Royal African Company to supply slaves. Ignoring the regulations limiting the *asiento*, the company cultivated a significant trade in smuggled goods and slaves. Thirteen thousand enslaved persons were transported by the company's ships between 1713 and 1718; sadly, the inefficient handling of the slave trade resulted in a high mortality rate among the slaves carried by the South Sea Company. The direct trade in goods was also mismanaged and did not see much profit.

The trade came to a stop when Britain's relationship with Spain weakened in 1718. The company directors were undaunted, however, and they shifted their focus almost immediately from trade to high finance: the refinancing of Britain's huge war debt at a lower rate of interest. In 1720 Parliament allowed the company to take over more than three-fifths of the national debt. The company sweetened the deal with the government by offering a cash advance of more than £7 million. The directors' plan was to convert the national debt into company stock. As it took over more of the debt, the company issued more and more stock. The company bribed a number of politicians in order to win these privileges. As long as its stock rose indefinitely, the scheme would work. With parliamentary backing, the directors thought they had a financial miracle.

To stir up business and interest in the company's stock, the directors publicized false stories of the company's success and the profits earned in the South Sea. A buying frenzy by wealthy British men and women with money to invest followed in the early months of 1720 and resulted in a sharp spike in the price of a share in the company. On January 1 the price stood at £128. It reached £330 by the end of March, and on June 24 it hit £1,050 a share. The directors held stock worth far more than the company's earning power, and just before the public realized it, many of them sold their shares.

The crash hit in September and by December the stock was valued at £128 again. Thousands of investors in Britain were ruined. Banks failed when they could not collect loans on inflated company stock. Hard currency was scarce. Houses stood half built and abandoned. Investigations and trials resulted in jail time for some and financial ruin for others. Although the crash had devastating consequences for investors, the Bank of England (the South Sea Company's competitor) averted a systemic threat by underwriting the South Sea Company's scam, thereby restoring Britain's financial stability. Some economic observers have compared modern market crashes (most recently the mortgage crisis of 2008) to the South Sea Bubble of 1720. Although each crisis and panic has its own profile, the similarity rests in the frenzy to invest in a potential profit. In the case of the eighteenth-century scandal, empire and the promise of trade in new and expanded markets in the New World lured investors.

Overseas trade continued to expand in the 1720s and 1730s, albeit more slowly as financiers found other ways to raise capital. The annual value of British exports grew by one-third and the value of imports by one-fifth. Fire destroyed Jonathan's coffee shop in 1748, but it was rebuilt and first renamed Stock Exchange and then the Stock Subscription Room. It was officially designated as the London Stock Exchange in 1801 and soon became the city's most important financial institution. In addition to the Royal Exchange, the city housed the Bank of England and Lloyd's Insurance Market, the sites and products of the financial revolution. Their investors included many Englishmen involved in the slave trade.

As a warehousing center, London afforded its residents all the luxuries money could buy. One in nine Londoners was a shopkeeper. The shops were stocked with goods from all over the world, as well as local items produced by weavers and dyers, spinners and cloth finishers. As mentioned above, the Port of London handled 80 percent of the country's imports, with spices, tobacco, sugar, silk, and tea featured among the products that came through. The demand for luxury goods among London's wealthy created a consumer society that mimicked Chinese, French, and Indian trends in fashion and design and set global tastes.

A Rapidly Growing Metropolis

London's booming growth in the eighteenth century led to the city's physical expansion beyond the city walls and into the suburbs to the north and south. The infrastructure of the city never kept up with the rapid pace of industrialization and population growth. London's sensory impact imprinted visitors with the pungent stink of inadequate sewers, and the pollution caused by the coal that fueled the city and its industries often shrouded it in its famous fogs. The cholera outbreak of 1854 was a direct result of the inadequacy of city services, especially the removal of human waste and the overcrowding of burials in churchyards.

Despite the racial, ethnic, and religious diversity that defined London, the nineteenth century saw a marked physical separation of the rich and the poor, and the middling sort was spread throughout the city. Different parts of the city were known for distinguishing characteristics depending on their social or occupational profiles. In the seventeenth and early eighteenth centuries, the East End became the home of manufacturing, brewing and distilling, sugar processing, and textiles. Later in the eighteenth century and into the nineteenth century, manufacturing moved out of London to avoid the high costs associated with the capital. Other groups of the poor took up residence in suburban parishes along the city's northern and western borders. The architecture of buildings and city neighborhoods clearly marked distinctions of class and social hierarchy.

GLOBAL ENCOUNTERS AND CONNECTIONS:
Diversity's Impact on London

While the wealthiest aristocrats made up only 2 to 3 percent of London's population, the middling sort—professionals, established merchants, and shop keepers—made up 20 percent. Of the remaining 80 percent, most (60 percent) experienced poverty and destitution for some part of their lives. They often turned to their parish for inadequate charitable relief during periods of unemployment, illness, or old age. Immigrants received parish relief, but they also set up their own relief societies. Societies set up by the Huguenot and the Jewish communities assisted their coreligionists in need. Black churches, pubs, and organizations created a sense of community and provided poor relief and other forms of support for Afro-Londoners.

Contact between these different social groups was feared because political and social tension between classes had intensified in the early part of the nineteenth century, during which time working people sought better parliamentary representation and universal male suffrage. One place where this contact did not lead to violence or extended debate was the Great Exhibition of 1851, the first world's fair, which was housed in Hyde Park in Sir Joseph Paxton's Crystal Palace. The Crystal Palace was a specially constructed building of glass, supported by a cast-iron frame that was large enough to house a row of elm trees on the site. Each element of the palace was significant. The building's girders represented a century of experimentation with iron construction. The glass manufactured by the Chance Brothers and Company, a glassworks near Birmingham, displayed the newest technology in glassmaking, which was the result of collaboration and competition among French, German, Austro-Hungarian, and British glassmakers. Chance Brothers became the first company to adopt the cylinder method to produce sheet glass, and eventually it became the largest British manufacturer of window and plate glass and optical glasses. The trees enclosed within the building reflected a new sense of human mastery of nature.

The Crystal Palace exhibition brought together products from all over the world and was intended to encourage international trade, especially within the British Empire. In addition to the engines, locomotives, and hydraulic presses, the exhibition displayed threshers, reapers, mowers, seed drills, and chemical fertilizers related to the latest advances in agricultural technology. The display of the products of empire included the 186-carat Koh-i-Noor diamond from India, as well as brass, bamboo, and textiles from China and India. European goods also appeared. The exhibit was not intended to sell products directly to consumers. Most of the items on display such as steam engines were intended for industry. However, the organizers of the exhibition wanted to make some profit on running it, so they opened it to the public, at a quite low admission price that even workers could afford. The exhibition's organizers were worried about admitting so much of the public, rich and poor alike, because they feared it would set off class antagonism and the vandalism of the machinery. Their fears were relieved once the tickets went on sale. Many more people bought cheap tickets to see the exhibition than they expected, and the crowds behaved in an orderly fashion. The exhibition was open six months, and during that time fully a fifth of the population of England visited it. The Great Exhibition of 1851 brought the empire home to Britain by displaying global and manufactured goods for visual consumption and flaunting the nation's technological, economic, military, and industrial power.

Although the record shows a diverse England, some contemporaries resisted the incorporation of the colonial experience into the metropole. Britain's imperial expansion and the diversity of its population were not always embraced by all of the city's occupants. However, those who envisioned a global empire directed, inspired, and led by a cosmopolitan metropole accepted that the mixing of different peoples and cultures was integral to the imperial experience and to their cosmopolitan aspirations. The relationship between colony and metropole, outsiders and insiders, foreigners and "good subjects" operated with a boundary defined opportunistically depending on the circumstances. Imperial relationships were continuously and repeatedly fraught with the tension and arbitrariness of the line drawn and constantly redrawn between those considered English, British, or imperial.

What follow are two examples of imperial encounters in London in the eighteenth century. These real people crossed paths in London in this time of dynamic change. In both instances, discomfort with racial, ethnic, and religious differences elevated these events into newsworthy occurrences. Embedded in these discussions was a debate about the implications of Britain's imperial expansion, specifically the reality of a religiously, racially, and ethnically diverse London populated by Jews, gypsies, Asians, Africans, Scots, Irish, Catholics, and nonconforming Protestants. London's diversity raised questions about the nature of Englishness as a cultural tradition and the relationship between the English nation and the British Empire. Both of these scandals played out in a legal setting and highlight the importance of law in British ideology. In both the Canning case and the Somerset case that follow, the intersection of English law and British imperial aspiration in the eighteenth century can be seen. Both tested the ideology of fairness and equality before the law so often praised as uniquely English and cited as proof of English superiority and the very reason for the British Empire.

London Encounters: Elizabeth Canning and Mary Squires (1753)

On New Year's Day in 1753, Elizabeth Canning (1735–1773), an eighteen-year-old servant maid, disappeared from her home in London's East End. She was apparently a victim of kidnapping. When she returned to her mother's home a month later, she explained her disappearance by accusing a woman, later identified as Mary Squires, a "gypsy," of arranging her abduction, attempting to lure her to a life of prostitution, and keeping her a prisoner fed only bread and water for twenty-eight days in a house in Enfield. In addition to her allegations against Mary Squires, Canning implicated Susannah Wells, a reputed brothel keeper. A young prostitute, memorably named Virtue Hall, who had been arrested along with Squires and Wells, testified that she was living at Wells' house in January and had witnessed Canning's capture. Based on this evidence, the two older women were arrested and accused of assaulting Elizabeth Canning and stealing her belongings. Squires was sentenced to death and Wells to six months in jail. Contradictory evidence presented at the trial, however, raised doubts about the facts of the case. An investigation by Sir Crisp Gascoyne (1700–1761), lord mayor of London, resulted in Virtue Hall recanting her testimony, and on May 21, 1753, Squires was granted a full pardon. Elizabeth Canning was brought to trial for perjury in April 1754; she was found guilty and transported to the American colonies.

The case immediately became a "trial of the century." A pamphlet war raged between the Canningites and the Egyptians, who defended the gypsy. They believed incorrectly that the gypsies who had first arrived in England at the beginning of the sixteenth century came from Egypt. This controversy generated an unprecedented amount of published material including broadsides, ballads, pamphlets, and prints.

Almost immediately after Canning's return, her story aroused doubt and suspicion. Detractors questioned how she could have been dragged the ten to twelve miles from central London to Enfield Wash without a single witness reporting it. They wondered how she had survived for so long on only a "quartern loaf" of bread and a jug of water and how she had disciplined herself to apportion the food so exactly. They asked why she had not come home earlier seeing as she was able to escape as soon as she decided to do so. Several of her earliest supporters dropped away after she was taken to Susannah Wells' home on February 1. Elizabeth could not find the stairs that led to the room where she was kept, and her description of the attic as dark with bare floors was belied by two windows and a "Quantity of Hay." Most glaring was Canning's dramatic change to her story. During the visit to Wells' home, Canning first saw and identified Mary Squires as the woman who cut her stays. Until then only Susannah Wells had been implicated and there had been no mention of the gypsy.

The trial narrative prominently featured Mary Squires, "gypsy," and stereotypes about gypsies played a central role in the recitation of the crime and its subsidiary details. Gascoyne responded to what he perceived as injustice and prejudice. His ostensible belief in the superiority of British law and liberty compelled him to defend the alien gypsy against Canning's allegations. Gascoyne paid dearly for his campaign, which led to his defeat in the next election for lord mayor and ultimately cost him his political career. His detractors saw his defense of Squires as a corruption of English law by the imperial project.

The stories surrounding Elizabeth Canning are marked by anxieties about sexuality, race, and nation, the geographical mobility of the protagonists insistently drawing attention to a fissured metropole, as well as to Britain's imperial project. English women were considered civilized, domestic, and sexually contained; women from warmer climates were represented as prone to excessive carnal desires and unrestrained sexual behavior. The representations of the women in the case, Elizabeth Canning and Mary Squires, produced a sharp definition of Englishness in which the native-born "white" woman emerged as a virtuous and honest victim, while the gypsy accused of running a prostitution ring, whether from the warmer Egypt or India, was portrayed as lacking all morality, credibility, or assimilability. This scenario demanded quite a leap of faith in the case of Canning, considering the disdain and suspicion with which servants were regarded in the eighteenth century. Even the mobility that exonerated Squires did not prove her innocence to readers and jurors in eighteenth-century Britain. Squires' very presence in England was threatening regardless of whether she had committed any crime against Canning. The written record left regarding the case exposed an unwieldy female autonomy that made a lie of conventions regarding English femininity, domesticity, chastity, and virtue and collapsed imagined spatial divisions within the metropole. Ultimately what propelled the Canning case into the headlines and the alehouses were discomforts associated with empire and the moral and social threat it posed through its multiplicity of sites and the mobile bodies that moved in its shadows and hidden spaces.

London Encounters: The James Somerset Case (1771–1772)

James Somerset was born in West Africa around 1741. When he was eight years old, he was bought by European slave traders and sold in Virginia to Charles Stewart, a Scottish merchant who later became receiver general of customs. Stewart (and Somerset as part of his household) frequently travelled among the northern American colonies, moving to Boston in 1764 and then to London in 1768. On October 1, 1771, Somerset, then about thirty years old, left his master's house and refused to return. He remained at large for two months before he was captured by slave hunters and, on Stewart's orders, delivered to the ship *Ann and Mary* on the Thames. Somerset was brought on board, confined in irons, and bound for sale in Jamaica, which had been part of Britain's holdings in the Caribbean since 1655. Abolitionists working on Somerset's behalf, calling themselves his godparents, publicized his situation and applied to William Murray, first earl of Mansfield (1705–1793) and chief justice of King's Bench, for a writ of *habeas corpus*. A writ of *habeas corpus* (Latin for "you have the body") is issued by a court of justice to someone holding another person in his custody. The writ directs the detainer to bring his prisoner to a court at a specified time for a particular reason.

Somerset's case attracted the attention of prominent abolitionist Granville Sharp (1735–1813), who framed it as a test of the legality of slavery in England. Its proceedings were followed closely by both West Indian planters and abolitionists. While the planters campaigned for a ruling that would recognize colonial laws relating to slavery and enforce them in the metropole, Sharp advocated a ruling forbidding slavery in England. Although it resulted in Somerset's freedom, Mansfield's ruling did not outlaw slavery in England, though some slaves and slave owners thought it did. Instead, Mansfield resolved only the writ of *habeas corpus*. He declared illegal the coerced transportation of slaves from England but remained silent on the general question of slavery in England and throughout the empire. In the face of British rhetoric about the rule of law and equality before the law, Mansfield chose not to take the opportunity to outlaw slavery. Instead, he favored a vague settlement that satisfied neither the proslavery forces nor the abolitionists. Mansfield reframed the debate as inconclusive. In his determination not to rule on the case, he only put off the unwelcome task.

It was precisely this lack of division or separation of Englad and its colonies and the arbitrariness of the lines that were drawn that prompted slave owners to organize in order to pursue a legal claim to their practice of moving their slaves between and among imperial sites, including London, Bristol, and Liverpool. The West Indian slave owners were just as interested as Sharp in using Somerset as a test case. West Indian planters bankrolled the case and refused all offers to settle out of court in the hopes of finally re-solving the question of slavery in England in their favor. Somerset's case brought the issue to the public's attention, but did not resolve the question of slavery's legality either in Britain or in the colonies. It was not until 1807 that Britain outlawed the slave trade and 1833 when it outlawed slavery in its colonies.

Why did Mansfield rule as he did? Beyond the threat to profits and white slaveholders across the empire, too strict a division between colonial and metropolitan law carried with it unintended consequences and high stakes. Making explicit the differences between jurisdictions risked exposing the fractures and fissures that divided the imperial system, or worse, imposing a formal rupture. An expansive ruling that spoke to broader issues such as the lawfulness of slavery would be received as an antagonistic act and might draw attention to the differences between the legal systems. It could set the laws and the cultures that produced them, enmeshed as they were in the eighteenth century, against one another, radically changing them both in unforeseeable ways.

Somerset's case reminded Britons everywhere that much of Britain's wealth was built on the slave trade and slave labor. It revealed glaring contradictions within Britain's legal institutions. The English (later British) government had sanctioned slavery in the colonies for at least two hundred years before the Somerset case came to court. In the eighteenth century, England was the world leader in the slave trade and the government accommodated and facilitated both slaveholding and the trading of slaves in ways that expanded the practices and maximized the profits garnered. Mansfield's Somerset decision continued (and nurtured) the fiction of an imperial regime that was separate from the domestic.

As this chapter and these cases illustrate, while London's influence was felt from the Americas to Asia, those locales made themselves equally felt in London. The trade of goods served as a vehicle for the encounters and interactions of people from around the world, contributing to both a clash and mixture of ideas and cultures.

ENCOUNTERS AS TOLD: PRIMARY SOURCES

The documents below are related to the chapter's discussion of the South Sea Bubble (1720) and the Somerset case (1771–1772). Both historical events developed as a consequence of Britain's imperial expansion and each of them had some connection to London as a financial center of the empire and to Britain's role in the slave trade. As you read, consider the questions of encounter that have been raised in the chapter.

"A South-Sea Ballad," by Edward Ward

The following ballad discusses the stock market crash and scandal called the South Sea Bubble. The author, Edward Ward (1667–1731), was a successful and prolific satirist whose work commented on a wide range of current events and often took aim at London's high society.

- What is the speaker's attitude toward the architects of the bubble?

- How does the author portray London's financial institutions and the commercial activity that made up so much of life in London at the time?

- Does the speaker seem sympathetic to those who lost fortunes?

- How does the speaker portray the relationship between imperial expansion and ethnic, racial, and religious difference?

- How does the ballad portray the nation?

- Is the speaker critical of capitalism?

I.

In London stands a famous Pile,
And near that Pile an Alley,
Where merry Crowds for Riches Toil,
And Wisdom stoops to Folly.
Here Sad and Joyful, High and Low,
Court Fortune for her Graces,
And as she Smiles or Frowns, they show
Their Gestures and Grimaces.

II.

Here Stars and Garters do appear,
Among our Lords the Rabble,
To buy and sell, to see and hear
The *Jews* and *Gentiles* squabble.
Here crafty Courtiers are too wise
For those who trust to Fortune,
They see the Cheat with clearer Eyes,
Who peep behind the Curtain.
[. . .]

V.

'Tis said, that Alchimists [sic] of old
Could turn a Brazen Kettle,
Or Leaden Cistern into Gold,
That noble tempting Mettle,
But if it here may be allow'd
To bring in Great and Small Things,
Our cunning *South Sea*, like a God,
Turns Nothing into All Things.

VI.

What need have we of *Indian* Wealth,
Or Commerce with our Neighbours,
Our Constitution is in Health,
And Riches crown our Labors:
Our *South-Sea* Ships have golden Shrouds,
They bring us Wealth, tis granted,
But lodge their Treasure in the Clouds,
To hide it till it's wanted.

VII.

Britain bless thy present State,
Thou only happy Nation,
So odly [sic] Rich, so madly Great,
Since Bubbles came in Fashion.
Successful Rakes exert their Pride,
And count their airy Millions.
Whilst homely Drabs in Coaches ride,
Brought up to town on Pillions.

VIII.

Few Men, who follow Reason's Rules,
Grow fat with South Sea Diet,
Young Rattles and unthinking Fools
Are those that flourish'd by it
Old Musty Jades and Pushing Blades,
Who've least Consideration,
Grow Rich apace, whilst wiser Heads
Are struck with Admiration.

IX.

A Race of Men, who t'other Day
Lay crush'd beneath Disasters,
Are now by Stock brought into Play,
And made our Lords and Masters.
But should our *South Sea Babel* fall,
What Numbers would be Frowning,
The Losers then must ease their Gall
By Hanging or by Drowning.

X.

Five hundred Millions, Notes and Bonds,
Our Stocks are worth in Value.
But neither lie in Goods or Lands,
Or Money, let me tell ye.
Yet tho' our Foreign Trade is lost,
Of mighty Wealth we Vapour,
When all the Riches that we boast
Consist in Scraps of Paper.

Source: Edward Ward, "A South-Sea Ballad: or, Merry Remarks upon Exchange-Alley Bubbles" (Edinburgh, 1720).

Extracts from Such as the Penal Laws, by John Fielding

John Fielding (1721–1780) was a magistrate in London and the half brother of novelist Henry Fielding. In 1751 he became a justice of the peace for Westminster, and then he assumed those duties for Middlesex in 1754. In the same year he became a court justice and advised the government on issues of law and order. Fielding is best known for his work to prevent crime. There was no organized professional police force in England in the eighteenth century, but Fielding organized the Bow Street office to try to gather and coordinate information about known criminals in and around London and later the whole country.

- What is Fielding's attitude toward West Indian planters who brought their slaves to England?

- Does Fielding object to slavery?

- How does Fielding describe the attitude of slaves who came to Britain with their masters?

- How does Fielding's warning about slaves in London relate to this project to prevent crime?

- Why is Fielding worried about exposing slaves to a "Country of Liberty?"

- How do you think Fielding felt about the British Empire?

The mixture of Foreign Servants with the English never fails to beget Jealousies, Quarrels and Disturbances in the Families where they live . . . it is clear to Demonstration to every impartial Mind that there cannot be a Conveniency that ought to be expected from a Servant, but what may be certainly found among those who are born and brought up in Great Britain: The immense Confusion that has arose in the Families of Merchants and other Gentlemen who have Estates in the West-Indies, from the great Number of Negro Slaves they have brought into this Kingdom also deserve the most serious Attention; many of these Gentlemen have either at a vast Expense caused some of these Blacks to be instructed in the necessary Qualifications of a domestic Servant, or else have purchased them after they have been instructed; they then bring them to England as cheap Servants, having no Right to Wages; they no sooner arrive here, than they put themselves on a Footing with other Servants, become intoxicated with Liberty, grow refractory, and either by Persuasion of others, or from their own Inclinations, begin to expect Wages according to their own Opinion of their Merits; and as there are not already a great Number of black Men and Women who have made themselves so troublesome and dangerous to the Families who brought them over as to get themselves discharged; these enter into Societies, and make it their Business to corrupt and dissatisfy the Mind of every fresh black Servant that comes to England; first, by getting them christened or married, which they inform them makes them free (tho' it has been adjudged by our most able Lawyers, that neither of these Circumstances alter the Master's Property in a Slave.) However it so far answers their Purpose, that it gets the Mob on their Side, and makes it not only difficult but dangerous to the Proprietor of these Slaves to recover the Possession of them, when once they are spirited away, and indeed it is the less Evil of the two, to let them go about their Business, for there is great Reason to fear that those Blacks who have been sent back to the Plantations, after they have lived from Time in a Country of Liberty, where they have learnt to write and read, been acquainted with the Use, and entrusted with the Care of Arms, have been the Occasion of those Insurrections that have lately caused and threatened such Mischiefs and Dangers to the Inhabitants of, and Planters in the Islands of the West-Indies; it is therefore to be hoped that these Gentlemen will be extremely cautious for the future, how they bring Blacks to England.

Source: John Fielding, *Extracts from Such as the Penal Laws as Particularly Relate to the Peace and Good Order of the Metropolis* (London, 1768), 143–144.

Further Reading

Blackburn, Robin. *The Making of New World Slavery: From the Baroque to the Modern, 1492–1800.* London: Verso, 1997.

Carswell, John. *The South Sea Bubble.* London: Alan Sutton, 1993.

Fox, Celina, ed. *London World City, 1800–1840.* New Haven: Yale University Press, 1992.

Games, Alison. *The Web of Empire: English Cosmopolitans in an Age of Expansion, 1560–1660.* New York: Oxford University Press, 2008.

Gerzina, Gretchen Holbrook. *Black London: Life Before Emancipation*, New Brunswick NJ: Rutgers University Press, 1995.

Langford, Paul. *A Polite and Commercial People: England 1727–1783.* New York: Oxford University Press, 1989.

Morgan, Kenneth. *Slavery and the British Empire: From Africa to America.* New York: Oxford University Press, 2007.

Nussbaum, Felicity. *Torrid Zones: Maternity, Sexuality, and Empire in Eighteenth-Century English Narratives.* Baltimore: Johns Hopkins University Press, 1995.

Porter, Roy. *London: A Social History.* Cambridge: Harvard University Press, 1995.

Wilson, Kathleen, ed. *A New Imperial History: Culture, Identity, and Modernity in Britain and the Empire, 1660–1840.* New York: Cambridge University Press, 2004.

Web Resources

Moving Here: 200 Years of Migration to England, www.movinghere.org.uk/.

The Proceedings of the Old Bailey, London's Central Criminal Court, 1674–1913, www.oldbaileyonline.org/index.jsp.

South Sea Bubble Resources in the Kress Collection at the Baker Library, Harvard Business School, www.library.hbs.edu/hc/ssb/.

The Trans-Atlantic Slave Trade Database, www.slavevoyages.org/tast/index.faces.

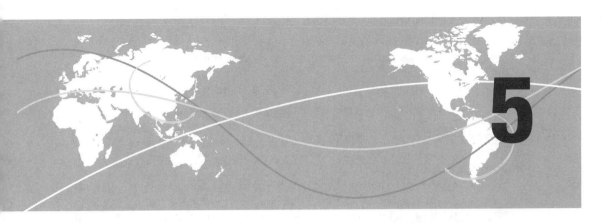

5

Gorée

At the Confluence of the Atlantic, Saharan, and Sahelian Worlds

(1677–1890)

TREVOR R. GETZ

O N A BRIGHT, WARM FALL MORNING I STEP OFF THE *chaloupe* (FERRY) FROM THE African mainland and onto the dock at Gorée Island. I'm not sad to leave the bustling metropolis of Dakar behind for a few hours. After two months, the pleasures of the Senegalese capital have worn off somewhat. The splendid French, Lebanese, and West African restaurants and the bustling nightclubs with their Afrobeat sound now just exhaust me, and even the relative calm of the national archives—one of the finest and best staffed anywhere—seems a bit stale and fetid. The busy, polluted streets are choking, and the daily cries of the Muslim *muezzins*, ringing of church bells, and construction jackhammers all jar me with their vibrations.

By contrast, Gorée is restful and welcoming. There are no cars whizzing by, no construction crews racing to build a new world-class hotel. Rather than concrete, the men on the street corners are mixing and pouring Moroccan-style tea. Down by the dock, their younger brothers are leisurely diving for coins thrown by the tourists into the small bay. On the dusty paths and roads behind them, the past is palpable—seen in the circular nineteenth-century prison and fortress Fort d'Estrees and the famous early-twentieth-century William Ponty School, where many of Senegal's elite were educated. Both are out-aged, however, by the eighteenth-century church and houses warming in the bright sunlight. On the bluffs above the small sandy-red town lies the Castel Fort; its big guns once fired on an American fleet during World War II. Now its turrets and bunkers are home to a community of Baye Fall, a Muslim brotherhood whose artistic, dreadlocked members expose the lie of the uniform, radical Islam depicted by conservative talk radio in the United States. They encourage me to sit on the once-powerful but now rusty rifled barrels and stare out to sea while they pour me the traditional three cups of tea—one sweet, one strong, one weak.

Most of the visitors who came off the *chaloupe* with me are here to explore the legacy of this island in one of the darkest chapters in human history—the Atlantic slave trade. Its traces are everywhere. From the sixteenth to the early nineteenth centuries, Gorée was an island full of the unfree—not only those waiting to be packed on board vessels for the deadly trip to Brazil and the Caribbean, but also others retained to labor for French merchant companies and the powerful *habitant* class of Africans and Euro-Africans who lived on the island itself. Many seemingly innocuous spots in the small town were once prisons for the enslaved—large commercial *captiveries* where captives from the African interior were warehoused while waiting for ships of the French Companie Royal du Sénégal, small one-room barred-window *barracoons* (slave sheds) owned by the local elite, and the official jails built to hold the "troublesome."

Both casual tourists and African American pilgrims focus much of their attention on the main site of memory for the island; the pink Maison des Esclaves (slave house), whose pleasant exterior hides a deep, dark dungeon with a small doorway facing out to sea—the notorious "door of no return." Ironically, the Maison may have never held captives, but rather food and drink supplies meant for the island's population. Nevertheless, it is the iconic marker of the time when Gorée was an island at the convergence of three worlds—the Saharan, the Sahelian, and the Atlantic—and a primary point of embarkation for one of the largest forced migrations in human history.

In this chapter we will explore the place of Gorée and its inhabitants, both free and unfree, in the transatlantic slave trade that reached critical mass in the seventeenth century and dwindled away only two hundred years later. Gorée was by no means the largest of the ports of embarkation for captive Africans entering the Atlantic world, but it was among the earliest, and its culture was among the most cosmopolitan, drawing as it did from Europeans, North Africans, and inhabitants of Senegambia and the wider Sahelian region of Africa. It is also one of the sites of memory where the echoes of the slave trade are easiest to hear today, preserved as they are in song, story, and architecture.

GORÉE AND THE WORLD: *Slavery's Wide Reach*

Gorée occupies a geographically unique position. The island sits just off the Câp Vert (Green Cape) peninsula jutting out into the Atlantic. This is almost the westernmost point in continental Africa, with the mouth of the Gambia River to the south being just marginally further west. To the east, the broad Sahelian plains of West Africa spread far into the continental interior. To the west, however, swirls a circle of ocean currents that brings cool water down from Europe along the west coast of Africa and then, around Gorée, turns westward to the Americas. To the north of Câp Vert, the coastal flats of Senegal slowly dry until—just past the Senegal River—the Sahara Desert begins.

These three great geographic and climatological features—the Atlantic currents, the Sahara Desert, and the grasslands of the Sahel—are joined in the area occupied by Gorée. They have helped to shape its history and its contemporary culture.

Gorée was at its height around 1770, drawing deeply on each of these features and contributing to them. Its inhabitants knew about and were influenced by revolutions in the Americas and France. Ships leaving the port travelled to the growing European trading cities of Marseilles, Toulon, and Liverpool. Others carried humans as cargo to the cities of the Caribbean and Atlantic America—Port au Prince, Salvador da Bahia, Kingston, and New Orleans. Gorée was meanwhile emulated by sister cities down the coast—Accra, Cape Coast, Calabar, Bathurst, and nearby Saint-Louis in Senegal, to name a few—yet it would always be the first Atlantic city of West Africa.

A Sahelian World

For most of the recent human past, Gorée and the Câp Vert peninsula were populated by people speaking languages that were the precursors of Wolof, the main language of Senegal today. In the late fifteenth century, when we begin our history of Gorée in this chapter, these speakers of Wolof formed the majority population of the massive Jolof Confederation, a decentralized but interconnected alliance of states that took up much of what is today northern Senegal. Gorée itself was probably never part of this confederation, however. Instead, its few inhabitants and those of nearby Câp Vert lived in small egalitarian societies politically centered upon committees of elders. Although speakers of Wolof, like their neighbors, they were seen as distinct because of their political organization and were known collectively by the name Lebu.

The Lebu and other speakers of Wolof were part of a vast community of people in western Africa who spoke related tongues and who interacted frequently with each other. Their languages, the so-called Western Atlantic group of African languages, at the time covered much of what is today Senegal and Guinea and were distantly related to the Mande languages of the state of Mali to the east. In fact, some of the outlying noble families of what is sometimes called the "Mali Empire" had occupied states just to the southeast of Gorée during the height of that state and continued to rule them in the fifteenth century.

Whether living in small independent communities or large states, the inhabitants of this Sahelian world were connected by trade, by politics, and by shared moral conceptions and social imaginations. Communities tended to respect each others' shrines and religions and sometimes even adopted their neighbors' gods and rituals. In general, however, gods were identified with local geographic features and even trees, and thus religion did not travel well. The major exception was Allah, introduced perhaps as early as the eleventh century by Muslims from north of the Sahara. By the sixteenth century, Allah and Islam were associated with those who travelled widely throughout the region, such as merchants, as well as with those who were literate, such as priests and kings.

For most people, however, religion was part of an identity that was rooted in belonging within a family or lineage. It is inaccurate to speak of local populations as belonging to ethnic groups or tribes for this period. Instead, the extended family was the level at which labor, protection, and identity was most commonly organized. In most communities of the Wolof, the Lebu, and their neighbors, it was the elders of the lineage group who assigned land and resources to young men and women, judged disputes, and led religious ceremonies. In the big states of the region, the extended family was the basis of political power as well. Leading lineages often competed to rule the state, and dynastic marriages between them were common.

Most of the speakers of Wolof were inhabitants of the allied states of the Jolof Confederation until its breakup in the seventeenth century, after which the area to the east of

Câp Vert was divided among several smaller successor states. The most important of these for the inhabitants of Gorée was Kajoor, a large state stretching along the coast toward the Senegal River. Kajoor and its smaller neighbor, Baol, were dominated by Wolof-speaking rulers but also contained a minority who spoke another Western Atlantic African language, Sereer. Both also had porous borders, and their frontiers were pockmarked by small egalitarian "republics," such as the Lebu of Câp Vert and communities of speakers of Sereer who lived in marshes and other marginal environments.

The Lebu and other speakers of Wolof, as well as the speakers of Sereer, shared a number of social institutions and practices, including a common understanding of the role of women in society. In this region, women had significant liberty and social independence, especially if they came from wealthy or important families. Economically, women were free to trade and acquire wealth as individuals, although, like men, they had obligations to the lineage as well. For example, members of extended families frequently shared the expense of paying for major ceremonies or laying out the funds for large projects like the building of a house. Evidence suggests that in the sixteenth century Lebu women, at least, could also pass on their wealth and possessions to their children, although this was unusual among speakers of Wolof. Generally, both Wolof men and women passed on most of their wealth to the extended family instead of directly to their children.

The Lebu were also more egalitarian than other Wolof speakers in that they held very few domestic slaves. In general, Wolof-speaking societies were divided into large groups. Most individuals were considered *jaambuur*, or "freemen," regardless of whether they were aristocrats or peasants. This group was distinguished from those who were not entirely "free." This latter group included some hereditary classes of artisans such as leatherworkers (*uude*), knowledge professionals such as the griot performer-historians (*gewel*), and blacksmiths (*tegg*). The term "castes" is sometimes applied to this group, since they were not enslaved but were set apart from *jaambuur* and not normally allowed to intermarry with them. We consider them to have been not entirely free because as individuals and families they were "attached" to *jaambuur* families and not able to relocate, to practice crafts other than those assigned to them, or in some cases to travel without permission.

Also in this second, unfree group were *jaam*, or "slaves." The *jaam* constituted probably less than 10 percent of society in Kajoor and Baol and even less in Lebu society. They were distinguished from the *jaambuur* in two ways. First, they were not socially independent, but rather were attached to freeborn individuals or lineages. Second, they were expected to exist without "honor." This meant that they had fewer rights, but also that they could act or be compelled to act in outrageous ways as dancers, singers, and concubines. Most, however, functioned as field or domestic workers, usually laboring five days a week alongside the family members to whom they were attached. They also worked in specific tasks, such as weaving, which were associated solely with *jaam*.

However, while we refer to them as slaves, the status and experiences of the *jaam* often differed substantially from slaves in North American society. First, the freeborn families to which the *jaam* were attached were obliged to feed and clothe them or risk losing honor themselves. Second, religious and cultural rules sometimes protected the *jaam* from mal-treatment. Third, although *jaam* status was hereditary, the *jaam* could often be assimilated into full status in the *jaambur* family to which they were attached, although this could take a great deal of time. In this way, the *jaam* lived lives very unlike the enslaved Africans relocated to the Americas, who were neither assimilated over time nor, usually, protected by extensive customary rules of behavior. As Islamic practices spread in the area, additional protections were provided to the *jaam*, especially to those whose owners converted and who converted themselves. These new rules were just one of many social changes shared by societies across the Sahel as Islam, like many other practices, moved around this vast West African "world."

The Senegal River and the Saharan "Sea"

Islamic religion and culture had entered the Sahelian region from across the Sahara Desert as early as the eighth century. A thousand years ago, as today, the Sahara was an obstacle to trade and exchange. This hadn't always been true. Ten thousand years ago, the Sahara was a wet grassland and the home of possibly the thickest population of humans on the planet. In the last few thousand years, however, it has dried considerably and its population moved to the north, east, and west. The descendants of those who went north and those who went south were probably cut off from each other for several hundred years. Then, in the seventh century CE, North African Berbers began to incrementally build routes across the desert with the aid of their camels. These Berbers were probably dissident Muslims seeking to escape pressure from the rulers of the North African coastline. Called Kharjites (meaning "those who secede"), they built the routes that connected North and West Africa. They were followed in the eleventh century by migrant Bedouins from the Arabian Peninsula who slowly made their way to Morocco and then south across the Maghreb to settle around the Senegal River and become the "Maures" of Mauretania. By the fifteenth century, the Sahara was crisscrossed by trade routes that carried gold and slaves north in exchange for salt from the Sahara interior and North African goods such as cloth, glass, ceramics, paper, and arms. In the process, ideas and worldviews also crossed this "sea" of sand.

The Senegal River was the westernmost end of the southern border of this sea, and some states of the Senegal areas, such as Bambuk, were involved in providing gold. As trade increased after the seventh century, so did cultural exchange. Many of the rulers of the region converted to Islam rapidly, and later the religion spread through merchant groups trading throughout the Sahel, including into Câp Vert. It was through these merchants that Islam reached the Lebu and other speakers of Wolof. It first took root among traders, but later, by the sixteenth century, it had become the religion of many of the rural peasantry as well.

Senegambia and the Emergence of an Atlantic World

Until this period, the population of the island of Gorée had probably always been small and impermanent. Lebu fishermen may have used the island as an occasional base, but in their safe, stable mainland society there was little reason for people to seek refuge on a small, dry island. In the late fifteenth century, however, a group arrived for whom Gorée seemed just the kind of secure, defensible outpost they needed.

It was the Portuguese who first established a permanent settlement on the island of Gorée as a stop on their effort to reach Asia via the southern route around Africa. (See Map 5.1.) Their arrival in the area was motivated by a desire to outflank their Moroccan rivals militarily and commercially. Although driven partly by a messianic mission of religious war and partly by political rivalry with the Muslim Moroccans, for most Portuguese ship captains and their funders the more important motivation was the desire to find the West African goldfields. The first Portuguese ships reached the Senegal River in 1445 and Gorée a few years later. Sailing back to Portugal against the southerly Canary currents was more difficult, but still possible. Moreover, within less than a century they

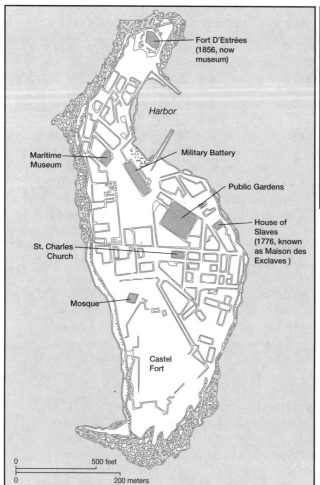

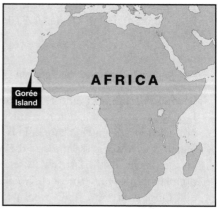

Map 5.1. Gorée

The Portuguese established a permanent settlement on Gorée in the late fifteenth century, and it soon served a pivotal role in the Atlantic slave trade, becoming a way station for enslaved peoples forced to take passage across the ocean and work on Brazil's plantations. Contemporary Gorée has maintained this history through the preservation of the House of Slaves and the Fort d'Estrées, which is now a national museum.

discovered that the westerly currents from Senegal could rapidly take them to the Americas—especially the Portuguese colony of Brazil. As this new colony became the center of a vast plantation system, the Portuguese also discovered that Africans enslaved in Senegal could be profitably put to work in the Americas. Thus began one of the darkest episodes of the human past—the Atlantic slave trade.

The operation and impact of the Atlantic slave trade on Gorée and local societies is discussed below, but it is important to note here that this trade was at the heart of the development of an Atlantic trading system tying Gorée to yet a third world. (See Map 5.2.) In the sixteenth and seventeenth centuries, Africans from Câp Vert, Kajoor, Baol, and far into the interior were brought to Gorée. Some stayed on the island, but others entered the

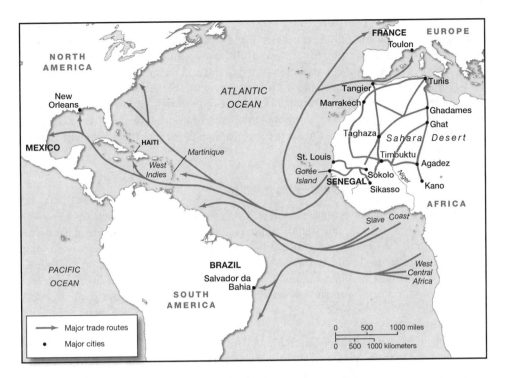

Map 5.2. Saharan, Sahelian, and Atlantic Trade Routes, 1705

The inhabitants of eighteenth-century Gorée lived at the junction of several trading worlds: a trans-Saharan network, a system of exchange across the Atlantic Ocean, and localized commerce within Senegambia. Geographically, Gorée was in an ideal position to take advantage of this confluence of trade.

Atlantic world as human cargo or as sailors, adventurers, or ship guards. In so doing, they helped to create a "Black Atlantic," whose numbers of migrants to the Americas outstripped those coming from Europe during this period.

In turn, significant numbers of Europeans came to Gorée to settle temporarily or permanently. At first these were largely Portuguese sailors, merchants, and officials. By the late sixteenth century, however, other Europeans arrived as well. This was the period of chartered companies, in which much overseas trade from Europe was run by groups of private investors who had been granted certain rights by their governments. The greatest of these in the sixteenth century was the Dutch East India Company (VOC), which may have purchased Gorée from Lebu leaders in 1588 in the midst of a conflict with Portugal. By the 1670s, however, the VOC was already being eclipsed by French and British companies. One of these, the French Compagne de Sénégal, seized the island in 1677. This act was made possible by events stemming from slave trade in the region, which was already in full swing as some Wolof-speaking rulers took the opportunity to profit from the sale of dissidents and ethnic minorities. Their raids had spurred a series of uprisings in Kajoor and other states known as the Marabout Wars (1673–1677), in which Muslim clerics led Wolof-speaking and Sereer-speaking peasants against the rulers who enslaved them. The turmoil weakened the Dutch traders in the region and laid the island open to French merchants.

French companies continued to rule the island for most of the next century until the British occupied it during the Seven Years' War (1758–1763). At the end of that conflict, the French returned and placed the island under an administration appointed by the French king. The permanent population of the island had meanwhile swelled to approximately one thousand residents, and it grew to almost double that by the end of the century. During this time, many additional people passed through on their unwilling way to the Americas. As an island, Gorée's population could not grow very fast, but additional settlements soon sprang up on the nearby mainland, in the area that later become the vast city of Dakar.

Cosmopolitan Gorée: *Signares and Habitant* Society

Aside from two brief interruptions, French companies and the French Crown ruled Gorée from 1677 to 1960. The island retained its importance as a commercial center for the region until the establishment of nearby Dakar as the terminus of a railway running into the interior in the 1880s. By that date, peanuts had become a vital asset for France, and Kajoor and Baol had become major producers of the crop. Dakar, with its deeper harbor and railway lines, rapidly eclipsed Gorée, whose significance and population began to decline. Thus the heyday of Gorée was the century-and-a-half period from the 1680s to the 1830s.

During this period, under French rule, local society was stratified into several classes, although there was a certain amount of social mobility between them. In terms of commercial and political power, the top tier of the system was populated by French civil administrators and the representatives of major French commercial houses. Yet the social bedrock of local society was classes known as *signares* and *habitants,* whose roots in Senegal were at least as deep as their connections to the Atlantic world and to Europe.

The term *signare* was often written in the eighteenth century as *nhara* and appears to have been derived from the Portuguese title *senhora*, indicating a woman of substance. Indeed, *signare* is a gendered term applied only to women. Evidence suggests that social and economic organization on Gorée during the eighteenth century was dominated by these women, some of whom were also politically very powerful.

The class of *signares* was born of the melding of Wolof and Portuguese worlds, institutions, and people beginning in the late fifteenth century. As early as the 1480s, there is evidence of Portuguese sailors settling in the region and marrying local women. Because women could inherit and pass on wealth and live economically independent lives in Wolof society, these early *signares* were able to act first as economic brokers smoothing trading relations between Europeans and local Africans and later as independent traders on their own behalf. By the eighteenth century, diarists and writers speak of communities of *signares* on Gorée and in other coastal communities as having large households and great quantities of trade goods and material wealth. In fact, they were accused by some French merchants of monopolizing the very best merchandise arriving from Europe and thus cutting deeply into the other merchants' profits.

It seems very likely that at least some of the women who became *signares* were of unfree descent (*jaam*), although it is known others came from important aristocratic Wolof, Lebu, and Sereer families. No matter what their origins, however, successful *signares* who parlayed their marriages to Europeans into commercial endeavors of their own came to dominate the island's social life. During the day, much of the business of the commercial town was carried out on Gorée's promenades, where *signares* followed by parasol-holding slaves slowly walked and discussed trade terms with each other. At night, great balls (*folgars*) were held by wealthy *signares* in their large two-story stone houses. European and African men vied for invitations to these events.

The marriages between *signares* and their European husbands were sometimes impermanent, since both merchants and civil servants frequently had to return to France or were posted to elsewhere in the Atlantic world. Nevertheless, they were taken very seriously. By the 1780s, such marriages followed very specific rules that brought together European and African practices. Weddings often took place at the island church, and they could also involve gifts from the groom to the bride's extended family, as was customary at that time in Wolof-speaking societies. It was understood that the children of these marriages could inherit from both their mothers and their fathers. Although the French Crown challenged this tradition between 1677 and the 1730s, it was ultimately unsuccessful in changing it.

Perhaps the most famous *signare* was Anne Pépin, who was the consort and commercial partner of the last royal governor of Senegal, the famous Chevalier de Boufflers. Pépin was a wealthy and powerful woman when she married the important but broke Chevalier, whose subsequent commercial enterprises she funded. She was well connected to important men, including her brother, who was a leader in the Euro-African community, and she corresponded with priests and merchants in Europe as well.

By the 1760s, *signares* and their children came to form the core of a wider social class known as the *habitants*. The term habitant merely means "inhabitant" in French, but in eighteenth-century Gorée it came to be applied to free persons of African or Euro-African (mixed) descent. In this period, *habitants* included independent traders, such as many of the *signares*, as well as artisans such as coopers (barrel makers) and such specialists as interpreters. In general, *habitants* chose to adopt certain markers of their status as members of "French" society—some were Catholics, and many adopted French language and dress. However, there was great diversity here, as some *habitants* were Muslim and others continued to speak Wolof and/or Portuguese as their first language(s). The one thing that tied most *habitants* together was their rivalry with the big French commercial houses that tried to monopolize trade at the expense of local traders. These companies also had a habit of alienating rulers and elites in Kajoor, the Maurish clans, and other local societies through their economic and political bumbling. In opposing them, the *habitants* were frequently allied with important groups and powerful individuals on the mainland, such as the king of Kajoor.

Along with French officials and merchants, the *signares* and *habitants* sat atop a cosmopolitan island society. Below them were *grumettes*, or African sailors from other parts of the western African coast who settled in Gorée, as well as Wolof-speaking members of various specialist castes, including not only smiths and leatherworkers, but also hairdressers and praise-singers. Underneath these classes were the slaves—domestic slaves and enslaved specialists who were rented out to ship owners and corporations as rowers or woodworkers, as well as captives meant for export to the Americas. A census taken in 1785 is revealing of the social stratification of the island. In addition to 116 habitants, it lists 522 "free blacks without property," 1,044 *jaam*, approximately 80 Europeans, and around 200 slaves being held for export. The last of these, the "export captives," were imprisoned for most of their stay in either one of the large *captiveries* (dungeons) of the town or in the sheds and basements of the houses of the wealthy.

GLOBAL ENCOUNTERS AND CONNECTIONS:
Gorée and the Legacy of the Atlantic Slave Trade

The two hundred or so "trade slaves" were representative of the many forced migrants enslaved in the region between the late fifteenth and early nineteenth centuries and sent to labor in the Americas on plantations and mines. Even though they were not for the most part able to leave written sources behind, they speak to us in various ways. The history of Gorée in this period cannot be told without them or the "domestic slaves" who lived permanently on the island.

The Rise of the Atlantic Slave Trade

The area around the Senegal River was the first major region of West Africa drawn into the Atlantic slave trade. The Mauritanian port of Arguin, which had probably been involved in the slave trade across the Sahara Desert, became an outpost of Portuguese slave traders as early as the 1460s, and both Saint-Louis at the mouth of the Senegal River and Gorée became sites of the trade soon after. However, Senegal and the wider region of Senegambia were not as fully integrated into the trade as other regions of western Africa, such as the Bight of Benin and Angola. In part, this probably had to do with successful opposition to the trade, especially in the form of Muslim brotherhoods that fought against slave-raiding elites in the eighteenth and nineteenth centuries.

Records suggest that the number of Africans enslaved on the mainland and passing through Gorée remained relatively level in the seventeenth and eighteenth centuries, at about 150 to 300 per year. There were brief periods of much higher numbers, however, as in the mid-1750s when years of famine caused economic and political unrest and a jump in enslavement. In most years, the majority of the captives came from deep in the interior. Some were brought from as far as the bend of the Niger River in modern-day Mali, although more were brought from the headwaters of the Senegal River and even from the region around the Gambia River. These individuals were forced to make long marches to Gorée. However, captives were also acquired from closer regions. It is clear, for example, that the rulers of Kajoor and at times Baol both opportunistically raided their own citizens, especially their Sereer-speaking minorities. Sometimes they merely saw this as a profit-making venture, although in other cases they were either attempting to quell dissidence or even to resolve succession disputes.

During this period, European merchants, as well as some *habitants* and *signares,* became wealthy through the slave trade, which devastated the surrounding region. This began in part with the breakup of the Jolof Confederation under the pressure of some coastal rulers such as the kings of Kajoor, who wanted to profit personally from the trade. These rulers began to build their own power based on the *ceddo,* groups of cavalry armed with guns, most of which were acquired from Europeans through the slave trade. These *ceddo* groups often, ironically, included slaves themselves. They raided peasant villages to acquire slaves. In turn, the peasants sought ways to organize in order to resist this practice. In the seventeenth century, they increasingly turned to the egalitarian Islamic brotherhoods as an ideology and structure for creating unity. Many of the great Islamic brotherhoods in Senegal—especially Muridiyya and Tijaniyya—began partly as a way for peasants to support each other in their fight against enslavement. Their new leaders were thus often great religious figures, or *marabouts.* This resulted in internal conflicts such as the Marabout Wars of the 1670s, which pitted peasants led by Islamic clerics against the armies of their own rulers.

These conflicts, as well as the more constant fear of small-scale slave trading, forced peasants to flee some of the most productive land in the region, which led to famine and possibly even depopulation. It has been argued that this in turn stunted the economic development of the region and made it ripe for the formal colonialism of direct rule by France that arrived in the late nineteenth century.

Slaving and Slavery in Cosmopolitan Gorée

Not all of the unfree individuals who came to Gorée during this period were on their way to the Americas. The island housed a large population of enslaved individuals who "belonged to" both Europeans and *habitants*. The conditions under which they lived and labored were different from those of European-style plantation slavery in the Americas and the *jaam* in Wolof-speaking societies, and yet drew from both. Because they usually lived in the same houses or compounds as their masters—although often on the ground level beneath the quarters of the household elite—these captives were often collectively known as "domestic slaves."

The number of domestic slaves on Gorée grew rapidly during the eighteenth century. Whereas there were probably only around 130 in the late 1740s, a census taken in 1767 lists 710 and another in 1775 lists 1,200. Thus, they probably formed around two-thirds of the population of the island during this century. Domestic slaves served various uses. Some worked around the house as maids, caretakers, cooks, or even attendants. Others were "rented" out for profit by their owners to companies and ships. Many of these were *laptots*, or rowers, who ferried goods and people from Gorée to the mainland and to ships. Others, however, were skilled artisans. All of these individuals were, to some degree, "chattel"—that is to say, they were signs of wealth and were treated as if they were property. Their masters and mistresses could, for example, take out loans by using their slaves as collateral.

Depending on their perceived value and on individual situations and agreements, the conditions in which domestic slaves lived varied greatly at Gorée. While they generally lived much better lives than the "trade slaves" held in close captivity, domestic slaves did not have the same social protections as were extended to the *jaam* on the mainland. However, the most valuable artisans among them were in some cases carefully protected as important investments by their masters. These included enslaved coopers, metalworkers, carpenters, and shipwrights, many of whom were the most skilled on the island. Yet it is clear that even they were often unhappy with their lot, as they participated in the numerous slave rebellions and escape attempts that are noted in the island's history in this period.

Abolition, Emancipation, Colonialism

As subjects of France, the inhabitants of Gorée were stirred by the French Revolution that began in 1789, although not all in the same direction. Many of the *habitants* and *signares* supported the Revolution because they hoped it would overthrow the big French trading companies often owned by aristocrats, which the *habitants* saw as oppressing them. Many of the domestic slaves of Gorée, meanwhile, had hopes that the Revolution would result in the abolition of slavery and were further stimulated by the great and successful slave rebellion in Haiti two years later. In fact, the new French Republic did abolish slavery in France, but it did not apply this abolition to Gorée and other external French colonies.

Unlike slavery within Gorée, however, the Atlantic slave trade slowly began to decline in the early nineteenth century. Britain abolished the trade beginning in 1807–1808. This was during the period of the Napoleonic Wars, during which Britain once again occupied Gorée, this time from 1803 to 1815. In the treaty that ended this conflict, France agreed to similarly ban the Atlantic slave trade, and in fact most slave traders thereafter had to smuggle their contraband captives out through hidden creeks and marshes, which led to their eventual abandonment of Gorée.

Nevertheless, slavery itself remained in practice in Gorée until 1848, when a revolution again swept the streets of Paris and ushered in a French government that included many leading abolitionists. This government decreed that all French soil, including Gorée, immediately freed those who touched it. The new decree came into effect on August 23, 1848, to great acclaim from the enslaved. Yet to the surprise of the governor of Gorée, most of the enslaved did not leave their masters. Instead, they remained with them, although probably on new terms as free renters or wage-earning dependents.

In the same period, a new commercial crop revolutionized commerce in the area. Peanuts, or groundnuts, grew well in the soil of Kajoor and neighboring areas, and peanut oil was in high demand in France for cooking, making perfume, and industrial production. Successive French governors tried to control these crops, at times by invading and attempting to occupy Kajoor, Baol, and other neighboring kingdoms. These occupations generally failed, however, and it was not until 1895 that France formally occupied the territory now known as Senegal. In the meantime, Dakar had come to eclipse Gorée as a port, and the island slowly faded into obscurity, only to reemerge in importance in the late twentieth century as it became a site for memory, tourism, and pilgrimage.

Yet, ironically, Gorée's transition into a backwater may have saved the traces of this earlier period. While Dakar turned into a sprawling, modern city of 2.5 million people and myriad skyscrapers, Gorée remains a sleepy island whose largest structures are churches, houses, and forts of the eighteenth and nineteenth centuries (along with a few big naval guns installed in the early twentieth century). Many these structures retain the *barracoons* and *captiveries* that once held enslaved humans for export, the permanent quarters of *jaam* and domestic slaves, and the grand ballrooms of the *signares*. Like the Gorée of earlier years, the island's society today is not self-sustaining. Unlike that earlier society, however, it is no longer a place that sends Africans to the Atlantic world, instead receiving their descendants and others as tourists and pilgrims.

ENCOUNTERS AS TOLD: PRIMARY SOURCES

This chapter has focused to some degree on the experiences of two groups on Gorée who lived at the intersection of the Atlantic and Sahelian worlds: *signares* and domestic slaves. These groups did not leave many written records despite their centrality to life on the island, and thus we have to search for their voices from within sources produced largely by French men. These sources do not usually effectively reveal the experiences and perspectives of African men and women. Because of both inexperience and bias, they often misunderstood what was happening around them and ignored important facets of daily life. Nevertheless, by carefully reading what they wrote we can gain some access to the lives of these Gorééans.

Description de la Nigritie, by Antione Edme Pruneau de Pommegorge

Among the most complete descriptions of the lifestyles and socioeconomies of the *signares* is the work of Antoine Edme Pruneau de Pommegorge, who wrote in the 1790s about his experiences in the 1760s. A French colonial official, Pruneau de Pommegorge spent twenty-two years in West Africa. At times, his description reads like an anthropologist's observations of a foreign society, complete with the value judgments of the author and a bit of sensationalism perhaps meant to titillate his audience. Yet he was also quite sympathetic towards the *signares* and the *habitants*.

Pruneau de Pommegorge's description of *signares* on Gorée and in the nearby outpost of Saint-Louis on the Senegal River raises a number of interesting issues. In reading it, consider his account of their economic activities.

- How are the *signares* connected to both Atlantic merchants and producers in the interior?

- How does the author evaluate their dress compared to that of French women of similar rank?

- Look at their lifestyles. How do they bring together West African and European practices in both major events (like weddings) and daily life?

The women . . . in general are strongly attached to the white men, and they could not better take care of them when they are sick. Most of them live in great wealth, and many of the African women themselves have thirty or fourty [sic] slaves, which they rent in the manner I have already described to the company. These domestic slaves every year take a voyage as sailors to Galam, and return to their mistresses with fifteen, twenty, even thirty weight of gold in return for two barrels of salt which their mistresses were able to embark duty free. With some of this gold, the women make jewelry, and the rest is used to purchase clothes, which they love, like women everywhere. Their clothing, usually very elegant, suits them well. They wear on their heads a blank kerchief very artistically arranged, over which they place a small black or colored ribbon. An ornamented chemise, a corset of taffeta or muslin, a skirt of the same [material] of the bodice, gold earrings and ankle chains, for they will wear no others, with red Moroccan slippers on the feet. Underneath the bodice they wear a bit of muslin two ells long, the ends of which dangle beneath the left shoulder. Thus dressed they go out in public, followed by one or two young [domestic slave or free] girls who serve as their chambermaids. [These are] likewise dressed although somewhat lighter and less modestly than in our own society. Their customs are different from ours, although once one is habituated such nudity makes less of an impression than if they were covered up.

The women thus escorted . . . frequently encounter a griot (a species of man who sings praises of one, in exchange for money); so he misses no opportunities to walk in front of them singing their praises with all the hyperbole he can muster, and some immodesties which they know, the women thus so flattered that if they have nothing left in their pockets to give him they fling their bits of clothing over them.

Next to fashion, the greatest passion of these women is their balls, or *folgars*, which sometimes go on to dawn, and during which all drink much palm wine, pitot (type of beer), and if they can get it French wine. The usual manner of applauding those who are the best dancers is to throw a cloth over them, which they return with a deep bow in thanks.

Many of these women are married inside the church and others in the style of the country, which consists in general of the consent of both parties and their parents or families. One may remark that these latter types of marriage are always more successful than the former as the women are more faithful to their husbands than might otherwise be the case. The ceremony which follows in these types of marriages is not in fact decent, unlike the good conduct of the women.

[In this ceremony] the morning after the consummation of marriage, the relatives of the bride come at dawn and take up the white cloth on which the couple have spent the night. If they find the proof for which they are looking they attach the cloth to a long pole like a flag and parade it all day in front of the town, singing and praising the new bride's chastity. But if they have not in fact found such proof, they quickly substitute one.

Source: Antione Edme Pruneau de Pommegorge, *Description de la Nigritie* (Paris: Chez Maradan, 1789), 3–8.

Notes de l'ordonnateur sur l'affranchissement des captives, by Guillet

If the ceremony above sounds barbaric, it must be pointed out that this displaying of the evidence of the virginity of the bride was more likely adopted from Portuguese or French, rather than Wolof, practices.

Reading to understand the lives of the *signares* is difficult, but it is even more complex for historians to try to comprehend the experiences and lifestyles of domestic slaves on Gorée. Sometimes they have to turn to sources that are not specifically about those topics, but rather are trying to make arguments for some policy or another. In the source below, for example, a French official is arguing against extending emancipation to the slaves of Gorée and Saint-Louis. Because he has such an obvious objective, it is not possible to consider this an "unbiased" assessment of life for domestic slaves. Nevertheless, we must rely on sources like these. In order to separate the propaganda from the evidence of what was actually happening, we must search for inconsistencies and pieces of information that expose the errors and fabrications of the author. Thus, when reading the source below, try to assess which pieces of information are merely meant to influence policymakers and which are actually helpful to the historian in figuring out what the lives of the enslaved were like at this time. Consider, for example, the three arguments against banning slavery on Gorée and Saint-Louis that were raised by a French commissioner named Guillet in 1836.

- Guillet begins by describing some of what he sees as the realities of slavery in the region and then makes a political argument as well. Is there a contradiction here?

- Consider on what basis Guillet is arguing in the first two paragraphs that slavery should be maintained. Then consider his fears that many slaves will desert their masters if slavery is abolished on the islands. Does this make sense? Why or why not?

There are a great many aged or ill domestic servants, incapable of any work and living with their masters, in some cases they [do no work but rather] serve as pure ostentation.

The best domestic slaves of Senegal, under the name *laptots*, navigate along the river or the coast, but the actual number of laptots more than suffices these two distinct navigations. Thus [in case of emancipation] the mass of these domestic slaves will be kicked out of their masters' houses.

We must not lose sight of the fact that Senegal is surrounded by diverse peoples among whom slavery is the norm. In their wars, these people consider prisoners of all ages and both gender as the most precious part of their loot, because they continually sell them to the inhabitants of Senegal [i.e. Saint-Louis and Gorée]. If we establish the principle that all slaves are freed by right of putting their feet on French soil, it seems likely that many slaves from the interior will desert [to the islands] in great number.

Source: Guillet, *Notes de l'Ordonnateur sur l'Affranchissement des Captives*, January, 29, 1836, National Archives of Senegal, File K6.

Further Reading

Barry, Boubacar. *Senegambia and the Atlantic Slave Trade*. Cambridge: Cambridge University Press, 1998.

Becker, Charles, and Victor Martin. "Kayor and Baol: Senegalese Kingdoms and the Slave Trade in the Eighteenth Century." In *Forced Migrations: The Impact of the Export Slave on African Societies*, edited by Joseph Inikor, 100–125. London: Hutchinson Press, 1982.

Brooks, George E. "The Signares of Saint-Louis and Gorée." In *Women in Africa: Studies in Social and Economic Change*, edited by Nancy J. Hafkin and Edna G. Bay, 19–44. Palo Alto: Stanford University Press, 1976.

Klein, Martin. "Servitude among the Wolof and Sereer of Senegambia." In *The End of Slavery in Africa*, edited by Suzanne Miers and Richard Roberts, 335–363. Madison: University of Wisconsin Press, 1988.

Web Resources

"Gorée and the Atlantic Slave Trade" (H-Net debate on Gorée and slavery), www.h-net.org/~africa/threads/goree.html.

UNESCO Virtual Visit of Gorée, http://webworld.unesco.org/goree/en/index.shtml.

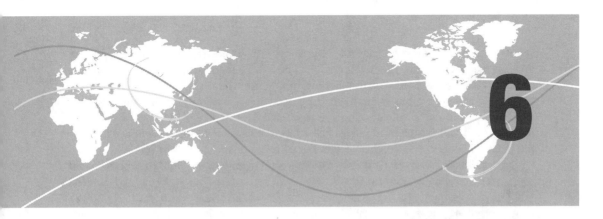

Paris

City of Absolutism and Enlightenment

(1700s)

CHARLES T. LIPP

L IKE SO MANY OTHER AMERICAN COLLEGE UNDERGRADUATE STUDENTS AT THE turn of the millennium, I first came to Paris carrying an overloaded backpack and clutching a rail pass in my hand after having saved up for a year. I was spending several days in the French capital with family members before hitting the rails and exploring the rest of the country. We felt a sense of cultural obligation, that Paris was a center of civilization and, so, was one of those places one just had to visit. We filled our days there by wandering the streets and visiting such touristy sights as the medieval cathedral of Notre-Dame. We chugged Orangina, rode the Metro, and commented sarcastically on the park trees trimmed into green squares in a display of French domination over nature. In short, we tried to absorb some sense of the city's fascinations. Of course, we also encountered its frustrations, including a grumpy waiter who chose to tip a bowl of soup over my back. Never question a café's potatoes.

Several years later I returned to Paris, this time as a graduate student studying aspects of France's history during the 1600s and 1700s, the French monarchy's height of power. I lived three hours by train to the east for my research, but came to the capital once a week to attend classes. After class and before my train ride home, I wandered Paris's streets once again. One spring day I walked from Notre-Dame west along the Seine River towards the Louvre, once the royal residence, now the famous art museum. The wing of the palace that borders the river is elegant, though understated. Turning into the main courtyard, however, I was overwhelmed by what I saw. The ornate sixteenth-century façade glowed in the warm sunshine and it seemed easy to imagine long-gone courtiers passing by. Studying kings and nobles helped me sense the old monarchy in a way I had not before. I felt closer to the people whose lives I was attempting to understand.

Paris was in so many ways *the* city of the eighteenth century. As capital of Western Europe's most dominant kingdom, France, Paris served as a political, social, and cultural model for other countries across the continent—a model that was exported around the globe as a consequence of European colonization. In the coming pages I will discuss two crucial aspects of Paris's eighteenth-century story that helped make it so central in European and global history: Paris as a reflection of royal efforts at state centralization, sometimes described as absolutism, and Paris as a, if not *the*, center of the European Enlightenment. Paris's leading role in these matters spurred much commentary. The Ottoman ambassador to France in the early 1700s spoke of an "infidel's paradise." Perhaps more directly, the playwright Pierre de Marivaux stated, "Paris is the world . . . the rest of the earth is nothing but its suburbs" (Jones, *Paris: The Biography of a City*, 178).

PARIS AND THE WORLD:
An Eighteenth-Century Political Capital

For most eighteenth-century French people, Paris was by far the biggest city they knew. At the beginning of the century, Paris's population numbered around 500,000; by 1789 it had grown to over 650,000. At the time, Paris was counted among the world's largest cities. In Europe, Istanbul, Turkey, and London, England, were larger, each with over 700,000 inhabitants by 1750. Beijing, China's capital, remained the greatest urban center in size, with around one million people. France's second-largest city, Lyon, had only around 150,000 residents. In fact, most urban centers in the kingdom had less than 20,000 people. In a country where nearly 85 percent of its 28 million inhabitants lived in small rural villages, Paris was unique.

In contrast to cities like New York, which grew thanks to its economic role, Paris's importance came from its status as a political capital, similar to places like Berlin in eastern Germany and Beijing. In the 1700s France dominated Europe politically, militarily, economically, and culturally. As a result, rulers across the continent imitated French kings, most obviously by building residential palaces outside their capitals to imitate Versailles, which had been built outside of Paris. It took an alliance of all of Europe's other major powers, along with a number of secondary powers, to defeat French armies in the early 1800s at the end of the Napoleonic Wars. By that point, French was the universal language for educated people in Europe and its current and former colonies, which served to spread French ideas worldwide. Paris stood at the center of all these developments.

As capital, Paris attracted the powerful, the wealthy, and those who wished to become one or the other. Increasing numbers of intellectuals and artists, craftsmen in luxury trades (such as goldsmiths), and large numbers of domestic servants also came to the city to service its small political elite. Up to 75 percent of Paris's population comprised workers of various sorts, including about thirty-five thousand master craftsmen and around forty thousand domestic servants. Many had come in search of employment. However, at least one-third of all Parisians lived in poverty, and this number sometimes rose to 50 percent in times of crisis. For many, life in the capital, though attractive, was difficult and fragile. In one sign of the harshness of Parisian life, it has been estimated that over seven thousand infants were abandoned at the city's Foundling Hospital yearly by the end of the eighteenth century. Most died. For all inhabitants, life in the city was dangerous because of high rates of death and disease. Still, people came. Many also returned to their original homes, either seasonally or permanently, establishing a cycle of immigration into and out of Paris. In fact, cities across the pre-industrial globe needed constant immigration because death rates outpaced birth rates.

Paris's new immigrants discovered a rather old city. The site had been occupied since before the days of Julius Caesar and the Romans. The city blossomed beginning in the 900s, when it became the royal capital. Paris developed on islands in and along the banks of the Seine River. The island of Île de Cité, upon which Notre-Dame Cathedral was built, formed the city's core. To the island's north lay the Right Bank, an area of royal buildings, including the Louvre Palace to the west and the Bastille prison to the east. The Left Bank, home of the university district, was to the south. In the 1700s much of Paris's street plan and buildings, including most of the cheaper housing, dated from the Middle Ages. In the city's center, defensive walls had created dark, narrow streets between densely packed buildings, and old houses filled the Louvre's courtyard and rose on many bridges. The walls had been removed in the late 1600s, which began a slow process of rebuilding and urban expansion. (See Map 6.1.)

City of Absolutism

Paris's history during the 1700s reflects concerted efforts by France's kings to centralize their power. In the centuries following the collapse of the Western Roman Empire in the 400s, Christian Europe witnessed a gradual decentralization of power. In contrast to places like China, in Europe once-public powers, such as waging war and raising taxes, became private property. This process began to slowly reverse in the late Middle Ages, in part because of technological changes like the introduction of gunpowder weaponry— technology that only central rulers could afford in large numbers. In France, following a century marked by religious civil war and several rebellions, the late 1600s saw a number of kings—Louis XIV (r. 1643–1715) most famously— argue that royal power should be absolute. By that, the monarchs meant that they should enjoy full power to impose law upon their subjects independent of all other human authority. Only in this way, they contended, could anarchy be prevented. At the time, wearied of social turmoil, many French residents agreed.

Absolute power never meant unlimited power, however. All kings acknowledged the limits imposed by Christian—particularly Roman Catholic—theology and custom. For example, France had three fundamental laws: the king must be Roman Catholic, he could never give core royal lands away, and the crown could never pass to or through a woman. Moreover, on a practical level, slow communications and a rudimentary infrastructure gave people who lived outside of Paris significant freedom of action.

The first fundamental law indicates the importance of religion to absolute rule and in Parisian life. Catholicism permeated almost every area of daily life in the city. Most people, for example, kept time by the ringing of thousands of church bells that marked the times for prayer. Throne and altar were mutually supporting institutions. The Church argued that God sanctioned royal rule and so legitimized the monarchy. The Church had even elevated medieval king Louis IX (r. 1226–1270) to sainthood (the city of St. Louis, Missouri, is named after him). For their part, French rulers throughout the 1700s gave the Church a number of crucial privileges. The Church enjoyed a near monopoly on

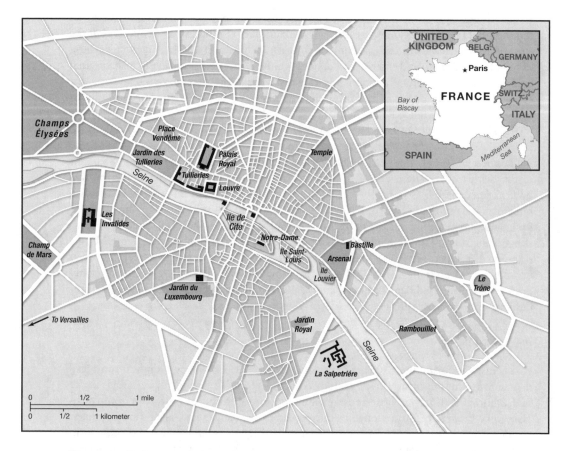

Map 6.1. Paris, ca. 1734

Paris originally developed on islands in and along the banks of the Seine River and grew to a densely populated city. Royal buildings lay to the north on the Right Bank of the river, and university buildings were built to the south on the Left Bank. The cultural and intellectual vibrancy of the city gave rise to Enlightenment ideas that inspired some in the French Empire to rise up and demand their own equality.

education. It was extremely wealthy, owning up to 10 percent of all cultivatable land in the kingdom, even though all the clergy together made up only around 1 percent of France's total population. Kings allowed the Church to levy a special tax called the tithe, which averaged 10 percent of ordinary people's gross income. Most of this wealth, it should be noted, flowed to the very top; most priests were middling to poor. Most importantly, the king helped to enforce Catholic orthodoxy. Protestants did not enjoy civil rights until 1787. Dissident Catholics faced persecution as well. Ideas that ran counter to official Church teachings could be censored.

In practice, absolute monarchy functioned through both coercion and compromise. During the 1700s, kings increased dramatically the weight of government on all levels of French society. At Versailles, many ceremonies involving the king emphasized to high nobles the monarch's elevated place. Taxes rose ever higher to finance a growing bureaucracy and almost constant warfare. The clergy and nobility enjoyed exemptions from most taxes, which fell disproportionally on those with fewer resources. Royal dictates and ambitions did not come without criticism, however. Much of this criticism was motivated by concerns over despotism, or encroachment on traditional liberties. During the time of medieval decentralization, groups within European society had gained particular privileges, and the exclusive right to enjoy them was defined as liberty. Prominent among these groups was the nobility, a small group of families that comprised about 1 percent of France's population. Their birth gave them rights to greater powers than others in society. Nobles, for example, had the exclusive right to carry a sword in public. In another example, only elected members of a craft guild, such as the goldsmiths, could practice that trade. (This vision of society as being composed of groups with unequal rights, in contrast to one with individuals equal under the law, is called corporate.) Therefore, at the beginning of the 1700s, social inequality was not just accepted but expected, and many social groups feared royal centralization might mean a loss of customary privileges.

In order to minimize resistance to their authority, French monarchs offered a compromise. In exchange for accepting greater central power, the highest positions in the state and the army were generally reserved for nobles. Nobles also gained a share of tax revenues. Moreover, all members of society saw benefits from stronger royal rule, particularly in terms of law and order. Violence and crime declined. In addition, monarchs maintained traditional policies of economic protectionism that were popular with the poor and struggling. At a time when the average Parisian ate around five pounds of bread a day, the French Crown ensured a steady supply of grain to the city at controlled prices. All of these policies led to a general acceptance of the growing state.

Throughout this transition, Paris served as a main setting and stage for state centralization. Although in the 1680s Louis XIV shifted the royal residence to Versailles, twelve miles southwest of the city, Paris remained the official capital. Foreign envoys from across Europe and places beyond, such as the Ottoman Empire and Siam, stayed in the city. As government expanded, kings began to organize their administration into specialized ministries, which represented an early form of cabinet government. The most important royal ministry, finance, was based north of the Louvre. The Supreme Court of Appeals met near Notre-Dame. Paris also housed academies for the arts and sciences that supported and established official standards for cultural and scientific production. Most famous was the Académie Française, created in the 1630s to regulate the French language. It based French upon the Parisian dialect. Over the next 250 years, rulers sought to eliminate other dialects within France and to export the official language to French colonies around the world. In that way, language itself aided state centralization and encouraged Parisian dominance over France and French-speaking areas of the globe.

Paris could not help being so central for, as capital, it fell under direct Crown control. Monarchical attention lay behind real and proposed changes in the city's appearance throughout the 1700s. In one notable instance, Louis XIV introduced widespread street lighting, which had not been seen in Europe since the 900s in Muslim Spain. In 1667 the king ordered thousands of lanterns be hung across Paris's narrow streets at night. Contemporaries viewed the lights as a progressive safety measure. Other programs designed to improve urban life and health followed. Arguing that confined spaces bred disease, royal officials replaced Paris's medieval walls with large, elegant boulevards, which soon became fashionable well-to-do districts, and new city squares. By the 1780s, the Crown ordered a minimum street width of nearly thirty feet and the demolition of the old houses on top of bridges. Other plans were made, including removing the old houses cluttering the Louvre's courtyard. Although done for health reasons, these projects directly affected Paris's poor, who tended to live in the oldest, and thus cheapest, areas of the city. Most plans only came to fruition in the 1800s, so in eighteenth-century Paris centers of power such as the Louvre remained close to areas of extreme poverty.

Despite the potential for social turmoil this proximity may have caused, Paris was considered a well-controlled city. In the 1500s and 1600s, Paris had seen riots, protests, and even rebellions. These ended under Louis XIV. By the 1780s, some commentators noted Paris's political apathy, especially in contrast to other European cities such as London. This seemed to prove the effectiveness of absolutism. Indeed, at the end of the 1700s, absolute monarchies dominated Europe's political landscape from Portugal to Russia.

City of Enlightenment

These developments occurred within a larger context, that of a broad social, cultural, and intellectual movement known as the Enlightenment, a term coined by eighteenth-century Europeans themselves. A diverse movement, the Enlightenment had some basic characteristics. At its core it marked a new way of understanding how the world—above all, the social world—worked. Earlier, based on Christian scripture, most European thinkers believed the world was created and continually acted upon by transcendent supernatural forces. God and Satan supposedly intervened in human life, and the world, it was long argued, remained fundamentally mysterious and unknowable. Christian churches, both Catholic and Protestant, had long spread such views with the support of state authorities. In stark contrast, some Enlightenment thinkers began to envision the universe as created by a divine being that then did not interfere with his creation. That creation, Enlightenment thinkers contended, was organized rationally according to universal principles and, thus, could be studied and understood by humans. Rather than relying on the authority of religious books like the Jewish Torah, the Christian Bible, or the Muslim Quran, people should form rational arguments based on close observation. Indeed, the Enlightenment subjected inherited beliefs to rigorous questioning and criticism. In short, because of their senses and their reason, humans could understand their world and, crucially, therefore improve it. Although generally optimistic about human ability to better society, the Enlightenment was not a naïve movement; it sought progress, not perfection.

Enlightenment ideas ranged from the radical to the conservative. The radical thinkers in some cases attacked organized religions, particularly Roman Catholicism. These thinkers questioned the validity of arguments, such as the truth of miracles, which could not be tested by human observation and reason. They saw organized religions as bastions of superstition preventing human progress. One book published in French in the early 1700s, for example, spoke of Moses, Jesus, and Muhammad as three imposters. Though certainly extreme, such views had effects on eighteenth-century religion. In the 1770s the pope disbanded the Jesuits, a highly influential monastic order that had launched a worldwide missionary campaign from Canada to China and defended stridently Catholic traditions. Some of the more conservative thinkers of the Enlightenment endorsed nobility and monarchy. They argued that only a single ruler could be powerful enough to enact rational reforms in the face of entrenched interests. Such ideas proved so popular that some historians speak of an eighteenth-century trend toward enlightened absolutism.

Similar to patterns observed during the Italian Renaissance, the Enlightenment appealed most to those in the middle to upper levels of society—those with the free time, the resources, and, perhaps most of all, the education to rethink their world. Therefore, the main participants in the Enlightenment included not only nobles, but also increasingly members of a social group known as the bourgeoisie. This group included professionals such as lawyers and doctors, as well as prosperous merchants. Most people, concerned with basic survival, worked. In addition, though enormous strides were made over the century, literacy rates remained low by today's standards. In France in the late 1780s, fewer than 50 percent of men and 30 percent of women could sign their marriage contracts.

The Enlightenment Contributes to a General Western Culture

The Enlightenment spread across Europe and its colonies in the Americas, affecting such disparate places as Philadelphia, Pennsylvania; Edinburgh, Scotland; and Saint Petersburg, Russia. By the nineteenth century, a general Western culture had been produced, one that emphasized confidence in human observation and reason leading to progress. This culture also emphasized the universality of that approach and the conclusions to which it led. Such beliefs encouraged Europeans to see themselves as different from and, at times, superior to, other peoples in the world. Some thinkers, for example, argued that differences in climate accounted for the presence of freedom and slavery in human societies. Paris was *the* center of this cultural production. As historian David Garrioch noted, Paris's role as a political capital ensured a large educated and affluent population that provided the critical mass necessary for an intellectual and cultural flowering. Enlightenment thinkers flocked to, came from, and continually thought about the city.

As a movement, the Enlightenment emerged out of a particular intellectual background that led Europeans in general and Parisians in particular to focus on improving human society and questioning past assumptions of how things worked. By the end of the 1600s, educated people were criticizing religious enthusiasm in the wake of almost a century of religious wars. These conflicts had erupted out of the Reformation, the division of medieval Christian unity. The 1600s also saw increased explorations of the workings of the natural world by a number of intellectuals, most famously English university professor Isaac Newton (1642–1727), whose theories seemed to indicate that the universe operated according to rational, and therefore understandable, laws. These explorations laid the foundations for what is now called the scientific worldview. By the early 1700s, people had begun to wonder if the human world functioned the same way.

The Enlightenment also emerged out of broad social and economic developments that directly involved Paris. For one, colonization and missionary efforts prompted Europeans to rethink their place in the world. Jesuit missionary writings about Canada and China, many published in Paris during the 1600s and 1700s, proved central in this respect. The accounts provided intellectuals models with which to compare Europe. These comparisons were sometimes quite critical. Those who viewed civilization as corrupting, including Jean-Jacques Rousseau, presented Native Americans as what were termed "noble savages," supposedly living pure, idyllic lives in the North American forests. Others, such as Voltaire, idolized China, seeing the Ming Empire as a state run by scholars in which organized religion played little role. China, it seemed, was led by the philosopher king that the ancient Greek philosopher Plato had advocated. To these thinkers, Confucius was an Enlightenment philosopher who happened to have lived far away during an earlier time. Needless to say, these views of the Chinese and of Native Americans were rather inaccurate. Rather than understand those societies on their own terms, Enlightenment thinkers constructed idealized and romanticized versions of them with which to support their arguments about reason and progress.

Rise of a Consumer Revolution

The Enlightenment also emerged out of a pivotal economic transformation that had major social consequences. By the early 1700s, developments such as improved infrastructure, agricultural specialization, and increased participation in global trade led to greater prosperity in Europe. This in turn led to what came to be called a consumer revolution, in which more products were available for consumption and more people willing and able to consume them. Paris was a center of this consumption because of its growing numbers of nobles, administrators, judges, and workers. Consumerism touched all levels of Parisian society. Economic historians argue that over the eighteenth century French workers saw their wages decline relative to inflation. The extent of that decline remains hotly debated. At the same time, historians studying post-death inventories have discovered that, by the end of the 1700s, luxury products such as beds and mirrors, once affordable only to the wealthy, became increasingly available at all income levels. In short, the material standard of living for all Parisians increased visibly. Parisian workers were able to afford these goods despite their declining wages through such strategies as working longer hours and more than one job and having multiple family members in the workforce.

Parisian consumerism displayed itself in two ways. First, throughout the eighteenth century, production of high-quality products like leather goods and fine textiles developed. By the end of the 1700s, luxury shops crowded Paris's fashionable districts, and Parisians engaged in a new pastime: window shopping. Paris had also become Europe's leading fashion center. Design houses sent dolls dressed in the latest styles out from Paris to France's provinces and abroad, and Parisian fashions could be found in closets from Philadelphia to Saint Petersburg. Second, Paris also developed as a market for goods produced elsewhere, including Chinese porcelain and colonial cash crops.

Cash crops, coffee and sugar in particular, were central to this growing consumerism in Paris. In the 1690s, the French established sugar plantations in their Caribbean colony of Saint-Domingue (modern-day Haiti). Within a century, Saint-Domingue was producing nearly 40 percent of the sugar sold on the European market. In fact, the French colony produced more sugar than all of Great Britain's Caribbean plantations combined. Sugar's popularity came, naturally, from its use as a sweetener for other products—above all, coffee. Originally imported from the Middle East, coffee became popular in Paris thanks to a trend started by the Ottoman ambassador in the 1660s. In the 1720s, coffee trees were introduced to France's Caribbean colonies—again, primarily Saint-Domingue. By 1789 that single colony produced more than half of Europe's coffee. Coffee production boomed over the 1700s with a related decline in cost. What had been an exotic luxury in Paris soon became an everyday necessity, workers and nobles alike considering a cup of coffee at the beginning of the day. The brutal exploitation of millions of enslaved Africans lay behind the surge in sugar and coffee production and consumption. By 1789 five hundred thousand slaves toiled in Saint-Domingue, and their average further life expectancy on arrival to the colony was only seven years.

In Paris, the growing consumption of sugar and coffee led to the establishment of coffeehouses, or cafés. In the 1710s, Paris had about four hundred cafés. Seven decades later, that number had increased more than threefold. One of the most notable examples of Paris's eighteenth-century cafés remains the Café Procope, located on the Left Bank off the Boulevard Saint-Michel. Founded in 1675, business boomed during the next century. In the mirrored confines of the café, waiters in supposedly Turkish clothing served patrons both famous and unknown. Another major site of coffee consumption was the Palais-Royal, a complex slightly north of the Louvre on the Right Bank. Built in the

1630s, by the 1700s it had passed to the dukes of Orléans, a younger branch of the ruling Bourbon dynasty. By 1781, in need of cash, the Palais-Royal's owners rented out shops and cafés in the galleries lining the palace's gardens, turning the space into a kind of mall. The growing numbers of cafés encouraged the development of a commercial press, as newspapers and magazines became standard features available to coffeehouse patrons.

The Appetite for Ideas

Along with the newspapers available for reading in Paris's cafés, another major product consumed over the 1700s was ideas. The ways in which these ideas were produced and spread were as important as their consumption. Sociability—the sharing of thoughts—characterized the Enlightenment. Its ideas developed mostly through collaboration and conversation, either in person or in print by reading and responding to what others wrote. Coffeehouses provided one venue for this intellectual exchange, but they were a completely masculine venue because contemporaries considered caffeine unhealthy for women, as it might excite them too much. Salons provided a more mixed arena in terms of gender. These were gatherings led by elite women in their own homes where intellectuals and well-connected persons came together to share witty exchanges about a wide range of matters. Women played a key role not just by hosting and arranging the guest list, but by choosing the topics of conversation. An initiation to a salon indicated that one had truly arrived in Parisian society. Among the most famous of these gatherings were those hosted in the home of Madame Geoffrin (1699–1777). Geoffrin established what was almost a class schedule for her salon, making Mondays the day to discuss arts and Wednesdays the day to discuss letters. Gatherings modeled on the Parisian salons spread among educated circles across Europe and the Americas.

Coffeehouses and salons changed Parisian society profoundly. Up until the 1700s, the groups a person belonged to largely determined social encounters. These groups included the clergy, the nobility, and the craft guilds, and each enjoyed exclusive privileges. In addition, these groups were arranged hierarchically. In contrast, entry into coffeehouses and salons came on an individual basis. Patronage of coffeehouses depended on one's ability to afford their wares. Invitation to a salon depended on one's conversational abilities. These, and similar venues such as Masonic lodges, served as sites of social mixing, where nobles and the bourgeoisie came together increasingly as equals. A vision of society based on individuals, not groups, emerged. By the 1800s, this Parisian vision dominated Europe and was spreading worldwide.

Central to this development was the notion of individual choice in terms of what products one wanted to buy and what ideas with which one wanted to agree or disagree. Thus, related to the changing social outlook was the notion of an impersonal "public" whose opinions mattered, and mattered more in fact than judgments imposed from above through institutions such as the royal academies. Parisian public opinion developed first as art criticism, especially of the regular shows of recent paintings held in the Louvre beginning in the 1730s. Those shows led to calls for the transformation of the palace into an art museum, and this project was accomplished by the end of the century. By that point, public opinion had moved from art to the discussion of politics and royal policy, which would have revolutionary consequences.

Among the major shapers of public opinion in Paris were a collection of celebrity intellectuals known collectively in French as the *philosophes*, or philosophers. Their backgrounds reflected the Enlightenment's diversity. For example, the Baron de Montesquieu (1689–1755) belonged to the nobility in southwest France. He moved to Paris in his early thirties and established a reputation as a political theorist. In his 1748 work *The Spirit of the Laws*, he argued that human laws reflected the societies that established them and, so, could be studied and improved if necessary. The book became the most widely read political treatise of its time. Montesquieu's younger counterpart Jean-Jacques Rousseau (1712–1778) also made a name as a political thinker. In *The Social Contract*, published in 1762, Rousseau claimed that political power should derive from the people and what he called their "general will." The general will was not the same as majority rule; by general will, Rousseau meant that which was in the best interests of the community as a whole and which would also be virtuous and right. Though these ideas proved influential later, at the time Rousseau became more popular as a sentimental novelist. Like Montesquieu, Rousseau was not originally from Paris. He was born in the Swiss city republic of Geneva. Unlike the baron, Rousseau came from an artisanal background. In eighteenth-century Paris, it was becoming possible for those from a variety of rungs on the social ladder to make a living writing.

Rousseau's one-time friend Denis Diderot (1713–1784) also had an artisanal heritage. Diderot arrived in Paris in the 1730s from eastern France and within a decade established a reputation as a witty intellectual and art critic. Diderot became the guiding force behind one of the greatest Enlightenment projects: the *Encyclopedia*, which offered a perfect illustration of the ideal of intellectual collaboration. Serving as general editor, Diderot convinced many of the *philosophes* to contribute articles. The work appeared in seventeen volumes published between 1751 and 1772, with an additional eleven volumes of images. The *Encyclopedia* aimed to gather all useful knowledge together and make it accessible to the reading public. In addition to articles on geography, manufacturing processes, and the like, the *Encyclopedia* also offered criticism of contemporary politics, society, and religion, reflecting Enlightenment questioning of tradition. Needless to say, the work proved controversial, particularly to religious authorities. One reason for this was that Diderot indirectly compared the Christian rite of the Eucharist to cannibalism.

Royal reactions to the Enlightenment varied. Censorship existed. Authors seen as too controversial because of their writings on politics and religion faced imprisonment at times, including Diderot. However, at the same time, well-connected members of the royal court, such as Louis XV's mistress Madame de Pompadour, supported and protected Enlightenment writers. More surprisingly, perhaps, the royal censor in the 1750s and 1760s, Guillaume-Chrétien de Lamoignon de Malesherbes (1721–1794), gave tacit permission to Diderot to continue the *Encyclopedia* project, even when it was officially banned by the crown as being antireligious and ordered burned in 1759 by the Parlement de Paris.

In fact, French kings, especially Louis XVI (r. 1774–1792), also saw much they liked in the Enlightenment. At their most basic level, some Enlightenment ideas offered ways to make government more efficient and effective and, thus, stronger. Moreover, throughout his reign, Louis XVI appealed to public opinion and tried to make his policies appear useful. That did not mean rejecting traditions of absolute rule, however. Unfortunately, these attempts to be simultaneously absolute and enlightened proved difficult to maintain. For example, Louis XIV came to power at a time of economic difficulty. In response, he appointed as his finance minister a *philosophe* named Turgot (1727–1781) who was a member of a group of economic thinkers known as the physiocrats. The physiocrats opposed traditional economic protectionalism and instead advocated free trade. They invented and popularized the term *laissez faire*, believing that less government regulation would spur economic growth. As finance minister, Turgot put this theory into practice and introduced a free trade in grain. Unfortunately, a series of poor harvests caused the price of grain to double—an increase that affected city dwellers and the poor the most. The public believed that the government had abandoned its role as social protector, and a series of riots that came to be known as the Flour War erupted in Paris and other cities during the spring of 1775. Military intervention quelled the riots; however, tensions remained between the king and his royal hopes of enlightened reform and the majority of the public, who viewed Louis's actions as harmful and—because free trade attacked traditional privileges—potentially despotic.

GLOBAL ENCOUNTERS AND CONNECTIONS:
Spreading the Ideas of a Modern World

These tensions led to a revolution by the end of the 1780s. In 1778 Louis XVI involved France formally in the American War of Independence (1775–1783). Seeking to humble Great Britain, an emerging commercial and political rival during the eighteenth century, the king had first supported the Americans secretly. French troops and ships contributed to British defeat in 1783. Seen as evidence of royal power and benevolence toward a new nation, the victory proved popular among the French public. However, French involvement in the war had unforeseen consequences. Only a few veterans, such as the Marquis de Lafayette, saw republicanism as a model useable beyond the specific circumstances of the United States. What truly affected France, though, was the cost of its involvement in the altercation. By the mid-1780s, France confronted bankruptcy, a financial situation made worse by a counterfeiting scandal that led to a credit freeze and by a series of bad harvests at the end of the decade. Louis pushed for far-reaching reforms and asked the nobility and clergy to agree to renounce their traditional tax exemptions. The two groups refused, saying that the request amounted to a despotic attack on their liberties.

Public opinion forced the king to call a meeting of the Estates General, a representative assembly that had not met since 1614. It was argued that only such a body could give legitimacy to the calls for reform. Louis asked his subjects at all levels to draw together lists of problems that should be addressed. The result was a massive expansion of political involvement. When the Estates General opened in May 1789, the issue of voting dominated the meeting. Traditionally, voting had been done by social group (the assembly was divided into three bodies representing the clergy, the nobles, and everyone else), but the Third Estate demanded individual voting that would reflect the sociability of Paris's coffeehouses and salons. In June 1789, after deciding traditional frameworks no longer worked, the Third Estate declared itself a national assembly and began to write a constitution for France. This move marked the beginning of the French Revolution, as it implied that sovereignty came first from the nation and that royal powers should be written down and, therefore, limited. Also implied was that the days of a society based on social groups enjoying exclusive privileges ruled by an absolute monarch were over. What was emerging was a new vision of politics and society based on the ideas and society of eighteenth-century Paris.

In fact, Paris dominated the Revolution during its first years. Reports of what was occurring in the French National Assembly traveled the twelve miles back to Paris daily and were discussed and debated. Most people, especially those in the middle to lower social levels, such as artisans and shopkeepers, embraced revolutionary change. In early July, news came that Louis XVI had moved his army toward the capital, and Parisians feared the worst—that the king would use force to end the Revolution. On July 14, 1789, a crowd seeking weapons moved across the city from the Palais-Royal to the Bastille, a royal prison and arsenal. Defended only by several hundred troops, the prison was quickly stormed and its governor beheaded. In the wake of this action, Louis XVI backed down. The violent action taken by Parisians ensured that political changes would not be undone.

In the wake of the Bastille a new symbol of France appeared: a tricolor flag that combined the red and blue of Paris with the white of the monarchy. By the end of the summer, a new vision of society, based in good part on Enlightenment theories, had emerged. It was constructed by citizens who saw themselves as equals and had a uniform governmental structure. The Declaration of the Rights of Man and Citizen was issued in August 1789, and moves were taken to eliminate longstanding differences in administration, justice, and taxation between the various regions of France. Ironically, these efforts helped build a more centralized state than Louis XVI could have ever imagined In October, Paris took control of the Revolution when a crowd of women demanding action over high food prices walked to Versailles and forced the royal family and the royal government to return to the capital, where they were continuously observed.

Over the next five years, the Revolution became increasingly radicalized because of the move to Paris. The spread of ideas through print that had begun in Enlightenment coffeehouses reached its zenith during the early Revolution. Parisians were inundated by literally millions of pamphlets and newspapers that espoused all political points of view. At the same time, political clubs emerged and offered spaces to continue printed debates in person. Two years after the Revolution began, nearly one thousand such clubs existed in Paris, and branches could be found across the country.

Between 1789 and 1791, the French National Assembly took steps to eliminate exclusive social privileges and to create a society of individuals equal in rights. In August 1789 it declared most noble privileges eliminated. In July 1790 it attempted to nationalize the Catholic Church, eventually demanding a loyalty oath to the Revolution on the part of priests. It was felt that church and state needed to be separated, considering how the clergy had long preached support for the monarchy. Though implemented for supposedly neutral and rational reasons, these actions led to public anger over the perceived attack on religion and to a number of nobles fleeing France and beginning to plot against the Revolution. In 1791 Louis XVI himself attempted to flee before being caught at the French border. The following year, a Parisian crowd stormed the Tuileries Palace, where the king had lived since 1789, and declared an end to the monarchy and the birth of a republic. Louis died by guillotine in the center of his capital in January 1793.

By that point, France was at war. In early 1792, the revolutionaries decided that foreign threats existed, and so the Revolution must become a universal movement offering liberty to all Europeans living under monarchical rule. The French declared preemptive war on Austria, the homeland of Louis XVI's queen, Marie Antoinette. This began a series of conflicts between France and most other European states that lasted until 1815 with the exception of only eighteen months of peace. No longer satisfied with merely transforming France, the revolutionaries now turned to transforming the world, and so the Revolution moved into its most radical phase. At that time, however, things looked dire for the Revolution. By 1793 Austrian and allied Prussian and British forces had invaded and occupied parts of France. Areas in the west and south had risen in rebellion against Paris, the west calling for a return of monarchy and religion and the south for a decentralized republic.

In this atmosphere of crisis, those opposed to the Revolution were declared to be in opposition to the general will and in need of being terrorized into conformity. So began the Reign of Terror. It ended in 1794 when revolutionary armies began to triumph over their enemies, foreign and domestic, ending the crisis and need for extraordinary rule.

Ultimately, in reaction to the extremism of the year of the Terror, a moderate republic came to power, one that was eventually taken over by Napoleon Bonaparte. Although Paris remained the capital of an increasingly centralized state, its influence over events in France was finished.

By this point, however, Paris's influence had become global. French armies swept over Europe during the 1790s, creating a number of so-called sister republics, primarily in the Netherlands and Italy. These republics were set up along French lines and so established revolutionary ideas across the continent. In Saint-Domingue, debate erupted almost immediately over how universal was the Declaration of the Rights of Man. In August 1791, after attempts were made to limit rights along racial lines, the slaves revolted and demanded their freedom. The resulting disruption of trade led to riots in Paris over the rising price of sugar. Within three years, in an effort to regain control, the French declared slavery universally abolished, becoming the first European nation to do so. (Napoleon later rescinded that abolition.) By 1804 Saint-Domingue's slaves defeated French troops that had been sent to force them back into the sugar fields and forged the nation of Haiti. In the 1800s and 1900s, other revolutionaries from Latin America to Russia looked to eighteenth-century Paris as an inspiration. Even those less radical adopted many of the ideas and ways of thinking about human society first developed in Paris, such as organizing society around individuals rather than privileged social groups.

Ironically, at the end of the 1700s, much of the world looked like it had in earlier centuries. China remained a dominant global power. The Muslim Ottoman Empire ruled over parts of three continents and controlled significant parts of the Mediterranean. Yet crucial changes had occurred. In 1800 Europeans stood on the cusp of a century and a half of global domination. Many of the ideas they spread around the world were centered on or reflected in Paris's history. French experiments with the relationship of state power to society and its evolution from absolute monarchy to revolutionary republic became models utilized by countries across the globe. Enlightenment ideas became seen as fundamental to "Western" civilization and as proof, it was believed, of European superiority. The modern world, in other words, emerged from the narrow, lantern-lit streets of eighteenth-century Paris.

ENCOUNTERS AS TOLD: PRIMARY SOURCES

The following documents provide a sampling of influential works reflecting influences and ideas coming out of Paris in the eighteenth century. From the writings of the Baron de Montesquieu and Jean-Jacques Rousseau to the formal Declaration of the Rights of Man, the Enlightenment's impact is evident on philosophy and, ultimately, government. These impacts can be traced from France to Haiti and other locations.

The Persian Letters, by [Charles-Louis de Secondat, Baron de] Montesquieu

The Baron de Montesquieu (1689–1755) came from southwest France, where he served as a judge before moving to Paris and making a name for himself as a political theorist. This selection comes from his earliest literary success, his 1721 novel *The Persian Letters.* Supposedly a collection of letters to and from two Persian travelers in 1710s France, the older named Usbek and the younger called Rhedi, the book satirized contemporary French society, and that of Paris above all.

- Does Montesquieu's characterization of a monarchy reflect Enlightenment thought?

- In what ways is self-interest the world's greatest monarch?

- How are luxury and poverty in Paris connected?

LETTER 102 (USBEK TO IBBEN, AT SMYRNA)

The greater part of the governments in Europe are monarchies, or rather they are so called: for I do not know whether there ever was one state truly so. At least, it is difficult that they should subsist long without being corrupted. It is a state of tension that always degenerates into despotism or into a republic. The power can never be equally divided between the people and the prince; that balance is too difficult to be preserved. The power must decrease on one side, while it increases on the other, but the balance is generally in favor of the prince, who is at the head of the armies.

LETTER 106 (USBEK TO RHEDI, AT VENICE)

Paris is, perhaps, the most luxurious city in the world, and where pleasures are most refined, and yet, perhaps, no people live harder than there. So that one man may live in luxury, a hundred must be continually laboring. A lady takes it into her head that she must appear at an assembly in a certain dress—from this moment fifty artisans have no leisure either to eat, drink, or sleep. She commands, and is more readily obeyed than our monarch, for self-interest is the greatest monarch upon earth. This great application to labor, this thirst to grow rich, runs through every rank [of society], from the artisans up to the greatest man. Nobody loves to be poorer than him who is next beneath him. You may see at Paris, a man who has enough to live upon until the end of the world, and who continually works, risking shortening his life, to scrape up, as he says, the wherewithal to live. The same spirit prevails through the whole nation, nothing is seen there but labor and industry.

Source: [Charles-Louis de Secondat, Baron de] Montesquieu, *The Persian Letters* (Edinburgh: Alexander Donaldon, 1773; originally published 1721; anonymous translation modified by Charles Lipp), 213, 223.

The Spirit of the Laws, by [Charles-Louis de Secondat, Baron de] Montesquieu

First published in 1748 and quickly translated into almost all major European languages, Montesquieu's work of political theory was read closely from North America to Russia. It became the most influential work on politics during the eighteenth century. Montesquieu argued that laws reflect the societies that produce them, both in terms of political systems, as seen in the first selection, and in terms of geography, as seen in the second.

- How is an absolute monarchy not despotic?

- How does climate shape politics and law, according to Montesquieu, and how does this outlook reflect Enlightenment thought?

BOOK II: OF LAWS DIRECTLY DERIVED FROM THE NATURE OF GOVERNMENT

The intermediate, subordinate, and dependent powers, constitute the nature of monarchical government, that is, that in which a single person governs by fundamental laws. I said, *intermediate*, *subordinate*, and *dependent*, powers. In fact, in monarchies the prince is the source of all power, political and civil. These fundamental laws necessarily suppose the intermediate channels through which the power flows: for if there be only the momentary and capricious will of a single person to govern the state, nothing can be fixed, and of course there is no fundamental law.

The most natural, intermediate, and subordinate power is that of the nobility. This in some measure seems to be essential to a monarchy, whose fundamental maxim is: *no monarch, no nobility; no nobility, no monarch*; but there may be a despotic prince.

BOOK XVII: HOW THE LAWS OF POLITICAL SERVITUDE HAVE A RELATION TO THE NATURE OF THE CLIMATE

Asia has properly no temperate zone, as the places situated in a very cold climate, immediately touch upon those which are exceedingly hot. . . .

In Europe, on the contrary, the temperate zone is very extensive. . . .

Hence it comes, that in Asia the strong nations are opposed to the weak; the warlike, brave, and active people touch immediately upon those who are indolent, effeminate, and timorous: the one must therefore conquer, and the other be conquered. In Europe, on the contrary, strong nations are opposed to the strong. . . . This is the grand reason of the weakness of Asia, and of the strength of Europe; of the liberty of Europe, and of the slavery of Asia. . . .

Africa is in a climate like that of the south of Asia, and is in the same servitude.

Source: [Charles-Louis de Secondat, Baron de] Montesquieu, *The Spirit of the Laws*, vol. 1 (Dublin: G. and A. Ewing, 1751), 18–20, 328–329, 334.

The Social Contract: or, The Principles of Political Rights, by Jean-Jacques Rousseau

Published in 1762, *The Social Contract* was not an immediate success. Readers at the time preferred Jean-Jacques Rousseau's sentimental novels. By the end of the 1700s, however, Rousseau's ideas were influencing political developments in France. The work had had a global impact over the past two hundred years and, because of the concept of the "general will," has been seen both as a call for democratic government and as a justification for totalitarianism.

- How do these ideas challenge eighteenth-century traditions?

- Where does political power ultimately come from?

- Is the "general will" democratic or totalitarian?

"To find a form of association which shall defend and protect with the public force the person and property of each associate, and by means of which each, uniting with all, shall obey however only himself, and remain as free as before." Such is the fundamental problem of which the *Social Contract* gives the solution.

If, then, we remove from the social contract all that is not of its essence, it will be reduced to the following terms: "Each of us gives in common his person and all his force under the supreme direction of the general will; and we receive each member as an indivisible part of the whole. . . . "

In order then that the social compact may not be an idle formula, it includes tacitly this engagement, which alone can give force to the others, that whoever shall refuse to obey the general will, shall be compelled to it by the whole body, which signifies nothing if not that he will be forced to be free. . . .

[T]he fundamental compact substitutes . . . a moral and legitimate equality for that which nature may have given of physical inequality among men; and while they may be unequal in strength or genius, they become equal by agreement and right.

[T]he general will is always right, and always tends towards public utility.

Source: Jean-Jacques Rousseau, *The Social Contract: or, The Principles of Political Rights*, Rose M. Harrington, trans. (New York: G. P. Putnam's Sons, 1893), 20–22, 26, 33.

Declaration of the Rights of Man and of the Citizen

On August 26, 1789, the French National Assembly approved the following declaration. Unlike the American revolutionaries, who passed the Bill of Rights after writing the Constitution, the French decided to establish a guiding set of principles first. It marked the culmination of Enlightenment political thought and presented a sharp break with the past.

- How do the declaration's ideas compare to those of Montesquieu and Rousseau?
- What is the relationship between law and rights?
- What kind of society does the declaration establish?
- To which social groups would these ideas appeal and why?

The representatives of the French people, organized as a National Assembly, believing that the ignorance, neglect, or contempt of the rights of man are the sole cause of public calamities and of the corruption of governments, have determined to set forth in a solemn declaration the natural, unalienable, and sacred rights of man . . . :

Article 1. Men are born and remain free and equal in rights. Social distinctions may be founded only upon the general good.

2. The aim of all political association is the preservation of the natural and imprescriptible rights of man. These rights are liberty, property, security, and resistance to oppression.

3. The principle of all sovereignty resides essentially in the nation. No body nor individual may exercise any authority which does not proceed directly from the nation.

4. Liberty consists in the freedom to do everything which injures no one else; hence the exercise of the natural rights of each man has no limits except those which assure to the other members of society the enjoyment of the same rights. These limits can be only determined by law.

6. Law is the expression of the general will. Every citizen has a right to participate personally, or though his representative, in its foundation. It must be the same for all, whether it protects or punishes. All citizens, being equal in the eyes of the law, are equally eligible to all dignities and to all public positions and occupations, according to their abilities, and without distinction except that of their virtues and talents.

10. No one shall be disquieted on account of his opinions, including his religious views, provided their manifestation does not disturb the public order established by law.

11. The free communication of ideas and opinions is one of the most precious of the rights of man. Every citizen may, accordingly, speak, write, and print with freedom, but shall be responsible for such abuses of this freedom as shall be defined by law.

16. A society in which the observance of the law is not assured, nor the separation of powers defined, has no constitution at all.

17. Since property is an inviolable and sacred right, no one shall be deprived thereof except where public necessity legally determined, shall clearly demand it, and then only on condition that the owner shall have been previously and equitably indemnified.

Source: James Harvey Robinson, ed., *Readings in European History, Volume II: From the Opening of the Protestant Revolt to the Present Day* (Boston: Ginn & Company, 1906), 409–411.

Further Reading

Doyle, William, ed. *Old Regime France: 1648–1788*. Oxford: Oxford University Press, 2001.

Garrioch, David. *The Making of Revolutionary Paris*. Berkeley: University of California Press, 2004.

Horne, Alistair. *Seven Ages of Paris*. New York: Vintage Books, 2004.

Jones, Colin. *The Great Nation: France from Louis XV to Napoleon*. New York: Penguin Books, 2008.

Jones, Colin. *Paris: The Biography of a City*. New York: Viking Penguin, 2004.

Roche, Daniel. *The People of Paris: An Essay in Popular Culture in the 18th Century*. Berkeley: University of California Press, 1987.

Web Resources

The Encyclopedia of Diderot and d'Alembert Collaborative Translations Project, University of Michigan, http://quod.lib.umich.edu/d/did/.

Gallica, French language sources on Paris and French history, Bibliothèque Nationale de France, http://gallica.bnf.fr.

Plan de Turgot: Paris en 1734 (map), http://plan.turgot.free.fr/plan_turgot/plan_turgot.php.

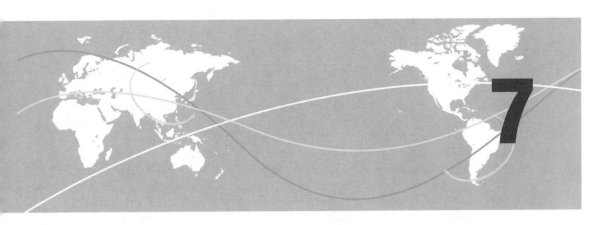

Calcutta

A Central Exchange Point for Widely Separate Worlds

(1700–1840)

Jonathan E. Brooke

ALCUTTA—OR KOLKATA AS IT WAS OFFICIALLY RENAMED IN 2001 AS A NOD TO its precolonial heritage—has long been a point of intersection and encounter, even before it became the "metropolis" of the British Empire in India, the hub of the Bengal Renaissance, or the bustling city it is today. Situated along the Hooghly River in the delta country of eastern India, fifty miles upriver from the Bay of Bengal, Calcutta served to funnel goods, people, and ideas in and out of the subcontinent. Its particular location, origins, and character have all contributed to create a cosmopolitan city with a rich and storied background.

I first became interested in Calcutta as a graduate student in history researching connections between British imperialism and Christian missions in the nineteenth century. There is, of course, a long tradition of romance associated with India and "the East," and through my sources Calcutta seemed to embody much of it. I was living and studying at the time in New Orleans, Louisiana, a city in many ways similar to Calcutta geographically, culturally, and historically, and this contributed in no little part to many of my notions of what the city must have been like two hundred years ago . . . *and what it might be like now.* A city near the mouth of a great river, situated for trade and interaction, whose very history and character was shaped by that circumstance. A city known for great luxury and great poverty, celebrated in turn for high and low culture, for glorious architecture and shadowy events.

I finally made it to Calcutta on my second trip to India, in early 2005, and it was in many ways exactly what I had imagined. Familiar images of streets packed with taxis, motos, scooters, rickshaws, bullock carts, and the occasional elephant confirmed it was indeed India. The juxtaposition of British formality against rambling alleys and residential quarters, massive old godowns, and squatters' camps confirmed it was the place I had been imagining all along. Though it sounds overly romantic, chugging down the Hooghly on a ferry, walking past neoclassical facades and through labyrinthine alleys in search of books, or strolling the open green space of the Maidan in the cool of the evening I could easily imagine the missionaries and officials I was studying doing the same thing in *almost* the same place.

Calcutta's contrasts reach back to the city's founding and are in many ways a product of the multiple levels of encounter reflected in its history. From the mid-eighteenth to mid-nineteenth century, Calcutta experienced great developments and controversies—commercial, administrative, educational, and cultural. Many of these developments shared common intellectual and ideological roots, which, through experimentation, conflict, and synthesis, were shaped by—and in turn shaped—the city of Calcutta itself.

CALCUTTA AND THE WORLD:
Connecting Commercial and Cultural Networks

The great Ganges River flows more than fifteen hundred miles from the Himalayas through the upper plains of India to the Bay of Bengal. Considered sacred in Hinduism, the Ganges, like other rivers around the world, has connected points on the subcontinent physically, culturally, and economically since ancient times. When it enters the state of West Bengal, the Ganges branches into its "delta," and the Hooghly River is one of its major outlets to the sea. Deep and navigable for almost its entire length, the Hooghly has long connected India with the broader commercial and cultural networks of Southeast Asia and the Indian Ocean. In the seventeenth and eighteenth centuries, European merchants also arrived to contribute to, expand, and enrich those connections.

On the fringes of the great Mughal Empire, which ruled most of North India from the sixteenth to the mid-nineteenth centuries, the city of Calcutta emerged from a cluster of fishing and weaving villages to become the metropolis of British India and the "second city" of the British Empire. Though it was situated on the edges of a broad malarial swamp on a singular piece of high ground, Calcutta was more importantly adjacent to a deepwater anchorage on the Hooghly River, and the products of Bengal—grains, cotton and silks, indigo, saltpeter, tea, and opium—produced great wealth for the Mughals, Bengalis, and Europeans alike. (See Map 7.1.) Calcutta's beginnings were rather humble, with East India Company merchants officially establishing in 1690 "factories"—warehouses and depots—on the site of a village called Kalicatta. These buildings were used to process and store the goods they planned to ship to Europe, China, and the Americas. Within a generation, however, Calcutta was becoming the hub of the entire region, and its location as a port city and gateway, as well as a growing administrative and cultural center, shaped the city's growth and character.

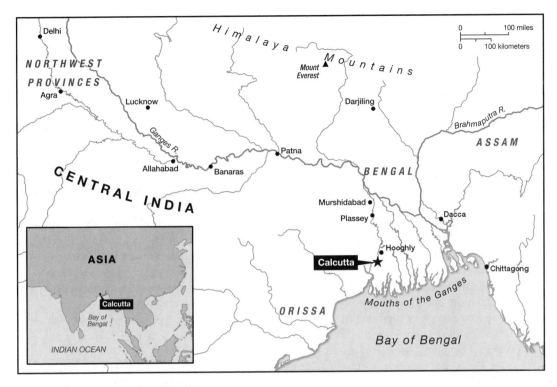

Map 7.1. Calcutta and the Ganges, Nineteenth Century

Calcutta's location along the Hooghly River and near the mouth of the Ganges contributed to its development as a hub for the region and as an active port city and cultural center that developed into a commercial powerhouse, drawing merchants from Europe and Asia to its shores. The British administered Calcutta as part of the East India Company throughout much of the eighteenth century, and curious Englishmen came to study Orientalism there.

Encounters on the Hooghly

Merchants of the British East India Company (EIC) made the greatest impact on the city. Established in 1600 by Queen Elizabeth I, the EIC was initially granted a monopoly on English trade in the Indian Ocean and beyond, especially with regard to spices and silks, but competition with the Dutch and Portuguese soon led English merchants to seek entry into mainland India. Successful negotiations with the Mughal emperor Jahangir in 1612 ushered in a new era for the EIC. Though initially interested only in trade and profits, the EIC's agents in India nevertheless soon found themselves continuously engaged in Mughal affairs, negotiating the complex hierarchies of the Mughal state through diplomacy and, more often, force of arms.

The new and expanded settlement of Calcutta flourished, and construction of Fort William—named for King William III of England—began in 1696. Though it was only completed in its full fortified form in 1717, the interior of the fort was quickly cluttered with warehouses and small homes for the British. Extensive ranks of small markets and dwellings for Bengalis and other Indians who had gravitated to the area were built outside the fort's walls. For decades the EIC had sought a *firman* from the Mughal emperor: his personal authorization to trade freely in Bengal. When this finally came, on New Year's

Eve 1716, it ushered in a period of rapid growth and development. The EIC became a vassal of the emperor, paying rents and taxes, and the massive revenues and profits gained by both the emperor and the EIC stimulated even more expansion and prosperity in the growing settlement of Calcutta. In addition to European merchants, agents, soldiers, and speculators, the growing port city drew people from the countryside who sought new freedoms and opportunities in the growing cash economy. They came to work the docks, warehouses, and markets; to transport goods; and to form the core of expanding service and civil needs. Many of the early Bengali "great families" of Calcutta were wealthy landowners who moved into the new metropolis in its early days and amassed huge fortunes by investing in building, finance, and trade.

By 1750 Calcutta boasted a population of 120,000 and had become a city of stately riverside mansions, as well as sprawling slums and suburbs—all watched over by the imposing Fort William. Thus, Calcutta as a city represented the increasing commercial, military, and cultural presence of the British on the eastern edge of Mughal authority. However, it also represented the increasing scope of British ambitions on a global scale: their expansion in India was being mirrored in the Americas, Africa, and even China, providing Britain's infant industries with raw materials as well as markets. Historians have debated whether this period, marked by mercantilism and competition, was separate from later, more overt imperialism by the British and their European counterparts, or whether it was a necessary prelude. To paraphrase English historian Sir John Seely, by the late eighteenth century it seemed that British power in India and elsewhere had been "acquired in a fit of absence of mind."

The wealth and power of the EIC in Calcutta and Bengal naturally drew the attention of longtime competitors and adversaries, including the French, the Dutch, and the Mughal *nawab* (governor) of Bengal himself. Despite further fortification and expansion of Fort William and the city's defenses, Calcutta was seized in 1756 by the *nawab*, leading to the infamous episode of the "Black Hole of Calcutta," in which over a hundred Europeans and Indians were imprisoned in the fort's small dungeon, few of whom emerged alive the next day. The city was famously recaptured by British lieutenant colonel Robert Clive in January 1757 with the assistance of wealthy Indian merchants and landowners and disaffected Mughal officials. It was Clive's final victory over the *nawab* in June, however, that transformed the position of the East India Company in Bengal and began a new era for the city of Calcutta and its inhabitants. By accepting a number of large personal rewards and titles, including the position of *nawab,* Clive effectively inserted himself—and thereby the EIC—into the political and commercial hierarchy of Mughal Bengal. Clive replaced the *nawab* with a sympathetic and compliant minor official named Mir Jafar and immediately began the construction of a massive new Fort William. The new fort covered almost two square miles on the banks of the Hooghly and was fronted by an open green space, or *maidan.* It was finally completed in 1773, and in the interim Calcutta had grown around it due to a steady stream of merchants, artisans, and laborers lured to the city by its reputation of easily gained fortunes. (See Map 7.2.) Meanwhile, military and diplomatic victories elsewhere resulted in similar growth in other Indian cities such as Bombay and Madras, as well as abroad in Africa and the Americas.

A Modern Babylon

Calcutta in the last decades of the eighteenth century was certainly a city of contrasts, much like any other large commercial, military, and administrative center. The city maintained a reputation as a place where fortunes could be gleaned by nearly anyone with

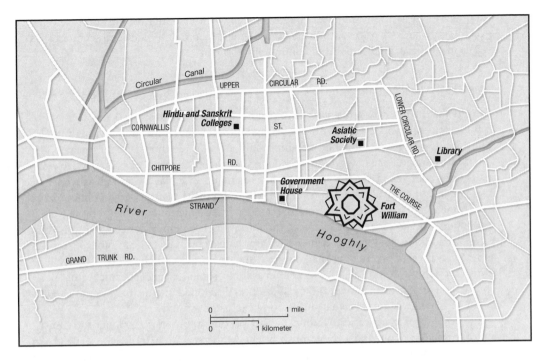

Map 7.2. Calcutta, ca. 1800

The British presence in Calcutta became evident throughout the eighteenth century and into the nineteenth as the city grew. British influence was reflected in new structures and spaces, such as Fort William and its surrounding maidan, and in organizations such as the Asiatic Society. The city also remained a vibrant locale for Indian learning, and Hindu and Sanskrit colleges served as educational centers for local residents.

some ambition and few scruples, as long as they could survive the climate, the diseases, and the temptations. Indeed, one historian has called Calcutta "a modern Babylon along the Hooghly," alluding to the city's grandeur and beauty, as well as the lifestyles of its European citizens. As one governor-general put it, "sloth, indolence, low debauchery and vulgarity" characterized many of the young East India Company clerks, called "writers," who came to India with dreams of fortunes and were then set to work at "the menial, laborious, unwholesome, and unprofitable duty" of copying receipts and ledger books in the offices and warehouses. Heavy drinking, gambling, horseracing, and pistol duels were commonplace despite constant campaigns aimed at maintaining a semblance of order and "civilized" behavior.

Although some of Calcutta's inhabitants resided in Garden Reach and the opulent European sections of the city, the vast majority lived in "black towns"—sprawling residential quarters and markets radiating out around the city. Many of these residents had migrated from the countryside in search of fortunes, wages, or even relief from the periodic famines brought on by the EIC's continuing exploitation of Bengal's vast agricultural resources. Here poverty and overcrowding presented a stark contrast to the marble columns and wealthy pastimes of the European quarters. However, many Indians in Calcutta profited handsomely from both the success of the British and the struggles of their own countrymen. Landowners, merchants, moneylenders, and professionals—Hindu and Muslim alike—represented an elite core of middle- and upper-class gentry that became known as the *bhadralok*. They would play an essential role in the economic growth and character of the city throughout the eighteenth and nineteenth centuries, as well as in its social, intellectual, and cultural development.

Orientalism and Anglicism

The city that had drawn so many types of people in its first hundred years was by the turn of the nineteenth century a city of developing and intersecting identities, with a population of almost a quarter million, including only about three thousand Europeans. The East India Company, like its Mughal predecessors, faced the challenge of effectively administering a large and diverse province while maintaining an *identity* as well as *authority*. As a small yet powerful minority, more interested in profits than imperial politics, many British merchants and officials found themselves in an environment that tempted them with luxury and power yet also alienated them from their counterparts and lifestyles back home. In addition, they had to contend with pressure and threats from other European and Indian powers, fluctuating markets, and their own increasingly insular society. The British viewed the responsibilities of administration from a particularly intellectual position, as well as a pragmatic one, and thus Calcutta developed into a city of not only commercial exchange, but intellectual and cultural exchange as well.

In the preceding centuries, Europeans had become more curious about "the East," and information about India drew much attention there. Within India, and Calcutta in particular, this curiosity had practical applications, such as the identification and study of languages, traditions, laws, and customs. This broad category of interest and investigation is generally known as Orientalism. The term's modern usage was coined by Edward Said in his monumental study *Orientalism* (1979), in which he argued that such "projects" were essentially means for Europeans to identify and manipulate sources of power in "the Orient." Orientalism was put to a variety of uses in India and elsewhere, and it would in many ways redefine Calcutta.

The human and financial resources brought to bear by the British in a city like Calcutta made such projects eminently feasible, and the city served at once as a site and as a catalyst for this process. European and Indian scholars, including translators, naturalists, and artists, came to work in Calcutta, and the decades straddling the turn of the nineteenth century saw prolific literary, scientific, and cultural developments in the city. As in other cities throughout history, wealth and power generated leisure time and a demand for entertainment and other pursuits, which helped lay the foundation for the unique character of Calcutta.

Ideas and administration were inextricably connected to one another from Calcutta's early days, and a synthesis of European trends influenced early British administrators. Informed by Enlightenment ideals of rationality and order, as well as by Romanticist visions of India's historical and social structures, they sought to administer Bengal by first understanding it. Enlightenment Europe had looked toward its "classical age"—the supposed glories of the Greeks and the Romans—to identify the sources of European civilization, law, and culture, and Orientalists in India applied this same "classicist" approach in India. They believed that India under the Mughals represented a corrupted version of its own classical age, now frozen in time and progress under despotic rulers and priests, but which could be restored and improved upon under British tutelage. They held that the Hinduism of contemporary India, and especially its Brahmin priesthood, were also corrupt and *corruptive* and deserved a guided return to ancient purity and nobility. Indeed, some historians have argued that it was at this point that a particularly British concept of "Hinduism" as a relatively homogenous belief system began to emerge, in part to set it apart from Mughal Islam and European Christianity (or Enlightenment secularism).

Hinduism by the eighteenth century reflected several thousand years of diverse philosophical and folk influences, including Vedic traditions, mythology, and devotional practices. Hindus worshipped many different deities and gods, all manifestations of the universal Brahma, thus underscoring the essential unity of all creation. They believed in the transmigration of souls, or reincarnation. British observers found distasteful some of the aspects of "popular" Hinduism, such as the worship of numerous gods and the concept of reincarnation, and recoiled at local practices such as blood sacrifices to Kali and *sati* (the burning of a widow on her husband's funeral pyre) in Calcutta and Bengal. These practices, the British argued, clearly reflected the worst aspects of Hinduism and needed to be eradicated if "progress" and modernization were ever to be successful in India. Many Indians, too, echoed these ideas and sentiments, and they would become instrumental in social and legal reforms in the following decades.

Scholarship as a Means Toward Government

Rational study and analysis of India's laws, traditions, and literature provided the British with a context for their own vision of their future rule of the region. Warren Hastings, the first governor-general of India (1773–1785), believed he had such a vision. Hastings believed that it was law that made man civilized, so it was law the English needed to impose in India in order to promote "the happiness of the vast population of this country." A combined application of ancient Hindu laws and more modern Muslim laws, applied to their respective populations, would ensure the appropriate conformity to British ideals and rule and encourage the potential of India's millions toward "progress" and "civilization." Under Hastings, EIC officials such as Nathaniel Halhed and William Jones devoted themselves to discovering what they hoped would prove the most ancient precedents for religious and legal traditions, which could be found and illuminated from the original texts of the *shastras*, Vedas, and Puranas.

"Discovering" such texts would allow the EIC free rein in its administration by freeing it from reliance on local intermediaries and legitimating their own interpretations. This, however, initially required the assistance and accommodation of Indian scholars: *pundits* (learned Brahmins), *munshis* (translators and secretaries), and *maulvis* (Muslim scholars). Reliance on these scholars, however, privileged those groups who were the "keepers" of the traditions and texts, and only when the British themselves were able to master Sanskrit and Persian could these early Orientalist designs be accomplished. In 1784 William Jones helped form the Asiatic Society to promote, collate, and disseminate Orientalist scholarship. The society, which still functions today as a center of scholarly activity in Calcutta, sponsored, published, and collected research by both Europeans and Indians on Indian languages and history, as well as on the natural and social sciences. This first official institution of Orientalism in Calcutta served as a model (and location) for many of the later intellectual and social developments in the city. It stands today as a library and museum and still functions as a center of scholarly activity along with its British counterpart, the Royal Asiatic Society, which has branches around the world. Together, these twin organizations serve as the root for extensive academic and scholarly work on India and much of the rest of Asia.

In 1786 Hastings was replaced as governor-general by Charles Cornwallis, who drew from his predecessor an emphasis on law and property and applied it in what came to be known as the "Cornwallis Code," a series of laws that rearranged property and tax structures along presumably "ancient" lines, but which rested on British Whig principles of stability and order based on the protection of property rights and landholding. These laws redrew village and farm boundaries and reorganized community structures by imposing fixed tax rates on landholdings and privileging the position of *zamindars* (landlords). Many rural Bengalis failed to meet the increasing tax demands of the EIC and were forced to move away from their farms and villages, swelling the population of Calcutta and increasing the already considerable wealth of absentee landholders and real estate speculators.

Within Calcutta itself, Cornwallis oversaw significant reforms intended to curb the excesses of company merchants and clerks, who had been allowed liberal personal trading privileges that they had naturally exploited by buying and exporting cargoes of grain, silks, and other commodities, often at the expense of the company's profit. Both the early Orientalists and the EIC's directors in London were increasingly concerned by such rampant corruption among the EIC's own employees, as well as by the continued reliance on Indians within the administrative and legal structures.

Cornwallis introduced a new policy of "Europeanization," replacing Indian intermediaries and functionaries with young new British employees who could be molded into responsible officials. The key to producing this new class of company men was knowledge of the laws and policies that were maintaining stability and profits in Bengal and an ability to impart that knowledge to the people of Bengal. This policy reflected a general shift throughout the early British Empire toward a general centralization of talents and responsibilities intended to ensure compliance and efficiency and to address the uniquely large-scale administrative challenges presented by Calcutta and Bengal.

Cornwallis's successor, Richard Wellesley, proposed a solution to these challenges that served multiple purposes. He planned to establish a college in Calcutta for training East India Company servants and administrators in the languages of India—Sanskrit and Persian, as well as the vernaculars—in order to eliminate their reliance on Indians and to further accomplish the effective implementation of British policies. Whereas Cornwallis had synthesized British and Indian ideas on land and property law, under Wellesley the EIC also took over every other level of administration. Moreover, Wellesley's own vision of rule rested on an emphasis on sound and moral governance and the promotion of duty over profit, with the intention of replacing the popular image of rapacious and irresponsible individuals draining India's wealth. Fort William College was established in 1800 and immediately began offering instruction in Indian languages, history, and jurisprudence, as well as in other traditional European subjects. Instruction was provided by a combination of British Orientalists (including the Baptist missionary William Carey) and native *munshis*, or translators, drawn from all over India. The college also became a hub of printing, stimulating other English and vernacular presses in Calcutta as well, which encouraged the spread of literacy and primary education in the city and beyond.

The products of translators, writers, jurists, and other scholars and printers circulated much farther than Calcutta, however, often piggybacking on growing British networks of printing and publishing. Travelling booksellers, theater troupes, public readers, and scribes had always played significant roles in Indian society, and an increase in material and subjects proved a boon to them and to their customers and clients. Moreover, interest in all things Indian—ancient and contemporary—continued in Britain and the rest of Europe, generating scholarly studies, as well as stories, poems, and plays for popular consumption.

Reforming Society and Saving Indian Souls

By the beginning of the nineteenth century, it seemed that the goals of the Orientalist "project" finally had been reached and British identity and authority established in Calcutta. But the notion of a singular "project" is misleading, as there were a variety of Orientalists in the city working toward different means and ends. Christian missionaries like William Carey, for example, had come to India to share the Gospel and saw obtaining knowledge of Indian languages, customs, and beliefs as the most expedient way to accomplish that. Until 1813 missionaries were officially prohibited from operating within company territories for fear that they might undermine the company's own goals and disturb that "happiness" that Hastings had envisioned for the company's Indian subjects. The small numbers of both missionaries and converts in the area generally rendered these fears moot. However, Wellesley superseded this policy and came to rely on Carey and his colleagues—and their printing press—as an indispensable factor in his own designs. Carey likewise relied on his position as a professor at Fort William to support his missionary activities.

Both of these Orientalist visions to gradually reform a society relied on education, whether it was used for effective administration and the uplifting of a civilization or for the salvation of Indian souls. With their obvious usefulness in the acquisition of wealth and position in Calcutta, literacy and numeracy—reading, writing, and arithmetic—in English and Bengali became increasingly desirable skills among Indian adults and their children, and the turn of the century saw rapid growth in local schools in the city. When the EIC's charter came up for renewal in 1813, a new clause was inserted by influential lobbyists in Parliament requiring the company to set aside ten thousand pounds a year expressly for local education, which began a new era in the city. This sum was multiplied tenfold in 1833. But this new emphasis on popular education also generated new ideas about its purposes and designs.

The development of new intellectual and political sentiments in Britain was increasingly finding applications in the now-secure position of the company government in India. A revival of Evangelical Christianity and the growth of liberalism challenged conceptions of the role of individuals and governments in improving society. Jeremy Bentham's popular "utilitarianism" emphasized simple, moral government and "useful knowledge" that promoted the happiness of the greatest number of people. These new ideas, when they made their way to Calcutta in the 1820s, seemed to remain intellectually and politically consistent with earlier strains of thought. British authority had been secured and employed by the rational application of knowledge by scholars and statesmen. Keepers of Indian traditions, such as Brahmins and *maulvis*, as well as wealthy Indian merchants and landowners, had cooperated in the extension of EIC authority and wealth—often at the expense of poor farmers, laborers, and the growing masses in Calcutta. Moreover, the anachronism presented by the contrasts of wealth and poverty in Calcutta had very public repercussions there and in Britain as well, and the lingering notion that the British had a responsibility to "improve" India continued to take a more definite shape in the first decades of the nineteenth century.

In contrast to the Orientalists, who had sought to synthesize Indian and British ideas, a new group of influential administrators and intellectuals known as Anglicists came to the fore in Calcutta, and the debates generated between the two schools of thought would last for decades. Anglicists such as James Mill (*History of British India*, 1817) and Thomas Macaulay ("Minute on Education," 1835) argued that English customs and institutions represented the greatest accomplishment of Western civilization and that the homogenizing English language itself held the most value for the future of India. Thus older, conservative views of British "paternalism" were combined with more liberal concepts of a responsibility—and ability—to transform and "improve" Indian society. The Anglicists offered a plan of "education" for Indian civilization so that it might one day no longer require a guiding hand. This plan was centered on the development of broad-based education in English language and literature, science and mathematics, and philosophy and politics. It represented a reversal of the "admiration" of the Orientalists for all things "classically" Indian.

This naturally concerned those Indian groups in Calcutta that had been privileged under the Orientalists and found themselves now threatened. Other Bengalis—particularly the *bhadralok*—knew that education, in English or otherwise, would be the tool to aligning themselves with the company government and maintaining their elite position in Calcutta society. In a purposeful (and perhaps self-conscious) reversal of Cornwallis' "Europeanization" of the civil service, an "Indianization" began, and wealthy Indians sought education and entrance into the system, which also significantly impacted the character and atmosphere of Calcutta.

The Bengal Renaissance and Young Bengal

Just as an "Oriental Renaissance" in Europe had been driven by Orientalism, a "Bengal Renaissance" emerged in Calcutta in the early decades of the nineteenth century, spurred by the British-driven cultural and intellectual developments of the previous years. The climate of curiosity and intellectualism, and especially the print culture that had emerged in Calcutta, had produced not only a demand for literate Indian civil servants and employees, but a lively literary culture as well. Though the Orientalists had initially focused on Sanskrit, Persian, and Arabic, the vernaculars also received a great deal of interest, especially after the turn of the century and the opening of Fort William College.

In contrast to perceived notions (on the part of the Europeans) of a monolithic and unchanging Hinduism, dynamic cultural and social shifts continued to affect Bengali culture, especially in Calcutta. An awareness and curiosity about literacy and education was also becoming popular. The 1818 establishment of the public library, which housed over eleven thousand volumes and manuscripts, reinforced the growing value Indians placed on vernacular education in their future development. Further developments in newspaper and periodical printing nearly outstripped other high-caste and socialite movements in terms of volume and impact.

The emphasis on "improvement" envisioned by Orientalists and Anglicists alike—and the tension generated between the two group's different interpretations of the concept—were manifested in 1826 with the opening of twin institutions for Indian students: Sanskrit College and Hindu College. The colleges initially occupied opposite wings of the same building. While Sanskrit College offered courses of study in ancient laws and literature, Hindu College taught English, Western literature, and Western science. Sanskrit College had been in operation under the East India Company in the city of Benares since 1791 (as had a parallel Muslim *madrassa* in Calcutta since 1780), but Orientalist officials had lobbied for decades for its removal to Calcutta. Hindu College, on the other hand, had been established in the city in 1816 by a wealthy Bengali named Rammohun Roy and was supported by the patronage of successful Indians and Europeans. It was within these two schools that a core of young Bengali intellectuals, known collectively as "Young Bengal," emerged to become literary and philosophical leaders who sought to create their own synthesis of Indian and English ideas.

Much of the driving force behind the Bengali Renaissance emerged from Orientalist scholarship and methods, now repurposed at the hands of Bengali scholars. Rammohun Roy himself might be considered an Orientalist, but he also embraced many of the philosophical and practical ideas of the Anglicists. Fluent in Sanskrit, Persian, and English as well as Bengali, he made his fortune working for the EIC and spent much of his time with government officials and Christian missionaries. Roy believed that much of value could be gleaned from Hindu scriptures and literature, yet he opposed the removal of Sanskrit College to Calcutta, fearing it would simply perpetrate what he saw as the corrupt "monasticism" of the Brahmin priesthood. Roy also believed that the forces of "modernization" were inescapable and promised great things for the future of India. He led a number of theological and social reforms, including the establishment of two philosophical societies and the official abolition of the practice of *sati*. Roy's ideas and his influence among the *bhadralok* remained strong within social and official circles and informed the interactions of the *bhadralok* with British reformers and politicians in Calcutta and Britain.

It was from Hindu College that the younger generation of Bengali intellectual and cultural leaders emerged, encouraged by the movements of reform and Westernization actively at work in Calcutta. The Young Bengal movement also reflected the mixture of influences and ideologies that had grown and changed with the city. Hindu College's English-language curriculum exposed its students to Western science and mathematics, as well as to Christian theology, Enlightenment philosophy, and Romanticist literature. At the forefront of this effort was a Eurasian named Henry Louis Vivian Derozio, who had been a clerk for the EIC before being hired to teach English at Hindu College in 1826. He had been captivated by the ideals of the French Revolution and English radicalism of the late eighteenth century, such as democracy, individualism, and redistribution of wealth (which would have landed him in prison in Calcutta a generation earlier), as well as the Enlightenment ideas of David Hume and John Locke that emphasized reason and empiricism. Thus, the benefits of an English education had exposed Derozio and his contemporaries to the ideas that had influenced the Orientalists in the first place.

Those Westernizing and modernizing influences had other, more visible effects; the young students' adoption of secular or Christian beliefs and outspoken rejection of Hinduism sat poorly with many influential figures and groups in Calcutta. Their adoption of Western dress—often in garish extremes—and consumption of beef and alcohol, combined with much carousing and youthful indiscretion, recalled the young EIC servants of Wellesley's day. Certainly the temptations of Calcutta worked on Young Bengal as they had on earlier students encountering a variety of cultures, pressures, and opportunities. But their reputation was not solely one of iconoclasm. Derozio was a distinguished English poet and journalist, and many of the other students and figures, including the influential Tagore family, led a revival of Bengali poetry and literature.

GLOBAL ENCOUNTERS AND CONNECTIONS:
The Fusion and Conflict of Ideas and Worldviews

By the 1840s the Young Bengal generation gave way to its successors, though the Bengal Renaissance continued to draw strength and energy from Calcutta's lively culture and institutions. The drive to reform and "improve," as well as to challenge traditions and outside influences, remained important to the city's intellectuals. Ishwar Chandra Vidyasagar had been a pupil at Sanskrit College, but on his own developed an appreciation of many of the same ideas popular among Hindu College students and reformers. He worked as a translator at Fort William College for several years before returning to Sanskrit College in 1850 as the principal and was a tireless proponent for Bengali-language education and literacy. Likewise, poet and journalist Michael Madhusudan Dutt carried on the progressive influences of Young Bengal and the Bengal Renaissance. Like his classmates at Hindu College, Dutt had initially scorned Bengali in favor of English literature and lifestyles, even converting to Christianity, but as an adult he felt challenged to write in Bengali as well as in English and successfully synthesized many Western and Indian literary styles. Influenced by Byron, Dutt's Bengali poetry and drama combined sonnets and epic cantos with Bengali meter and Indian themes, and he is remembered as one of the founders of modern Bengali literature. As a result of the efforts of Dutt and Vidyasagar and those of other intellectuals and writers, the Bengal Renaissance continued through the nineteenth century, spreading literacy, education, and cultural expression from Calcutta throughout Bengal and abroad.

In less than two centuries Calcutta had grown from a fortified trading post to a metropolis, the administrative capital of Britain's Indian empire, and the economic center of the broader empire. But it had also grown as a site of encounter between merchants and artisans, priests and missionaries, rulers and subjects, and, most importantly, between ideas and worldviews. The intersections of faiths, languages, and histories had an indelible effect on the growth of the city and on its role in the wider world.

The Hooghly River had brought together villages and towns throughout Bengal and had drawn Europeans into their world beginning in the sixteenth century. As those connections developed and grew, so did demand for Indian goods and presence within the subcontinent itself. The merchants and officers of the British East India Company established Calcutta as an entrepôt, a place for exchange and communication between two widely separated worlds, but as Calcutta grew those worlds were drawn ever closer together. Varying tastes in architecture, goods, entertainments, and ideologies influenced and drew from each other to create a truly cosmopolitan environment characteristic of port cities and capitals around the world.

Trade and diplomacy also brought warfare and politics, and Calcutta increasingly became a hub of power and money, as well as a new center of administration and rule. British traders and Indian merchants grew wealthy from the vast agricultural and industrial production of Bengal and beyond, while the increasing burdens on the rural population this created flooded Calcutta with new inhabitants in search of opportunities. The city was also a site of intellectual and ideological exchange, as British administrators initially wrestled with Indian social and legal structures and attempted to utilize Hindu and Muslim texts and traditions to solidify their new positions of authority. This favored traditional elites like Brahmin priests and wealthy landholders, but also revealed the ambivalent nature of early British rule in India.

Later rulers in Calcutta favored a more direct approach in administration, emphasizing English language and institutions as the city's foundation and future direction. An emphasis on "progress" and modernization was reflected in the wealth and prosperity of Calcutta. This prosperity, however, was contrasted with widespread poverty, which led to movements of reform and "improvement" from inside India and from Britain. As education and literacy spread across all social levels and boundaries, the tensions between tradition and modernity—and East and West—continued to negotiate and resolve themselves into unique products of cultural identity and expression. From the early nineteenth century to the present, Calcutta has clearly reflected its precolonial and colonial pasts—its British influences as well as its Bengali identity.

The sources below reveal the attitudes and perspectives behind the Orientalist-Anglicist debates in Calcutta. In the first document, Governor-General Wellesley proposes the establishment of Fort William College. In the second document, Thomas B. Macaulay argues before Calcutta's Supreme Council that government funds should be utilized for English-language schools. In the third, Raja Rammohan Roy describes his early interests and the development of his personal ideology and philosophy. As you read them, consider not only the main arguments of each side, but also their respective positions on British responsibilities in India.

"Minute in Council at Fort William," by the Marquis Wellesley, Containing His Reasons for the Establishment of a College at Calcutta

This first document discusses Lord Wellesley's rationale for creating Fort William College: to reform the East India Company's loose regulations on young employees in India and to train a new generation of civil servants and administrators. Consider the governor-general's attitudes toward current practices and his vision of the EIC's future role in India.

- What are the qualities Wellesley hopes the college will instill?

- What particular purposes will these qualities serve?

The British possessions in India now constitute one of the most extensive and populous empires in the world. . . . Those provinces . . . which are under the more immediate and direct administration of the European civil servants of the Company, are acknowledged to form the most opulent and flourishing part of India, in which property, life, civil order, and religious liberty, are more secure, and the people enjoy a larger portion of the benefits of good government, than in any other country in this quarter of the globe. The duty and policy of the British Government in India therefore require, that the system of confiding the immediate exercise of every branch and department of the government to Europeans educated in its own service, and subject to its own direct control, should be diffused as widely as possible, as well with a view to the stability of our own interests, as to the happiness and welfare of our native subjects. . . .

The civil servants of the English East India Company, therefore, can no longer be considered as the agents of a commercial concern; they are in fact the ministers and officers of a powerful sovereign. . . . Their studies, the discipline of their education, their habits of life, their manners and morals, should therefore be so ordered and regulated as to establish a just conformity between their personal consideration, and the dignity and importance of their public stations, and a sufficient correspondence between their qualifications and their duties. Their education should be founded in a general knowledge of those branches of literature and science, which form the basis of the education of persons destined to similar occupations in Europe. To this foundation should be added an intimate acquaintance with the history, languages, customs, and manners of the people of India, with the Mahommedan [Muslim] and Hindu codes of law and religion, and with the political and commercial interests and relations of Great Britain in Asia. . . . They should be well informed of the true and sound principles of the British constitution, and sufficiently grounded in the general principles of ethics, civil jurisprudence, the laws of nations, and general history, in order that they may be enabled to discriminate the characteristic differences of the several codes of law administered within the British empire in India, and practically to combine the spirit of each in the dispensation of justice, and in the maintenance of order and good government. . . .

The early education of the civil servants of the East India Company is the source from which will ultimately be derived the happiness or misery of our native subjects; and the stability of our government will bear a due proportion to its wisdom, liberality and justice. . . . The junior civil servants must therefore continue to embark for India at the age of fifteen or sixteen, that they may be tractable instruments in the hands of the government of the country,

that their morals and habits may be formed with proper safeguards against the peculiar nature of the views and characteristic dangers of Indian society; that they may be enabled to pass through the service before the vigour of life has ceased, and to return with a competent fortune to Europe, while the affections and attachments which bind them to their native country continue to operate with full force; and lastly, that they may possess regular, reasonable, and certain means of attaining the peculiar qualifications necessary for their stations. . . .

Under all these circumstances the most deliberate and assiduous examination of all the important questions considered in this paper, determined the Governor-General to found a collegiate institution at Fort William by the annexed regulations.

Source: Letters of the Marquis Wellesley Respecting the College of Fort William (London, England: J. Hatchard, 1812).

"Minute on Indian Education," by Thomas B. Macaulay

This famous document from Thomas B. Macaulay, a former member of Parliament in England and the law member of the EIC's Supreme Council of India from 1834 to 1838, is one of the most well-known examples of early British imperial ideology. Produced thirty-five years after Wellesley's appeal (above), Macaulay's own appeal for English instruction represents a clear shift in opinions on education.

- What value does Macaulay place on Indian languages and knowledge?
- What purpose(s) does he envision for the introduction of English knowledge?
- With what potential consequences?

A sum is set apart *"for the revival and promotion of literature, and the encouragement of the learned natives of India, and for the introduction and promotion of a knowledge of the sciences among the inhabitants of the British territories."* . . . We have a fund to be employed as Government shall direct for the intellectual improvement of the people of this country. The simple question is, what is the most useful way of employing it? . . . All parties seem to be agreed on one point, that the dialects commonly spoken among the natives of this part of

India contain neither literary nor scientific information, and are moreover so poor and rude that, until they are enriched from some other quarter, it will not be easy to translate any valuable work into them. It seems to be admitted on all sides, that the intellectual improvement of those classes of the people who have the means of pursuing higher studies can at present be effected only by means of some language not vernacular amongst them. . . .

What then shall that language be? One-half of the committee maintain that it should be the

English. The other half strongly recommend the Arabic and Sanskrit. The whole question seems to me to be, which language is the best worth knowing? . . . I have no knowledge of either Sanskrit or Arabic. But I have done what I could to form a correct estimate of their value. I have read translations of the most celebrated Arabic and Sanskrit works. I have conversed, both here and at home, with men distinguished by their proficiency in the Eastern tongues. I am quite ready to take the oriental learning at the valuation of the orientalists themselves. I have never found one among them who could deny that a single shelf of a good European library was worth the whole native literature of India and Arabia. The intrinsic superiority of the Western literature is indeed fully admitted by those members of the committee who support the oriental plan of education. . . .

How then stands the case? We have to educate a people who cannot at present be educated by means of their mother-tongue. We must teach them some foreign language. The claims of our own language it is hardly necessary to recapitulate. . . . Whoever knows that language has ready access to all the vast intellectual wealth which all the wisest nations of the earth have created and hoarded in the course of ninety generations. It may safely be said that the literature now extant in that language is of greater value than all the literature which three hundred years ago was extant in all the languages of the world together. Nor is this all. In India, English is the language spoken by the ruling class. It is spoken by the higher class of natives at the seats of Government. It is likely to become the language of commerce through-

out the seas of the East. . . . Whether we look at the intrinsic value of our literature, or at the particular situation of this country, we shall see the strongest reason to think that, of all foreign tongues, the English tongue is that which would be the most useful to our native subjects. . . .

I think it clear . . . that we are free to employ our funds as we choose, that we ought to employ them in teaching what is best worth knowing, that English is better worth knowing than Sanskrit or Arabic, that the natives are desirous to be taught English, and are not desirous to be taught Sanskrit or Arabic, that neither as the languages of law nor as the languages of religion have the Sanskrit and Arabic any peculiar claim to our encouragement, that it is possible to make natives of this country thoroughly good English scholars, and that to this end our efforts ought to be directed. . . .

In one point I fully agree with the gentlemen to whose general views I am opposed. I feel with them that it is impossible for us, with our limited means, to attempt to educate the body of the people. We must at present do our best to form a class who may be interpreters between us and the millions whom we govern—a class of persons Indian in blood and colour, but English in tastes, in opinions, in morals and in intellect. To that class we may leave it to refine the vernacular dialects of the country, to enrich those dialects with terms of science borrowed from the Western nomenclature, and to render them by degrees fit vehicles for conveying knowledge to the great mass of the population.

T[homas] B[abington] Macaulay,
2nd February 1835.

Source: Bureau of Education, *Selections from Educational Records, Part I (1781–1839)*, edited by H. Sharp (Calcutta, India: Superintendent, Government Printing, 1920. Reprint, Delhi, India: National Archives of India, 1965), 107–117.

"Autobiographical Sketch," by Rammohun Roy

In this final document, Rammohun Roy describes the development of his theological, intellectual, and educational principles. Roy published this "sketch" as a letter in several British periodicals and papers, as well as in Calcutta. Consider his purposes in doing so and who his potential audience might be.

- What influences on his thoughts and life does Roy reveal through his letter?

- What are some reasons for his "continued controversies" with Hinduism and Brahmins throughout his life? What outcomes do you think he envisioned?

My ancestors were Brahmins of a high order, and, from time immemorial, were devoted to the religious duties of their race. . . .

In conformity with the usage of my paternal race, and the wish of my father, I studied the Persian and Arabic languages, these being indispensable to those who attached themselves to the courts of the Mahommedan [Muslim] princes; and agreeably to the usage of my maternal relations, I devoted myself to the study of the Sanskrit and the theological works written in it, which contain the body of Hindoo literature, law and religion.

When about the age of sixteen, I composed a manuscript calling in question the validity of the idolatrous system of the Hindoos. This, together with my known sentiments on that subject, having produced a coolness between me and my immediate kindred, I proceeded on my travels, and passed through different countries, chiefly within, but some beyond, the bounds of Hindoostan, with a feeling of great aversion to the establishment of the British power in India. When I had reached the age of twenty, my father recalled me, and restored me to his favour; after which I first saw and began to associate with Europeans, and soon after made myself tolerably acquainted with their laws and form of government. Finding them generally more intelligent, more steady and moderate in their conduct, I gave up my prejudice against them, and became inclined in their favour, feeling persuaded that their rule, though a foreign yoke, would lead more speedily and surely to the amelioration of the native inhabitants; and I enjoyed the confidence of several of them even in their public capacity. . . .

My continued controversies with the Brahmins on the subject of their idolatry and superstition, and my interference with their custom of burning widows, and other pernicious practices, revived and increased their animosity against me; and through their influence with my family, my father was again obliged to withdraw his countenance openly, though his limited pecuniary support was still continued to me. . . . After my father's death I opposed the advocates of idolatry with still greater boldness. Availing myself of the art of printing, now established in India, I published various works and pamphlets against their errors, in the native and foreign languages. . . .

The ground which I took in all my controversies was, not that of opposition to *Brahminism,* but to a *perversion* of it; and I endeavoured to show that the idolatry of the Brahmins was contrary to the practice of their ancestors, and the principles of the ancient books and authorities which they profess to revere and obey. Notwithstanding the violence of the opposition and resistance to my opinions, several highly respectable persons, both among my own relations and others, began to adopt the same sentiments.

I now felt a strong wish to visit Europe, and obtain by personal observation, a more thorough insight into its manners, customs, religion, and political institutions. I refrained, however, from carrying this intention into effect until the friends who coincided in my sentiments should be increased in number and strength. My expectations having been at length realized, in November 1830 I embarked for England, as the discussion of the East India Company's charter was expected to come on, by which the treatment of the natives of India, and its future government, would be determined for many years to come, and an appeal to the King in Council, against the abolition of the practice of burning widows, was to be heard before the Privy Council; and his Majesty the Emperor of Delhi had likewise commissioned me to bring before the authorities in England certain encroachments on his rights by the East India Company. I accordingly arrived in England in April, 1831.

Source: Rammohun Roy, *The English Works of Raja Rammohun Roy: With an English Translation of "Tuhfatul Muwahhiddin"* (Allahabad, India: The Panini Office, 1906), 223–225.

Further Reading

Ahmed, A. F. Salahuddin. *Social Ideas and Social Change in Bengal, 1818–1835*. Leiden: E. J. Brill, 1965.

Dutta, Krishna. *Calcutta: A Cultural History*. Northampton, MA: Interlink Books, 2008.

Inden, Ronald. "Orientalist Constructions of India." *Modern Asian Studies* 20, part 3 (1986): 401–446.

Kopf, David. *British Orientalism and the Bengal Renaissance: The Dynamics of Indian Modernization, 1773–1835*. Berkeley: University of California Press, 1969.

Marshall, Peter J. *The British Discovery of Hinduism in the Eighteenth Century*. Cambridge: Cambridge University Press, 1970.

Moorhouse, Geoffrey. *Calcutta: The City Revealed*. New York: Penguin Books, 1984.

Oddie, Geoffrey. *Imagined Hinduism: British Protestant Missionary Conceptions of Hinduism, 1793–1900*. New Delhi: Sage Publications, 2006.

Stokes, Eric. *The English Utilitarians and India*. Oxford: Oxford University Press, 1959.

Web Resources

Banglapedia: The National Encyclopedia of Bangladesh, www.banglapedia.org.

Calcuttaweb: A Guide to Kolkata (Calcutta), Bengali and West Bengal, www.calcuttaweb.com.

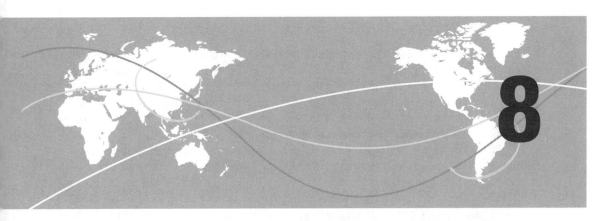

Shanghai

From Chinese Hub Port to Global Treaty Port

(1730–1865)

CHRISTOPHER A. REED

RAWN BY A PERSONAL INTEREST IN OLD BRITISH COLONIAL PORTS AND A professional, scholarly one in the history of global communism (China's Communist Party was born here in 1921), I first visited Shanghai as a backpacking tourist in the summer of 1991. I passed a few days in the old Astor Hotel, marketed in its heyday as "the Waldorf-Astoria of Shanghai." The Astor, or rather the Huangpu Hotel as it was known when I stayed there, had recently been converted into an international youth hostel by the People's Municipal Government, which then managed all of the socialist city's real estate. The hotel's large residential rooms, which had originally housed visiting British Empire types and American businessmen, politicians, and reporters, were now all broken up into single-sex dormitories. Each dreary-looking room held perhaps twenty iron-frame beds, but two-story banquet rooms glimpsed through locked hallway doors hinted at the hotel's long-gone sumptuousness.

My own room at the hotel quickly turned into a place of encounter. Among my roommates were Pakistani peddlers—intriguing but also a little unnerving—who claimed to have crossed the Hindu Kush on foot. Hitchhiking through Afghanistan and then China's Muslim northwest, they had supported themselves by selling their wares along the road before finally arriving overland in Shanghai (translated as "Above the Sea"). Here, these vagabonds were picking up new goods to finance their homeward journeys. Sharing the room with us were also many Europeans, Australians, and a few North Americans. Feeling very adventuresome, at least until we listened to the Pakistanis, most of us spent a few days here quietly in quest of our own "Old Shanghai." Afterwards, we all moved on to other less-storied destinations and accommodations.

At 250,000 souls in 1842, when the first groups of Westerners arrived, Shanghai was already one of the twenty most populous cities in the Qing Empire (itself physically and demographically larger than today's United States). To the foreign interlopers of those days, such as Great Britain, France, and the United States (whom the British later called "coat-tail imperialists" for their tendency to avoid military engagement while insisting on a share of any spoils), Shanghai offered ready access from and to the sea, shelter from typhoons, easy trading opportunities, and secure real estate. For these reasons and more, as the city was incorporated into Western-defined global trading networks, Shanghai's Huangpu River also became equated with the city.

From this river, our hostel acquired its name and, in the period from 1730 to 1865, Shanghai gained its identity as a crossroad of empires and an international emporium. Most of this period lies outside the era of Shanghai's direct involvement with Western trade, which was restricted by European knowledge and navigational mobility prior to 1760. In that year, the so-called Canton System limited Western trade to the southern city of Canton (from the Portuguese "Cantaõ;" today Guangzhou) in order to make it more manageable. The conclusion of the First Opium War (1839–1842) ended the Canton System. The Treaty of Nanjing, named after the Yangzi River city west of Shanghai, then opened four new ports to Western trade, including Shanghai, which made a total of five.

A modern industrial and trading colossus throughout the late nineteenth and twentieth centuries, metropolitan Shanghai was nonetheless quite tarnished and shabby in 1991. Marketed before 1937 to Westerners as the "Pearl of the Orient," Shanghai when I arrived combined elements of its Chinese-imperial and Western-colonial pasts with more recent changes initiated by the Communist Revolution of 1949 and by Beijing's post-1978 policy of "openness" and market-oriented reforms.

Across the street from the Astor/Huangpu Hotel was the old Soviet consulate, looking very austere and spooky. Built by the ill-fated Tsarist government in 1916, it harkened back to an era when the Bolshevik Revolution of 1917 had inspired acolytes worldwide. Like the hotel, the consulate still looked out onto Suzhou Creek, known historically as the Wusong River. If the Astor could be said to have gazed in a friendly way toward the former British consulate across the Wusong, one could well imagine that the Soviet one, topped after 1917 by its red hammer-and-sickle flag, must have seemed to glare at the walled British compound flying its Union Jack. Beyond, along the Anglo-American Bund (a Hindustani term for "embankment" picked up by British traders en route to China), stood colonial-capitalist citadels from the late nineteenth and early twentieth centuries. These included former shipping and insurance offices, banks, the customs house, and even an old English-language newspaper building.

The pre-1949 Bund ended at the Shanghai Club, where British *taipans* (trading company tycoons) once lounged against its legendary Long Bar, cooled by Indian-style punkahs (overhead fans) as they sipped their *stengahs* (whisky and soda water, derived from the Malay term for "half" possibly learned in Malacca) and gazed at the Huangpu River. On the far side of the Shanghai Club began the French Bund, which wrapped along the river's shoreline near the formerly walled confines of Chinese Shanghai. Most of these buildings are still there today but are dwarfed by skyscrapers built since 1991.

In 1991 the Wusong River was little more than a dingy, malodorous barge canal. Imagining the waterway once serving as a rippling superhighway linking Lake Tai, the Grand Canal, the ancient canal city of Suzhou (Marco Polo's "Venice of the East"), and the East China Sea took real effort, yet that is what the guidebooks insisted it had been. To today's visitors, as to the Western aggressors of the nineteenth century, the Huangpu River—half a mile across in the city and flowing north to join the Yangzi River twelve miles downstream—seemed a far more likely candidate for acclaim.

Yet history details the role of the Wusong and its watery web of tributaries, including the Huangpu, in fostering inland travel and trade. By the 1830s and 1840s, however, Shanghai was merging riverine and coastal trade in a way that suggested the city could also serve as a significant point of connection with global trade. The foreign hydraulic engineers who then dredged, widened, and mapped the Huangpu to the point where it seemed to be the main channel and the Wusong its tributary were merely building with modern technology and science upon a long history of reconfiguring the wet and dry parts of Shanghai's landscape.

SHANGHAI AND THE WORLD: Crafting a Global Treaty Port

A thousand years ago, much of the land around present-day Shanghai was still underwater. From the beginning of the Common Era, the Yangzi estuary, then situated much farther to the west than it is today, had been depositing its sediment and extending the deltaic network on which Shanghai sits at a rate of perhaps one mile every seventy years. Ever since that time, Shanghai has been defined by water, both fresh and salty. Changes in the man-made landscape in turn influenced innovations in the local economy.

Dikes were built in 713 CE and 1172 CE to create pockets of dry alluvial land that, after being enlarged, formed Shanghai's present land area. For a long time this reclaimed land remained too saline and sandy for much rice cultivation, but it did provide a footing for cotton cultivation and, in turn, textile manufacturing. Prior to cotton's arrival from India in about the tenth century, Chinese had clothed themselves in other fibers, such as silk, hemp, flax, and ramie. After the second dike was built, however, peasant farmers in southeastern Jiangsu Province began growing cotton on the newly reclaimed flat, lowlying acreage between the Wusong and Huangpu Rivers. Thanks to the invention of a cotton gin and other agricultural technologies in the early 1300s, cotton cultivation and basic processing became the centerpiece of the local economy.

In the more advanced southwestern parts of Jiangsu Province, a medieval industrial revolution soon germinated that featured larger, heavier looms and more specialized products. Suzhou, the axis of a watery latticework of canals centered on the Grand Canal, connected the former imperial capital Hangzhou in the south with Tianjin and Beijing in the north. Suzhou now became China's silk and cotton textile manufacturing center, making it, in effect, the southeastern terminus of the Silk Road (that is thought more conventionally to end at Xian).

From Hub Port to Treaty Port

Inevitably, water routes became vital arteries of communication in the Yangzi River delta (hereafter Jiangnan) region, creating the geographic, political, cultural, and economic landscape that Shanghai Chinese and nineteenth-century Western residents took for granted. What is now called the Huangpu River then rose near the border with Zhejiang Province and supplied a southerly eastbound channel connecting the western Grand

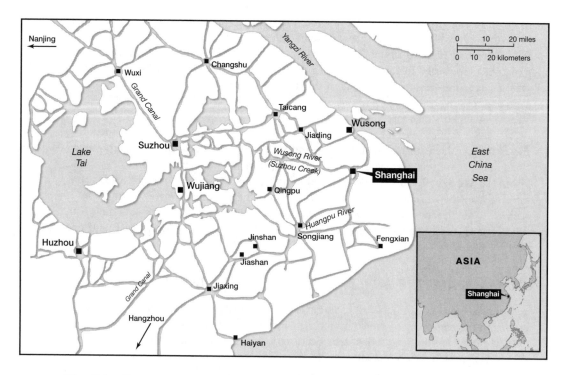

Map 8.1. Jiangnan with Waterways, ca. 1600

Shanghai, situated on reclaimed land, was located at the center of a domestic and international system of freshwater and saltwater shipping. Early waterways, both natural and man-made, linked Shanghai's cotton-growing districts to Jiangsu Province's manufacturing zones around Suzhou, situated on the north-south Grand Canal that led to Beijing. Long before oceangoing British opium merchants had even heard of Shanghai, inland waterways provided access to the domestic and international maritime trade of the China coast.

Canal regions with the delta ones near Shanghai. Draining the fens, marshes, and creeks of southern Jiangsu, the Huangpu grew into a substantial tributary of the far older Wusong River. The two flowed together in front of the latter-day Soviet and British consulates. (See Map 8.1.)

Shanghai in the Chinese Empire

In the period covered by this chapter—1730 to 1865—China was ruled by the ethnically Manchu Qing dynasty, which had been established in Beijing in 1644 after the collapse of the ethnically Han Ming one (1368–1644). Throughout much of this period, and certainly from 1760 to 1842, Qing Shanghai provided a place of encounter for Chinese and non-Western outsiders. This trade and exchange took place in a city that first gained administrative and economic shape in the imperial state in the late thirteenth century, when, under the newly founded Mongol Yuan dynasty (1279–1368), Shanghai County was created from older administrative units. Formerly merely a market center, Shanghai City now doubled as the county seat within Jiangsu Province. Both of these events, which gave Shanghai an official position in Chinese administration, helped the city flower under the Yuan, the Ming, and the Qing, although this ascendancy was by no means linear or direct.

Late Ming maps reveal a nearly circular wall built to protect the town from predators known as *wokou* (Japanese pirates). Anticipating the multinational European force of the nineteenth century, the sixteenth-century *wokou* actually included Japanese, Koreans, and even Chinese. All roamed the China coast from Shandong Province southward, robbing, burning, and kidnapping. Beginning in the 1550s, as part of a broader empire-wide wall-building trend, local Shanghai scholar-official elites led the townsmen in erecting the city's earth-and-masonry walls and digging a moat. The wall remained in place until the end of the Qing dynasty in 1911.

Although Westerners first arrived in southern China in the late 1500s, they came in small numbers and largely showed respect and/or awe for the vast and wealthy Ming Empire; this stance was maintained well into the eighteenth century. By the nineteenth century, however, many Westerners held a radically different view, one that led to small wars of choice against China in pursuit of trade and quick fortunes. These wars resulted in, among other phenomena, the creation of treaty ports. Treaty ports (or concessions) were self-contained, self-governing units of territory exempt from Chinese law and run by their non-Chinese occupants. These occupants were in turn protected by warships supplied by their home governments.

Shanghai's Evolving Urban Landscape

When "treaty-port Shanghai" began to appear in the mid-nineteenth century, the Chinese city's walls concretely outlined the administrative differences between the three evolving urban communities of the Chinese city; the French Concession northeast, due north, and west of it; and the merged Anglo-American International Concession beyond. In particular, the planned, "modern" city of the International Concession, with its broad, straight streets worked into a grid bordered by the Bund and the Wusong, allowed the British and Americans the conceit of calling their concession the "Model Settlement," in contrast to the labyrinth of narrow, brick-paved streets in the Chinese city.

However, unlike other British colonial towns, no real provision was made here for green spaces. The Bund's Public Gardens, as the strip of open land along a short stretch of the river would become known, really could not compare favorably with, for instance, the Chinese walled city's vast Suzhou-style garden called the Yuyuan (Leisured Garden). The initial inspiration for the Yuyuan's construction lay in China's Confucian culture (with filial piety at its core), which was dominant in government, administration, and personal relationships. Built by a filial son who bought land close to the City God Temple and employed a famous Suzhou garden designer of the day, the garden was completed in 1577 and dedicated to the memory of the son's father, who had directed the city wall construction. In 1760 the Sea Merchants Guild, one of the oldest and most respected guilds in the city, rescued the two-hundred-year-old Yuyuan. The guild bought it from the owners, descendants of the bureaucratic scholar-official elites who had built it, and donated it to the City God Temple for public use. The garden, surrounded by elaborately decorated walls of its own, now covered some eleven acres at the center of the five-hundred-acre walled city. Its purchase by wealthy shipping merchants signaled their growing importance in local affairs in eighteenth-century Shanghai.

Measuring a mile across the circular ramparts and three miles around them (about the same size as the walled City of London), the city of Shanghai was sparsely populated when the Yuyuan was first plotted. At least four sizable canals or streams irrigated the city from east to west and served as sources of transportation and drinking water and even as sewers. All were interwoven via north-south channels and finally spilled into the Huangpu. Streets and intersections were festooned with more than sixty tall *pailou* (commemorative arches) honoring persons such as chaste widows or sage officials.

The City's Religious Influences

Religion in early modern Shanghai included a vast array of public and private cults. Some were related to the universalistic religion of Buddhism, which first arrived in northern China via the Silk Road in the first century and then in central China by the third or fourth century. Conversely, Daoism, a native Chinese philosophy and religion, dated to the classical period. Others were related to universalistic philosophies such as Confucianism, which long before had spread eastward to Korea and Japan and southward to Vietnam. Still others were purely local, such as the city god and local ancestral cults. To the extent that Shanghai had a planned ritual center comparable to those in northern China (such as Xian) that served both official and popular functions, it was the City God Temple.

The city god—which was, like many local Chinese cults, inspired by an actual scholar who was then honored by the first Ming emperor—provided the county magistrate in his forbidding *yamen* (government compound) a spiritual partner with whom he could confer. (Like other Chinese urban centers, Shanghai then had no mayor per se). Perhaps in a symbolic effort to undermine the cult at the center of the urban community, the *wokou* burned the City God Temple, but it was rebuilt at the same time as the walls and moat, over which the city god was believed to reign. Nearby was the Temple of Confucius, which was affiliated with the county-run Confucian academy. The former was destroyed in the mid-1850s by Chinese insurgents but rebuilt. Like the City God Temple, it survives today.

Complementing the City God Temple and Confucian Temple but located outside the city walls was the elegantly adorned mariners' temple dedicated to Tianhou (Empress of Heaven); the original eleventh-century Buddhist complex at Longhua, rebuilt in the late 1500s, which still flourishes today; over a hundred smaller Buddhist centers; several Daoist shrines; and ubiquitous private ancestral altars. In the late Ming period, Paul Xu Guangqi, a high Beijing official and Catholic convert who worked with famous missionary Matteo Ricci, built a Catholic church outside the city's north gate. Although it was torn down in the late 1600s, memory of it nonetheless formed the basis for France's nineteenth-century claim, as "Protector of the Faith," for the compensation that led to what became known after 1842 as the French Concession. Involvement with Buddhism and Christianity prior to the Treaty of Nanjing had already tied Shanghai to world religious habits, however.

Shanghai's Resurgent Economy and Treaty Port

Although the Manchu conquest of 1643 and 1644 was devastating to some nearby centers, Shanghai, surrounded as it was by water, survived those years without profound dislocations. More importantly, its economy recovered quickly, due to policy decisions made by the new Manchu overlords in Beijing. In 1684 the Qing emperor lifted the old prohibition on maritime commerce imposed by the Ming in an effort to close the coast to the *wokou*. Soon after, dynastic administrators opened southern coastal customs stations: Canton in Guangdong Province, Quanzhou in Fujian, and Ningbo in Zhejiang. In Jiangsu, Songjiang crowned a network of some twenty provincial stations that included

Shanghai. The customs offices were probably intended to capitalize on the expansion of trade and the growth of a merchant class in the overwhelmingly agrarian Qing Empire.

Unlike the three customs offices on the southeast coast, known merely as *haiguan* (maritime customs stations), those in Jiangsu were identified as *jianghaiguan* (river and maritime customs stations). Reflecting the complex interplay of the river and ocean waters and high levels of trade throughout Shanghai's home province, these Jiangsu stations, alone among the four provinces, collected both river and maritime (including coastal and international) customs, indicative of the area's important position in both. In 1730 the main *jianghaiguan* office moved to Shanghai, which already possessed sole responsibility for coastal customs collection. Two years later, when the new *daotai* (prefect) arrived to take up residence, Shanghai was well on its way back to the economic prominence it had held before the fifteenth-century relocation of the Ming capital from nearly Nanjing to distant Beijing. A port town in an empire that had turned its back on the sea, Shanghai had then found itself marginalized.

The new *daotai's* office, with its red customs house located on the Huangpu bank, now assumed formal responsibility for collecting duties on international commodities such as bird's nests (for soup) from Java (in modern-day Indonesia) and knives, paper, and even tobacco from Japan, which had acquired seeds from the New World via the Philippines. It also collected tariffs on domestic trade. The *daotai* was joined by two administrators subordinate to him—the subprefect for coastal defense and, below the subprefect, the county magistrate—but still not by a city mayor due to the Qing interest in thwarting the emergence of an independent corporate urban mentality that might undermine central rule from Beijing.

Not surprisingly, the Confucian academy carried on as before the Manchu ascendancy, and so did the Confucian Temple. However, reflecting new merchant wealth, the county academy was now joined by three private ones, two of them founded during the Qing period (the last in 1865, when it grafted Western-style mathematics and natural science onto the conventional Confucian curriculum). Eleven philanthropic institutions also depended on the private largesse of the recently invigorated merchant community and that of older local landowning imperial degree-holders. Two new religious cults flourished, one of them that of Guandi, to whom a new temple was consecrated in 1730.

As Shanghai historian Linda Cooke Johnson explains, Guandi was technically the god of war, but he now also came to be venerated by traveling merchants as the patron of trustworthiness and loyalty. Both virtues were important to men who disliked turning to the *yamen* courts for contract or other adjudications. Johnson also observes that the establishment of the Guandi cult at Shanghai clearly reflected the growing influence of southern, especially Fujianese and Cantonese, temporary residents in Shanghai in the Qing period. Like the older Tianhou cult of mariners, which also began in south China, the cult of Guandi was officially sanctioned and regulated by the Manchus. Learning from earlier dynasties, they recognized both cults as useful in governing coastal areas.

Between 1730 and 1839, during the long Manchu peace that was aborted by the First Opium War, Shanghai's commercial middlemen and brokers, with only a weak political administration to restrain them, flourished as never before. Apart from the official Confucian administration, which imposed a largely theoretical ideological unity on the vast Qing Empire, the Manchu court adopted what Adam Smith later called a laissez-faire philosophy when it came to the economy. In the eighteenth century, China's population also doubled from 150 million to some 300 million, inflating consumer demand. Thus, in eastern Jiangsu, "King Cotton" quickly revived in response to market growth. Along with the world's largest population, Qing China now also boasted the world's wealthiest pre-industrial national economy. No longer marginalized as it had been in the late Ming period, Shanghai was now in the thick of it.

Shanghai began to move out of the freshwater network of the Grand Canal and take greater advantage of its coastal access to both north and south China via the steadily dredged middle and lower Huangpu River. Southern Chinese religious cults in Shanghai notwithstanding, three-fourths of Qing Shanghai's trade—Jiangsu yarn, thread, and textiles; Anhui paper, ink, and Qimen tea; Zhejiang hams and green Longjing tea; and fine Yixing teapots and Jingdezhen porcelain—went north. In return, Shanghai gained the northern agricultural products needed to feed its people and the high-grade soy-cake fertilizer demanded by local cotton growers. This north-south trade turned on highly specialized exchanges previously absent from the city's history.

The Rise of Merchant Guilds

Even before the Qing lifted prohibitions on coastal trade in 1684, Shanghai had drawn maritime shippers from Shandong Province and southern Manchuria (Guandong). The northerners, perhaps intimidated by the local Wu language, which was unrelated to their own northern ones, and by sharp local business practices, created a protective trade association (*gongsuo*) early in the new dynastic era. In 1685 Shanghai's local merchant shippers responded by forming the Sea Merchants Guild (*huiguan*), presumably to protect their own trade in cotton and fertilizer.

Like Britain's late-nineteenth-century Shanghai Club, the Sea Merchants Guild provided accommodations for members in its premises along the Huangpu. Unlike the Shanghai Club, however, the guild's operations were not confined to provisioning. Its wealthy members built their own Tianhou temple, guildhall (containing a grand courtyard stage), wharves, shipbuilding yards, and dry docks. By managing its corporate resources wisely, the guild retained its influential position in Shanghai for over two hundred years.

It was, after all, the wealthy Sea Merchants Guild that in the 1760s purchased the eleven-acre Yuyuan garden and donated it to the City God Temple. By then, the temple had been rebuilt several times, ever more elaborately in the elegant carved dark-wood and white-stucco Jiangnan style. In the absence of a European-style *bourse* (exchange) sanctified by the (nonexistent) municipal government, the Yuyuan's pavilions and halls were quickly populated by a fraternity of associations such as the Finance Guild, which in the 1800s came to represent more than one hundred Chinese-style banks, and Shanghai's other trade associations. Other parts of the garden opened to the public as teahouses and social centers. One of them, the five-sided Wuxing Teahouse, accessed in the middle of a pond via a zigzag bridge, eventually became associated with an English design motif—Willow pattern—that extended Europe's eighteenth-century *chinoiserie* craze well into the twentieth century. As with the earlier aristocratic fashion, this industrial-age bourgeois *chinoiserie* promoted a Western fantasy of China's culture. Somewhat out of step with reality, it nonetheless helped to establish Shanghai's centrality in the Western image of China.

Inside the walled Qing city, "shophouses" (with retail operations on the first floor and housing on the second) now lined the narrow streets. Both local residents and outsiders bustled about, necessitating new residences, workshops, and retail establishments. Specialty-trade lanes and districts of the sort found in contemporary European centers were common. Between 1760 and 1842—the era of the Canton System—when Western machine-made goods could enter China only through the southern city and had to travel the hundreds of miles to Shanghai overland, such commodities were still plentiful enough to support specialized retailers in the city. Although there is no detailed information, as is typical with imported goods anywhere, these goods probably appealed in their novelty to a small but well-off class of consumers comprised, perhaps, of wealthy merchants similar to the kind of Shanghainese who later embraced all sorts of post-1842 trade with the West and produced the treaty port's distinctive hybridized urban consumer culture. Across town, local weavers and cotton dealers found their spaces. Printers and bookstores wisely assembled around the county school. Curio and gift shops occupied the city's northern district, and pawnshops were scattered throughout Shanghai. Private silk and tea merchants predictably opened their storefronts near their representative trade association.

During the eighteenth and early nineteenth centuries, trade associations and guilds came to define Shanghai much more than did religion or government. Significantly, during this period Shanghai outgrew its walls and experienced a form of early modern "suburbanization." Locals usually claimed sites within the city walls, and outsiders, flocking to Shanghai to cash in on its expanding urban economy, were relegated to or chose locations between the moat and the Huangpu River.

Unlike the guilds, which built grand compounds on surplus land outside the city walls and supplied a full range of social services to their members, the trade associations typically occupied more modest inner-city quarters. Linda Cooke Johnson has determined that, between 1796 and 1821, Shanghai merchants founded at least eleven trade associations, with the majority situated in or near the Yuyuan garden. Shanghai's economy flourished even as the Canton System banned Western traders from coming to the city.

Apart from the Guandong-Shandong Trade Association and the Sea Merchants Guild, which both dated informally from the 1600s, other guild-like organizations began to increase in the 1730s, perhaps as a response to the new *daotai* and other government offices. The Zhejiang and Shaoxing City Trade Association, whose members engaged in a broad spectrum of activities from finance to charcoal production to butchering, built its headquarters within the walls in 1736. The Anhui tea merchants' guild shipped tea north to Tianjin and Beijing via both the canal and open-sea routes. Although long active in the city, they did not establish a headquarters until 1755. A little later, Fujianese merchants and shippers built their guildhall. Clearly, Qing Shanghai provided a place of encounter for outsiders from all over Asia and China (if not yet from the West).

Johnson has also found that, by 1821, there were a dozen guilds (as opposed to trade associations) in Shanghai. Only one, however, was located physically inside the city. Much like the future French and Anglo-American citadels would, the rest looked out on the Huangpu, the source of prosperity for all. Clearly, Shanghai would be a far larger and richer city when threatened by nineteenth-century Western warships than it was when plundered by sixteenth-century *wokou*.

Shanghai's Economic Prosperity Turns to Depression

Despite the fact that no Westerner visited Shanghai until 1832, already in the 1780s Shanghai's banking accounts were tallied in Mexican silver dollars, a reflection of the port's incorporation into the broad international currents of East Asian and even transpacific trade. By 1834, despite exclusion since 1760 from Canton's trade with British and other Western merchants, Shanghai's total trade volume is estimated to have doubled that of Canton; it may even have equaled that of London, then the center of the West's international trade networks.

Shanghai certainly benefited from the so-called Daoguang Prosperity, named after the new Qing emperor, which lasted from 1821 to 1835. This phase coincided with the silting of the Grand Canal, by means of which the river fleet had been transporting tribute (or tax) rice to Beijing. With the inland route impassable, tribute rice now followed the northern coastal route, which was already familiar to Shanghai's shipping firms. In addition, tribute rice shipping brought a new form of business—and perhaps thirteen hundred more vessels per year—to Shanghai and the coast.

However, in 1830 an empire-wide silver shortage caused by an imbalance in foreign trade in Canton led Jiangnan-area bankers to adopt the so-called Suzhou System, which pegged China's paper currency to opium prices. This silver shortage and the response to it indicates that the illegal British-owned narcotic refined from Indian poppies was shifting the balance of trade in Britain's favor and was already a significant part of the Shanghai area's economy despite Shanghai's distance from Canton. Then, effective 1834, Britain ended its East India Company's monopoly on trade with China. Because foreign traders temporarily stopped visiting Canton, the southern city drastically reduced purchases of the Shanghai area's cotton textiles (including the early modern world's equivalent of dungaree, the khaki-colored "nankeen" that was named after the city of Nanking). Shanghai's Daoguang Prosperity quickly plunged into the Daoguang Depression.

In the 1830s, with its quarter of a million inhabitants—a third of them temporary residents from elsewhere—Shanghai was far smaller than London, England (1.7 million people); Beijing, China (at least one million); and Tokyo, Japan (one million). It was about half the size of Canton (513,000), but it was larger than Mumbai, India (around 235,000), and New York City (202,500). Still a major manufacturing and processing center, Shanghai also proffered river and canal access to inland towns and large cities, as well as a safe haven for coastal and international trade. These considerations strongly influenced the British decision to include Shanghai among the five ports stipulated in the Treaty of Nanjing when it ended the First Opium War and the Canton System of trade. Direct trade with Westerners now brought new forms of economic and demographic growth, augmenting preexisting trade with East and Southeast Asians and coastal Chinese. After 1842, however, Shanghai's identity changed radically as a divided and tripartite—Chinese, Anglo-American, and French—administrative matrix was placed over the formerly Chinese-only administration.

GLOBAL ENCOUNTERS AND CONNECTIONS:
Treaty-Port Encounters at Shanghai

Clearly, amphibious Shanghai, with its agricultural hinterland and its circular-walled and canal-crossed city, had a complex history prior to the Westerners' appearance in the 1840s. Shanghai had long been a domestic and international trading center. In the late eighteenth and early nineteenth centuries, when Western trade was confined by Manchu *diktat* to the southern city of Canton, the Huangpu River continued to provide berths to coastal ships from northern and southern China, Japan, Liuqiu (also known as the Ryukyu Kingdom, a Chinese dependency until 1879 when it was forcibly annexed by Japan), and Korea. Almost everyone except Westerners traded in Shanghai, the hub port and central customs city for the teeming Jiangnan hinterland—an area that included the richest and most productive districts in the world's wealthiest empire.

However, in 1765, in the same decade in which Shanghai's Sea Merchants Guild donated the Yuyuan garden to the City God Temple, Scotsman James Watt sparked the Industrial Revolution while strolling on Glasgow Green. His invention of the steam engine's separate condenser eventually made feasible Glasgow's and Manchester, England's industrialized textile mills, as well as Britain's steam navy and its worldwide gunboat diplomacy. Britain was now able to dispatch its modern, industrialized armed forces around the world and, within a few decades, to control a quarter of the globe outright. With the help of its merchant adventurers, the Royal Navy, and a responsive Parliament, Britain (and other trading nations who imitated its industrial advances) soon reversed its unfavorable balance of trade with China and brought the mighty Qing Empire to its knees through force of arms, trade, and Christianity. Meanwhile, with Western merchants flocking to Shanghai, the city and its port benefited from China's steady reversals, a fact that later condemned the city in the eyes of nationalistic twentieth-century reformers and revolutionaries.

Chartered by the English queen Elizabeth I in 1600, the British East India Company (EIC) first arrived in China in 1689 and held the British monopoly on the China trade—chiefly silk and cotton textiles, tea, and porcelain—until 1834. For much of that time, Manchu China conducted its own maritime trade via a lightly regulated multiple-port system that reversed late Ming policies and allowed traders to put in at coastal ports largely of their own choosing. In 1760, exasperated by problems caused by unruly Western traders, the Qianlong emperor confined them all to a seasonal trade in Canton. Withdrawing from the riskier modes of the China trade, the EIC then subcontracted so-called country traders such as Scotsman William "Iron-Headed Old Rat" Jardine to transport commodities on the routes between its possessions in Bengal, India, and Canton. Both the EIC and the multinational country traders now became complicit in selling the illegal (by Chinese law) narcotic—Bengal opium—that reversed Britain's China trade imbalances. "Recreational" narcotics such as opium created their own customer base that was willing to pay ever-higher prices, and, as a result, Britain's and other Western traders' balance sheets with the Chinese Empire appeared to improve.

Bridling at the Qing emperor's restriction of Western trade to Canton, Western free-booters like "Old Rat" Jardine, now a member of Parliament, called for war, if necessary. Their objective was to force "free trade" onto China and, by abolishing the Canton System, to lead a return to the pre-1760 multiple-port trading system. The country traders got their wish in 1839, when hostilities erupted along China's southern coast, sparked by a Qing "drug tsar" who destroyed British opium stores on the bank of the Pearl River opposite Canton. That conflict spread to Shanghai, which was identified by "Old Rat" Jardine as an essential prize, in June 1842. British warships en route to Nanjing invaded the Huangpu, possibly in search of a backdoor route via the Wusong River to the empire's former capital.

When the British ships arrived at the mouth of the Huangpu, the river was stoutly defended by the Wusong batteries. However, the British guns quickly silenced them. The British commander then divided his forces: marines marched overland and the fleet ascended the Huangpu. Each group set its sights on walled Shanghai twelve miles upstream. When they reached the Wusong River, perhaps half a mile north of the city, Qing defenders again fought back, and, for the second time, the British responded with superior force. Shanghai, defenseless and threatened from both the river and the land, capitulated without additional shots being fired. Many of its residents fled; four thousand British and Sepoy (Indian troops under British officers) soldiers quickly replaced them and erected tents in the Yuyuan garden. They looted Shanghai and molested its remaining inhabitants for four days before sailing for Nanjing.

Later that summer, the First Opium War ended when Britain threatened to bombard Nanjing and the Qing court capitulated. Britain and China then signed the Treaty of

Nanjing, the first of numerous nineteenth-century "unequal treaties," so termed because all the benefits went to the Western aggressors. Very soon after the conclusion of hostilities with Britain, American and French shippers, both of which had also long been active in the Canton and opium trades, clamored for treaties similar to Britain's. They got them in 1844, along with the added American stipulation of extraterritoriality, which rendered all Americans exempt from Chinese law. The "treaty system" initially opened five (and eventually nearly one hundred) ports, including Shanghai, to the West. In addition to the treaty ports, it also established extraterritoriality for all Westerners and the nineteenth century's version of "most favored nation" status, which extended benefits won by a single Western power to all. China found itself facing what is known in European diplomatic history as "the nightmare of coalitions" (*la cauchemar de coalitions*) and lost its ability to play one aggressor off against another.

Until British warships penetrated the Huangpu defenses at Wusong, Shanghai had not experienced war, terror, or plunder since the last of the sixteenth-century *wokou* had departed. Chinese reactions to this first unequal treaty simmered for a long time before boiling over. When they did, the outcomes were related to the population's discovery, as a byproduct of the Western invasion, that the Manchu order was vulnerable. The Small Swords, for example, who would occupy Shanghai in 1853, were made up of southern (particularly Cantonese) militants apparently acting in sympathy with another, far larger anti-Qing uprising known as the Taiping Heavenly Kingdom (1851–1864), which took thirty million lives. The Taipings, whose insurgency began in southern China and eventually touched nearly all eighteen Qing provinces, came into existence as a result of the Treaty of Nanjing. (Coincidentally, the Taipings established their capital at Nanjing, initially hoping for support from the Westerners downriver in Shanghai.) The treaty gave Christian missionaries free access to the five ports, and it was in Canton that the leader of the Taipings first learned of Christianity from a fiery Tennessee Baptist lay preacher. Taiping followers included many who had lost work when Canton was abandoned by Western traders for the other four treaty ports, including Shanghai.

"Opening" Shanghai to Western Trade While Creating a Tripartite Treaty Port

In the immediate wake of the Treaty of Nanjing, in early November 1843, Britain's new consul, Indian Army captain George Balfour, arrived via steamship to "open" Shanghai to Western trade. Transported from the Huangpu into the city by sedan chair, he was officially received by *Daotai* Gong Mujiu. Later, a visiting Cantonese merchant approached Balfour and offered for rent a fifty-two-room mansion that could do double duty as consulate and residence. Although Balfour accepted the offer, the British merchants accompanying him opted to live outside the crowded Chinese city. Unfamiliar with the Western concept of a consulate, *Daotai* Gong treated it like a guild, holding the consul himself responsible for Western customs receipts.

Three years later, in 1846, Balfour was replaced by Rutherford Alcock. Abandoning the inner-city "guild," Alcock claimed the trapezoidal site that became the new British consular compound in 1852; extensive dredging and sandbagging were needed to prevent the Wusong and Huangpu Rivers from eroding it. Although the Americans tried to create a separate concession on the north bank of the Wusong, where the Astor Hotel and Soviet consulate later rose, their small numbers rendered these efforts futile. Therefore, they blended into the emerging British "model settlement" and even began to ape the British colonial mindset, eventually producing the hybrid Anglo-American "Shanghailander." These Anglo-American Westerners acquired a bellicose mentality of entitlement that remained in place until 1949 and the city's liberation by the Communists' peasant army.

French consul Charles de Montigny arrived exactly four years to the month after Balfour. By then, the British settlement was prospering, albeit slowly. Montigny had been preceded by Catholic missionaries, who had built the baroque Cathedral Church of Saint Francis Xavier in the *huiguan* district between the city walls and the Huangpu. Montigny started by living in a house rented from Catholic missionaries who had already settled around the tomb of the late Ming Catholic convert Paul Xu Guangqi. In these ways, the various Westerners laid the foundations for the tripartite treaty port of the future.

Into the late 1840s, Shanghai continued to experience the downward economic spiral that had begun with the Daoguang Depression. Initially, Britain's textiles and other imports did not sell as well as the merchants had earlier insisted they would. Nonetheless, the British merchants concluded that the First Opium War and the inconveniences of their life in Shanghai had all been worth it when they found they could buy the same export silks in Shanghai for 35 percent of the price they had been charged in Canton. Exports of tea and silk increased in the early 1850s, however, and the British paid for them with illegally imported (and, therefore, duty-free) opium, with its industrial extracts morphine and heroin on the horizon. Opium hulks (ships used as warehouses) soon anchored in the Huangpu, setting Shanghai on its way to becoming the central narcotics entrepôt of East Asia, much as Singapore, Batavia (Jakarta), Manila, and Saigon were (or soon would be) in colonial Southeast Asia. As it amounted to three-quarters of the value of all foreign imports, opium's profitability suggested the need to legalize it sooner rather than later, which provided a motive for the Second Opium War (1856–1860).

As the Shanghai-area economy gradually recovered, the Chinese-, English-, and French-speaking communities began to withdraw from each other, prompted first by early uses of gunboat diplomacy and then by Anglo-French distrust of each other. In 1844, to enforce a diplomatic point but thereby setting an unfortunate precedent, Consul Balfour threatened the *daotai* with gunboats. By the time Alcock arrived, "gunboat diplomacy" was part of the new jargon being created in Shanghai, along with pidgin ("business") English. In the same year, the *daotai*'s office opened a separate "Western trade only" customs house, like the Chinese one also painted red but located north of the eight-to-ten-foot-wide Yangjing Creek that effectively separated the French Bund from the British one. Within two years, according to Linda Cooke Johnson, Western traders no longer had any reason to enter the Chinese city. They relied instead on their new and separate customs house.

In 1853, when the Small Swords entered and occupied the Chinese city, British, American, and French soldiers carefully preserved their neutrality. At the same time, the British took responsibility for collecting the Western customs tariffs on behalf of the *daotai*. After suppression of the Small Swords by Qing troops in 1855, the Manchu court permanently entrusted the collection of foreign customs to a new, British-run *"daotai"* (in Chinese eyes), eventually known to Westerners as the inspector-general (I.G.) of the Imperial Maritime Customs. This system of taxation with its two sets of authorities, built on the system Balfour had adopted and similar to the tax "farming" (delegating) long followed by Chinese guilds, was extended to other treaty ports in 1858. The I.G. had the long-term effect of making successive Chinese governments financially dependent on the British payments of customs duties. Understandably, the Chinese Communists abolished the system in 1950.

In 1854, reflecting the growing reality of Shanghai as a partitioned city of "native" and "European" zones (see Map 8.2), the British formed a municipal council for their now-expanded concession (at 470 acres, it was slightly smaller than the historic Chinese city but continued growing until it was far larger). The Treaty of Tianjin, signed in 1858 to end the first phase of the Second Opium War, enhanced Western privilege and reinforced the sense of duality. The 1860 Convention of Beijing, which ended the Second Opium War, legalized opium imports, thereby establishing the basis for many Shanghailander fortunes. Four years later, the French, finding administrative cooperation with the British (and Americans, who had merged their concession into Britain's a year earlier) awkward, established their own separate council. The following year, in 1865, taking advantage of the new legal environment in the Anglo-American International Concession, the Hong Kong and Shanghai Banking Corporation (today's HSBC Bank) began operation. Soon its Scottish managers, the Keswick family (descended from "Old Rat" Jardine), began to profit from the Qing dynasty's ever-increasing war indemnities and foreign loans.

After losing two wars in twenty years to the British, French, and Americans (who did in fact aid the British in the Second Opium War), the Qing now tried to modernize, with Shanghai at the center of the effort. For example, as part of its first official attempt to industrialize and thereby fulfill its fundamental obligation of better protecting China, the Qing court initiated the costly Self-Strengthening Movement (SSM; 1861–1895). In 1865 the SSM brought the Jiangnan Arsenal (the world's largest such establishment after its construction by British and American military engineers) to the banks of the Huangpu just south of the walled city. At the same time, it necessitated further foreign debts to the Qing dynasty and service fees to the British bankers.

The Tripartite System Marks a New Phase in Sino-Western Relations

Against the geographical, political, cultural, and economic background underlying the Qing emperor's decree of 1730 that made Shanghai the eastern coast's *jianghaiguan* (river and maritime customs station), by 1865 Shanghai was well on its way to becoming a global treaty port. In the period covered by this chapter, as evidenced by the eighteenth-century proliferation of trade associations and guilds, Chinese merchants increased substantially in number and wealth; their purchase of the Yuyuan and the decision to hand it over to the City God Temple is indicative of their growing influence vis-à-vis the old scholar-official elite and local government. However, the commercial and manufacturing economy of which they were masters also made the customs port an attractive prize to Western "free traders" such as "Old Rat" Jardine. Jardine and others like him leveraged the First Opium War to pursue an end to the Canton System restrictions, as well as additional special ports for Western traders. In the case of Shanghai, the protected harbor also proffered riverine access to the most productive districts in the world's largest pre-industrial economy.

It took the Second Opium War, fought after Jardine's death, before Shanghai became the El Dorado sought by the British and other Western traders. Once the Taipings were suppressed in 1864, however, Western imperialists felt even more strongly than they had in 1843 that the difficulties they had faced had been worth it. In that same year, the tripartite administrative system of the treaty port was established and remained in place until the 1940s; Jardine's descendants would long profit from the treaty-port arrangement via HSBC. A new phase in Shanghai's (and China's) history was now to begin, one founded on Sino-Western banking, commerce, real estate, modern industry, Christianity, and military force, as well as on segregated racial, ethnic, religious, and linguistic administrations.

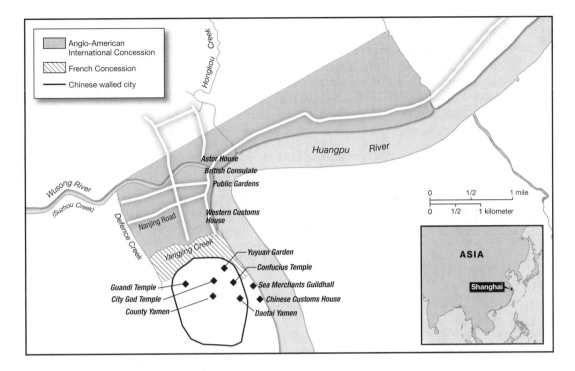

Map 8.2. Tripartite Shanghai, ca. 1880

In the wake of the Treaty of Nanjing (1842), the port of Shanghai combined territories claimed by France and jointly by Great Britain and the United States. Together with the old Chinese city, they made up the three administrative zones of the city. All were situated on the western bank of the Huangpu River, which provided access to the Yangzi River estuary twelve miles to the north and, beyond it, to the East China Sea. The treaty-port system of which Shanghai was the crown jewel lasted until the 1940s and was enforced with military power arrayed in ships berthed along the Huangpu, each flying the flag of its home country.

ENCOUNTERS AS TOLD: PRIMARY SOURCES

The following primary sources cover the years from 1842 to 1854. This "period of adjustment" began with a war of choice prosecuted by Great Britain against Qing China. It was marred by the British plundering of walled Shanghai and the Yuyuan and later by gunboat diplomacy. It ended with the unilateral British decision to create an administrative unit separate from the Chinese one. The Treaty of Nanjing, the first of multiple "unequal treaties" forced on China by Western powers, did not provide for such arrangements, but Britain's decision did create the foundation for the merged Anglo-American Concession, the French Concession, and the Shanghailander mentality discussed earlier.

The Treaty of Nanjing

The Treaty of Nanjing ended the First Opium War (1839–1842). In the view of the British, it was signed aboard the HMS *Cornwallis*, moored in the Yangzi River near Nanjing. In the Chinese understanding, however, the treaty was signed in a small temple just outside the northwest gate of walled Nanjing—the same temple from which legendary eunuch and Muslim admiral Zheng He had departed for the Indian Ocean in the early fifteenth century. Among other provisions, Qing China agreed to indemnify Britain between four and five million pounds sterling for destroyed opium stores and to open to trade the five ports of British choosing mentioned in the document. The following excerpt comes from the British version of the treaty. In 1844 the Americans and the French leveraged similar treaties named after Wangxia, near Macao in southern China west of Hong Kong.

- What did the British gain from taking over the responsibilities detailed in the treaty?

- In light of the long history of administrative experience in China generally, and in Shanghai in particular, and based on this document, why might the Shanghai *daotai* (prefect) of 1843 have been justified in regarding the British consulate as a *huiguan* (guild) much like any other in Shanghai?

- Based on what you've read in the chapter, why might the British have been reluctant to fill that role?

ARTICLE II

His Majesty the Emperor of China agrees that British subjects, with their families and establishments, shall be allowed to reside, for the purpose of carrying on their mercantile pursuits, without molestation or restraint at the cities and towns of Canton, Amoy [Xiamen], Fuzhou, Ningbo, and Shanghai, and Her Majesty the Queen of Great Britain, etc., will appoint superintendents or consular officers, to reside at each of the above-named cities or towns, to be the medium of communication between the Chinese authorities and the said merchants, and to see that the just duties and other dues of the Chinese Government as hereafter provided for, are duly discharged by Her Britannic Majesty's subjects.

Source: Harley Farnsworth MacNair, *Modern Chinese History: Selected Readings* (Shanghai: The Commercial Press, Ltd., 1927), 175–176.

Memorial: The Acting (Military) Viceroy of Jiangsu and Jiangxi Provinces and the (Civil) Governor of Jiangsu Sun Shanbao Reports that American Ships Have Been Refused Permission at Shanghai

In the nineteenth century, the British often called the Americans "coat-tail imperialists" because they refused to join the fighting against the Chinese Empire yet claimed the same benefits that the British had wrung from the Chinese. In fact, the legal ground for these benefits was the Most Favored Nation Clause introduced into a revised British treaty. In the following memorial (a formal style of written communication between administrators and the Qing court), Viceroy and Governor Sun Shanbao sheds some light on this phenomenon, on the Chinese perception of the Americans, and on his view of problems that would likely arise if the tariff regulations for trade at the four ports outside of Canton (including Shanghai) were not sorted out quickly. Remember that, although signed in August 1842, the Treaty of Nanjing was not ratified until early summer 1843, and British consul Balfour did not arrive in Shanghai until November 1843. The ships mentioned were possibly clippers, sleek and fast, that were designed to move low-volume, high-value commodities such as tea and opium.

- What does this document suggest about the maritime reach of the American merchant marine in the early decades of the nineteenth century?

- Based on the events described in this document, what were the goals and motives of the Americans in spring 1843? Do you think the Americans behaved appropriately?

- Which Chinese officials confronted the American ships and do you think they felt the Americans behaved in a reasonable fashion?

- Knowing what you now do about the First Opium War, does this document suggest that the Americans merchants were, in fact, "coat-tail imperialists?" If so, why did they end up in this role?

- Based on this document, how must the attitudes of the Shanghai-area authorities have changed in the space of a year or two? What might have caused the change? Further, what precedents were being set with respect to the future of Shanghai's treaty-port relations with the Americans and, by implication (because of the Most Favored Nation Clause), with all Western traders?

- Although by this time use of the term "barbarian" to refer to foreigners was purely *pro forma* in official communications, if the Americans had seen this document, how might they have reacted to this terminology? Why?

It is humbly observed that on March 3 of the present year [1843], outside Wusong harbor, there arrived three barbarian ships intending to go to Shanghai to trade. It seems that they were American ships. The military and civil district (officials) notified them that, as the tariff was not yet fixed nor wharves built, it was not convenient to proceed to trade. The said barbarians . . . anchored outside the harbor. . . . Later, on the 15th, another barbarian ship came. It . . . was also an American ship. . . . On April 11 again a barbarian ship, taking advantage of the wind and a favorable tide, sailed from Wusong to the outskirts of the city wall of Shanghai. The . . . local officials went on board and found on inquiry that it was a "Flowery Flag," that is, American ship, laden with goods and coming here from the Philippines to trade. The said officials explained that they still had no notice regarding the customs agreement. The said barbarians agreed to return to [Canton] and wait for word. On the 15th, they sailed away.

Source: Earl Swisher, *China's Management of the American Barbarians: A Study of Sino-American Relations, 1841–1861, with Documents* (New Haven: Yale University for the Far Eastern Association and Far Eastern Publications, 1953), 116–117.

Memorial: Xu Naizhao, Governor of Jiangsu, Reports on British, Americans, and Frenchmen at Shanghai during the Small Swords Uprising

Historians regard the Small Swords as local allies of the Christian-inspired, millenarian Taiping insurgency, whose rebellion against the Manchus and their Han Chinese supporters originated in southwestern Guangxi Province in 1851. By 1853 the Taipings reached the Yangzi River and installed their government at Nanjing, where it remained until the movement was destroyed by Qing troops in 1864. The Small Swords seized control of the walled city of Shanghai in 1853 and were suppressed by imperial troops in 1855. The memorial makes clear that the Qing officials' duties were complicated by the Western presence and voice via the printed word at a time of internal disorder. In the document, "English" means "British."

- Western historians typically state that the Westerners at Shanghai remained neutral with regard to the Small Swords. Does this document suggest otherwise and is this claim of the Western historians significant?

- How might the presence of the Westerners have destabilized Shanghai and made the *daotai*'s job more difficult?

- Why is the *daotai* concerned about the opinions being set forth in the Hong Kong Chinese-language and Shanghai English-language newspapers?

- Why might the *daotai* have concluded that the "English barbarians" were the most "difficult to manage?" In this conclusion, might his knowledge of history (including the *wokou* of the late Ming period and the 1842 attacks by the British on Wusong and Shanghai) have influenced his understanding of contemporary events?

The English barbarians are arrogant and intractable and have long been so. Since the opening of the Five Ports to trade, they have increasingly vaunted themselves. The honest people of Canton became steadily [and] increasingly resentful. . . . [A]t Shanghai, the popular temper has been mild, and the people have not been antagonistic. The said barbarians are greatly pleased at this situation, vastly different from Canton, and have constantly courted popular favor. Their purpose is particularly questionable. [Shanghai *daotai*] Wu Jianzhang is thoroughly conversant with barbarian psychology. . . . The American and French barbarian chiefs have also repeatedly spoken of this [English arrogance]. Wu Jianzhang has therefore secretly allied with the American and French barbarian chiefs in order to isolate the strength of the English barbarians. . . . [From September 3 to October 3, 1853] the rebels began to attack [Chinese] officials. . . . The rebels regarded the barbarians as close allies; the barbarians regarded the rebels as profitable customers. The feeling of all English barbarians was merely fear that Shanghai hostilities would stop.

Furthermore, [Westerners] who read Chinese . . . published a journal [in Hong Kong] called . . . *News from Far and Near*. Regarding the motives and actions of the [Taiping leader] . . . the said journal regarded them as rather well ordered. It was most mischievous. [What's more], there is a [British] newspaper printed [at Shanghai]. [The weekly *North China Herald*] makes the extreme statement that "Chinese are hard to reason with and it is only by threatening them with force that we can gain our ends." As it is circulated among the various countries, the barbarian chiefs get ideas therefrom. . . . Its harm had been most extreme.

It is noted that [Western] trade at Shanghai began with the English barbarians. In this trade, the English barbarians are the greatest and the American barbarians are second to them. The French barbarians regard religion as the most important and their interest is not in gain. The lesser countries, adhering to England, the United States, and France, are about five or six. They are not uniformly good or bad, but the English barbarians are the most inscrutable and most difficult to manage.

Source: Earl Swisher, *China's Management of the American Barbarians: A Study of Sino-American Relations, 1841–1861, with Documents* (New York: Octagon Books, 1972), 203–204.

Further Reading

Bergere, Marie-Claire. *Shanghai: China's Gateway to Modernity*. Stanford: Stanford University Press, 2009.

Elvin, Mark. "Market Towns and Waterways: The County of Shanghai from 1480 to 1910." In *The City in Late Imperial China*, edited by G. William Skinner, 441–474. Stanford: Stanford University Press, 1977.

Johnson, Linda Cooke. "Shanghai: An Emerging Jiangnan Port, 1683–1840." In *Cities of Jiangnan in Late Imperial China*, edited by Linda Cooke Johnson, 151–182. Albany: SUNY Press, 1993.

———. *Shanghai: From Market Town to Treaty Port, 1074–1858*. Stanford: Stanford University Press, 1995.

Jones, Susan Mann. "The Ningpo *Pang* and Financial Power at Shanghai." In *The Chinese City between Two Worlds*, edited by Mark Elvin and G. William Skinner, 73–96. Stanford: Stanford University Press, 1974.

Pan, Lynn. *Shanghai Style: Art and Design Between the Wars*. South San Francisco: Long River Press, 2008.

"Shanghai: Sights in the City," *North China Herald* (Shanghai), no. 439, December 25, 1858.

Van Slyke, Lyman P. *Yangtze: Nature, History, and the River*. New York: Addison-Wesley, 1988.

Wei, Betty Peh-t'i. *Shanghai: Crucible of Modern China*. Hong Kong: Oxford University Press, 1987.

Web Resources

Shanghai, ChinaDiscover.net, www.chinadiscover.net/china-tour/shanghaiguide/china-shanghai.htm.

Shanghai historical maps, www.earnshaw.com/shanghai-ed-india/tales/t-oldmap.htm.

Shanghai history, ShanghaiCentral.com, www.shanghai-central.com/shanghai%20history.html.

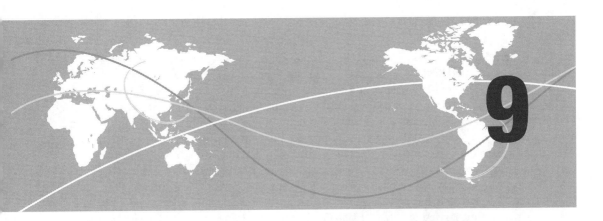

Algiers

A Colonial Metropolis Transformed to a Global City

(ca. 1800–1954)

JULIA CLANCY-SMITH

MANY AMERICANS FIRST ENCOUNTER ALGIERS BY VIEWING THE 1965 ITAL-IAN film *The Battle of Algiers*, directed by Gillo Pontecorvo, who cast local people as actors in the city's markets, cafes, and the famed Qasbah. Shot in black and white on location with a hand-held camera to lend documentary authenticity and released only three years after Algeria won its independence from France, *The Battle of Algiers* narrated the 1957 struggle that erupted within the capital of French Algeria between the National Liberation Front (FLN) and colonial troops as France's global empire collapsed. When I was attending university, *The Battle of Algiers* was already becoming a cult film, and it whetted my appetite to know more about the city, Algeria, and North Africa in general. While I was a Peace Corps volunteer in Tunisia during the 1970s, I had the opportunity to travel around Algeria and subsequently made the country's history the focus of my dissertation and scholarly research.

By the early twenty-first century, Algiers had grown into the third most populous urban area in North Africa—only Cairo and Casablanca are bigger—with nearly five million inhabitants in the greater metropolitan region. It stretches as far as the eye can see along the Mediterranean coastline to the west of the Bay of Algiers for nearly ten miles. In

Arabic the city's name, *al-Jaza'ir*, means "the islands," which refers to several islets that at one time dotted the bay, conferring upon it strategic value. However, since the early colonial period, these islands have either been connected to the mainland by causeways or removed by harbor modernization. Despite its phenomenal growth since independence, today's Algiers still bears the physical and cultural marks of its precolonial, and particularly its colonial (1830–1962), past in terms of built environment and organization; some urban quarters resonate with the epic conflict of 1957 that brought the "Algerian question" to world attention. Savvy tourists familiar with Pontecorvo's film seek out the upper city, or Qasbah, which rests on ancient ruins dating back to classical antiquity, but whose main attraction is the vertical mazes of Moorish houses, blind alleys, and small lanes where the most riveting action of *The Battle of Algiers* took place. Yet many visitors are visibly disappointed by the Qasbah's dilapidated state; much of it is falling into ruins and it ranks as one of the most insalubrious urban quarters of North Africa.

The second part of Algiers still boasts the wide public squares and grid-like boulevards of the colonial city, built after the French army's 1830 invasion. Stretching beyond the historic urban core are extensive modern suburbs, which now cover most of the surrounding Metidja plain and do not normally tempt tourists. Dating largely from the post-1962 era, these suburbs manifest processes and problems found across the globe in terms of rural-to-city migrations, unrestrained urbanization, and ecologically unsupportable population densities. Indeed, obtaining sufficient daily potable water for household use in Algiers is difficult, although the climate is relatively benign, with abundant seaborne rainfall. Previously known as Algiers "la Blanche" or "the White City," because its older Arab quarters appeared as white-washed cubical formations to travelers arriving by sea, the city's name conjures contradictory images, emotions, and meanings. (See Map 9.1.)

This chapter traces the city's evolution from its earliest origins until the war for independence, with an emphasis on the developments from the nineteenth to the mid-twentieth centuries. Numerous wide-ranging, often contradictory, forces entangled the city and its hinterland with much larger transnational connections and transformations—from the regional and global influences of French Algeria to Algiers' role as an urban planning model to the city's social experimentation during the interwar years (1918–1939). With the outbreak of the war for independence in 1954, the city experienced unspeakable violence involving both civilians and military personnel; it also became a global inspiration for popular resistance to settler colonialism. During decolonization, Algiers became a model for African and Asian independence struggles for justice and dignity, as well as the tragic emblem of the colonial city. The end of France's North African empire also resulted in massive, forced, south-to-north trans-Mediterranean migrations, which still exert considerable torque on French and European politics in the twenty-first century.

ALGIERS AND THE WORLD:
The Convergence of Peoples and Cultures

Like Carthage to the east, Algiers was founded by the Phoenicians as one of their trading colonies along the North African coast. Established around 1200 BCE, this particular commercial outpost, named Ikosim, was where the marine quarter of Algiers is now located. Arab-Muslim conquests overtook much of the region in the late seventh century, but North African ports such as Algiers continued to trade with other commercial hubs in the Mediterranean, irrespective of religion. Notably, one of these hubs was the Byzantine Empire's capital city, Constantinople, one of the most active harbors during the Middle Ages. Archeological evidence from contemporary Istanbul has revealed eighth- and

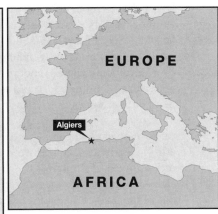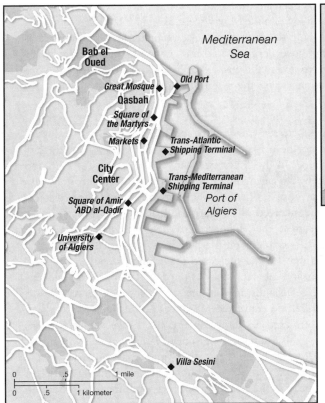

Map 9.1. Algiers

This map shows the precolonial and colonial urban topography of Algiers, which after 1830 tended to expand to the south of the Qasbah district along the Mediterranean. The modern port facilities seen here contain docking facilities and ferry terminals and were gradually constructed during the nineteenth century until Algiers resembled an African version of the French port of Marseille. The establishment of rapid regular steamship transportation between France and Algeria reduced the time of travel between the two sides of the sea dramatically and facilitated the movement of Algerian migrant workers and colonial troops to France.

ninth-century cargo ships transported, among other things, amphorae manufactured in the Maghrib that were sold to merchant-importers in the city on the Bosporus. By this period, the Islamization of Algeria and the rest of North Africa was nearly complete; Christianity and its churches had died out by the twelfth century, although important Jewish communities continued to exist.

Algiers remained a small, relatively unimportant town, eclipsed by Constantine and Tunis to the east and cities such as Tlemcen to the west, until the sixteenth century, when thousands of Muslims and Jews expelled from Spain during the centuries-long Reconquista or from elsewhere in Europe sought refuge there. That same century witnessed titanic struggles for mastery of the Mediterranean basin between two superpowers—the Hapsburg and the Ottoman Empires—and the North African coastline became a critical site in these maritime conflicts. In 1514 Spain seized one of the offshore islets, el Peñon, in the Bay of Algiers. The notables and populace of Algiers begged two Greek privateers in 1516 to drive the Spaniards from the strategic Peñon Island. Barbarossa, also known as

Khayr al-Din, took Algiers in 1541, expelled the Spaniards, and placed Algiers under the authority of the Ottoman sultan, Süleyman the Magnificent. By 1574 Tunisia and what is known today as Libya (Tripolitania in the period) had also come under Ottoman rule as provinces administered by military governors and soldiers sent from Istanbul. The *beyler-beys* (governors-general), later promoted to the position of *deys* or regents of Algiers, constructed an Ottoman fort and a palace on the steep hills above the port, as well as a number of mosques.

Algiers represented a major Mediterranean port for the Ottoman navy. Its geographical position along the fluid borders between Christianity and Islam, the eastern and western Mediterranean, and between northern Africa, the Sahara, and the sea earned the city the sobriquet of "Bulwark of Islam." In the Mediterranean world, the seventeenth and eighteenth centuries were marked by corsair raids and privateering, and Algiers grew into one of the most formidable corsair republics tied to the Ottoman Empire. The privateering, or corsair, system might be conceived of as maritime brigandage; most cities or states, Christian or Muslim, adjacent to the Mediterranean actively participated in the seizure of ships, crews, passengers, and goods on the high seas. This method of forced population and commodity exchanges further increased the ethnic diversity of Algiers, which may have boasted fifty thousand inhabitants in its heyday. Renegades and adventurer-sailors from the Italian or Greek islands, the Balkans, and elsewhere served the Algerian state in maritime raids and battles, converted to Islam, and melded with the local Arab-Berber populace through intermarriage. Many converts played a central role as intermediaries between European consuls established in Algiers, Tunis, and Tripoli and local Ottoman authorities or Muslim notables. Corsairing financially underwrote the Ottoman Algerian state because maritime profits were high, whereas wringing sufficient agricultural surplus from the peasantry in the countryside or pastoral nomads in the high plains and desert was difficult and costly.

The vast majority of the Christians seized on the high seas or from coastal villages, however, were employed as slaves in various capacities—as galley rowers or in domestic service—or were bartered as captives in the trans-Mediterranean ransoming economy, which involved both Muslims and Christians. Social actors such as renegades occupied fluid spaces between Islam and Christianity, between Ottoman and European states, thereby blurring and complicating categories. The centuries-old practice of incorporating Christians into the fabric of North African society represented an important element in Algiers' intense involvement in the Mediterranean.

Another important current of trade, conquest, and both forced and free migration crisscrossed the Sahara for centuries. Merchants from the Sahara and West Africa had long journeyed to North African cities for commercial purposes; with the Islamization of sub-Saharan Africa, Muslim pilgrims and scholars traveled north to Islamic centers such as Cairo, Tunis, or Fez. However, from the ninth to thirteen centuries, the growth of the Ghana Empire in southern Mauritania progressively linked trans-Saharan trade and trade across seas. Lacking adequate gold supplies, Mediterranean economies exchanged salt and other products for Western African gold and slaves through chains of trade intermediaries. Large numbers of enslaved Africans were forcibly sent to northern Africa to serve as domestic servants or slave concubines; some labored in Algerian oases. From the tenth to the nineteenth centuries, an estimated six to seven thousand enslaved persons were transported north each year for distribution in slave markets found from Morocco to Egypt. As it was not directly situated on the principal routes crossing the desert, Algiers acquired sub-Saharan products and enslaved peoples via chains of entrepôt cities in the south. As was true of Tunis, some enslaved Africans were shipped from Algiers or other North African ports to eastern Ottoman lands, mainly for employment in household service. The French conquest of Algeria and abolition of African slavery in 1848 drastically reoriented trans-Saharan commerce in human beings and African commodities. In any case, by the eighteenth century's close, the trans-Saharan trade was in decline and the Mediterranean-wide corsair political economy and culture were in eclipse as new kinds of states and economic systems arose on the sea's northern limits.

New Empires and Encounters

In 1798 a French fleet and army under Napoleon Bonaparte conquered Egypt in an ephemeral occupation that ended in 1801 after Ottoman-British armies expelled French forces. Napoleon's invasion of Ottoman Egypt, while short-lived, utterly transformed relationships between the Ottoman Empire, North Africa, and the European Great Powers. The invasion's aftermath sparked state-led reforms and modernization from Istanbul to Cairo to Tunis and beyond. It also set the stage for British-French rivalry in the region, which lasted until World War II, as well as for French cultural and/or political domination of the nineteenth-century Middle East and North Africa. In 1801 Great Britain seized the strategic Maltese islands from the French army, which made the British into a redoubtable Mediterranean power and increased British interest in the Ottoman regency of Algiers. At the same time, Napoleon's adventure in Egypt and Syria, as well as the publication of the multivolume, lavishly illustrated *Description de l'Égypte*, sparked generalized European interest in North Africa and the Middle East, an interest that gave birth to full-blown Orientalism in literature, art, and scholarship. (The term Orientalism refers to the depiction of Eastern, mainly Muslim, societies by Western artists, writers, and literati who portrayed in print and in visual media these cultures as different and thus inferior.) The *Description* served as a model for the later multivolume *Tableau de la situation des établissements français dans l'Algérie*, published annually from the 1830s on, which further fed European interest in Algeria and North Africa. Moreover, just as Napoleon had brought a purloined Arabic printing press to Egypt, so one of the warships moored off Algiers in 1830 had on board an Arabic press for the French army to issue communications to the city's inhabitants. Thus, the 1798 expedition could be viewed as a military dress rehearsal for 1830; Egypt provided an imperial template for colonial Algeria in the way that Algeria was used as a model and countermodel for later French imperial expansion in Asia and Africa in terms of immigration/settler policies and methods to put down anticolonial resistance. Finally, European commerce, banking, transportation, and law increasingly became the "Trojan horse" of creeping imperialism in adjacent North African states, principally Egypt, Morocco, and Tunisia, even prior to the imposition of formal colonial rule over these Muslim states. In order to grasp the profound transformation wrought by French colonialism upon the city of Algiers, one needs to consider its history prior to 1830.

From Ottoman Port to Colonial Metropolis

Travelers arriving by ship in the port of Algiers prior to July 1830 would have remarked that the urban spaces, activities, and residents were more or less contained within the traditional walls of the Ottoman-Arab and Islamic city perched on a hill overlooking the Mediterranean. The city was divided into two major sections: the upper, which largely contained residential quarters, and the lower, which boasted congregational mosques with law courts attached to them, Ottoman administrative offices, large markets, and military garrisons. Most important was the Janina Palace in the lower town, which served as the headquarters for the ruler, the *dey*, until 1817. Ottoman notables lived in mansions surrounding the palace that conformed to local architectural norms. One key principle of social organization was the *hawma*, or neighborhood, whose outer edges were fluid but whose inner core was often determined by the dominant ethnicity or religion of its inhabitants rather than by social class. Because of its nature, the port had always sheltered a heterogeneous population of sailors, dock workers, merchants, and traders.

The city's population was estimated at about forty thousand in 1829, while the country's total population was about three million. Resident European traders and diplomats comprised by far the smallest foreign group, with no more than one hundred individuals, but their numbers increased dramatically after 1830 due to largely spontaneous labor immigration from southern Europe. France's invasion in 1830 utterly transformed the city's social organization, meaning, and aesthetic; the logic of empire demanded such.

During the Napoleonic Wars, Algerian grain had been exported to France for provisioning the army. However, the Algerian state had never been remunerated for its wheat shipments, and the conflict over unpaid debts persisted until 1827 when Husayn Dey, the Ottoman-appointed ruler of Algeria, demanded the hefty sum of eight million francs from France. During an altercation at his palace in Algiers, the *dey* allegedly struck or tapped the French consul, Alexandre Deval, with his bejeweled fly whisk. Declaring that France's national honor had been besmirched, French monarch Charles X imposed a blockade in June 1827 on all Algerian ports, bringing trade between France and Algeria to a virtual halt. In Istanbul, the sultan attempted to bring both parties to the peace table and the conflict to a diplomatic conclusion, which was standard practice in the period. Ottoman emissaries and ships were repeatedly dispatched to Paris and Algiers to smooth things over—to no avail.

Until the summer of 1830, few observers in Europe or the Ottoman Empire had anticipated a French invasion of Algeria, much less a long-term military occupation. The major impetus for overseas military ventures was domestic—the political woes of the increasingly unpopular French monarch. Charles X faced a rising tide of liberal opposition to uncurbed monarchy, and a distraction was needed to save his throne. General Count Louis de Bourmont organized the expedition during the spring of 1830, claiming that a rapid military victory against Algiers would assure the royalist party in France of triumph in the elections of July 1830. Prior to the expedition, it had been calculated that no more than ten thousand troops would suffice to take Algiers and its hinterland; by 1847, some one hundred thousand French soldiers were committed to the unfinished task of "pacifying" the population. The July elections in France placed the antiroyalists firmly in power in the Chamber of Deputies. Violent popular demonstrations in the streets of Paris forced Charles X to abdicate on August 2, 1830. His commanding general, Bourmont, was forced into exile in Spain; he had been wrong on all counts. This was by no means the last time that events in Algeria would topple a government in France.

On May 25, 1830, an enormous French fleet of some six hundred ships bearing over forty thousand military and support personnel left Toulon, eventually landing on June 12 at a small bay known as Sidi Ferruch, some twenty miles to the west of Algiers. After a series of battles with Algerian-Turkish forces that were overwhelmed by the French firepower and manpower, the army reached Algiers on July 4. The next day, Husayn Dey capitulated and agreed to the terms imposed by the French commander. Taking with him court officials, retainers, his family, and thirty thousand gold coins, the former ruler was allowed to sail across the Mediterranean a few days later for a new life in Naples; most of the Turkish army and state officials were deported. Three centuries of Ottoman rule in

Algeria had come to an end. This event sparked decades of bitter imperial competition between France and Great Britain—and later Italy—for control of northern Africa and the Mediterranean coastline for commercial, political, and strategic reasons. And after the opening of the Suez Canal in 1869, the region became even more critically important.

As quoted by John Reudy in his 2005 *Modern Algeria: The Origins and Development of a Nation*, the French declared that "the exercise of the Muslim religion shall be free. The liberty of the inhabitants of all classes, their religion, their property, their businesses, and their industry shall remain inviolable. Their women shall be respected." In flagrant violation of the agreement, the army seized private, state, and religious properties, looted homes, destroyed mosques and buildings, pillaged the treasury, burned the state archives, and expropriated agricultural land. Thousands of city inhabitants fled their homes, although a few native elites chose to collaborate with the invaders. The most radical colonial urban interventions were effected in the lower town, where part of the principal markets were destroyed to construct a vast, open square, the Place d'Armes (later renamed Place du Gouvernement), where the army could parade. In 1832 the military began systematically demolishing Ottoman-Islamic Algiers, renaming streets and neighborhoods, digging up Muslim cemeteries for road building, and converting mosques into barracks or churches. One of the most beautiful buildings, the al-Sayyida Mosque (reconstructed by the Ottomans in 1794 in conformance with Algerian architectural aesthetics), was completely razed. The destruction of religious edifices and their conversion to profane uses— some mosques were employed as stables—created enduring animosity of native inhabitants toward the colonizer.

The ancient core of the city was ripped open to make way for European structures and monumental spaces until modern Algiers resembled Marseille in Africa. Indeed, some urban historians argue that Georges-Eugène Haussmann (1809–1891), a French civic planner who oversaw the rebuilding of Paris between 1852 and 1870, was inspired by the earlier example of colonial Algiers, notably the wanton destruction of historic quarters. The violent remaking of Algiers was a novelty because earlier imperial rulers, notably the Ottomans, had largely left intact the city's built environment or expanded upon preexisting structures and forms of urban social organization.

From 1830 on, tens of thousands of French and non-French nationals, impoverished peoples from around the Mediterranean, poured into first the Algiers region and later the coastal regions in search of land, booty, and employment. Subsequently, state and private emigration societies were organized in Paris to recruit worthy settlers—skilled, sober, virtuous—from targeted European populations, such as the Swiss and Germans, to offset settlers in Algeria from nations regarded as morally or politically objectionable, notably the Maltese, who were British subjects, and the Sicilians. By 1850 the European population of Algiers was estimated at about 56,000; it would continue to grow until by the interwar era French or European inhabitants numbered around 733,000. Most Europeans tended to reside in the lower city, near the port, or in the new quarters created by the army after 1830, while Arab Jews and Muslims remained in the *madina* and Qasbah districts. By far, the single largest immigrant group came from Spain and the Balearic Islands; during the global droughts that began in the 1880s, ten of thousands of Spaniards relocated to Algeria in search of a better life, especially in the agricultural field. However, while the total number of Spaniards in Algeria remained high, by World War I most Spanish emigrants set out for the Americas.

Gender and national stereotypes thus played a pivotal role, since communities or nations known for their respectable women and hard-working males were recruited. Algeria was also employed as a military and civilian penal colony. In June of 1852, twelve women arrested during popular uprisings against Louis Napoleon's 1851 coup d'état were trans-ferred involuntarily from the Saint-Lazare Prison in Paris to Algeria. Hundreds more were eventually transported; some forced to stay for years in exile. Among the women sent across the sea to rid the French capital of turbulent elements was Pauline Roland (1805–1852), an educated feminist, Socialist, Radical Republican, and mother of three. Roland's life demonstrates the connections between the French Empire and Algeria. After settling in Paris in 1832, Roland became involved with the feminist movement, which brought her into the circle of novelist George Sand, among others. Roland also agitated for sexual equality in education, for women's right to work, and for labor unions. Her ac-tivism got her into trouble with Napoleon III's autocratic government. In 1850 she was arrested and imprisoned in France until July 1851, when she was forcibly transported to Algeria. The employment of colonies as prisons dated back to the pre-revolutionary French Empire, but the Algerian experience reinvigorated the practice; for example, nineteenth-century French Guyana borrowed penal laws and incarceration methods de-veloped in Algeria at the time.

As the number of immigrants to Algeria climbed, Algiers, Oran, and Bône came to have majority European populations and to spatially and architecturally resemble French cities in terms of urban patterns, institutions, and social organization.

Rising Resistance to Colonial Rule

The political future of Algeria remained contested for a decade as some political fac-tions and parties in France called for immediate and total evacuation, while others, mainly the military, demanded increasing numbers of men, armaments, and resources to combat fierce Algerian resistance. Charles X's successor, King Louis-Philippe (r. 1830–1848) wavered for a time, which allowed local military officers, speculators, for-tune hunters, and carpetbaggers in Algeria to seize the initiative. This had far-reaching and long-lasting consequences for the nature of colonial rule because many of the legal, social, political, and cultural practices and policies that governed Algiers for decades were worked out on the ground in the early conquest period. Algeria's uncertain politi-cal future changed dramatically when General Thomas Robert Bugeaud was named governor-general in December 1840, after eight of his successors had proven unequal to the task of ruling the country. He embarked on a scorched earth policy, employing guerilla warfare tactics aimed at crushing Algerian opposition. While the last native re-bellions were not put down until 1871, Bugeaud's approach effectively opened the way for military colonization and agricultural exploitation in the Algiers region and along the Mediterranean coast. In consequence, the country became a vast army camp; many French officers and European mercenaries trained there. Military considerations took precedence over social or political policies, and the officers of the Arab Bureau created in 1841 exercised largely unlimited administrative power over the native population. Therefore, Algeria from 1830 until 1870 was principally a department of the French Ministry of War. Violence against Algeria's diverse inhabitants became institutionalized, enshrined in law, practice, custom, and culture from the start, notably in the region's le-gal system, which maintained the native peoples in a state of quasi-permanent legal ex-ception or inferiority.

Once the Algiers region was pacified by 1840, the French army moved to progres-sively subjugate, mainly by force but at times by treaty, the country's northern regions. Protected by a brutal climate, distance, and difficult terrain, the oases and peoples of the deep Sahara proved more resistant but for the most part were subdued by the late nineteenth century. From 1848 on, Algeria was legally and administratively attached to France, and in 1881 it was made an overseas extension of the metropole. Decades of military campaigns invariably unleashed disease and famine, disrupted village and peasant economies, and led to demographic decline among native Algerians; many thousands relocated to adjacent Muslim countries. Algerian opposition to foreign rule was fierce and endured until 1871, assuming a number of different guises, from jihads to tribal rebellions to millenarian revolts.

France discouraged industrialization since Algeria was to serve as a source of agrarian products—wheat, olive oil, and wine—and mineral wealth, as well as functioning as a market for goods produced in the mother country. Ultimately, Algeria became the crown jewel of France's global empire and an emblem of great power status, a measure of national and international dignity despite determined local resistance. The impetus for new colonial holdings, particularly in the rest of North Africa, the Sahara, and West Africa, was to no small degree dictated by France's drive to defend its first Afro-Mediterranean possession against other European rivals. In reality, the "Scramble for Africa" by European colonial powers began not in 1878 but rather in 1830.

In 1889 naturalization laws were passed in France and applied in Algeria, making French citizens out of many, but not all, Maltese, Sicilian, Spanish, and other non-French residents claiming European descent. The term *pied-noir* (black feet), of uncertain origins, came to designate these people, many of whom were poor whites and most of whom resided in cities or towns. In the countryside, settlers planted wheat and unsuccessfully experimented in export cash crops such as cotton and tobacco, unsuitable to Algeria's soils and climate. When global wheat prices began plummeting, there was a steady increase in viticulture, or grape cultivation, especially after phylloxera destroyed French vineyards in 1878, and wine became Algeria's most important export. The transformation from subsistence farming into a focus on a market-oriented crop that the Muslim population did not consume because alcohol consumption is forbidden by Islam utterly undermined the traditional rural economy. European-owned colonial estates favored the more lucrative viticulture sector. This in turn encouraged rural-to-urban migrations by former Algerian cultivators and also endangered local food supplies, unleashing cycles of devastating famine.

For the settlers, viticulture became an essential component not only of their livelihood but also of their identity, although the underlying reasons for the expansion of this sector of the colonial economy, which directly competed with French wine production, were political. Born in Algeria, celebrated French writer Albert Camus (1913–1960) came from this very social class—his father had worked in a vineyard until he was mobilized to fight in France in 1914, where he died. Camus's impoverished family then moved to the popular Algiers working-class suburb of Belcourt, although his education eventually propelled him into the ranks of the Parisian intellectual elite. By about 1900, a profound transmutation occurred among European settlers as a hybrid collective identity crystallized, one whose political project was proclaimed by the notion of *Nous Algériens*—"We the Algerians." This ideology held that European Algerians constituted a cultural race distinct from both the "inferior natives" and the racially degenerate, even effeminate, French in the metropole. A manifestation of this identity was the fact that the European settlers displayed an aggressive racism toward indigenous Muslims and Jews, virtually without parallel in Tunisia or Morocco, which became French protectorates in 1881 and in 1912, respectively. Nevertheless, colonial racism marked all European empires by the late nineteenth century, although legally, politically, and socially those racial attitudes played out differently in different places. Between 1872 and the 1906 census, the number of

Europeans residing in France's African departments soared from 245,000 to over 800,000, but only about 35 percent of that total was actually French in origin, a supreme irony.

From the 1870s on, the Paris parliament, under pressure from French Algerian delegates, enacted a series of exceptional laws designed to place Muslims in a state of permanent legal inferiority. Known as the Code de l'indigénat (Indigenous Peoples Law Code), its provisions were absent from French law; these extraconstitutional regulations rendered illegal and punishable a long list of infractions, such as traveling without written permission or neglecting to properly register births or deaths. Admitted into the code was the *corvée*, state-imposed unpaid labor obligations, which only added to the misery and humiliations of rural society. Enhancing the armature of legal disability was the right of administrative detention, which conferred extraordinary power on the governor-general to incarcerate Muslims deemed undesirable; often individuals were labeled as "undesirable" for insignificant reasons such as not displaying adequate respect to local French police officers. Many of these legal and extralegal measures for controlling the native population lasted well into the twentieth century. Nevertheless, institutionalized legal exceptions were not confined to Algeria—indeed, some were exported to other French possessions; for example, the "Indigenous Code" was imposed on Nouvelle-Calédonie in the southwest Pacific, which had disastrous effects on the local Kanak populations. Thus, we see how legal regimes developed by the colonial government in Algiers influenced distant places and peoples.

The Great War and the City Transformed

By the eve of World War I, Algeria had come to represent a template for white settler rule in imperial projects across the globe, particularly in terms of colonial law and administrative practices. In addition, the country served as a colonial laboratory for experiments in urbanism, with numerous projects carried out in or proposed for Algiers, and other experiments were also carried out in the fields of medicine, psychiatry, photography, and agricultural mechanization in grain-growing regions. However, the failures of French Algeria were patent by the period to those who wished to see them. Claims of France's civilizing mission—to bring European enlightenment to the natives—were contradicted by high rates of illiteracy among Algerian children and by the Muslims' refusal to convert to Christianity. In some other French possessions, notably Tunisia after 1881, Algeria served as an imperial countermodel—a lesson in what *not* to do, particularly in terms of granting French nationality to European settlers. In Morocco, declared a French protectorate in 1912, colonial legislation was passed that forbade the wanton destruction of indigenous historic monuments, a policy clearly aimed at avoiding what had earlier transpired in Algiers. In addition, the pauperization of the native population, paradoxically combined with rapidly accelerating Muslim birth rates, produced widespread misery and internal migrations that fed political unrest, culminating in movements for national independence around World War I. Demographic realities deeply troubled the official mind of imperialism in all settler colonies where Europeans or whites ruled over larger indigenous populations whose numbers expanded because of basic improvements in modern public health. (See Map 9.2.) Long after the French military had crushed nineteenth-century rural resistance movements, colonial society was seized by sporadic waves of panic that linked Muslims to perceived increases in banditry, criminality, and general lawlessness—fears that justified colonial political and legal repression. But the constructed image of the Algerian woman also played a part.

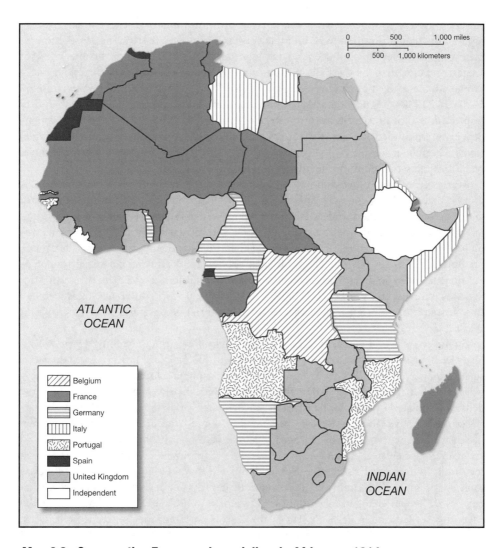

Map 9.2. Comparative European Imperialism in Africa, ca. 1914

By the outbreak of World War I, the vast majority of the African continent had been seized and controlled in various ways by seven major European nations. As is clear from the comparative map, Great Britain and France held the largest colonial territories, but not necessarily the richest, because Portugal claimed the Congo. While much of the continent was partitioned among European states during the "Scramble for Africa," which accelerated after 1881 and lasted until 1914, the 1830 French invasion of Algiers and conquest of Algeria set the process of colonial expansion in motion.

For Europeans in this period, the most visible cultural markers of "Oriental civilizations" or "Muslim societies" were their women and artisanal products, both increasingly on display and available to Western consumers and audiences. In Algiers, the spread of photography, first introduced by the military during the 1850s, resulted in a proliferation of photographers' studios that spawned a visual trade in women; photographs-cum-obscene postcards featured alleged Algerian prostitutes in inviting poses and postures, rendering them accessible to European male spectators. While other European colonial powers also eroticized colonized women in photographs, paintings, and other visual or cultural media, the French focus upon Algerian Muslim women was exceptional. Photography and colonialism thus were intimate traveling partners. In 1896 newsreel cameramen went to Algiers to film scenes, such as ships in the great harbor, "native" market scenes, and of course the Qasbah's teeming streets. Algiers was cast as a mysterious backdrop, with the native population serving as "props." This visual legacy continued into the 1920s and 1930s, when the first Algerian fiction films were released. The more than fifty feature films shot in Algeria from this period until the outbreak of the war for independence were intended for French viewers and validated the country's "eternal" colonial status. For modern empires, the camera proved critical because of its alleged objective, scientific ability to communicate images and ideas to vast audiences.

Moreover, exotic women and native handicrafts were among the most popular exhibitions at that peculiarly characteristic institution of nineteenth-century Europe—the world fair or colonial exhibition. Indeed, the interior of an Algiers "native home" was recreated in Paris for onlookers in one such exhibition. Despite efforts to faithfully reconstruct traditional artisans' workshops from Algiers at the 1900 exposition in the French capital, one singular element was missing—women as producers. Portraying colonized women as essential to household economies might undermine the dominant image of Muslim females as purely sexual markers of Islam's irreconcilable cultural differences; this ideology was utilized by the European settlers to deny political rights to Algerians until after World War I.

By the eve of World War I, the rural-to-urban migratory impulse within Algeria was already well advanced, bringing the countryside into the *bidonvilles*, or squatter quarters, surrounding Algiers and other major cities. In the capital, colonial officials increasingly worried about rising native settlement in the Qasbah district, which became the most densely populated quarter in the entire city. Adequate work was scarce in Algiers for unskilled male native laborers; to feed their families, some Arab or Berber Muslim women began working as servants for Europeans. While data on Muslim women in household service remains elusive, and the exact nature of their employment, as well as its impact on the family and society, is still unclear, it is significant that a feminine wage-laboring class took shape by the beginning of the twentieth century, soon after a male proletariat emerged. The war changed many things. Between 1914 and 1918, an estimated 170,000 Algerians served under France's flag in the European killing fields—some voluntarily, other forcibly. Upon demobilization and return, the former soldiers, who had anticipated some recognition from France for their sacrifice and devotion, instead experienced discrimination and disenfranchisement, which in turn fueled the anticolonial movements. Even prior to the war, severe labor shortages in France were offset by the importation of Algerians after 1905 to work temporarily in factories, notably in oil and sugar refineries located in Marseille, where unionized European laborers originally from Italy or elsewhere in the continent engaged in labor protests; in effect, impoverished Algerians were employed as "strike breakers."

During World War I, some 173,000 North African civilian workers, the vast majority of them Algerian, labored principally in French state-owned factories, which immensely aided the war effort in Europe. But with peace, they were forcibly repatriated, largely because colonial lobbies in the Maghrib opposed the siphoning off of cheap labor to the metropole. The war inadvertently created the conditions for the later massive, south-north labor migrations to France and Europe, which caused problems of social justice, law, and cultural assimilation still found in today's European Union. Therefore, pauperization, internal rural-to-urban migrations within Algeria, and military service made trans-Mediterranean expatriation conceivable to the Algerian peasantry. The experience of war and industrial wage labor laid the groundwork for organized labor union movements centered in Algiers, which merged with various ideological strands of nationalism. By the post–World War I era, demands for independence began to be publicly articulated in Algiers and across the country.

Final Ruptures? From French Territory to Independent State

Europeans comprised three-quarters of Algiers' population by the 1930s, but the number of natives residing in shantytowns skyrocketed, and by 1948 some thirty-five thousand people lived in 120 *bidonvilles* on the city's perimeter. In this same period, the notion and practice of "master plans" for urban administrators came into vogue worldwide. During the 1930s, French architects and municipal authorities regarded Algiers (and Rabat) as sites for experimentation in these new ideologies of constructed social space and built environment. Collective attention came to be focused on the marine quarter adjacent to the harbor, which housed a motley assortment of impecunious Europeans, largely from Malta, Spain, and Sicily, and native Algerians, including Arab Jews. It may be that political calculations were intertwined with urban planning, because dockers constituted the proletarian base of the Algerian Communist Party, created in October 1936. Many lived in miserable conditions in the overpopulated Qasbah or the marine quarter, where they encountered socialist or communist ideologies and union organizing; they were galvanized by the formation of a new socialist government in France, the Popular Front, in 1936.

Among these radical urban planners, Le Corbusier proved the most controversial because he proposed extensive demolitions in the marine quarter and the construction of skyscrapers and an immense bridge over Arab residential neighborhoods, which would have effectively segregated the native population from the European one. While his plan was not implemented, it demonstrates clearly the close link between imperialism, modernity, and urban planning. Nevertheless, the razing of parts of the lower town began and continued through World War II. By 1945 hundreds of buildings and shops had been demolished and some eleven thousand people forcibly displaced. The destruction of the city was likened to Hiroshima by a leading Algerian intellectual, Omar Racim.

Epilogue: The End of French Colonialism

The occupation of France by Nazi Germany from 1940 on resulted in the collapse of the Third Republic. The Allies (British and Americans) captured Algeria and Morocco as part of the North African campaigns that began on November 8, 1942. Allied forces established headquarters in Algeria and were regarded as agents of emancipation; both Allied and Axis radio stations broadcast Arabic-language programs promising liberation for colonial peoples in North Africa. Fierce Allied battles were waged against German and Italian armies first in Libya and then in Tunisia; the eventual expulsion of Vichy French colonial officials from Algeria, Morocco, and Tunisia humiliated France. Thus, World War II brought the *coup de grace* to French colonialism not only in North Africa and the Middle East but also worldwide, and it exerted a tremendous impact on Algeria, Algiers, and the various strands of the nationalist movement.

In the midst of the war in June 1941, Charles de Gaulle's provisional French government-in-exile offered independence to French-ruled Syria and Lebanon, a diplomatic move that was supported by British colonial authorities in the Middle East; this fed the independence movement in Algeria. The French army's humiliating defeat at the Battle of Dien Bien Phu in Southeast Asia in May 1954 signaled the end of France's empire in that part of the globe and constituted a watershed in the annals of decolonization because a non-European anticolonial movement, which had begun as a guerrilla operation, had overwhelmed a modern Western power on the field of battle. Drawing on this lesson, the National Liberation Front (FLN) coordinated a series of attacks across Algeria, targeting symbols of French rule, on All Saints Day, November 1, 1954. The French army and special forces hit back hard, unleashing a bitter eight-year struggle that left three million Algerians displaced in military concentration camps, destroyed eight thousand villages, and killed at least five hundred thousand people, the vast majority of them civilians.

Over the next several years, Algiers suffered waves of general strikes, served as a war zone, and endured massive military repression; tens of thousands of people were arrested, many of them tortured, and thousands were killed or disappeared. In June 1962, less than a month before Algerian independence, the French terrorist group Organization of the Secret Army (OAS) torched the Algiers University library, destroying over one hundred thousand books. This act of intellectual terrorism became a potent symbol for Algerian independence that was memorialized by images of the destruction on postage stamps specially issued by numerous Muslim states. Algiers was becoming an international symbol of a city torn asunder by empire's violent demise. At the same time, a mass exodus of almost all French citizens or European nationals emptied the country of its former technocrats, cadres, and administrators. Nearly one million people were "repatriated" to a France that they did not know because many families had resided in Algeria for generations. In 1962 the former colonial Place du Gouvernement, the heart of colonial Algiers, was renamed Square of the Martyrs. One hundred thirty-two years of French colonialism had ostensibly ended, but many grievous challenges lay ahead.

GLOBAL ENCOUNTERS AND CONNECTIONS:
A Reconquest of Civil Society and Modernity

In Algiers the *madina* (city), or traditional urban core, was progressively undermined by the combined forces of modernization, imperialism, and settler colonialism. In the pre-1830 era, the upper limits of the city around the Qasbah had been home to local notables, both Jewish and Muslim. By 1914 these residential areas sheltered a rural subproletariat that had been socially and culturally marginalized by the capitalist colonial economy. Nevertheless, after World War I, the old city, portrayed as "backward" and premodern, progressively became home to complex forms of modern associative life in music, sports, and culture that nurtured the emergence of an Algerian civil society and fed the nationalist movements. In a sense, by embracing institutions of civil society and modernity, which were being worked out worldwide in the period, the native population of Algiers began to repossess their city in a sort of moral reconquest. In contrast, modern Algiers exerted considerable influence not only on the rest of the Maghrib but also upon Dakar and other cities in French West Africa, where urban planners either emulated the Algerian model or viewed its experience as a cautionary lesson in what not to do. In the period between world wars, the city represented a site for experimentation in modern urban forms, ideologies, and practices that culminated during the last decade of the occupation in massive, now crumbling, social housing projects.

World War II and France's humiliating loss of Vietnam in 1954–1955 made it vital to retain Algeria; France granted Tunisia and Morocco independence in 1956 in order to suppress the Algerian rebellion. The French military's systematic torture of Algerian civilians during the war, including the rape of thousands of women, brought the issue of human rights and torture to world consciousness. Thus the city, and its infamous Villa

Sesini, where French paratroopers tortured Algerian militants and their French or European allies, came to incarnate global colonial violence after the international media brought human rights abuses to light. That violence inspired a number of writers, activists, and literati to oppose the war; figures such as Simone de Beauvoir, Henri Alleg, and Frantz Fanon, whose meditation on race and the colonial situation is found below, published tracts exposing and denouncing the violations. Even today, the exact number of Algerians killed during the eight-year conflict remains disputed. The years of violence, as well as the declaration of the Algerian Republic, resulted in the massive departure of former European settlers who were "repatriated" mainly to France and represented one of the largest trans-Mediterranean population movements of the post–World War II era.

Finally, the "Algerian question" became a major Cold War issue, not in the least because huge quantities of crude oil and natural gas were discovered in the Sahara in the mid-1950s, which was one of the principal reasons that France sought to retain its African possession. In the postcolonial era, the Algerian regime assumed a leadership position in the third world bloc and in Pan-Africanism, offering inspiration to revolutionary movements and leaders; American black radical Malcolm X visited Algiers in 1964 shortly before his death.

From ancient Phoenician trading outpost to Ottoman naval station to colonial metropolis, Algiers has retained its historic significance as a major maritime shipping center even after the demise of empire. The dual historical processes known as "end of empire" and "decolonization," however, should not be confused; Algeria provides a critical example of this. In contemporary Algiers, official urbanism schemes have yet to break away from many of their colonial antecedents in urban planning. More revealing are contemporary economic and commercial relationships. The city's hinterland has become a bustling refueling station for petroleum and, above all, natural gas, which is now sold principally to Europe, notably to companies such as Gaz de France, Enagas of Spain, and Distrigaz of Belgium. Indeed, France is one of Algeria's major trading partners.

ENCOUNTERS AS TOLD: PRIMARY SOURCES

This section contains a pair of related documents from the 1830 French invasion. The first reflects an Algerian poet's expression of grief, while the second presents an official French pronouncement on measures to be taken during the city's military occupation. The final document contains reflections on decolonization and the racialized relationships between the colonizer and the colonized.

Ballad by Sidi 'Abd al-Qadir

The first document reflects the perspective of city inhabitants and comes from the pen of a religious student, Sidi 'Abd al-Qadir, who composed this popular ballad lamenting the fate of his city and of Islam; it continued to be sung by other bards into the next century. Note the caustic reference to "Agha Brahim," part of the Turkish military government ruling Algeria that failed to defeat the invaders; ordinary Algerians looked in vain to Istanbul for military assistance in 1830.

• How were the events of July 1830 remembered by the inhabitants of Algiers?

• What did the invasion look like to natives in the capital city?

- What metaphors did the poet employ to express his anguish?

> I am grieved, o world, about Algiers!
> The French march on (toward) her
> > With troops whose number (only) God knows.
> They have come in vessels which cleave the sea;
> > It is not a matter of a hundred vessels, or two hundred,
> > Mathematics does not understand.
> Those who counted wore themselves out;
> > O Muslim, you would have said they were a forest!
> They swam ashore; but, the dogs, as soon as they faced the port,
> > Saw the cannons aiming at them,
> > And they went toward Sidi-Farruj [west of Algiers]
> > Burj al-Fanar [lighthouse tower] had terrified them!
> Soon the sea and the waves became swollen,
> > In order to vomit on our shores the French, sons of Ilja [sons of European slave women].
> From all sides they were seen stomping about;
> > Time called them and they came:
> > It is known that everything has its time.
> The Agha Brahim [Turkish military commander] hastened to mount his horse
> > with his flags, his music, and his foul-mouthed Turks.
> Arabs and Kabyles joined in,
> > Horsemen and foot soldiers charged,
> > The battle became hot, Oh my brothers!
> Its fire raged through Sundays and Mondays,
> > And the volley fell on our warriors.
> Death is worth much more than shame:
> > If the mother of the cities is taken,
> > What will you have left, Oh Muslim?
> Be patient, do not be frightened,
> > Death is our share,
> > We are all its prey.
> Death in holy war *(jihad)*
> > Is life in the other world.

Source: Alf Andrew Heggoy, *The French Conquest of Algiers, 1830: An Algerian Oral Tradition* (Athens: Ohio University Center for International Studies, 1986), 20.

Bulletin Officiel des Actes du Gouvernment

This pronouncement made by the occupying French army soon after 1830 declared that land, houses, and businesses belonging to the inhabitants of Algiers were subject to seizure and encouraged Algerians to inform on each other with the promise of reward. Juxtaposed, these two documents raise a number of questions.

- In contrast to the first document, what were the objectives and possible motivations of General Clauzel's proclamation and how would the inhabitants of Algiers have reacted to such orders?

- What impact would these regulations have exerted upon the city itself?

ALGIERS: SEPTEMBER 8, 1830

Art. 1. All houses, stores, shops, gardens, lands, places, and establishments whatsoever formerly occupied by the Dey, the beys, or Turks who have left the territory of the Regency of Algiers, or which are managed for their accounts, as well as those belonging in any way whatsoever to Mecca or Medina, revert to the public domain and shall be managed for its profit.

Art. 2. Persons of any nation who are holders or tenants on the said properties are obliged within three days to file declarations indicating the nature, location, and consistency of the domains of which they enjoy the use of management, together with the amount of the income or rent and the time of the last payment.

Art. 3. This declaration shall be transcribed onto registers opened for this purpose by the municipality.

Art. 4. Any person subject to this declaration who fails to file it within the time prescribed shall be condemned to a fine that shall not be less than one year's revenue or rent of the undeclared property, and he shall be constrained to the payment of this fine by the severest penalties.

Art. 5. Any individual who reveals to the French government the existence of an undeclared domain property shall be entitled to half the fine incurred by the delinquent party.

Proclaimed by Clauzel, General in Chief,
French Army in Algeria.

Source: Government General of Algeria, *Bulletin Officiel des Actes du Gouvernment*, vol. 1, 9 (Paris: Imprimerie Royal, 1834–1854); translated from the French in John Ruedy, *Land Policy in Colonial Algeria* (Berkeley and Los Angeles: University of California Press, 1967), 39–40. Republished in Robert Landen, *The Emergence of the Modern Middle East: Selected Readings* (New York: Van Nostrand Reonhold, 1970), 150–151.

The Wretched of the Earth, by Frantz Fanon

The following document is a selection from a work published in 1961 in French as *Les damnés de la terre* by Frantz Fanon (1925–1961). Born on the Caribbean island of Martinique, which was a French colony (and remains today a French territory), Fanon was of mixed racial origins; his father descended from African slaves, while his mother was of Native American, European, and African descent. After serving with the Free French, anti-Vichy forces in North Africa during World War II, Fanon went to study psychiatry and medicine in France. In 1953 he was assigned to the Blida-Joinville Psychiatric Hospital in Algeria, where he was practicing when the Algerian revolution began in November 1954. He joined the FLN liberation front (Front de Libération Nationale), which resulted in his expulsion from Algeria in 1957. In evaluating this document, it should be remembered that Fanon was writing during the events of the war, which greatly influenced his view of the situation.

- How did Fanon define decolonization?

- Why did he appear to condone violence and what are his moral arguments for the use of violence in the colonial context?

- How does Fanon portray the colonial city and the relationships between the people residing in the same space?

National liberation, national renaissance, the restoration of nationhood to the people, commonwealth: whatever may be the headings used or the new formulas introduced, decolonization is always a violent phenomenon. At whatever level we study it—relationships between individuals, new names for sports clubs, the human admixture at cocktail parties, in the police, on the directing boards of national or private banks—decolonization is quite simply the replacing of a certain "species" of men by another "species" of men. Without any period of transition, there is a total, complete, and absolute substitution. . . . We have precisely chosen to speak of that kind of tabula rasa which characterizes at the outset all decolonization. Its unusual importance is that it constitutes, from the very first day, the minimum demands of the colonized. To tell the truth, the proof of success lies in a whole social structure being changed from the bottom up. . . . The need for this change exists . . . in the consciousness and in the lives of the men and women who are colonized. But the possibility of this change is equally experienced in the form of a terrifying future in the consciousness of another "species" of men and women: the colonizers.

Decolonization, which sets out to change the order of the world, is, obviously, a program of complete disorder. But it cannot come as a result of magical practices, nor of a natural shock, nor of a friendly understanding. Decolonization, as we know, is a historical process: that is to say that it cannot be understood, it cannot become intelligible nor clear to itself except in the exact measure that we can discern the movements which give it historical form and content. Decolonization is the meeting of two forces, opposed to each other by their very nature, which in fact owe their originality to that sort of substantiation which results from and is nourished by the situation in the colonies. Their first encounter was marked by violence and their existence together—that is to say the exploitation of the native by the settler—was carried on by dint of a great array of bayonets and cannons. The settler and the native are old acquaintances. In fact, the settler is right when he speaks of knowing "them" well. For it is the settler who has brought the native into existence and who perpetuates his existence. The settler owes the fact of his very existence, that is to say, his property, to the colonial system. . . .

In decolonization, there is therefore the need of a complete calling in question of the colonial situation. If we wish to describe it precisely, we might find it in the well known words: "The last shall be first and the first last." Decolonization is the putting into practice of this sentence. That is why, if we try to describe it, all decolonization is successful. The naked truth of decolonization evokes for us the searing bullets and bloodstained knives which emanate from it. For if the last shall be first, this will only come to pass after a murderous and decisive struggle between the two protagonists. That affirmed intention to place the last at the head of things, and to make them climb at a pace (too quickly, some say) the well-known steps which characterize an organized society, can only triumph if we use all means to turn the scale, including, of course, that of violence. . . .

The colonial world is a world divided into compartments. It is probably unnecessary to recall the existence of native quarters and European quarters, of schools for natives and schools for Europeans; in the same way we need not recall apartheid in South Africa. Yet, if we examine closely this system of compartments, we will at least be able to reveal the lines of force it implies. This approach to the colonial world, its ordering and its geographical layout will allow us to mark out the lines on which a decolonized society will be reorganized.

The colonial world is a world cut in two. . . .

The zone where the natives live is not complementary to the zone inhabited by the settlers. The two zones are opposed, but not in the service of a higher unity. Obedient to the rules of pure Aristotelian logic, they both follow the principle of reciprocal exclusivity. No conciliation is possible, for of the two terms, one is superfluous. The settlers' town is a strongly built town, all made of stone and steel. It is a brightly lit town; the streets are covered with asphalt, and the garbage cans swallow all the leavings, unseen, unknown and hardly thought about. The settler's feet are never visible, except perhaps in the sea; but there you're never close enough to see them. His feet are protected by strong shoes although the streets of his town are clean and even, with no holes or stones. The settler's town is a well-fed town, an easygoing town; its belly is always full of good things. The settlers' town is a town of white people, of foreigners.

The town belonging to the colonized people, or at least the native town, the Negro village, the medina, the reservation, is a place of ill fame, peopled by men of evil repute. They are born there, it matters little where or how; they die there, it matters not where, nor how. It is a world without spaciousness; men live there on top of each other, and their huts are built one on top of the other. The native town is a hungry town, starved of bread, of meat, of shoes, of coal, of light. The native town is a crouching village, a town on its knees, a town wallowing in the mire. It is a town of niggers and dirty Arabs. The look that the native turns on the settler's town is a look of lust, a look of envy; it expresses his dreams of possession—all manner of possession: to sit at the settler's table, to sleep in the settler's bed, with his wife if possible. The colonized man is an envious man. And this the settler knows very well; when their glances meet he ascertains bitterly, always on the defensive, "They want to take our place." It is true, for there is no native who does not dream at least once a day of setting himself up in the settler's place.

Source: Frantz Fanon, *The Wretched of the Earth.* (New York: Grove Weidenfeld, 1965), 35–39. Translated by Constance Farrington.

Further Reading

Çelik, Zeynep. *Urban Forms and Colonial Confrontations: Algiers under French Rule.* Berkeley: The University of California Press, 1997.

———, Julia Clancy-Smith, and Frances Terpak, eds. *Walls of Algiers: Narratives of the City in Text and Image.* Seattle: University of Washington Press, 2009.

Clancy-Smith, Julia. *Mediterraneans: North Africa and Europe in an Age of Migration, c. 1800–1900.* Berkeley: University of California Press, 2011.

——— and Frances Gouda, eds. *Domesticating the Empire: Race, Gender, and Family Life in French and Dutch Colonialism.* Charlottesville: University Press of Virginia, 1998.

Heggoy, Alf A. *The French Conquest of Algiers, 1830: An Algerian Oral Tradition.* Columbus: Ohio University Press, 1986.

Hoerder, Dirk. *Cultures in Contact: World Migrations in the Second Millennium.* Durham: Duke University Press, 2002.

Lazreg, Marnia. *The Eloquence of Silence: Algerian Women in Question.* London: Routledge, 1994.

Ruedy, John. *Modern Algeria: The Origins and Development of a Nation.* 2nd ed. Bloomington: Indiana University Press, 2005.

Web Resources

Julia Clancy-Smith, "Imperialism in North Africa," *Women in World History*, the Center for History and New Media Project, George Mason University, http://chnm.gmu.edu/wwh/modules/lesson9/lesson9.php?s=0.

"Walls of Algiers: Narratives of the City," 2009 Exhibition, the J. Paul Getty Museum, Los Angeles, California, www.getty.edu/art/exhibitions/algiers/.

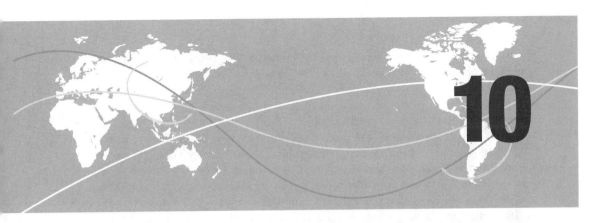

10

Gallipoli

War's Global Concourse

(1915)

EDWARD J. ERICKSON

FOR SUCH A STRATEGICALLY AND HISTORICALLY IMPORTANT PLACE, THE Gallipoli peninsula in modern-day Turkey is surprisingly remote. By car, the tip of the peninsula (Cape Helles) is a five-hour trip from the Istanbul airport, and tourists find it sometimes difficult to get there. However, were you to journey to the peninsula on April 25 of any given year, you would find it packed with visitors from a number of countries—Australia, New Zealand, the United Kingdom, France and, of course, Turkey itself. Moreover, every April these visitors often include heads of state, ambassadors, university rectors, soldiers and, as always, hundreds of casually dressed young people on walkabout. April 25 is Anzac Day, the national day of Australia, and every year this holiday brings Australians to Gallipoli by the cartload.

The word Anzac is a shortened term for the military formation known as the Australian and New Zealand Army Corps (ANZAC), and since 1915 it has been one of the words used to describe a person who is Australian. In the cold, dark, predawn hours of April 25, 1915, during World War I, twenty-five thousand Australians and New Zealanders (who are often called "Kiwis") stormed ashore on a narrow, shelf-like cove to attack the Ottoman Turks huddled in their trenches overlooking the beaches. It was the first modern amphibious operation of the twentieth century, and the men of the two infantry divisions of the ANZAC believed they were about to alter world history. Instead, they failed. Over eleven thousand Anzacs and Kiwis never returned home, and most are buried in well-tended graves on the peninsula. Twenty-five thousand more were wounded.

I've been to the Gallipoli peninsula a dozen times or so. I'm a historian, and I suppose that I'm connected to the peninsula in an intellectual way, which springs from my lifelong passion for military history, as well as from my professional writing. Yet, more than that, I'm connected to the place in a raw and emotional way as well. You see, I'm also an old soldier, and when I walk the ground there my mind hears the crump of incoming artillery and the stutter of machine guns raking the dead ground. As in the Leonardo DiCaprio movie *Titanic*, my mind's eye shifts between the past and present, and just by blinking I can see the khaki-clad Anzacs, overloaded with their heavy packs, struggling up the high bluffs to meet the Turks waiting somewhere above. It's always an emotional experience for me, and the dead seem to call from their graves in the carefully manicured commonwealth cemeteries. The echoes of history are there.

In my current position I travel to the peninsula with my students, who are officers in the United States Marine Corps. It's their job to land on hostile shores like those Anzacs did almost one hundred years ago, so I have occasion to talk about how hard it was then and how equally hard it is today. We talk about those men and what they did in 1915, and we all understand that if the United States Marines had to do something similar today, some of them would also wind up in the well-tended graves of our own national cemeteries. Conversations about such encounters transcend rationality and go to the emotional root elements of combat. If you visit Little Round Top in Gettysburg, Pennsylvania, or Omaha Beach in Normandy, especially in the company of a veteran, you might hear the echoes of history and feel these emotions yourself.

This chapter illustrates the importance of geography in understanding how war creates global convergences between peoples. The location of the Gallipoli peninsula itself created the dynamics of encounter between old empires and young democracies. Moreover, this chapter highlights the essential timelessness of war, whether we like it or not, as a component of both the human condition and collective human memory. The consequences of this campaign ensured that World War I lasted longer than it might have, thus leading to "a peace to end all peace," the effects of which still afflict the world.

GALLIPOLI AND THE WORLD:
A Strategic Point of Global Convergence

The Gallipoli peninsula is located on the European side of the Dardanelles Strait, which is itself a part of a larger group collectively called the Turkish Straits that link the Aegean Sea and the Black Sea. (See Map 10.1.) The other components of this geographic group are the Sea of Marmara and the Bosporus Straits farther to the north. The Dardanelles Strait is about forty miles in length and is dominated on the west side by the rugged and commanding heights of the Gallipoli peninsula. In ancient times the peninsula was known as Chersonesus Thracica or the Thracian Chersonese. On the opposite side, the Asian shore and its hinterland are lower and less rugged. The strait is hourglass in shape and narrows to a width of only two thousand yards at its waist at modern Eceabat. The peninsula itself is sparsely inhabited aside from Eceabat, containing only the large town of Gallipoli and a few small villages. It is hot and dry in the summer, cold and damp in the winter, and for most of history has simply been home to farmers and fishermen.

Why then might the place itself be important at all? It is a fair question and easily answered. The Dardanelles Strait is the access point to and from the Black Sea. In geographical military terms, it is called a "choke point" (other similar choke points include

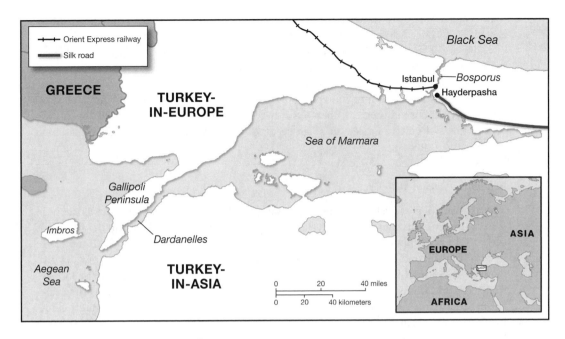

Map 10.1. The Turkish Straits

The Turkish Straits comprise the Dardanelles (which lead from the Aegean Sea in the south through the Sea of Marmara) and end in the north as the Bosporus enters the Black Sea. The ancient city of Constantinople (the modern Turkish city of Istanbul) lies in a strategic location where both the Orient Express Railroad and much older Silk Road stopped, and it has been a hub of world commerce for thousands of years. Equally strategic in location, the Gallipoli peninsula, southwest of Istanbul, was a pivotal point of control for the competing British and Turkish armies during World War I.

Gibraltar, the Suez Canal, and the straits of Malacca), and therein lies its strategic importance. Today the Turkish Straits carry the heaviest volume of shipping traffic of any waterway in the world. This has been so throughout history. The Gallipoli peninsula has high ground from which control over the straits may be exerted, and thus control of the peninsula has strategic value. This unfortunate happenstance of geography has, in turn, brought armies to this place since the dawn of civilization.

On the Asian shore lie the ruins of Homer's Troy, and while elements of the *Iliad* may be dismissed, there were surely wars waged there in the eleventh or twelfth century BCE. These wars are thought to have been fought over trade routes and access to the Black Sea. Classically the Dardanelles Strait was called the Hellespont, and in 480 BCE the Persian king Xerxes I built floating pontoon bridges over it so that his armies might invade Greece. In 334 BCE, Alexander the Great crossed in the opposite direction, stopping briefly at Troy to visit oracles and make sacrifices. Romans and Byzantines subsequently crossed the strait at Gallipoli, as did the Christian crusaders marching east toward Jerusalem in the 1100s. They were followed by the Ottoman Turks traveling in the other direction in a wave of conquest in the early 1400s. Shortly after the conquest of Constantinople in 1453, Sultan Mehmed II ordered the construction of twin fortresses at the narrows, one of which—Kilitbahir Kalesi (which translates to "Lock on the Sea Castle")—still stands on the peninsula at Eceabat.

In spite of the Ottoman conquest, the population of the peninsula remained mostly Greek, with Ottoman military garrisons sprinkled around the forts and towns. These medieval-like fortresses decayed over the following centuries until 1807, at which time a British fleet under Admiral Sir John Duckworth broke through the defenses into the Sea of Marmara. The Ottomans recognized the vulnerability of the peninsula and gradually improved the defenses and brought them to modern standards. By 1900 there were a dozen forts lining the strait, armed with a hundred heavy ship-killing cannon. The Balkan Wars of 1912–1913 brought more cannon and more soldiers to the peninsula, and as many as ten thousand men lost their lives there in those years. The peninsula has never been a place of culture or beauty or grace; from time immemorial it has always been a place of encounter and of war.

Gallipoli's Place in Memory

The assassination of Archduke Francis Ferdinand in Sarajevo, combined with the alliance system, imperialism, and militarism, slid an unsuspecting Europe into war in the summer of 1914. In November of that year, the Ottomans went to war with the Triple Entente of Britain, France, and Russia in an attempt to preserve their failing empire. However, by joining the German-led alliance, the Ottomans, in turn, unleashed the might of the industrialized world on itself. Over the winter events arose that brought war back to the Gallipoli peninsula. Firstly, the western front in Europe devolved into a stalemated killing machine from which no decisive result appeared possible. Secondly, the Ottoman grip on landlocked Russia prevented the Russians from exporting grain and from importing critical ammunition and war supplies. Russia began to weaken. This caused London to consider ways to fight the war at lesser human cost while opening a supply route to Russia. The aged and tottering Ottoman Empire, sometimes called the "sick man of Europe," appeared to be an easy target. Recent history appeared to validate this idea, as the Russians had taken most of the Caucasus region in 1826 and 1877, the British had taken Egypt and Cyprus, the Italians had taken Libya, and the Greeks, Serbs, and Bulgars had conquered almost the entire Balkan peninsula in 1913. The truncated remains of the Ottoman Empire included not just Turks, but Jews, Armenians, Greeks, and Kurds, as well as millions of refugees from the lost territories.

Winston Churchill, then first lord of the British Admiralty, advanced the idea in January 1915 that the Royal Navy might fight its way through the strait and bombard Constantinople, forcing the Ottomans to surrender. Once accomplished, Russia might be resupplied and its armies reequipped. This was strategic thinking on a grand scale that leveraged traditional British sea power and promised to conserve lives. The British war cabinet launched its navy against the Gallipoli peninsula. But all attempts to break through the Ottoman defenses failed and, after losing a number of battleships to Ottoman underwater mines, the war cabinet decided to launch an amphibious attack using land forces.

Once again armed men from distant lands encountered one another on the Gallipoli peninsula. The land campaign began on April 25, 1915, with amphibious landings on five beaches on the peninsula and on one beach on the Asiatic side. It involved seventy thousand men from the United Kingdom (including Scots, Irish, and Welsh), Australia, New Zealand, and France (including North Africans). (See Map 10.2.) About half of the men were prewar regulars and the rest were enthusiastic volunteers. The Ottomans had a similar number of men, and their conscripted army included Turks, Arabs, Kurds, and a number of smaller minorities. The senior officers on both sides were well trained, but the junior officers often lacked military education and experience. The British army

was styled the Mediterranean Expeditionary Force, and some of its units were
full of well-known young men educated in
Britain's universities. Poet Rupert Brooke
(who was famously known as "the hand-
somest man in England"), athlete Bernard
Freyberg, wealthy American expatriate
Johnny Dodge, prime minister's son Ray-
mond Asquith, and brilliant author Patrick
Shaw-Stewart were chief among them.
These men and others like them, products
of a Victorian and Edwardian classical education, instilled a famously literary bent
to the expedition and were inclined to
think of themselves as the descendents of
Achilles and Agamemnon—after all, Troy
itself was just across the strait!

The expedition began with a carefree
confidence borne of inexperience and a
general contempt for "Johnny Turk." All of
that ended shortly after dawn on April 25,
when the pitiably equipped Turks held
their position and the killing began. The Allies scarcely made it off the beaches, and
the fronts froze in place, with a "no-man's-
land" developing between the trenches as
the dynamics of war in the twentieth cen-

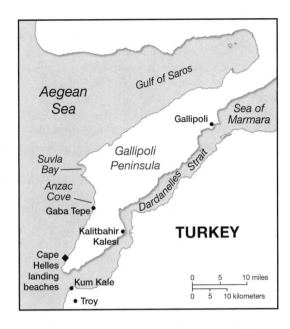

Map 10.2. The Gallipoli Campaign of 1915

*Just before dawn on April 25, 1915, the British landed at the tip of
the Gallipoli peninsula, while the Australians landed just to the north
of Gaba Tepe. The firmly entrenched Ottoman Turks were able to
hold them to the beaches. The ruins of Homer's Troy lie on the Asian
shore, just south of Kum Kale.*

tury imposed themselves at Gallipoli. The quiet peninsula was blasted with high explo-
sives and the campaign dragged on inconclusively. In August the British launched a
second amphibious assault on the peninsula just to the north of the ANZAC beachhead
at Suvla Bay in an attempt to outflank the stubborn Ottomans. By this time the number
of men engaged had grown to almost half a million.

The nature of the fighting reflected the horror of early-twentieth-century conflict,
which was characterized by trench warfare. The distance between the opposing trenches
on the peninsula ranged from several hundreds of yards to as little as twenty. It was suici-
dal to raise one's head above the parapet, and the soldiers rigged periscope sights to fire
their rifles. However, it would be incorrect to use the fighting at Gallipoli as a metaphor
for the emerging trench warfare of the age. In truth, the campaign there was fought at a
much lower tempo and at lower levels of intensity than what was happening in France in
1915. Gallipoli was a soldier's battle. It was not what is known as *materialschlacht* (a war
of armaments), characterized by millions of shells and hundreds of machines. Both the
Allies and the Ottomans were short of artillery shells and, as a result, rifles and machine
guns were more heavily relied upon. Shelling on the peninsula was episodic, rather than
continuous as in France, and luck played more of a role in whether one was wounded or
not. Moreover, poison gas and tanks were not used in Gallipoli, and the battles took on a
more human dimension.

Unlike the mass anonymity of the western front, individual personalities emerged on
the Gallipoli peninsula, and in this regard it was more like the battles of the previous

century. Reinforcing this point, most of the time the combatants at Gallipoli observed archaic rules of war, making this a *kreig ohne hass* (war without hate), in that they did not massacre prisoners and observed truces to evacuate wounded and bury the dead. Atrocities and war crimes were almost unknown on the peninsula. It then came to pass, amidst the violence, that the soldiers of each side evolved a grudging respect and admiration for their adversaries. "Johnny Turk" became a term of affection rather than one of derision. And, in a sense, the battles were "clean" in that there were no civilians involved; the Ottomans had withdrawn them from the battle space earlier. While the battles there were brutal, they were not as soul shattering or as punishing as those raging in France in the same year. In the end, the casualties from the Gallipoli campaign numbered about a quarter of those from the Marne, Verdun, and the Somme. As a consequence of these factors, the veterans of the Gallipoli campaign were inclined to remember their experiences and their adversaries in a more favorable light than their counterparts elsewhere in the war.

The campaign was widely reported in the newspapers, and a vocabulary and a nomenclature entered the popular mind in Britain and in the antipodes. Gully Ravine, V Beach, Lone Pine, and Kirthia became household names in those areas and on the Ottoman side as well. The Ottomans also began to make references to Zengindere (Rich Man's Valley) and Kanlisirt (Bloody Ridge).

Heroes emerged—at W Beach the Lancashire Fusiliers famously won "six VCs before breakfast" (the Victoria Cross is Britain's equivalent to the American Congressional Medal of Honor), and the Ottomans lionized Corporal Seyit, who loaded and fired a giant naval gun alone in the smoldering rubble of Fort Rumeli Mecidiye. The campaign dragged on into the fall before the British decided that it was unwinnable and that the men and resources might be used to better effect elsewhere. Finally in December they abandoned the Anzac beachhead and pulled out of Cape Helles at the peninsula's tip on January 6, 1916. The campaign was over. It destroyed the political career of Winston Churchill, who was blamed for the disaster and forced from office in disgrace, but created a favorable reputation for a little-known Ottoman colonel named Mustafa Kemal (later known as Atatürk). Casualties remain hard to estimate but were roughly equal. Each side lost about sixty thousand men and suffered another one hundred thousand wounded, although these losses were far more serious for the smaller Ottoman Empire than the larger British and French Empires. By this time, any hope that the war might be brought to a rapid and cheap conclusion was dead, since the campaign was a clear win for the Ottomans.

World War I continued until 1918, and the Ottoman possessions in the Caucasus region, Palestine, and Mesopotamia were the scenes of much bitter fighting as the Ottomans continued to engage millions of Allied soldiers. In the end, the exhausted Ottoman Empire collapsed under the weight of Allied offensives. The war, however, never returned to the Dardanelles, and after the campaign the Ottomans recovered the abandoned debris of the invasion force and went about preparing for a future attack that never came. The peninsula reverted to the quiet backwater that it had been before the Allied landings. Many thousands of Allied dead were already buried in temporary cemeteries, and the Ottoman dead were simply buried in mass graves. Thousands of corpses, intact and otherwise, however, remained to be discovered and buried, a process that the Ottoman garrison began immediately. The bodies were sometimes physically locked together in death in a macabre aftermath of hand-to-hand combat. Such was the nature of the fighting. After the armistice in 1918, the Allied nations all sent graves registration teams to the peninsula to account for the dead, as well as to begin the process of formally acquiring land for permanent commonwealth cemeteries.

Gallipoli as a Place of Mourning

The new Turkish Republic arose from the ashes of the dismembered Ottoman Empire and formally occupied the peninsula in 1923. Over time many of the residents were allowed to return, but most of the Greeks were relocated to Greece itself in the vast population swaps of the postwar world. By the early 1930s, the Commonwealth War Graves Commission, as well as its French counterpart, had constructed a dozen permanent cemeteries in the Cape Helles and Anzac beachheads. The Turks maintained their mass graves but accounted for all of their casualties man by man. Memorials and monuments were built there by both nations and by veterans' organizations. Over the course of the decade, then through World War II and long into the Cold War, the Turkish army occupied the peninsula and prepared its defenses to meet first the Nazis and then the Soviets. Civilians were prohibited from entering most of the military zones, which remained largely as they had been left in 1915. At the end of the Cold War in 1991, however, the peninsula was demilitarized, which enabled the construction of a large international battlefield and peace park.

Gallipoli today occupies a unique place among the historic battlefields of the world because it is very nearly intact as it appeared in 1915. The signatures of modernity have encroached on every battlefield in the world today—strip malls, gas stations, condominiums and the like crowd in and erode both time and place. Sadly, most of the world's battlefields are cluttered and fenced in to such an extent that it is hard to imagine that a battle was ever fought there. Gettysburg in the United States is a notable exception, as the United States National Park Service struggles to maintain the historical integrity of the site. Gallipoli, however, avoided the contamination of modern human activity.

The Allied cemeteries are now counterbalanced by Turkish ones. The Allied monuments and memorials of the 1920s and 1930s have been supplemented by a number of counterpart Turkish monuments commemorating the Ottoman effort. The Ottoman soldiers buried in mass graves have been exhumed and reburied in individually marked graves. Unfortunately, their names are largely unknown. The most dominant memorial remains the massive, square-pillared Turkish one overlooking the Dardanelles. Modern roads crisscross the peninsula and allow for easier access to the landing beaches and to the sites of the battles that raged there. Indeed, it may be said that the Gallipoli peninsula today has become, by design, a place of memory and a place of mourning.

Gallipoli: Looking Back, Looking Forward

In many ways the Gallipoli campaign was a coming of age for Australia and New Zealand as these nations entered the mainstream of the twentieth century. The battles and associated losses served to drive the peoples of those nations to build national identities and a sense of national pride. Britain had asked for help from her commonwealth, and the selfless and immediate response was instrumental in the survival of the British Empire. This was a critical affirmation for the governments and peoples of the former colonies. Likewise, the campaign was important for the Ottomans as it served notice on the Western imperialist powers that the Ottomans were back in the game. The Turks inherited this legacy, and Gallipoli served as a sort of national turning point from being humiliated as the "sick man of Europe" to being known again as an opponent of some worth. For the British, however, the campaign was a wholesale disaster—human casualties and lost prestige aside, its government nearly collapsed, the failure caused the high command to divide into opposing strategic camps, and instead of shortening the war the campaign encouraged the Ottomans to increase their efforts, thereby broadening the conflict in the Middle East. Moreover, the long war nearly bankrupted Britain, weakening it and starting its long slide from imperial empire to small nation-state.

In the years since the end of World War I, the Gallipoli experience and its remembrance have been an important part of the building of friendly relations between the Turks and their former enemies. For many years after the war, it was not uncommon for British, Australian, and New Zealand veterans groups to visit the peninsula and join with Turkish veterans groups for commemorative observances. Reciprocally, Turks went to London, Canberra, and Wellington to pay tribute there as well. Old soldiers and their commanders forged strong friendships in the first half of the twentieth century. The celebration of Anzac Day on the peninsula, held within sight of the landing beach and its cemetery, became institutionalized and drew the presidents and prime ministers of four countries. In effect, a lasting and transgenerational friendship has been embedded into the collective consciousness of the nations that spent the blood of their young men on the Gallipoli peninsula. Although the survivors themselves are now long dead, the tradition continues, and April 25 remains a day of memory and mourning on the peninsula.

One of the remarkable things about this memory in Turkey today is the strong attachment that modern Turks have to their former enemies. This deep friendship carries over to embassies around the world. Turkish ambassadors attend the Anzac Day remembrance at the Australian embassy, and the Australian ambassador likewise attends the Turkish embassy's annual Atatürk lecture remembering that great leader's demise. To this day it remains a source of pride in both countries when one can say that one's ancestor fought at Gallipoli.

One of the more significant outcomes of the Gallipoli campaign was the emergence of a cadre of seasoned and capable battlefield generals such as Mustafa Kemal Atatürk, Fevzi Çakmak, and Yakup Şübaşı, who later led the nationalist army to victory in the Turkish War of Independence in 1922. There were about forty of these men, and they became division, corps, and army commanders in the forces that drove the Greeks and Allies out of occupied Anatolia after the end of World War I. Under Atatürk's determined leadership, they helped established the modern Turkish state as a secular republic with a democratic constitution.

In truth, since the 1880s the school-trained officers of the Ottoman army were the engine of modernity that dragged the empire into the twentieth century. It is unlikely that Atatürk could have implemented his reforms without their support. These reforms included a modern, French-styled secular law code; the establishment of a genuine parliament; universal childhood education; the emancipation of women and their inclusion in higher education, medicine, and government; the creation of a Western alphabet to replace the Ottoman Turkish Arabic script; electrification; and industrialization. In 2011 Turkey had the sixteenth-largest economy in the world and was a rising cultural and industrial hegemon in the Middle East. Modern Turkish historians have come to view modern Turkey as an outcome of the processes begun by a cadre of leaders seasoned in the cauldron of Gallipoli.

GLOBAL ENCOUNTERS AND CONNECTIONS:
The Modern Legacy of Gallipoli's Combat

The Gallipoli campaign reflects the essential non-Western struggle to combat European imperialism through the development of a program of Westernization and modernization. It may be argued that much of the success of the Ottoman army in the Gallipoli campaign was the result of reform efforts undertaken to modernize the military in the wake of the Ottoman defeat in the Balkan Wars of 1912 and 1913. (During these wars the Ottomans lost their most productive province, which they had held since the 1400s.) This modernization was, for the most part, a function of the influence of a political party called the Committee of Union and Progress but more commonly known as the "Young Turks." The Young Turks were led by the triumvirate of Enver Pasha, Taalat Pasha, and Cemal Pasha. They really were quite young men, highly educated and fluent in European languages and dedicated to the Westernization and modernization of the moribund Ottoman Empire. They were committed to the restoration of Ottoman power and to regaining the ability to throw off the economic and military domination of the imperialist European powers.

Rather than rejecting European ideas and technology, the Young Turks embraced them. In this they took encouragement from the example of the Japanese Meiji Restoration as that region struggled to build an educated and industrialized nation-state. Of particular note was the impact of Japanese military and naval victories, as their forces shattered their Russian counterparts in the Russo-Japanese War of 1904–1905. The Japanese example had a profound effect and proved conclusively that non-Europeans could defeat Europeans when they were comparably equipped with modern weapons and training. The Ottoman high command eagerly studied the reports of its officers who observed the great battles of Port Arthur and Mukden and used the lessons contained in them to reconstruct the obsolescent Ottoman army along modern European lines. By 1915 the Ottoman army could stand toe-to-toe with Europeans and win on the battlefield, something that had not happened since the early seventeenth century. In truth, the victory at Gallipoli validated the Young Turks' efforts in clear but brutal terms.

Gallipoli's Legacy as a Failed Strategy in Global War

It may be argued that the failure of the British campaign in 1915 was monumentally significant in changing the course of World War I by setting the conditions that led to the overthrow of the czar and to the Russian Revolution. This stemmed from the Russian Empire's principal strategic problem in 1915, which involved its geographic isolation from its allies and its world markets. Russian grain from the Ukraine, the empire's main export, could not be shipped through the Ottoman-controlled Turkish Straits. This in turn reduced foreign revenues to a trickle. Making things worse, the antique Russian industrial base could not supply the army with adequate amounts of the modern equipment of war—artillery, machine guns, aircraft, shells, and ammunition. The Russian army had surplus manpower but could not equip or supply its soldiers.

The strategic intent of the Gallipoli campaign was to secure a sea-lane to the Russian Black Sea ports, thus allowing the Russians to export and sell their grain and then use the revenues to purchase and import war material and weapons. When the campaign failed, the Russian army became progressively weaker, and casualties mounted as the czar's poorly equipped soldiers tried to fight off the well-trained and well-armed German army.

The catastrophic defeats and losses suffered by the Russians led directly to a collapse of national will, the March revolution, and the abdication of the czar. With no end in sight, the continuance of the war by Alexander Kerensky's government set the conditions that enabled V. I. Lenin to overthrow the regime in October 1917. The British failure at Gallipoli drove nails in the coffin of the czar's empire.

Advancements in War in the Twentieth Century

The Gallipoli campaign was the first great amphibious invasion of the modern age. The British had no experience in landing a force of seventy thousand men on an enemy shore and, as such, it was largely an *ad hoc* affair involving a large variety of expedient measures. For example, steam launches towed clumsy barges packed full of men to the shore, whereupon the men leapt over the sides onto the sand. In one case, a ship named the *River Clyde,* carrying several thousand men, was rammed intentionally onto a beach and the men were slaughtered by machine gun fire as they tried to climb out of the ship. Commanders remained behind on the battleships, trying to assist by directing naval gunfire and were thus unable to lead their men forward. The evacuation of casualties was problematic, as was the resupply of such basics as food and water.

After the war, the Royal Marines and the United States Marine Corps studied the failures and came to understand the tactical lessons learned, from which modern amphibious fighting doctrines emerged. The resource-rich Americans then developed specialized equipment to support these new doctrinal ideas. Examples included amphibious vehicles; landing craft with bow doors that dropped on the beach; armored tank-carrying, flat-bottomed ships that beached on the sand; ship-to-shore radios; and specialized aircraft that could be used as aerial artillery. As the Allies went on the offensive in World War II, this equipment and the lessons learned from Gallipoli proved invaluable in the massive invasions that were necessary to bring land forces to bear against the Axis powers. The Allied amphibious operations in Italy and Normandy, in France (D-Day), and in the Pacific at places like Iwo Jima and Okinawa created iconic images of World War II. To a large extent these operations were successful because the Allies had the right mix of specialized equipment and fighting tactics needed to get off the beaches quickly. The lives lost at Gallipoli were, in some sense, an expensive investment in intellectual understanding about the nature of war in the twentieth century, which in turn enabled the Allies to defeat the Axis powers in World War II.

Gallipoli's Contributions to Foundation Myths and Identity

All nations and peoples have foundation myths that form the basis for their shared identities. Often these foundation myths encourage and propel a sense of nationalism as well. The American myth focuses on self-reliance and taming the frontiers, which frame the American identity of rugged individualism. Americans believe that they are somehow a different kind of people, and the concept of American exceptionalism is based on this. Similarly, the Gallipoli campaign formed a major component of the foundation myths of Australia and New Zealand.

Campaigns such as Gallipoli placed amateur Anzac soldiers under rigid and class-conscious British officers, who observed strict military and social protocols. Making things worse, the Australian volunteers were impressive physical specimens in comparison to their conscripted, and, quite often, underdeveloped and slight British comrades. As the war progressed, the ANZAC came to be characterized as ill-disciplined but so curiously reliable in combat that the men could be used as shock troops. The consequent high casualties then drove the evolution of a mythology: first, the imperialist British Empire came to rely on its white colonial subjects as cannon fodder in a pointless series of European wars. Second, the British failed to recognize the superior soldierly qualities of the Anzacs—their physical prowess, individualism, and initiative. Lastly, uncaring and incompetent British generals recklessly threw away the lives of colonial soldiers in order to save British lives. Cumulatively, these ideas created the feeling that the British had, very carelessly and very intentionally, wasted Anzac and Kiwi lives. After the war, awareness coalesced in popular memory of what might be termed antipodal countertraits to British military regulation and rigidity. Today Australians consider themselves egalitarian, informal, and irreverent. They have an image as a muscular and independent people, and they have become strongly nationalistic in their own right. The evolution of identity from colonial subject to Australian and New Zealander, arguably, was born in the Gallipoli perimeter.

Gallipoli's Effect on History

American historian Dr. George Cassar asserts that more books have been written in English about the Gallipoli campaign than any other campaign in World War I. The reason that this is so, in this author's view, derives from the proposition that the campaign presents the greatest "what if?" of that war. Indeed, Churchill's strategic design to end the war rapidly by succoring Russia and defeating a key German ally had real possibilities, and it seemed close to success on at least three occasions (March 18, April 25, and August 6, 1915). In retrospect and to a much greater degree, Gallipoli seems so much more achievable than the Marne, Verdun, or the Somme. In our popular memory, Gallipoli has become the singular campaign that might have succeeded. What if it had? Imagine a shortened war without the millions of subsequent casualties, imagine the Russian czar remaining in power, imagine a negotiated peace without the indignities of Versailles, imagine a more moderate settlement in the Middle East, and imagine a world without the Soviet Union, fascism, and Nazism. Imagine an entirely different twentieth century—ahistorical, to be sure—but, just imagine . . .

ENCOUNTERS AS TOLD: PRIMARY SOURCES

What happened on the Gallipoli peninsula in 1915 was, in many ways, the inevitable result of its strategic location. In this regard, it is the place itself that matters. Gallipoli has always been a contested nexus—a place where armies come together and a place where men die. Throughout history, men have come from distant places such as ancient Persia and Greece, medieval and modern Britain, India, Australia, and even Newfoundland. Gallipoli is misty with antiquity, littered with ancient ruins, and pockmarked with the shell craters of more modern killing machines. Time and era, therefore, seem less important than place.

This section contains three primary source documents that illustrate the importance of Gallipoli as a place of encounter. The first document is a poem by a British officer for whom the peninsula is a place linking him directly to the past. The second is a private letter from a British civilian war correspondent that advocates actions to be taken in the then-future of 1915. The third document relates the experiences of an Ottoman soldier in captivity who encounters a British officer and fellow Gallipoli veteran and reflects on human nature and the memory of wartime experiences.

Achilles in the Trench, by Patrick Shaw-Stewart

The English public-school men of the British Mediterranean Expeditionary Force understood the import of Gallipoli's connections to time and place. The most vivid exposition of this connection between the past and present (at least as it was in 1915) is found in Patrick Shaw-Stewart's poem *Achilles in the Trench*, in which he returns to the trenches on the peninsula after a three-day rest on the nearby island of Imbros. The poem articulates the combat soldier's sense of his own inability to change his destiny. The brilliant and literate Shaw-Stewart was killed in action in France later in the war.

- Who was Achilles and how does his experience relate to that of Patrick Shaw-Stewart?

- What did Shaw-Stewart mean by "fatal second Helen, Why must I follow thee?"

- How does Shaw-Stewart use shared experiences to draw the past and present together?

I saw a man this morning
Who did not wish to die
I ask, and cannot answer,
If otherwise wish I.

Fair broke the day this morning
Against the Dardanelles;
The breeze blew soft, the morn's cheeks
Were cold as cold sea-shells

But other shells are waiting
Across the Aegean sea,
Shrapnel and high explosive,
Shells and hells for me.

O hell of ships and cities,
Hell of men like me,

Fatal second Helen,
Why must I follow thee?

Achilles came to Troyland
And I to Chersonese;
He turned from wrath to battle,
And I from three days' peace.

Was it so hard, Achilles,
So very hard to die?
Thou knewest and I know not;
So much the happier am I.

I will go back this morning
From Imbros over the sea;
Stand in the trench, Achilles,
Flame-capped, and shout for me.

Source: Patrick Shaw-Stewart, *Achilles in the Trench*, 1915, http://nauplion.net/trench.html.

Personal Letter from British War Correspondent Ellis Ashmead-Bartlett to British Prime Minister Herbert Asquith, dated September 8, 1915

Dissent in wartime is not a new part of the human condition. As the Gallipoli campaign began to go bad for the British in the late summer of 1915, there were individuals who believed that the true facts, as they saw them, ought to be brought to the attention of the decision makers in London. One such man was Ellis Ashmead-Bartlett, a journalist and correspondent on the Gallipoli peninsula, who thought that the entire campaign was a hopeless waste of men's lives, time, and resources. He had been heavily censored previously by the British commander, General Sir Ian Hamilton, who did not want Ashmead-Bartlett's pessimistic opinions heard in London. Seeking a way around this censorship, Ashmead-Bartlett took it upon himself to write a personal letter to British prime minister Herbert Asquith, and he entrusted his letter to the care of Australian correspondent Keith Murdoch, who was on his way to England. Up until this time the British government had received only positive reports from General Hamilton, but Ashmead-Bartlett's frank and discouraging views so alarmed Asquith that he turned against the campaign and advocated withdrawal.

Ashmead-Bartlett's letter was a damning indictment of the campaign and was particularly critical of General Ian Hamilton's leadership of the army. Not only did the military campaign fail, the public awareness of its mishandling was a leading cause in the collapse of Asquith's liberal government in the spring of 1916. In many ways, Ashmead-Bartlett's uncensored report was the 1915 equivalent of the 2011 WikiLeaks controversy and reflects the impact that uncensored reports may have on world events.

- How does Ashmead-Bartlett view the prospects for the British campaign to take the Dardanelles?

- What is the problem as he sees it?

- Would you consider Ashmead-Bartlett a patriot or a traitor? Please explain.

- To what extent is Ashmead-Bartlett similar or different from Daniel Ellsberg (the Pentagon Papers) or Bradley Manning (WikiLeaks)?

SEPTEMBER 8TH 1915

Dear Mr. Asquith,

I hope you will excuse the liberty I am taking in writing to you but I have the chance of sending this letter through by hand and I consider it absolutely necessary that you should know the true state of affairs out here. . . .

Personally I never thought the scheme decided on by Headquarters ever had the slightest chance of succeeding and all efforts now to make out that it only just failed owing to the failure of the 9th Corps to seize the Anafarta Hills bear no relation to the real truth. The operations did for a time make headway in an absolutely impossible country more than any general had a right to expect owing to the superlative gallantry of the Colonial Troops and the self-sacrificing manner in which they threw

away their lives against positions which should never have been attacked.

The main idea was to cut off the southern portion of the Turkish Army by getting astride of the Peninsula from Suvla Bay. The Staff seem to have carefully searched for the most difficult points and then threw away thousands of lives in trying to take them by frontal attacks.

The failure of the 9th Corps was due not so much to the employment of new and untried troops as to bad staff work. The generals had but a vague idea of the nature of the ground in their front and no adequate steps were taken to keep the troops supplied with water. In consequence many of these unfortunate volunteers went three days in very hot weather on one bottle of water and were yet expected to advance carrying heavy loads and to storm strong positions.

The army is in fact in a deplorable condition. Its morale as a fighting force has suffered greatly and the officers and men are thoroughly dispirited. The muddles and mismanagement beat anything that has ever occurred in our Military History.

The fundamental evil at the present moment is the absolute lack of confidence in all ranks in the Headquarters staff. The confidence of the army will never be restored until a really strong man is placed at its head. It would amaze you to hear the talk that goes on amongst the Junior commanders of Divisions and Brigades. Except for the fact that the traditions of discipline still hold the force together you would imagine that the units were in an open state of mutiny against Headquarters.

The Commander in Chief and his Staff are openly spoken of, and in fact only mentioned at all with derision. One hates to write of such things but in the interests of the country at the present crisis I feel they ought to be made known to you. . . .

It is no use pretending that our prospects for the winter are bright. We do not hold a single commanding position on the Peninsula and at all three points Helles, Anzac and Suvla Bay we are everywhere commanded by the enemy's guns. This means that throughout the winter all the beaches and lines of communication to the front trenches will be under constant shell fire. Suvla Bay is especially exposed. The Turks are firing a fair amount of ammunition but it is obvious they are feeling the shortage or else are carefully husbanding their supply otherwise they could shell us off the Peninsula at some points altogether.

No one seems to know out here what we are going to do in the future and I am so afraid we shall drag on in a state of uncertainty until the season is too far advanced for us to make proper preparations to face the coming winter in a certain measure of comfort and security. . . . I have only dealt with our own troubles and difficulties. The enemy of course has his. But to maintain as I saw stated in an official report that his losses in the recent fighting were far heavier than ours is a childish falsehood which deceives no one out here. He was acting almost the whole time on the defensive and probably lost about one third of our grand total.

You may think I am too pessimistic but my views are shared by the large majority of the army. The confidence of the troops can only be restored by an immediate change in the supreme command. Even if sufficient drafts are sent out to make good our losses we shall never succeed operating from our present positions. . . .

I have taken the liberty of writing very fully because I have no means of knowing how far the real truth of the situation is known in England and how much the Military Authorities disclose. I thought therefore that perhaps the opinions of an independent observer might be of value to you at the present juncture. I am of course breaking the censorship regulations by sending this letter through but I have not the slightest hesitation in doing so as I feel it is absolutely essential for you to know the truth. . . . Hoping you will therefore excuse the liberty I have taken.

Believe me

Yours very truly

E. Ashmead-Bartlett
The Rt. Hon. H. H. Asquith
10 Downing Street

Source: "Ellis Ashmead-Bartlett's Letter to Prime Minister Asquith," September 8, 1915, www.firstworldwar.com/source/ashmeadbartlett_letter.htm.

"The Battle of Anzac Cove, Gallipoli," by Ali Demirel

These are the 1981 recollections of ninety-six-year-old Ali Demirel from Biga-Gundogdu Village, Turkey, who served in the Ottoman 27th Infantry Regiment at Gallipoli. Demirel was captured by the British in Palestine later in the war, and he begins this part of his narrative with the experience of marching into a prisoner-of-war camp.

- What do you surmise happened to the British officer lamed at Gallipoli?

- How would you explain the evolving relationship between captor and prisoner in this particular case?

- What factors contributed to this relationship?

- How would you characterize the relationship that developed after two years?

The British has divided us into convoys of thousands. We have walked for eight days and arrived at Egypt. There were twelve sections enclosed by wire. I was in the fourth section, where I have stayed for two years.

It was in our first days; a lame British officer came. He was walking with a stick. We were standing. He had a translator. The translator shouted:

"Is there anybody from the 27th Regiment?"

I thought to myself that they cannot kill me and stepped forward.

"I am," I said.

The lame officer came nearby; he kissed my hands and eyes. I think he was the commander of the prisoners. God knows; he made me comfortable. He gave a private tent to me. Moreover, he said, "take two friends of yours."

Later I have learnt that he was wounded in the Anzac Cove. He was so scared. The translator told that the British were very frightened because they thought the Turks would kill all of them. Anyway, he paid me twenty Turkish pounds salary every month. He also gave me eighty boxes of cigarettes every week. He told me "sell them and make money."

He came to my tent very often. I made him a chest out of German screens and coated it with velvet, like a Turkish dowry chest. Also, I have made him two pairs of half boots by tearing the British boots. I even fixed the nails using my hands. He gave me two Ottoman golden coins. He has written, "Made by the prisoners" on the chest and taken to Britain. He talked rarely.

Source: Ali Demirel, "The Battle of Anzac Cove, Gallipoli, 25 April 1915," http://alh-research.tripod.com/Light_Horse/index.blog/2010599/the-battle-of-anzac-cove-gallipoli-25-april-1915-ali-demirel-account/.

Further Reading

Cassar, George H. *Kitchener's War: British Strategy from 1914 to 1916.* Washington, DC: Brassey's Inc., 2004.

Erickson, Edward J. *Gallipoli: The Ottoman Campaign.* Barnsley, England: Pen & Sword Books, 2010.

Haythornthwaite, Phillip J. *Gallipoli 1915.* London: Ospry Press, n.d.

Holt, Tonie, and Valmai Holt. *Major and Mrs. Holt's Battlefield Guide Gallipoli.* Barnsley, England: Leo Cooper, 2000.

James, Robert Rhodes. *Gallipoli*. New York: Macmillan, 1965.
Macleod, Jenny. *Gallipoli: Making History*. London: Frank Cass, 2004.
Prior, Robin. *Gallipoli: The End of the Myth*. New Haven, CT: Yale University Press, 2009.
Strachan, Hew. *The First World War: Volume I: To Arms*. Oxford: Oxford University Press, 2001.

Web Resources

ANZAC Tradition, Australian War Memorial,
    www.awm.gov.au/commemoration/anzac/anzac_tradition.asp.
Canakkale Turkish Martyrs' Memorial (Abide), Gallipoli, Turkey,
    www.ww1cemeteries.com/other_cemeteries_ext/canakkale_memorial_abide.htm.
Diaries, Memorials, and Personal Reminiscences, The World War I Document Archive,
    http://wwi.lib.byu.edu/index.php/Diaries,_Memorials,_Personal_Reminiscences.
First World War Diaries, Australian War Memorial,
    www.awm.gov.au/collection/war_diaries/first_world_war/class.asp?levelID=78.
FirstWorldWar.com, http://www.firstworldwar.com/battles/gf.htm.
Lone Pine Memorial, Turkey,
    www.ww1cemeteries.com/other_cemeteries_ext/lone_pine_mem_turkey.htm.
100 Events of the Gallipoli Campaign, www.anzacsite.gov.au/5environment/timelines/100-
    events-gallipoli-campaign/august-december-1914.html.
Reports on Gallipoli, The World War I Document Archive,
    http://wwi.lib.byu.edu/index.php/Reports_on_Gallipoli.

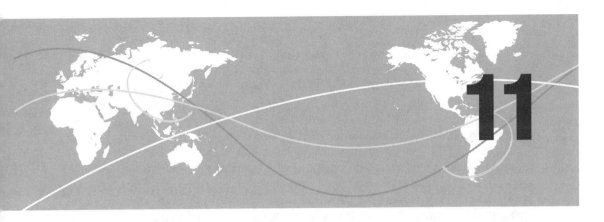

St. Petersburg

The Russian Revolution and the Making of the Twentieth Century

(1890–1918)

ELAINE MCCLARNAND MACKINNON

THE MAJESTIC CITY OF ST. PETERSBURG WAS THE CAPITAL OF THE RUSSIAN Empire from 1712 to 1918. Built on the shores on the Neva River, it owes its existence to the will of Tsar Peter I, Russia's visionary ruler, who saw it as his "window to the West"—an outlet to the Baltic Sea and to Europe. It is an architectural treasure paying tribute to Peter's imperial imagination—a truly magnificent city, romantically situated on a series of islands crisscrossed by rivers and canals, with stunning palaces, theaters, and churches. Yet it is also a reminder of the Russian state's penchant for pursuing its goals regardless of the human cost. The site chosen for the city was marshy, damp swampland, situated on the sixtieth parallel, the same as southern Alaska. The area proved to be pestilential and prone to bitterly cold winds, frequent ice storms, and periodic flooding. It exacted a high death toll from the very beginning. Peter conscripted hundreds of thousands of peasants to build the city from scratch, and over two hundred thousand died from disease, exposure, and starvation.

My first encounter with St. Petersburg came in the summer of 1991. I was a graduate student working on my dissertation, and I came to interview Russian historians and gather research materials. Regrettably, I did not make it in time for the famed "White

Nights" of June, when the city enjoys twenty-four hours of daylight and people forsake sleep so as not to miss a moment of this enchanting period. As a Westerner, I fell instantly in love with the city's European flavor and architecture. I walked for hours along the Neva and its adjoining canals. I kept expecting to run into the city's frenetic founder himself as I explored what was once known as Zayachi Island, the original site for the city and for its first building, the Peter and Paul Fortress; Peter personally laid the first stone in 1703 and supervised much of the construction. This, along with the Admiralty naval yards, formed the historic center of the city; other signature buildings date from later periods but reflect Peter's desire to see European facades on Russian shores. I loved to gaze from the opposite shore at the blue Baroque-style Winter Palace, designed by the Italian architect Rastrelli during the reign of Empress Elizabeth, Peter's daughter, and at the glittering dome of the nineteenth-century St. Isaac's Cathedral. I would then cross over to meander down the main thoroughfare, the Nevsky Prospect, ideal for window shopping with all of its storefronts and markets. This was the original artery of the city, running from the Admiralty quarter to the Alexander Nevskii Monastery, designed to display spatially the link between God and tsar.

My visit coincided with the changes wrought in the Soviet Union by Mikhail Gorbachev's reforms. I traveled on the night train from Moscow, sharing my compartment with an elderly Russian man who told me of his fondness for American cowboy stories and the Wild West. My hostess in St. Petersburg took me all over the city and to the magnificent palaces located around its periphery. As a student of twentieth-century Russian history, I wanted to see the monuments of the 1917 revolutions, the Smolny Institute where the October Revolution began, and the battle cruiser *Aurora* that fired the famous shots on the Winter Palace. But my new Russian friends wanted to show me literary Petersburg: the streets and alleyways familiar to its famed writers Nikolai Gogol and Fyodor Dostoevsky and the residences of its beloved poets Alexander Pushkin and Anna Akhmatova. My only glimpse of revolutionary St. Petersburg came at the Winter Palace, when they showed me the door through which Alexander Kerensky, the head of the Provisional Government (Vremennoye Pravitel'stvo Rossii), passed as he fled the Bolshevik takeover.

During a later visit I confronted perhaps the most tragic moment in the city's past when I saw the areas devastated by the Nazi blockade during World War II, and my hostess's father recounted for me his family's struggle during the ensuing starvation that took over a million lives. This kindly man could not understand my vegetarianism and penchant for jogging and why anyone who could have meat so easily would not want it, and in a moment of exasperation told me that I would have made a perfect prisoner under Joseph Stalin since I only wanted to eat bread and drink hot tea. For me, St. Petersburg is always a living history lesson, allowing me to step back into multiple layers of Russia's past whether I am studying its public façade or reaching into the lived experiences of its human population. It is a city still linked by its architectural treasures with the power of the Russian tsarist state, and yet, as we will explore in this chapter, it was also the scene of its violent overthrow by frustrated women, striking workers, and mutinous soldiers.

ST. PETERSBURG AND THE WORLD:
Revolution and the Making of the Modern World

After its founding as Russia's portal to Europe, St. Petersburg grew into a truly cosmopolitan capital city at the forefront of modern trends in art, literature, music, and especially ballet. Throughout its cafés and salons there was a readiness for experimentation and a tremendous creative energy that reached all the way to Paris, London, and Berlin.

Although Russia experienced late industrialization, with economic modernization coming only in the 1880s and 1890s, nonetheless by 1900 a person could walk down the Nevsky Prospect and feel as though he or she was strolling through any major European city with fancy shops selling foreign items such as perfumes, exotic delicacies, and the latest fashions. Leading artists, musicians, and writers from all over the world were coming to St. Petersburg, and Russian artists in turn were meeting with great success on foreign tours. Scientists working in St. Petersburg universities and academies of science were pioneering new studies in behavioral science, chemistry, and other disciplines and forging connections with leading research institutes outside of Russia.

St. Petersburg was a major center of Russian industrialization, and as such it was an enormous magnet for foreign industrialists, businessmen, and managers from Germany, France, Belgium, Austria, and England. They owned a large share of the city's industry, as foreign capital and expertise played a major role in Russia's industrial drive. Many French and British investors owned Russian government bonds, as well as mines, factories, and large industrial plants. In fact, much of the economic power in St. Petersburg was concentrated in foreign-owned enterprises. Thus, true to its founder's wishes, the city had indeed become the empire's link to the outside world. For many, St. Petersburg was the face of Russia, despite the fact that in reality, St. Petersburg with its modernist European-style architecture and voluminous factory smokestacks was far removed from the villages of rural Russia where the majority of Russians still lived as the twentieth century dawned.

But, as this chapter will show, perhaps St. Petersburg's greatest link to modern world history was the fact that it became the setting in 1917 for two epochal revolutions. (See Map 11.1.) The first of these toppled the Romanov dynasty that had ruled Russia for over three hundred years, and the second established the world's first socialist government. To paraphrase the words of the famous American observer of the revolutions, reporter John Reed, the events in St. Petersburg "shook the world," opening the door to a monumental clash between two major ideologies of the twentieth century—capitalism and communism. The popular masses who rose up in the streets of St. Petersburg and across the Russian Empire, as well as the revolutionary leaders who sought to harness them, were inspired by democratic and egalitarian ideals that trace their roots to the Atlantic revolutions of the late eighteenth century and to nineteenth-century European socialist visionaries who sought to replace private property and capitalist competition with communal ownership and cooperation. Many in 1917 believed they were carrying out the predictions of German radical philosopher Karl Marx, who in his 1848 pamphlet *The Communist Manifesto* called for workers to rise up against their exploitive bourgeois factory owners, abolish private property, and establish economic as well as political equality. Socialism had found fertile soil in Russia, where communal traditions and egalitarian values were deeply rooted in rural life and culture, and by 1914 there were several different strands of socialist political movements focused either on peasants as the key revolutionary force (the Socialist Revolutionaries) or on factory workers (the Russian Social Democratic Workers Party, which in 1903 split into two branches, the Mensheviks and the Bolsheviks).

This chapter will trace this year of revolution in Russia, 1917, through the streets of St. Petersburg, which in 1914 was renamed Petrograd to provide a more Russian-sounding name after war with Germany had begun. It opens with the initial strikes and mutinies of February (March, by the Gregorian calendar, which the tsarist regime had never adopted) that overthrew the last Russian tsar, Nicholas II, and then moves through the tumultuous summer and fall as the liberal democratic Provisional Government

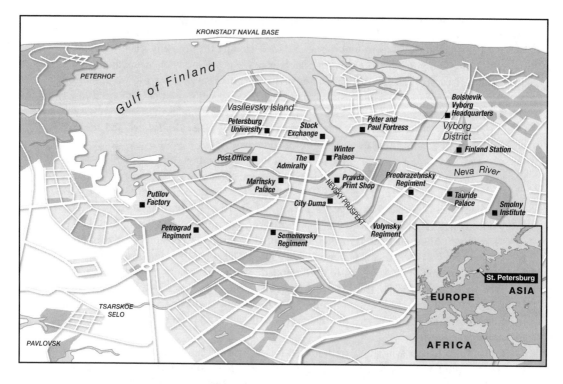

Map 11.1. St. Petersburg, 1917

St. Petersburg's historical significance as Peter the Great's "window to the West" is demonstrated here, as the city's location was situated on the Gulf of Finland and connected to Europe via the Baltic Sea. Also visible are the locations in the central districts of the city where the February and October Revolutions took place. The workers' districts were on one side of the Neva River and the soldiers' regiments on the other, while in the center were tsarist state buildings and wealthy palaces. In February 1917 the workers and soldiers converged on the central districts and took possession of many of these structures for their own revolutionary purposes.

struggled to maintain authority. It culminates in the October Revolution (November by the Gregorian Calendar) that saw the Bolshevik Party, a branch of Russian Marxism founded by Vladimir Lenin and officially renamed the Communist Party in 1918, overthrow this embattled government in the name of direct rule by workers, soldiers, and peasants.

This chapter draws from the pioneering work of historian and geographer James H. Bater on the history of modern St. Petersburg to show revolution as stemming from the impact of modernization, particularly rapid industrialization, in a traditional society governed by a stubborn autocratic ruler who refused to reform politically or socially. To maintain its great power status, Russia had to develop modern industry, but the tsar rejected the need for political liberalization despite growing demands from an emerging civil society. Added to this already incendiary formula were the massive economic, social, and demographic problems caused by Russia's entry into World War I. Thus, what occurred in the streets of St. Petersburg was an explosive encounter of nineteenth-century ideals and expectations with twentieth-century urban realities and the dislocations of modern war.

Prelude to Revolution: Industrialization, Modernization, and World War

St. Petersburg in 1917 was the largest city in the Russian Empire, with an estimated 2.4 million inhabitants. In addition to being the political and administrative capital, it was a major center for banking, commerce, and manufacturing. As a port city connected to the Baltic Sea, St. Petersburg served as the trade entrepôt for the whole empire, linking Russia to the world through its railway terminals and grain and stock exchanges. St. Petersburg was a religious capital as well, with major Orthodox Christian cathedrals, but, as a reflection of Russia's multinational makeup, it also became a focal point for Islam in the early twentieth century with the building of the Cathedral Mosque, the largest in Europe.

Also starkly visible were the inequities that fueled Russia's revolutionary upheaval. Its neighborhoods embodied the extremes of imperial grandeur and mass impoverishment characterizing tsarist society. Aristocratic families enjoyed palatial homes and apartments in the central districts, while just across the Neva, within view, were the crowded, unhealthy, working-class slums of the Vyborg district, ridden with mud, raw sewage, and poor roads. What distinguished St. Petersburg was the fact that the rich and the poor lived in close proximity to each other, heightening awareness of the gulf between them. Unlike in major cities such as London, Paris, and Berlin, neighborhoods segregated by class did not develop to the same extent in St. Petersburg, partly due to the inadequate development of public transportation. The poor had to be able to walk to work, and since most of the factories built after 1860 were located in or near the central city and its islands, this meant that the majority of the population lived within the official city limits. Thus, they saw on a daily basis the luxurious dwellings and the impressive imperial palaces owned by the aristocracy and upper-middle-class residents, who, unlike their counterparts in the West, did not move out to suburban areas. Class segregation did exist, but was not as much by neighborhoods as by floors. Even in the wealthiest districts one could find rich and poor sharing the same building. But the poor found themselves living in the wretchedly damp and cold cellars, which were frequently flooded, or on the very top floors, which had perpetually leaking ceilings. Also located within such prestigious neighborhoods as the Admiralty were large military garrisons. Segregation existed there in terms of public access—garrison soldiers and worker-migrants from the countryside found themselves barred, along with dogs, from parks and gardens.

What exacerbated these extremes was the explosive industrial growth that began after the emancipation of the serfs in 1861. By 1913 St. Petersburg housed nearly one thousand factories for industries that included metalworking, paper and printing, and food production. There was hardly any section of the city where you could not at least see or smell a factory or mill. This fueled in turn a major increase in population. Between 1850 and 1914 the city's population expanded from a little over five hundred thousand to more than two million. The increase was mainly due to the seasonal influx of thousands of migrants from the countryside who came seeking work; slightly less than one-third of the city's inhabitants in 1910 had been born in St. Petersburg. Many of these laborers were unmarried, male, and unfamiliar with the urban environment. Rural migration into the city and the workforce was certainly not an unusual pattern in global industrialization. But what distinguished the Russian case and contributed to volatility was the fact that the rural migrants retained close ties to their home villages, often returning seasonally to work in the fields and retaining proprietary rights in the village. This meant that urban workers remained in close touch with the problems and resentments of the countryside, where peasants fumed over high taxes and inadequate allotments of land. It also slowed the process of assimilation into urban mores and habits.

An additional source of tension was the fact that the urban population was growing exponentially but municipal services lagged considerably. St. Petersburg stood far behind comparable cities such as Berlin, New York, and Paris in the development of adequate housing, clean water, or transportation. Thousands were homeless, and in 1914 as many as one-fourth of inhabitants did not have access to running water. The central quarters of the city were so congested that some had to rent a hallway, or even a single corner or a bed in a room. The number of people living within single apartments was twice what it was in Paris or Vienna. The naturally cold and damp climate exacerbated the misery of the poor. The urban environment with its filthy cesspools and polluted water triggered perpetual outbreaks of cholera, typhus, diphtheria, tuberculosis, and pneumonia. Consequently, death rates in St. Petersburg exceeded those of any other major city in the Russian Empire, Europe, or the United States.

But the revolution was not just about poverty. St. Petersburg was at the forefront of Russian urbanization (less than one-fifth of the empire's population lived in cities in 1914) and in rising labor militancy. Nearly 70 percent of its population could read and write in 1910, which was double the rate found in most parts of Russia, though still well below the 90 percent rate found in Britain, France, Norway, and Sweden. Through growing access to modern forms of mass media—particularly the press—literate workers increasingly knew about gains being made by their counterparts in England and Western Europe, such as the right to strike, an eight-hour workday, and collective bargaining. It is also significant that St. Petersburg had the highest concentrations of workers in the world; factories tended to be much larger than they were in the United States and Europe and employed more persons. More than two-thirds of the city's workforce labored in enterprises with more than a thousand workers, including the Putilov Metal Works that employed over thirteen thousand. Workers' close proximity at home and work facilitated the spread of radical ideas, such as those circulating from European socialist parties and trade union movements that encouraged a greater sense of class consciousness and the entitlement of workers to rights, respect, and greater control over the conditions of their labor. Russian Menshevik and Bolshevik agitators consciously targeted these large enterprises with high concentrations of both skilled and unskilled laborers and found them to be prime recruiting grounds for teaching Marxist notions of class struggle and egalitarianism. Workers in these enterprises developed a strong class identity and embraced symbols of European socialism, such as May Day celebrations honoring labor. Among the most militant sectors in 1917 were the highly concentrated northern industrial areas across the Neva from the Winter Palace—the Vasilevsky, Petersburg and Vyborg districts.

The city had already been a cauldron for revolution in 1905, when desires for social justice and political liberalization drove workers, peasants, and middle-class elites to try unsuccessfully to overthrow Tsar Nicholas II. The tsarist regime survived thanks to the continued loyalty of the military and minor liberal concessions, including establishment of Russia's first parliament, the State Duma. But, weak in mind and will, Nicholas II could not accept his role as a constitutional monarch and refused to work with the Duma. He wanted Russia to stay politically and socially what it had been for centuries, a society dominated by the aristocracy, but due to modernization there were factory workers and middle-class professionals demanding rights and representation in public affairs. His oppressive responses to strikes and mass discontent earned him the nickname "Nicholas the Bloody."

What brought Russia to the brink of revolution again in 1917 was a confluence of these conditions of political discontent and social inequity with the outbreak of war in 1914. World War I for Russia was a disaster that brought catastrophic losses, inflation, and bureaucratic bungling. Early enthusiasm for the war quickly dissipated as the casualties mounted (over four million by August 1915), as did food and fuel shortages. The war disrupted railway service—the lifelines of the city that delivered its food, coal, iron, and oil. Nicholas II compounded the situation by taking over command of the armies and leaving political control largely in the hands of his wife, Empress Alexandra, and her disreputable adviser, the Siberian "holy man" Grigory Rasputin. This peasant-born healer had won Alexandria's undying devotion through his uncanny ability to control the bleeding of her only son and Nicholas's heir, Alexei, who suffered from hemophilia. But Rasputin's dissolute behavior and political incompetence discredited the regime even further. Nicholas rejected efforts of the Duma and other public organizations to assist in the war effort. Major defeats in battle led to serious losses of territory and men. By 1916 over five million soldiers were either dead, wounded, or had been taken prisoner. The tsar's disastrous leadership alienated every sector of society, including the highest ranks of the Russian military.

February 1917: The Revolution Begins

The winter of 1916–1917 brought intense cold, continued shortages of food and fuel, and mounting unrest. On January 9 and February 14, tens of thousands of workers, angry over the failure of wages to keep up with rising prices, went on strike. Revolution, though, did not come until one week later. It began in the streets of the Vyborg district when women workers spontaneously burst out in frustrated protest—they were tired of working long days and then standing in endless lines for bread that usually ran out before they could buy it. On February 23 women textile workers took advantage of a socialist holiday, International Women's Day, to march through the streets calling for bread and an end to the war. The women began inciting their male counterparts to join them, and as the day progressed, more and more factories shut down as workers rushed out to join the growing demonstration. Soon the disturbances spread toward the center, the left bank of the Neva River, where the government resided along with the wealthy upper classes. Strikes, meetings, and demonstrations swept across the city. By February 26, the third day of protest, there were over two hundred thousand people in the streets, and violence began to break out in accompaniment to cries of "down with the tsar."

What turned these popular street disturbances into a revolution was the mutiny of the soldiers, who on February 26 had been ordered by the tsar to suppress the disorders. Instead, on the following day, the members of the elite Volynsky Guard Regiment changed history when they chased down and shot their commanding officer and then rallied other garrison units to do the same. Many of these soldiers were of peasant and working-class origin, and they were weary of the war and their harsh treatment by aristocratic officers. Now both sides of the Neva were aflame with armed protest as soldiers and workers converged to attack symbols of tsarist authority, such as prisons and barracks, and to tear down portraits of Tsar Nicholas II. At the Tauride Palace, soldiers cut the tsar's profile from its picture frame and held it high on the point of a bayonet. This act, like the others, represented a form of revolutionary pageantry, seen first in the French Revolution, wherein the masses display their ascendancy through the destruction of symbolic and personalized vestiges of authority. The act of the soldiers in the Tauride is reminiscent of the behavior seen in the streets of Paris after the taking of the Bastille in the summer of 1789, when the masses beheaded the commander of the fortress and paraded his head on the end of a bayonet. It was also duplicated decades later when Soviet power disintegrated in Eastern Europe and in the former Soviet Union and people tore down hundreds of statues of Communist Party leaders.

The masses had initiated the revolution, but now key elites sought to gain control over the streets. High-ranking military commanders and Duma politicians shared mass disaffection with the tsar, and they hoped to use the unrest to bring about a change in leadership that could turn the tide of the war. The Tauride Palace, located close to the barracks of the mutinous garrison regiments on the government side of the Neva, had served since 1906 as the seat for the Duma. Here, on February 27, 1917, a group of Duma leaders proclaimed the formation of a temporary committee to establish authority. Rather than carry out the tsar's orders to suppress the revolution militarily, the army commanders supported the Duma and joined their voices to those from the streets demanding the tsar abdicate. In a lone train car, stranded on his way from the eastern front of World War I, where Russian armies had been battling German and Austrian forces, Nicholas II, the last tsar of Russia, surrendered his throne, not just for himself but also for his son and heir, Alexei. Power then passed to the Duma leaders, who set up the Provisional Government, which declared its mandate to be to continue the war while preparing for a democratically elected constituent assembly that would craft a new Russian state. This provisional government committed itself to liberal democracy and the rule of law. It initiated a series of sweeping reforms, including the release of all political prisoners and the establishment of civil liberties, but it refused to make any major changes in property rights, labor relations, or the war policy until the convening of the much-anticipated constituent assembly.

Simultaneously, in a different wing of the Tauride Palace, workers and socialist party activists formed a rival institution, the Petrograd Soviet of Workers' and Soldiers' Deputies. The word "soviet" in Russian means "council," and this organ of direct popular control had first emerged in the Revolution of 1905 as a strike committee but then took over many duties of municipal administration. Though forcibly suppressed, the memory of this grassroots institution proved enduring, and in 1917 workers revived it as their own political instrument. From the beginning, there was deep distrust among many workers and soldiers for the Provisional Government, even though it contained a socialist minister, Alexander Kerensky. Those forming and supporting the Petrograd Soviet viewed it as a necessary overseer, keeping a watchful eye on the unreliable class elements of the new government, which was predominantly gentry and upper middle class in composition. This situation came to be known as "dual power" and it would prove fatal to the authority of the Provisional Government, particularly when the soldiers joined the Petrograd Soviet and it issued what became known as "Order No. 1." This order effectively subordinated military units to the Petrograd Soviet, limited the authority of officers, and provided for elected soldiers' committees. "Dual power" reflected the social polarization that would impair efforts to forge a liberal democratic outcome for the February Revolution.

In the weeks following the tsar's abdication, the masses grew angry and disillusioned as the Provisional Government failed to respond to their expectations that the revolution would usher in long awaited social changes, land for the peasants, economic betterment, and a negotiated end to the unpopular war. Consequently, they turned to the Petrograd Soviet as the means to achieve their goals. Ironically, though, for most of the spring and summer of 1917, the Petrograd Soviet was led by moderate socialists, Mensheviks and Socialist Revolutionaries, who had no intention of directly taking power from the government. In fact, in the course of the spring they chose to join the Provisional Government, and in so doing compromised their revolutionary credentials in the eyes of the radicalizing workers, soldiers, and peasants. Moderate socialists did not believe Russia was ready for socialism, in part because they adhered literally to Marxist doctrine, which projected that socialist revolution was only possible after a society passed through a liberal democratic phase. But they also feared that a socialist government would alienate Russia's Western allies, possibly strengthening the German war effort, and prompt a right-wing military coup from within Russia.

Evidence of the growing divide between the Provisional Government and the masses can be seen in the conflicting ways in which each identified with the traditions of the French Revolution. For all groups in 1917, there was a desire to adapt revolutionary symbols and rituals, but revealing differences surfaced. From the beginning, the Provisional Government viewed itself as a successor to the liberal middle-class leaders of the French Revolution and adopted its festivals, the French revolutionary song "The Marseillaise" as the new national anthem, and the French practice of addressing one another as "citizen" (*grazhdanin*) and "citizenness" (*grazhdanka*). Workers, on the other hand, more often self-identified with the socialist-minded *sans culottes* of the revolution, the urban shopkeepers and artisans who helped push forward the most radical policies of the French Revolution, including price controls and direct democracy. They also preferred the term "comrade" (*tovarishch*) to "citizen" or "citizenness." In addition, socialists preferred the rival revolutionary socialist anthem "The Internationale," written in 1871 during the Paris Commune, over the "The Marsellaise."

Meanwhile, in the course of 1917, the other Marxist-based political party, the Bolsheviks, adopted policies that gained them increasing popular support. Prodded by their founder, Vladimir Ilyich Lenin, the Bolsheviks came to emphasize Marxism as a flexible tool for achieving political power and less as a projection of historical development. Before the summer, the Bolsheviks had played only a minor role. Lenin was in exile in Switzerland and only returned to Russia in April on a sealed train financed in part by the German government in hopes that he would oppose World War I upon arrival. The Bolshevik leaders in Russia had been tentatively supporting the Provisional Government, but, once Lenin returned, the party began calling for all power to be transferred to the people in the form of these revolutionary councils, or soviets, and for an end to the war. In his first public speech as he stepped off his train, Lenin called for a second revolution to unseat the bourgeoisie, a socialist revolution. He and his followers developed slogans with great mass appeal—peace, land, bread, and all power to the soviets. In June and July a series of demonstrations and violent protests broke out in the streets of Petrograd as radicalized soldiers, sailors, and workers called for the Petrograd Soviet to take power and bring an end to the war. Though Lenin and the Bolsheviks did not initiate these demonstrations, they did support them, and they became the target of the government's crackdown. The Provisional Government released information accusing Lenin of being a German spy, and the public outrage drove Lenin to flee to Finland and led to the arrests of other Bolshevik leaders such as Leon Trotsky. But the social gulf that existed between the government and the radicalized masses only widened as the war dragged on and the economy worsened. Those who had taken to the streets in February were still hungry, they still faced inflation and long lines, and now they were losing their jobs as more and more factories closed. Business owners and industrialists, after initially agreeing to reforms, began to resist further demands for higher wages and eight-hour workdays. They claimed that with the war and economic collapse, their only recourse was to shut down operations. So unemployment grew while real wages, production, and investments plummeted. Public disapproval of the Bolsheviks proved only temporary. Their class-driven explanations for the war resonated with the masses that were already deeply resentful of the upper classes and their privileges. The Bolsheviks explained it as a capitalist war conducted by a capitalist government for its own interests and called for workers to take control of the factories. By September the Bolsheviks had won majorities in the soviets of Petrograd and Moscow. The Bolsheviks also increased their popularity in late August by helping to suppress a poorly organized attempt at a military takeover led by Russian military commander General Lavr Kornilov. The Provisional Government, now headed by socialist Alexander Kerensky, successfully aborted this coup but had to turn for help to Bolshevik-influenced soldiers, sailors, and worker militia units. Kerensky ordered them to be given arms to put down the coup. Afterwards they held on to their weapons and in October used them to topple Kerensky himself.

October 1917: The Second Revolution and the Collapse of the Provisional Government

Most countries in Europe and the United States had welcomed the February Revolution and the removal of the autocratic tsarist regime; they pledged support to the development of democracy in Russia, but their primary attention was on the war—the western front with its continued stalemate or the sands of the Arabian desert where T. E. Lawrence and Arab forces were overturning Ottoman rule in the Middle East. European countries had their own domestic troubles, with thousands of workers taking to the streets to protest the war; in France thirty thousand French soldiers mutinied and refused to return to the damp and deadly trenches. At the same time that the February Revolution was occurring, the United States under President Woodrow Wilson was preparing to enter the war, prompted by the German decision earlier in 1917 to resume unrestricted submarine warfare. Very few had heard of Lenin and the Bolsheviks, and many dismissed the notion that they had any chance of coming to power. But the Allied nations and the United States contributed to that very outcome by insisting that the Provisional Government stay in the war; this fatal decision is what helped seal its fate. The Provisional Government could not simultaneously resolve Russia's pressing social problems and wage war, and the fact that the Bolsheviks promised an end to the war proved to be very appealing to the weary masses of the Russian Empire.

The Great October Socialist Revolution, as it came to be called in the Soviet Union, took place October 25–27 (November 7–9) and was different from the February Revolution in its dynamics but not in its root causes: social polarization, popular anger over the war, and continued economic distress. The overthrow of the Provisional Government was not a spontaneous street movement; it was a conscious act set in motion by the Bolshevik leadership. More than any other politician in 1917, Lenin was intent on taking power, convinced that World War I, which he called an imperialist war, had created conditions for an immediate socialist revolution and that revolution in Russia would then spark similar movements in more advanced industrialized nations. Lenin also believed that Russia had the most essential element for carrying out revolution in Russia—the revolutionary vanguard party, which could take decisive action in the name of the people. But there was also mass support for the Bolsheviks to take power because workers, peasants, and soldiers believed that at long last the Bolsheviks would allow them to take control of their workplaces, to own the land that rightfully belonged to them, and to realize their natural rights of equality, dignity, and self-rule.

In the end, it was Kerensky who initiated this chain of events. On October 24 he ordered Bolshevik presses to be shut down, and this provided justification for the Bolshevik-controlled Petrograd Soviet to activate its newly formed Military Revolutionary

Committee (MRC); this body, ostensibly formed to defend Petrograd against impending German invasion, now acted to "defend" the revolution by seizing control of all means of communication and transportation in the city, including bridges, railway terminals, and postal, telephone, and telegraph offices. Although this was in part a defensive act, the insurrection became during the course of the night of October 24 a conscious drive to take power. Some historians attribute this to Lenin, who insisted that the MRC must immediately overthrow the Provisional Government. Thereby October 25, which dawned damp and cold, became a day of revolution. Kerensky fled the city in a car borrowed from the US embassy. The cruiser *Aurora*, led by Bolshevik sailors from the nearby Kronstadt naval base who had defied orders to go out to sea, fired blank shots at the Winter Palace while a contingent of workers and soldiers made their way inside. They arrested the government ministers who were holed up in the palace with a paltry defense force. In later years the "storming" of the Winter Palace took on mythic proportions. The October Revolution in Petrograd was virtually bloodless, as were similar seizures of power across Russia, with the exception of Moscow, where there were over a thousand casualties. The Bolsheviks formed a new executive body, which they entitled the Council of Peoples' Commissars, and the new government signed an armistice with Germany; nationalized land, industry, and assets; and held elections for the Constituent Assembly. The masses that had helped the Bolsheviks gain power could feel that the hopes of February were finally being realized.

Fatefully, what then ensued was something very different. The Bolsheviks dispersed the Constituent Assembly when it met for its one and only session on January 18, 1918. Rather than rule through soviets, the Bolsheviks created a one-party state run by a massive bureaucracy. With the outbreak of civil war in 1918, Lenin's primary goal became the centralization of power in the party apparatus, not empowering workers through factory committees or through soviets. The democratically elected Congress of Soviets and even the Council of Peoples' Commissars were eclipsed in power by the party, and eventually, by 1929, by Joseph Stalin, who created one of the century's most brutal personal dictatorships. Yet the Soviet Union, the country that emerged from revolution, nonetheless represented an unprecedented political experiment based upon a belief that social justice was more important than capitalist profit, and through its command economy it managed to develop into an economic superpower surpassed only by the United States in its productive capacity. Its existence unquestionably created new sets of challenges, possibilities, and problems for humankind in the twentieth century.

The city that gave rise to the revolutions of 1917, St. Petersburg, would itself be abandoned by the new ruling elite. Lenin and the government fled the invading Germans in March 1918, taking a special train to Moscow where they set up their new state, the Soviet Union, behind the walls of the old Kremlin. The tumultuous civil war that began soon thereafter took a harsh toll on St. Petersburg, and its population dropped to as low as 799,000 in August 1920. Nonetheless, streets were renamed to honor the revolution, and giant posters proclaimed the unity of workers, soldiers, and peasants. When Lenin died in 1924, the government changed the city's name to Leningrad. Utilities, public transportation, and bathing facilities were subsidized, and workers moved into subdivided properties that were once the exclusive homes of single wealthy families. But, despite their role as the standard bearers of revolution, the people of Leningrad would suffer much in the coming decades. Communist Party leaders, particularly Stalin, seemed to distrust the city, whose radicalized masses had risen up against two governments. Undoubtedly this unease was exacerbated in 1921 when the sailors from the nearby Kronstadt naval base, who had been among the most staunch supporters of the Bolsheviks, mutinied in protest against the failure to establish democratic rule. The regime ruthlessly suppressed the revolt. Then, in the 1930s and 1940s, the city became a direct target of Stalin's policies of terror, and mass arrests decimated the population. Even more deadly was the terrible blockade ordered by Adolf Hitler during World War II, during which over a million citizens died from starvation, disease, and exposure. To its credit, after the war the Soviet government rebuilt the city and resurrected its ghostly ruins and abandoned streets; it became a productive economic center, generating a considerable percentage of the Soviet Union's gross national product. But many felt that the city was neglected and underfunded, and the population overwhelmingly voted in 1990, when offered the chance, to discard Lenin's name and return to that given it by its founder, St. Petersburg. As we look at it today in the twenty-first century, St. Petersburg is a venerable monument to the resiliency of the Russian people, outlasting revolution, oppression, starvation, and, most recently, a troubled economic and political transition.

GLOBAL ENCOUNTERS AND CONNECTIONS:
The Echoes of Revolution Past and Future

What happened in 1917 in St. Petersburg certainly transformed Russian history, but it also reverberated across the globe. The world now had its first alternative to capitalism and liberal democracy, and much of the history of the twentieth century evolved in response to it. These epochal events erupted as a junction of intersecting currents reaching back as well as forward in world history. They were the product of problems, hopes, and visions rooted deep in Russian history, but were also part of a larger European tradition of revolution. The bourgeois social and political order enshrined in modern constitutional monarchy and liberal parliamentary systems, which had come out of the English Glorious Revolution and the Atlantic revolutions, was increasingly challenged in the nineteenth century by socialist notions of a society based on egalitarianism, direct democracy, and the abolition of property. Russian revolutionaries saw themselves as acting in the name of the same principles of liberty, equality, and fraternity that had inspired the French Revolution, but they increasingly believed they were carrying these ideas to their full fruition. Lenin emerged arguing that the world had changed from what it had been during the earlier periods of revolution, and he used Marxism to declare that the time was ripe for world socialist revolution and that it was backward Russia, in the context of an imperialist world war, led by a vanguard party, that could light the spark. The Bolshevik success in achieving power in a largely agrarian society and establishing a workable alternative to market capitalism echoed across the globe, providing exploited peoples in Asia and Africa with an ideal as well as a means for overthrowing oppressive colonial and imperial regimes. Lenin emphasized the importance of national liberation movements as part of the world socialist revolution, and in 1919 he founded the Communist International, or Comintern, to facilitate assistance to colonial peoples fighting subjugation and degradation.

The events that led to the collapse of the Russian Empire were also connected globally to larger processes of imperial collapse precipitated by the destabilizing forces of modernization, nationalism, and world war. In addition to the Russian Empire, the German, Austro-Hungarian, and Ottoman Empires also imploded amid the carnage of World War I. In the immediate aftermath of the October Revolution, as these empires collapsed, similar upheavals occurred. There were short-lived attempts to create soviet-style republics in Hungary, Slovakia, Bavaria, and Munich; in Germany the November revolution unseated the kaiser and established an interim government headed by the Social-Democratic Party, though its leaders staved off a coup attempt by radical Communists. Even in the United States, the events in Russia helped spur the most powerful wave of strikes in the country's history in 1919–1920. Although all efforts in this period to emulate the Bolsheviks ultimately failed, the echoes of the St. Petersburg events nonetheless rang on. Many intellectuals in the West felt that the old order had been proven bankrupt, and they were impressed by early Bolshevik campaigns for cultural transformation, literacy, and modernization. Under Stalin the Soviet Union's model of centralized economic planning achieved rapid industrialization and overcame the massive German invasion in World War II. Despite its brutally coercive nature, it provided an option to developing nations in Africa, Asia, and Latin America, many of which associated imperialism with capitalism and Western liberal democracy.

Above all, the revolutions in Petrograd had their greatest resonance in backward agrarian societies that sought to break free from Western imperialism and achieve national unity—namely China, North Korea, Vietnam, and Cuba. After 1917 Chinese intellectuals seeking national unification turned to Marxism and founded a Leninist-style vanguard party. One of its leaders, Mao Zedong, geared it toward the peasantry rather than the workers, but he borrowed much from the Leninist and Stalinist models in terms of organizational strategies, mass mobilization, and propaganda. Likewise, Vietnamese leader Ho Chi Minh founded a Leninist party after studying in Russia and working in China for the Comintern, and he believed fully in the importance of a vanguard party for organizing and leading a national movement for independence.

The Russian revolutions also changed history by prompting fears in the West of domestic communist movements against property and capitalism, which in the 1920s and 1930s fueled support for fascist parties in Italy, Germany, and Spain. At the same time, fascist leaders such as Benito Mussolini and Adolf Hitler borrowed freely from the Bolshevik model, including the one-party state, mass propaganda techniques, and a command economy. Following World War II, despite having been allies in the war against Hitler, the Soviet Union and the United States turned their ideological differences into the Cold War, a global struggle for power and economic influence along with a massive arms buildup including nuclear weapons.

For the city of St. Petersburg, or Leningrad as it became known, its place in modern world history will remain centered around the revolutions of 1917. Its struggles to recover from civil war and terror diminished its global economic significance, and culturally many of its greatest artists perished in Stalin's purges, or, like composer Dmitri Shostakovich or poetess Anna Akhmatova, found themselves creatively stymied by oppressive and overbearing censorship. Although its heroic stance against the German blockade in World War II helped turn the tide of that conflict and inspired millions elsewhere to stand resolute, in the aftermath, as the Cold War took shape, the sacrifices of the city were largely forgotten in the West. Interest revived after Stalin's death, when restrictions were lifted on foreign travel to the Soviet Union, and many found Leningrad appealing with its European-style architecture and Venice-like canals. The global reach of the city also lies in the contributions of its former residents who left Russia after the 1917 revolutions and whose artistic talents subsequently enriched Western arts and letters. These included writer Vladimir Nabokov, composer Igor Stravinsky, poet Joseph Brodsky, and ballet dancer and choreographer George Balanchine, who eventually emigrated to New York City and helped introduce audiences to what has become now a quintessential American Christmas custom, the Nutcracker Ballet, with music by the great Russian composer Peter Ilyich Tchaikovsky. In so many ways, the world of the twentieth century was indeed a product of 1917 in St. Petersburg.

As this chapter has noted, the Russian revolutions of 1917 had a far-reaching impact. The documents selected here illustrate the dynamics of revolution in Petrograd and how events in Russia inspired and influenced future revolutionary leaders.

Resolution on the Crisis of Authority and the Current Moment

The following selection includes a resolution passed by workers in the summer of 1917. It is the resolution of a meeting of workers in twenty-seven enterprises from the Peterhof district of Petrograd held on July 27, 1917. The references to revolutionary democracy and the dangers of tyranny, along with the references to slavery, reveal a common language that has been forged through over a century of revolution and reform in Europe and the Atlantic world. Take note of the ways in which these workers seem to have assimilated the language of intersecting traditions of resistance to oppression, including the French revolutionary tradition, Marxism, and even possibly abolitionist movements across the globe.

- What does the revolution mean to these workers? What, in their minds, are the major threats to the revolution?

- How do Marxist social categories and class analysis factor into their depiction of the world war?

- Do you believe these workers would support the Bolshevik Revolution in October?

- What elements of class consciousness come out in this resolution? How do these statements help one to understand why the Provisional Government was not able to hold on to power in 1917?

- What weakened the Provisional Government, as reflected in these statements?

Recognizing the extremely critical condition of the Russian revolution when an adventuristic offensive has led inevitably to serious defeat at the front and to the disintegration of the revolutionary army, and when the war, artificially and criminally prolonged by the ruling circles, is leading the exhausted army into new and dangerous adventures, when under the influence of bloody carnage, bankers' speculation and factory and plant owners' sabotage, the agricultural and industrial collapse mounts, pushing the country toward total exhaustion and ruin, when under pressure from the counter-revolutionary bourgeoisie, the Black Hundreds, and the command staff of the army, the leading majority of the Soviets is shamefully retreating and surrendering its positions one after another to its enemies, when through the shameful resurrection of the death penalty [by the Provisional Government] and field courts-martial arrests and violence threaten to shed the blood of the people's conquests, when with the criminal connivance of the ruling parties the tested leaders of the revolutionary democracy have been betrayed, when before our very eyes, instead of the chains of autocracy, a new slavery has been forged and there has been a wild outburst of tyranny—the working class cannot remain silent, and we, workers from the small enterprises of the Peterhof district, having listened to a report by members of the Soviet of Workers' and Soldiers' Deputies,

Griaznov and Travnikov, about the current situation, consider it our duty to state:

1. The new coalition "combination" of the Provisional Government is frankly doomed to failure and to a new downfall in the near future, as four months of a chronic crisis of authority have shown fully the entire senselessness of democracy's policy of appeasement with the counterrevolutionary imperialist bourgeoisie. . . .

2. A government of unlimited irresponsibility toward the Soviet of Workers,' Soldiers,' and Peasants' Deputies cannot enjoy the confidence of the people, for in this situation the presence of the Soviets, which alone are capable of saving the country, is reduced to nil. The refusal of responsible factions in the Soviets to participate in the organization of [state] power is an act of political suicide that we wholeheartedly protest. . . .

With respect to the crisis of authority, we declare that only a revolutionary authority that rests on the proletariat and the poorest strata of the peasantry can facilitate the country's move toward saving the revolution; therefore our immediate task is the irreconcilable struggle for the interests of the very poorest people and for concentrating all authority in the hands of the revolutionary proletarians', soldiers', and peasants' Soviets, which alone can reinforce and extend the gains of the revolutionary people.

Source: "Resolution on the Crisis of Authority and the Current Moment," in *Voices of Revolution, 1917*, Mark D. Steinberg (New Haven: Yale University Press, 2001), 189–190. Documents translated by Marian Schwartz.

"On New Democracy," by Mao Zedong

The following selection is from an essay written by Chinese communist leader Mao Zedong in 1940 in which he is promoting communism as the way forward for China in its struggle for national unity and autonomy. At the time, in addition to battling Japanese invaders, the Chinese Communist Party was fighting for power in a civil war against the Nationalist Party, or the Guomindang. Note how Mao situates China within the framework of the world socialist revolution as proclaimed by Lenin in 1917.

- What connections is Mao Zedong making between the Chinese communist movement and the October Revolution of 1917 in Petrograd?

- What significance does Mao Zedong impart here to the October Revolution?

- Why does Mao declare that China is no longer part of the bourgeois-democratic world revolution, but instead is part of the proletarian socialist world revolution?

- What connection is Mao making here between anticolonialism and the October Revolution of 1917 in Petrograd?

IV. THE CHINESE REVOLUTION IS PART OF THE WORLD REVOLUTION

The historical characteristic of the Chinese revolution lies in its division into the two stages, democracy and socialism, the first being no longer democracy in general, but democracy of the Chinese type, a new and special type, namely, New Democracy. How, then, has this historical characteristic come into being? Has it been in existence for the past hundred years, or is it of recent origin?

A brief study of the historical development of China and of the world shows that this characteristic did not emerge immediately after the Opium War, but took shape later, after the first imperialist world war and the October Revolution in Russia. Let us now examine the process of its formation.

Clearly, it follows from the colonial, semi-colonial and semi-feudal character of present-day Chinese society that the Chinese revolution must be divided into two stages. The first step is to change the colonial, semi-colonial and semi-feudal form of society into an independent, democratic society. The second is to carry the revolution forward and build a socialist society. At present the Chinese revolution is taking the first step. . . .

A change, however, occurred in China's bourgeois-democratic revolution after the outbreak of the first imperialist world war in 1914 and the founding of a socialist state on one-sixth of the globe as a result of the Russian October Revolution of 1917.

Before these events, the Chinese bourgeois-democratic revolution came within the old category of the bourgeois-democratic world revolution, of which it was a part.

Since these events, the Chinese bourgeois-democratic revolution has changed, it has come within the new category of bourgeois-democratic revolutions and, as far as the alignment of revolutionary forces is concerned, forms part of the proletarian-socialist world revolution.

Why? Because the first imperialist world war and the first victorious socialist revolution, the October Revolution, have changed the whole course of world history and ushered in a new era.

It is an era in which the world capitalist front has collapsed in one part of the globe (one-sixth of the world) and has fully revealed its decadence everywhere else, in which the remaining capitalist parts cannot survive without relying more than ever on the colonies and Semi-colonies, in which a socialist state has been established and has proclaimed its readiness to give active support to the liberation movement of all colonies and semi-colonies, and in which the proletariat of the capitalist countries is steadily freeing itself from the social-imperialist influence of the social-democratic parties and has proclaimed its support for the liberation movement in the colonies and semi-colonies. In this era, any revolution in a colony or semi-colony that is directed against imperialism, i.e., against the international bourgeoisie or international capitalism, no longer comes within the old category of the bourgeois-democratic world revolution, but within the new category. It is no longer part of the old bourgeois, or capitalist, world revolution, but is part of the new world revolution, the proletarian-socialist world revolution. Such revolutionary colonies and semi-colonies can no longer be regarded as allies of the counter revolutionary front of world capitalism; they have become allies of the revolutionary front of world socialism.

Source: Mao Zedong, "On New Democracy," January 15, 1940, accessed online through the Marxists Internet Archive, www.marxists.org/reference/archive/mao/selected-works/volume-2/mswv2_26.htm.

Further Reading

Acton, Edward. *Rethinking the Russian Revolution*. Edward Arnold: London 1990.

Fitzpatrick, Sheila. *The Russian Revolution*. New York: Oxford University Press, 2008.

Kowalski, Ronald. *The Russian Revolution, 1917–1921*. New York: Routledge, 1997.

Marples, David R. *Lenin's Revolution: Russia, 1917–1921*. London: Pearson Education, 2000.

Rabinowitch, Alexander. *The Bolsheviks Come to Power: The Revolution of 1917 in Petrograd*. Chicago: Haymarket Books, 2009.

Thompson, John M. *Revolutionary Russia, 1917*. 2nd ed. Prospect Heights, IL: Waveland Press, Inc., 1989.

Wade, Rex. *The Russian Revolution, 1917*. New York: Cambridge University Press, 2000.

Web Resources

Alexander Palace Guide to Russian History Websites, www.alexanderpalace.org/index.html.
Alexander Palace Time Machine, www.alexanderpalace.org/palace/.
The Empire That Was Russia: The Prokudin-Gorskii Photographic Record Recreated,
     www.loc.gov/exhibits/empire/.
Mapping Petersburg, http://stpetersburg.berkeley.edu/index.html.
Nevsky Prospect photographs from pre–World War I,
     http://stpetersburg.berkeley.edu/olga/olga_splash.html.
The Russian Revolution: A Gallery of Photos,
     www.nevsky88.com/SaintPetersburg/Revolution/.
Saint Petersburg 1900: A Travelogue, www.alexanderpalace.org/petersburg1900/intro.html,
     including a photograph of the Nevsky Prospect,
     www.alexanderpalace.org/petersburg1900/36.html.
Seventeen Moments in Soviet History, www.soviethistory.org/.
Virtual Tour of St. Petersburg, www.saint-petersburg.com/virtual-tour/index.asp.

Bibliographic Note

In addition to the works included in the Further Reading section at the end of the chapter, the following sources provide information and analysis of particular relevance to the topics discussed in the chapter: James H. Bater, "St. Petersburg and Moscow on the Eve of Revolution," in *The Workers' Revolution in Russia, 1917: The View From Below*, ed. Daniel H. Kaiser (Cambridge: Cambridge University Press, 1987), 20–57; J. H. Bater and R. A. French, eds., *Studies in Russian Historical Geography*, vol. 2 (London: Academic Press, 1983); James H. Bater, *St. Petersburg: Industrialization and Change* (Montreal: McGill-Queens University Press, 1976); Stephen G. Marks, *How Russia Shaped the Modern World: From Art to Anti-Semitism, Ballet to Bolshevism* (Princeton, NJ: Princeton University Press, 2003); David Priestland, *The Red Flag: Communism and the Making of the Modern World* (London: Penguin Books, 2009); Robert Weinberg and Laurie Bernstein, *Revolutionary Russia: A History in Documents* (New York: Oxford University Press, 2011); William G. Rosenberg, "Russian Labor and Bolshevik Power: Social Dimensions of Protest in Petrograd after October," in *The Workers' Revolution in Russia, 1917: The View From Below*, ed. Daniel H. Kaiser (Cambridge: Cambridge University Press, 1987), 98–131; Steve A. Smith, "Petrograd in 1917: The View from Below," in *The Workers' Revolution in Russia, 1917: The View From Below*, ed. Daniel H. Kaiser (New York: Cambridge University Press, 1987), 59–80; Ronald Grigor Suny, "Revising the Old Story: The 1917 Revolution in Light of New Sources," in *The Workers' Revolution in Russia, 1917: The View From Below*, ed. Daniel H. Kaiser (Cambridge: Cambridge University Press, 1987), 1–19; Solomon Volkov, *St. Petersburg: A Cultural History* (New York: Free Press, 1997).

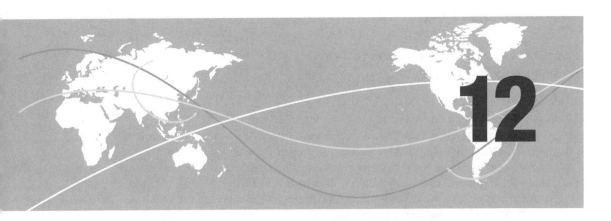

Kinshasa

Confluence of Riches and Blight

(1800s–1900s)

DIDIER GONDOLA

A T FIRST GLANCE, KINSHASA, THE CAPITAL OF THE DEMOCRATIC REPUBLIC OF Congo, seems to have cruised through the Cold War impervious to the turmoil that wreaked havoc in the rest of the country, as the newly independent republic was transformed into one of the fiercest battlegrounds of the war. Conflicts, atrocities, and unrest ravaged the eastern half of the country and took their toll not only on armed combatants but also on unarmed civilians and on the region's pristine flora and fauna. Hemmed in by the Great Lakes, eastern Congo boasts some of the world's most abundant and rich mineral ores, including cobalt, copper, manganese, diamond, gold, uranium, tin (cassiterite) and coltan (columbium-tantalum). But eastern Congo seems doomed by what political scientists have termed "resource curse." Kinshasa, however, has always been shielded from military disturbances due to its westernmost location in an area of the country devoid of vast mineral deposits. Yet the capital of Congo has borne the brunt of the mineral conflicts and ethnic unrest that have thwarted the country's development since it gained independence from Belgium in 1960.

I was born in Kinshasa in 1966, a few months before its name changed from Leopoldville to Kinshasa. The city had been originally named after Belgian king Leopold II, who controlled the so-called Congo Free State until 1908 and, according to Adam Hochschild's bestselling book, *Leopold's Ghost: A Story of Greed, Terror, and Heroism in*

Colonial Africa (1998), established there a slave labor system that claimed the lives of eight million Congolese. Growing up in Kinshasa in the late sixties and seventies was no different from coming of age in any other metropolis of the Global South. One's sense of place was informed by the township where one lived rather than by the city itself or what lay beyond its confines. Urban identity was rather parochial and not yet shaped by the global cultural currents that now crisscross the world via texting, Facebook, CNN, and MTV. By the early 1970s, Kinshasa was no longer this tropical Klondike (a town created overnight, usually as the result of a gold rush) that attracted white colonists from all corners of Europe to strike it rich. Nor did it resemble the late colonial city with its newly and neatly designed housing projects for Africans, the inconspicuous presence of African women in the public arena, and its curfew that barred Africans from milling about the business district and European quarters after sunset. Back then, the feeling—which also percolated in sociological and demographic studies done at the time—was that of a city *en devenir* (in transition). Because the city sprawled so much as a result of cascading waves of rural migrants, newcomers who lived on the outskirts tended to depend more on the rural economy rather than on urban activities. In an ongoing process, the city itself was gradually shedding its colonial appearance to become one of the most paradoxical Global South megalopolises: a city in perpetual flux both in terms of its geographical growth and its social makeup.

I returned to Kinshasa in the late 1980s—after spending a decade in Paris, France—as a graduate student, determined to recover fragments of my youth by devoting my life to making sense of Kinshasa's postcolonial growth. I discovered a different place from the one I'd left. The city had expanded well beyond its original limits, with the great majority of its population living on the fringes. These newcomers had no access to urban amenities. Their quality of life lagged well below what we usually associate with life in the city. Nowhere was this disparity more abysmal than among the youth population, which by then accounted for about 60 percent of the total urban population. Kinshasa had grown not only to become one of a handful of African cities that had reached the one million-population milestone, but also a city of youths. It had retained its vocation as a place of encounters, yet there was more to the vibrancy and youthfulness of the city than met the eye. In fact, Kinshasa had become a vast melting pot of cultures. Thrown into an already rich cultural crucible, where traditional and modern patterns had given birth to hybrid threads, these cultures in turn radiated across Africa and Europe like spokes on a wheel. Take Congolese popular music, for example. It sprang up in Kinshasa in the post–World War II period as the city became home, or at least a temporary residence, to an international population. Kru men came from Liberia, Nigeria, and Sierra Leone to fill positions in private companies such as Huileries du Congo Belge (palm oil), a subsidiary of Unilever Overseas created by the Lever brothers, and they brought highlife along with their job skills. Black American troops who were stationed in the coastal city of Matadi and in Leopoldville during World War II introduced jazz to an already saturated musical scene. From across the Congo River, in neighboring Brazzaville, came the French accordion music and French Caribbean rhythms that so enthralled Congolese audiences. I became particularly interested in these popular genres, not just because they registered the changes that have affected the city, but also because they served as anchors that harnessed the aspirations of Kinshasa's youths for urban modernity while connecting them to global trends and the global zeitgeist (spirit of the age).

One of the largest cities of the Global South, and Africa's third-largest metropolis (next to Cairo and Lagos), Kinshasa exhibits startling paradoxes and hubris with its slums in the shadow of luxurious residences, high unemployment, large contingents of disenfranchised youths, HIV/AIDS prevalence, and crumbling infrastructures, all juxtaposed with vibrant and resilient urban cultures. This chapter traces the history of Congo's capital city from the early precolonial settlements of the nineteenth century onward, paying attention to its role during decolonization and the Cold War period and examining how its inhabitants have coped with underdevelopment and the impact of regional conflicts taking place around the Great Lakes area since 1994. With an emphasis on geographical location, political and social functions, trade, and colonial occupation, readers will be able to describe and discuss how space shapes urban experience and how the city becomes ultimately a place where larger political and international stakes are played out.

KINSHASA AND THE WORLD:
A Tropical Klondike Offering Vast Resources

To understand the importance of Kinshasa, it helps to begin with geography. The story of an original settlement near a river that sprawls to become a thriving metropolis has long been part of history. Kinshasa stands as one of these numerous cities that owe everything to their location. This is where the powerful Congo River stretches into its last navigable expanses, Malebo Pool—which covers nearly three hundred square miles with Mbamu island, fourteen miles long, flanked in the middle—before it furiously rushes down toward the sea in a succession of cataracts, falls, and rapids. (See Map 12.1.) Before colonization, any travel from that point on to the coast had to be managed by human porters, since pack animals in this tropical area were prone to trypanosomiasis (sleeping sickness), and transporting canoes overland, to bypass the cataracts, amounted to a titanic task. This geographical feature forced traders coming from the upper Congo area to make a stop at Malebo Pool and trade. It also promoted Malebo Pool to an important demographic hub that may have sustained at least fifty thousand people by the time the first European explorers ventured into the area at the end of the nineteenth century. Tio fishermen and Bahumbu agriculturists shared the area and set up several settlements on both sides of Malebo Pool. Ntamo, Ndolo, Lema, and Nshasa (which gave its name to the city) were among at least sixty villages and trading centers that dotted the lower banks of Malebo Pool. These centers attracted Bobangi ivory carvers from the forested north and Bazombo and Bakongo traders who came as far as the Loango coast to trade salt, cloth, European secondhand clothes, pottery, glassware, copper, guns, and gunpowder in exchange for ivory and slaves. In contrast to the coast and the interior of the Congo basin, where kingdoms had formed in earlier times, Malebo Pool exhibited small chiefdoms where "big men" held sway over trading hubs. Many, however, wielded little power and acted as *primus inter pares* (first among equals) rather than as potentates.

That the French and the Belgians chose to establish the capitals of their respective colonial domains by Malebo Pool rather than on the coast, as was the case along the entire Atlantic coastline, stands as a testimonial to Malebo Pool's geographic attractiveness and importance. In the early 1880s, European explorers trekked across the Congo basin to reach Malebo Pool. By all accounts, these explorers were probably the last group in a tradition that began in the fifteen century with the "discovery" of the Americas. Thus, the Congo basin stood as the last frontier for European exploration. Because they came in small numbers, these explorers were hardly seen as a threat. In fact, Malebo Pool's "big men" offered them hospitality and curried favor with them, unaware that under the guise of commerce and exploration these newcomers were laying the groundwork for colonial scramble. By the early 1890s, most of the Tio and Bahumbu villages had been

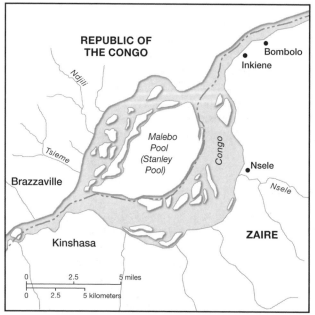
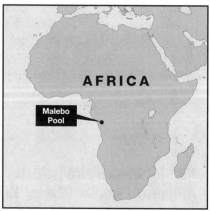

Map 12.1. Kinshasa Malebo Pool

Straddling the banks of the Malebo Pool, the largest expanse on the Congo River, Kinshasa and Brazzaville have mirrored each other from the time they served as bustling precolonial hubs to their colonial integration as the world's closest capitals to their postcolonial trajectory as the most populous transborder metropolitan area in the world. They have registered and borne the brunt of most of the political, social, and economic changes that shaped the global era.

either destroyed or forced to move upstream to make way for European settlements. French and Belgian colonizers exploited longstanding rivalries between the Tio and some of their trading partners and foes. The colonizers evicted the natives from their strongholds and replaced their villages with makeshift camps for the new colonial labor that arrived initially from the lower Congo area. Whole villages had to abandon the land of their ancestors and leave under the threat of military force.

Initially, Europeans followed the same pattern as the original occupants by locating their settlements on the two most advantageous sites, Ntamo (Kintambo or Leo II) in the west and its twin sister Nshasa (Kinshasa or Leo I) in the east. Only when the capital of the Belgian colony moved from Boma to Leopoldville in 1923 did the two European centers of Leo I and Leo II merge into a single urban district. With this new administrative function came an unprecedented urban boom in other areas as well. European visitors who came to Kinshasa, whether from Europe or just from French Brazzaville across the Congo River, seldom failed to marvel at the hustle and bustle of this colonial Klondike. Visiting the city for the first time in 1923, Belgian journalist Pierre Daye noted, "The way I felt upon my arrival in Kinshasa can be best described as *une impression d'américanisme* ['as if one were in an American city']." On any parcel of land that could be grabbed from despondent African residents, Europeans erected residential and administrative buildings, schools, and hospitals; laid roads and bridges; and built parks and military camps.

Cogs in a Colonial Economy

With perhaps the exception of Luanda, Angola, the urban upsurge that Leopoldville witnessed during the 1920s was unrivaled in Central and Equatorial Africa. In keeping with a longstanding policy that harkened back to the ignominious days of the Leopoldian Congo Free State, Leopoldville welcomed all European would-be colonists, regardless of their nationality. Just as in the Americas, Australia, and Algeria, downtrodden Europeans hoped for a reversal of fortune in the colonies and banked on commerce or a career in the military as a means to move up the social ladder. British, French, Italian, Portuguese, and Greek fortune seekers and adventurers, along with a smattering of Indians and Pakistanis, flocked to the city in such great numbers that the European population more than doubled between 1924 (1,224) and 1929 (2,766). Some never struck it rich but eked out a living as bartenders, day laborers, or—worse—hustlers.

For Africans, moving to Leopoldville presented a different challenge and afforded them with few opportunities. To begin with, African men were turned into alienated cogs in a colonial economy that operated neither for their benefit nor for that of the colony itself. Their labor, as well as the wealth of the colony, was siphoned off through an intricate conveyer belt that ran through Leopoldville and finished its course in Belgium. Furthermore, African workers that vied for lower-level positions in the colonial economy chafed under deplorable living and working conditions. Yet these jobs allowed them to earn cash to pay the newly imposed poll tax. Belgian colonial ideology so stressed the notion that the city was, as one colonial author put it, "entirely the creation of the new masters of the continent, [an] absolutely novel introduction in an entirely virgin land," that until World War II Africans were considered strangers to the city.

With this ideology in mind, the Belgian colonizers confined Africans in temporary settlements and barred single African females from moving to and residing in Leopoldville. For example, in 1928 Leopoldville contained only 358 African women that were legally married, yet there were nearly five thousand single women who had been literally smuggled into the city. Many offered sexual and maid services to male workers in exchange for money, shelter, or food. Not surprisingly, European employers faced many challenges retaining their African workers, who often quit their jobs unexpectedly or did not return the next day. This was the price to be paid for stacking the deck against African laborers and keeping them in wretched urban conditions. But the attractive power of the city as a repository of colonial modernity, coupled with rural poverty, contributed to the high numbers of labor migrants to Leopoldville throughout the colonial period, as it did elsewhere in places such as Cairo, Mexico City, and Bombay.

Kinshasa's Division into Two Urban Spaces

By the end of the 1920s, the city had acquired its main geographic and demographic features, with two primary urban spaces. The European city (*la ville européenne*) spread in a long corridor along the Congo River. It consisted of a business district and European residential areas located in Kalina and two main industrial poles around OTRACO (Office des Transports Coloniaux), a publicly owned company operating railway, port, and river transport and transit in the colony, and the CHANIC shipyard. OTRACO and CHANIC were both located on opposite ends of the European corridor, at equidistance from Kalina.

Further inland, separated from the European city by several military camps and a prophylactic belt of greenery that served the role of buffer zone, the native townships (*cités indigènes*) stood in stark contrast to the European residential areas. Here municipal developers committed fewer resources, influenced as they were by the notion that African settlements could serve only as pools of laborers for the city's growing economy and nothing more. Thus, while European settlements stood on higher grounds overlooking Malebo Pool, African housings were built in lowland areas prone to flooding and infested by mosquitoes.

The European city enjoyed paved roads, running water, and adequate sewerage systems. The African townships had none and resembled the villages that these migrants had left behind. Before World War II, few Africans would dare challenge a colonial order that reigned supreme through an arsenal of coercive measures, including segregation, curfews, and an ubiquitous police force (known as the Force Publique).

World War II and Decolonization

World War II marked a watershed in the struggle for decolonization in Africa and Asia. As England and France, the two main colonial powers in Africa, reeled from the devastation caused by the war, African war veterans, workers, and activists, fueled by nationalism, stepped up their demands for more social and political rights. The Belgians for their part ignored Congolese grievances. Yet after the Great Depression, which in the Belgian Congo lingered until the beginning of the war, the ebb and flow of African migrants became a cause for concern, a liability rather than an asset to economic recovery. Time and again, European employers stressed the importance of stabilizing the African manpower in order to recover the ground lost to the Depression. Improving living and working conditions for the plethora of African migrants that moved to Leopoldville became not only a priority but a condition for economic progress and the preservation of the social and racial order. Indeed, Leopoldville's population more than doubled during the war, increasing from 46,884 in 1940 to 96,116 in 1945.

Even though urban experience for both Europeans and Africans continued to be defined by blatant inequalities in terms of housing, urban amenities, and job opportunities, the postwar period proved to be a turning point of seismic proportion that yielded lasting changes. During the war, African troops fought battles in the British-led East Africa campaign against the Italian army and even as far away as Burma. At home, Congolese peasants and workers labored to the brink of exhaustion to meet the Allied forces' demand for vital resources, especially after South Asia fell into Japanese hands. Some Congolese took advantage of the absence of many mobilized European residents who left the colony for the war front to jockey for some mid-level positions in the colonial administration and in private companies, which would not have been available to them if not for the shortage of white colonial workers. Those men, long confined in subaltern and menial positions in spite of their skills and aspirations, were dubbed *évolués* (literally, those colonial subjects who had "evolved" through education, Christianization, and monogamy) in the Belgian colonial parlance. Many came out of the Catholic schools that trained the Congolese elite. They quickly moved into managerial positions that became vacant, determined to hone their skills and test the limits of Belgian paternalism.

Colonial authorities, for their part, felt indebted to the Congolese for contributing to the war effort. In neighboring French Congo the pace of reforms sped up, climaxing in General Charles de Gaulle's appointment of Félix Eboué, a black Frenchman from Guyana, as governor-general and the momentous Brazzaville Conference of 1944, which set in motion decolonization reforms in the French Empire. Following the independence of India in 1946, the British also introduced some political reforms, albeit limited ones, in the Gold Coast (Ghana). Yet in the Belgian Congo, gradualism remained the order of the day. For example, the Belgians decided to appoint Africans to municipal offices rather than having them elected. Following this timid reform, appointments were made in the major cities of the colony. In Leopoldville, Henri Bongolo, a war veteran, became the first African chief of the Cité Indigène de Léopoldville (Native Township of Leopoldville) on January 1, 1946. The position was purely honorific and required that he faithfully collaborate with and report to the colonial municipal authority. His duties included helping with demographic census and tax collection and keeping track of the swelling number of migrants arriving daily in the African townships. Bongolo was among a growing number of *évolués* who had risen from the ranks by taking advantage of postwar policies that replaced the benighted, and often racist, attitudes that presided over the disenfranchisement of large segments of the African population in the prewar period.

To accommodate this emerging African elite, which numbered more members in Leopoldville than in other urban centers in the colony, Belgian authorities implemented a number of policies. Meritorious Africans could vie for new housing thanks to public subsidies that helped finance housing projects that sprouted throughout the *cités indigènes*. At the helm of this urban project was the OCA (Office des Cités Africaines), a public, nonprofit housing agency. In all, the OCA built nearly twenty thousand units distributed evenly in several newly designed African townships in Leopoldville, including Renkin, Christ-Roi, Yolo-Nord, Yolo-Sud, Pierre Wigny, Max Horn, Général Moulaert, Lemba-Est and Lemba-Ouest. Starting in 1948 some *évolués* could also apply for a *carte de mérite civique* (civic merit card) that entitled its holders to certain rights and privileges that other Africans did not have. Among these were the right to purchase and consume wine in bars and restaurants and the right to move about the European city during the curfew.

The *carte de mérite civique* and its upgraded equivalent, the *carte d'immatriculation*, rested on the premise of colonization as a civilizing mission. Whereas the former vindicated progress toward civilization, the latter, which was bestowed upon just a handful of Africans (only 120 Congolese held the card in 1956), put its recipients on par with Europeans. *Immatriculés*, as the members of the latter group were officially recognized, enjoyed the same rights as Europeans. Yet in the eyes of African masses they were nothing but *mindele ndombe* (Kikongo for "whites with black skins"), a versatile label of both praise and contempt.

It should come as no surprise that the people who bore the full brunt of the colonial system were also the ones that played a decisive role in its demise. While the *évolués* acquiesced in the Belgians' project to delay independence indefinitely, it was the masses of uneducated and disenfranchised Leopoldville youth that dealt colonization its biggest blow. In December 1955 Antoine Van Bilsen, a Belgian professor of colonial legislation at the University Institute for Overseas Territories in Antwerp, Belgium, proposed a plan with a thirty-year timetable calling for a gradual emancipation of the Belgian Congo. Under Van Bilsen's plan, Congolese would be granted self-government in 1986 after the obligatory training of an African elite to take full command of government. The plan was immediately greeted with enthusiasm by the Congolese *évolués* but rejected by the majority of other Congolese. Dealing with a fractured urban population, mobilized along ethnic lines rather than political ones, the colonizers made no concessions except for a timid foray into municipal reform that in 1957 granted administrative rather than political power to a handful of elected African burgomasters in the *cité indigène*. This was a far cry from development in French and British colonies, which either had obtained independence or had been granted meaningful political rights, including citizenship and parliamentary representation.

Then, on January 4, 1959, the Congolese populace took to the streets to force the colonizers' hand and demand "*indépendance immédiate*." Leopoldville had never before witnessed such widespread uprisings. These anticolonial riots went unabated for four days, subsiding only after additional troops were brought in from other parts of the colony. The January insurrection loomed large in the decolonization process for several reasons. First, it single-handedly moved the issue of independence to the top of the colonial agenda, compelling the Belgians to move haphazardly from reluctance to grant independence according to a thirty-year timetable to urgency to free their colony within a year. Second, it forced the Congolese political leaders to adopt a more radical anticolonial stance, as "*indépendance immédiate*" became the only possible outcome that could win them the support of the masses. Lastly, it consecrated the importance of Leopoldville as a site of indiscipline, a volatile milieu where discontent could easily coalesce into widespread urban riots. But more importantly, Leopoldville, which historically positioned itself as a commercial hub, became a highly politicized place where power could be won and lost— a site that registered and influenced Congo's trajectory. This pattern was hardly unique in Africa. From Accra (Ghana) to New Delhi (India), independence was won not just because of political pressure exercised by political activists, but also because people took to the streets and met colonial violence with mass violence and a sense of sacrifice.

GLOBAL ENCOUNTERS AND CONNECTIONS:
A Central Root for Resources and Inequity

That Congo served as a linchpin for some of the most significant economic revolutions the world has witnessed in the last five hundred years is a view supported by an abundant literature. From the time hundreds of thousands of captives were snatched from the Congo basin to toil on the plantations of the New World to its later role as a supplier of raw materials for the industrial revolution in the nineteenth century, the nuclear revolution, and now the digital revolution, the area has been highly coveted for its seemingly inexhaustible resources. Since the time of Belgian king Leopold II, who held Congo as his private property for over two decades without ever once setting foot there, the West has viewed Congo's resources as a global cornucopia rather than a national patrimony. Thus, when Congo became independent on June 30, 1960, Belgium quickly signaled that it intended not only to preserve its economic interests there but also to guarantee the West's unrestricted access to Congo's mineral bonanza.

On June 30, 1960, Congo's new government mirrored a typical European political system, with a head of state (President Joseph Kasavubu) endowed with executive powers but governing through a prime minister (Patrice Lumumba) responsible for forming the cabinet, and a bicameral legislature (senate and chamber of representatives). The system, however, failed to operate as planned, not just because both Kasavubu and Lumumba vied for more control of the executive branch, but also due to Congo's involvement in the Cold War. After World War II, tensions rapidly escalated between the United States and the Soviet Union as they fought to spread their spheres of influence globally through propaganda, espionage, rivalry at sports events, diplomatic and military alliances, proxy wars, deployment of strategic weapons, and a nuclear arms race, which taken together constituted the Cold War. In addition to Germany, Cuba, Korea, and Vietnam, Congo stood as a contested Cold War battleground.

In the Cauldron of the Cold War

Any discussion of Leopoldville's involvement in the Cold War is bound to miss the mark if the narrative focuses solely on the polarizing figure of Lumumba. To be sure, Lumumba served as a catalyst that set in motion international forces that undermined Congo's independence from the get-go. As it became obvious following the demonstrations of January 1959 that independence loomed imminently on the horizon, Leopoldville witnessed the meteoric rise of several political leaders who used the city as their base. For Lumumba, a nonnative, Leopoldville represented perhaps the crucible of modernity with its hubris and its many contradictions. It certainly constituted the high point of a career that started quite modestly in his native Katako-Kombe province, took him to Stanleyville (now Kisangani), and catapulted him to the helm of a country that could not be governed as a sovereign nation because of its abundant natural resources. The fact that he belonged to the relatively small Tetela ethnic group may have partly accounted for his vision of a unified Congo at a time when most Congolese politicians heavily relied on ethnic constituencies. It was in Leopoldville that Lumumba created the Mouvement National Congolais (National Congolese Movement) to counter the federalist agenda of political parties such as the ABAKO (Association des Bakongo), which had most Bakongo rallying behind Joseph Kasavubu. Yet Leopoldville was caught in the web of the Cold War for reasons that had less to do with internal ethnic politics than with international economic interests that have continued to shape Congo's predicament even to this day.

While for the United States Congo mattered on account of its abundant mineral wealth, for the Soviet Union gaining influence and building a communist, anti-Western bloc outweighed all economic concerns. It was in fact this neocolonial agenda that ignited the powder keg that led to Congo's descent into the doldrums of the Cold War. At the celebration of independence in Leopoldville, Belgian king Baudoin I, speaking on behalf of Western powers, all but hinted at Belgium's intention to leave the Congolese to their own devices. After extolling the virtues of Belgian colonialism and praising the "genius" of his great granduncle Leopold II, Baudoin told a mystified audience that the Congolese owed Belgium a debt of gratitude. Independence, he insisted, was the "crowning" of the civilizing work accomplished by selfless Belgian pioneers in behalf of the Congolese masses. "Don't mortgage the future with hasty reforms," he admonished. "And don't replace the structures Belgium hands over to you until you are certain you can do better. . . . Don't be afraid to turn to us. We will remain by your side to advise you and train your technicians and civil servants."

Prime Minister Lumumba, who was not slated to speak at the event, flouted that protocol after President Kasavubu's rather timid speech. By vowing "to see to it that the soil of our country really benefits its children," Lumumba unwittingly challenged the established capitalist order. Lumumba's riposte, though couched in the anticolonial language that gave momentum to nationalist movements across Asia and Africa, unsettled powerful interests vested in Congo's mineral wealth. Immediately following the speech, Congo became, as Argentine revolutionary Che Guevara later noted in his diary, an "immense field of struggle." With the backing of the United States, Belgium fomented the secession of Congo's richest province, Katanga, and fueled separatist sentiments in the diamond-rich province of Kasai. With Lumumba facing secessionist threats, a tug of war with President Kasavubu, an invasion by Belgian military forces, and Western plots to eliminate him, he appealed to the United Nations before turning to Moscow for help.

As these tumultuous events unfolded and threatened to dissolve the new country, tens of thousands of refugees from central and eastern Congo flocked to Leopoldville. Many came from war-torn areas to escape wanton acts of violence perpetrated by all belligerents, including the Armée Nationale Congolaise (the Congolese army). How the city registered these dramatic changes is better gauged by looking at the swelling numbers of its population. In 1960 Leopoldville had already reached its capacity with four hundred thousand residents. The postwar wave of residential expansion that witnessed the creation of new townships never kept up with the unprecedented demographic boom. By 1967 the population had surged to an estimated nine hundred thousand, with no new additional housing development. While old timers crowded the areas of the *cité indigène*, now only known as the *cité*, newcomers had to settle for substandard housings in the city's far-flung margins. Their urban experience hardly befitted the idea of modernity that many envisioned. In particular, young people who left their rural homes beckoned by the social and cultural opportunities that emerged with the end of colonization felt disenchanted with the city's propensity to marginalize its youths.

Without access to education and training and with few if any opportunities for employment, young people channeled their quest for modernity into other avenues. They transformed 1950s and 1960s Leopoldville into a vibrant cultural scene that witnessed the birth of several popular genres in areas such as music, fashion, painting, and street culture. Many young people coped with urban life only by joining gangs of "cowboys" that shaped street culture in 1950s Leopoldville. In the 1960s, as the city agonized in the throes of the Cold War, these gangs were no longer influenced by Hollywood Western films (as was the case in the 1950s) but increasingly reflected the turmoil that had beset the country. With names such as ONU (UN), URSS (USSR) and Ambassade des Juifs (Jewish Embassy), and leaders who styled themselves with emblematic monikers of Dag Hammarskjoldr, Billy Khrushchev, Néron (Nero), Tarzan, and Godzilla, Leopoldville's gangs mirrored the international violence that wreaked havoc in Congo. At a time when political and social upheavals gradually eroded traditional norms, youth gangs ushered in new standards of manliness within their respective townships, standards that often involved ubiquitous violence (including sexual violence), drug consumption, magical rituals, and sartorial ostentation. The legacy of this youth culture continues to saturate Kinshasa's urban culture and to serve as a behavioral repertoire for many young urban residents.

Kin-La-Belle, Kin-La-Poubelle

While this cultural blossoming peaked, allowing young people to assert their agency in the realm of popular cultures, it also became increasingly perilous for them to fully express themselves once Congo was caught in the clutches of the Cold War. The assassination of Lumumba in 1961 paved the way for the rise of one of the most brutal and protracted dictatorships in Africa. When Joseph-Désiré Mobutu came to power in 1965, following a Western-backed coup, Congo was still reeling from five years of rebellions, ethnic strife, and political instability. Mobutu, a former freelance journalist and army officer who worked for Lumumba and then plotted to have him eliminated, was handpicked by Washington to serve as its most loyal Cold War proxy in Africa. With the backing of the US government, the "Guide," as Mobutu liked to be called by his people, created a regime that blended disparate political symbols and ideologies, from the French Revolution to Mao's Great Leap Forward. For example, after a visit to Mao's China in January 1973, Mobutu adopted the Mao suit, with its recognizable close-fitting, stand-up collar, and banned the Western suit and tie. The *abacost* (a shorthand of the French "*à bas le costume,*" meaning "down with the suit"), as this Congolese version of the Mao suit was dubbed, symbolized Mobutu's attempt to eradicate the legacy of colonialism and the influence of Western culture while extolling the virtues of *authenticité*. In his own words, *authenticité* purported to "discover our personality by reaching into the depths of our past for the rich cultural heritage left to us by our ancestors." While in many former colonies leaders strengthened economic as well as cultural ties with former colonial powers, in Congo Mobutu charted a course that was not seen elsewhere except in Tanzania under President Nyerere's *ujamaa* (African socialism).

In Mobutu's mind there was no insurmountable contradiction between promoting "ancestral" values and using *authenticité* to reclaim Lumumba's legacy and forge national unity. And as long as he satisfied the West's insatiable demand for Congo's mineral resources he could run the country as he saw fit without much interference from the international community. With the support of the West and once all political opposition was stifled, Mobutu implemented a series of "authentic" policies intended to bolster his personal regime. In 1972 Christian and Western first names were banned in favor of "authentic" ancestral names ("post-names") that people added after their family names. Setting the example as "Father of the Nation," he renamed himself Mobutu Sese Seko Kuku Ngbendu Wa Za Banga. Gone were also *monsieur* and *madame*. Instead, Zairians had to address one another by *citoyen* and *citoyenne* (citizen), as had been the custom of the French revolutionists. By then other name changes had already taken place, including those of places. Perhaps some of the most sweeping changes came on October 27, 1971, when Mobutu ushered in the "Day of the Three Zs" by christening the country Zaire, along with the national currency and the main body of water, the Congo River. But the impetus had started early on in his reign when in May 1966 Leopoldville became Kinshasa.

During Mobutu's long rule (1965–1997), Kinshasa witnessed some dramatic changes, becoming in the 1990s one of the largest cities of the Global South and Africa's third-largest metropolis (next to Cairo and Lagos). Its population, close to eleven million to date, is larger than those of neighboring nations of Congo, Gabon, and the Central African Republic combined. Together with Brazzaville, Kinshasa displays two important features. They are the world's two closest capitals, separated only by a stretch of four kilometers across the Congo River, and stand as the most populous transborder metropolitan area in the world with a combined population of nearly twelve million inhabitants. While Brazzaville remains tied to its colonial past, as a slow-paced, administrative backwater— its colonial name never changed—Kinshasa has long lost most of its late colonial charm and appeal as a bustling yet orderly city.

When Mobutu took over, the city, in spite of the general political and social mayhem, showed resilience and quickly sloughed off the ethnic tensions that flared up in the wake of independence. This was due in no small measure to Mobutu's determination to depoliticize the city. Kin-la-Belle (Kin-the-Beautiful), aptly named because of the vibrancy of its cultural life, its lively markets, craft stores that catered to Western tourists, and scenic promenades along the Congo River, endeared itself to the hearts of its residents as a city too enthralling to hate. Enshrined in Congo's unofficial constitution was Mobutu's own version of *panem et circenses* (bread and circuses): "Happy the people who sing and dance" came to define the essence of *mobutisme*, the state ideology. From the colorful pageants praising him whenever a foreign dignitary visited Kinshasa to the hundreds of dance bars blasting Congolese rumba night and day to the Sunday church services that made music and dance the centerpiece of worship, Kinshasa pulsated with vibes and hubris.

Political cheerleading was of high importance in Mobutu's Zaire, and it required an organized structure. For this purpose, the regime set up a state agency, MOPAP (Mobilisation, Propagande et Animation Politique), which opened its main office in Kinshasa.

With an endowed budget rumored to have consistently dwarfed the state's expenditures for both education and health, MOPAP acted as a base, extending its roots in all areas of public life, from public schools, where the morning prayer was dropped for the formulaic praise to Mobutu, to churches, public offices, stadia, and markets. Performers strove to outshine one another with the most riveting compositions and performances celebrating the "Guide." Those who caught his attention were handsomely rewarded and often coopted within the regime's officialdom.

Perhaps the most emblematic example of this festive frenzy was Kinshasa's international annual fair (FIKIN), which first opened its doors on June 30, 1969. The FIKIN used to attract huge crowds of Congolese and expatriates with its international pavilions showcasing the latest innovations from all over the world and with its amusement park, food courts, fashion shows, and concert halls. It once epitomized Kinshasa's vibrancy and buttressed its claim to "beauty." Today the city desperately tries to shake off its infamous nickname of Kin-la-Poubelle (Kin-the-Trash-Bin). It has been plagued not only by mounds of uncollected garbage littering the roads and sidewalks, but also by sprawling *favellas* (slums) that are the result of waves of refugees fleeing war, violence, and rape along the country's eastern border. Kin-la-Poubelle stands also as a metaphor for the city's ills. It was in Kinshasa that the earliest known case (1959) of HIV/AIDS was identified, and problems stemming from bad governance and corruption on both national and municipal levels continue to cripple this African megalopolis and to hamper any meaningful urban renewal.

Kinshasa: A Tale of Many Cities

It does not take too long for visitors to notice Kinshasa's blatant inequalities, a common trait of most cities of the Global South from Bombay to Rio de Janeiro. The poor in Kinshasa rarely escape their far-flung slums to venture downtown. Urban survival in these slums, where people constantly battle diseases, malnutrition, flooding, and erosion, is a testimony to the resilience and resourcefulness of Kinshasa's downtrodden masses. While much of this poverty is certainly engineered by local failures, there is no doubt that the legacy of colonialism and external interferences have played an equally devastating role. For over three decades, Washington continued to buoy Mobutu's regime and to turn a blind eye to human rights abuses, corruption, and kleptocratic practices. As long as Mobutu abided by the Cold War arrangements, successive American administrations, from John F. Kennedy to George H. W. Bush, secured International Monetary Fund and World Bank loan packages for their protégé and shielded the regime from media scrutiny. In return for this protection, Mobutu ensured that Washington had unlimited access to Zaire's mineral reserves and safeguarded US ideological, diplomatic, and military interests in Africa. For instance, in the late 1970s and throughout most of the 1980s, as the United States battled Soviet influence in Angola, Zaire's southern neighbor, Mobutu allowed the Central Intelligence Agency to funnel weapons through the country's military bases to arm a pro-Western rebel group (UNITA) that had vowed to unseat the Soviet-friendly regime in Luanda (Angola's capital).

The most lasting legacy of the Cold War, however, continues to be the lack of accountability and the overreliance on mineral exports. Mobutu and his successors hardly conceived their power as emanating from the people; instead they saw it as something to be maintained by force. Since the economy remains entirely dependent on the export of natural resources, the state's revenue, as well as its political capital and legitimacy, comes from abroad. One cannot jockey for the position of president unless one has strong Western support. Because of colonization and Cold War politics and economic imperatives, Congo has been confined to the producing end of raw materials, fueling several economic revolutions in the process, and remains at the receiving end of manufacturing production. In Kinshasa, as in other Congolese urban areas, private industries never expanded except for a few processing plants held by foreign businesspeople (Lebanese, Greeks, Italians, Indians, and, more recently, a growing number of Chinese). As a result, virtually everything, from cars down to underwear, must be imported from the outside. Until the 1980s, thanks to the preservation of neocolonial ties, Europe fulfilled the city's needs for manufactured goods. But as of late, cheaper goods have come from Guangzhou and Dubai, the latter being the favored destination of savvy Congolese businesspersons. For residents of Kinshasa (Kinois), Dubai has become a byword for cornucopia and development, while Guangzhou remains synonymous with cheap, unsafe, and subpar goods. It is indeed in line with the serendipitous arrangement of our global economy that Dubai, a Middle Eastern locale with no prior connection with Kinshasa, has come to embody the ideals of progress, modernity, and plenty for millions of Kinois.

ENCOUNTERS AS TOLD: PRIMARY SOURCES

The following two documents contrast the views of the Congolese on their past and future and on a Cold War power invested in that future going a certain way. Patrice Lumumba speaks out against the virtues of Belgian colonialism, while a US diplomat responds to the perceived threat of a Congo that receives support from the Soviet Union.

Independence Day Speech, by Patrice Lumumba

Patrice Lumumba, Congo's prime minister, gave this speech on Independence Day before a large crowd of guests and foreign dignitaries, including Belgian king Baudoin. The speech was hastily written as Lumumba listened with anger while King Baudoin spoke, extolling the virtue of colonization and charting a blueprint for Belgian's continued involvement in Congo's affairs. While many people have praised the speech and continue to revere its fiery, nationalistic rhetoric, others have blamed it for alienating Western backers and thus derailing Congo's newfound independence from the beginning.

- Given the context of the Cold War described in this chapter, which elements of Lumumba's speech may have stoked Western fears of a communist takeover in Congo?

- Overall, what is Lumumba's portrayal of the colonial encounter? Compare it with what you know about European colonization in Africa and elsewhere. What would be a more nuanced portrayal of European colonization in Africa?

- In what sense was this speech couched in the Pan-African language of the 1950s and 1960s and therefore meant to appeal to a broader African audience, not just to Congolese constituencies?

Victorious fighters for independence, today victorious, I greet you in the name of the Congolese Government. All of you, my friends, who have fought tirelessly at our sides, I ask you to make this June 30, 1960, an illustrious date that you will keep indelibly engraved in your hearts, a date of significance of which you will teach to your children, so that they will make known to their sons and to their grandchildren the glorious history of our fight for liberty.

For this independence of the Congo, even as it is celebrated today with Belgium, a friendly country with whom we deal as equal to equal, no Congolese worthy of the name will ever be able to forget that it was by fighting that it has been won [applause], a day-to-day fight, an ardent and idealistic fight, a fight in which we were spared neither privation nor suffering, and for which we gave our strength and our blood.

We are proud of this struggle, of tears, of fire, and of blood, to the depths of our being, for it was a noble and just struggle, and indispensable to put an end to the humiliating slavery which was imposed upon us by force.

This was our fate for eighty years of a colonial regime; our wounds are too fresh and too painful still for us to drive them from our memory. We have known harassing work, exacted in exchange for salaries which did not permit us to eat enough to drive away hunger, or to clothe ourselves, or to house ourselves decently, or to raise our children as creatures dear to us.

We have known ironies, blows that we endured morning, noon, and evening, because we are Negroes. Who will forget that to a black one said "tu," certainly not as to a friend, but because the more honorable "vous" was reserved for white alone?

We have seen our hands seized in the name of allegedly legal laws which in fact recognized only that might is right.

We have seen that the law was not the same for a white and for a black, accommodating for the first, cruel and inhuman for the other.

We have witnessed atrocious sufferings of those condemned for their political opinions or religious beliefs; exiled in their own country, their fate truly worse than death itself.

We have seen that in the towns there were magnificent houses for the whites and crumbling shanties for the blacks, that a black was not admitted in the motion-picture houses, in the restaurants, in the stores of the Europeans; that a black traveled in the holds, at the feet of the whites in their luxury cabins.

Who will ever forget the massacres where so many of our brothers perished, the cells into which those who refused to submit to a regime of oppression and exploitation were thrown [applause]?

All that, my brothers, we have endured.

But we, whom the vote of your elected representatives have given the right to direct our dear country, we who have suffered in our body and in our heart from colonial oppression, we tell you very loud, all that is henceforth ended.

The Republic of the Congo has been proclaimed, and our country is now in the hands of its children. Together, my brothers, my sisters, we are going to begin a new struggle, a sublime struggle, which will lead our country to peace, prosperity, and greatness.

Together, we are going to establish social justice and make sure everyone has just remuneration for his labor [applause].

We are going to show the world what the black man can do when he works in freedom, and we are going to make of the Congo the center of the sun's radiance for all of Africa.

We are going to keep watch over the lands of our country so that they truly profit her children. We are going to restore ancient laws and make new ones which will be just and noble.

We are going to put an end to suppression of free thought and see to it that all our citizens enjoy to the full the fundamental liberties foreseen in the Declaration of the Rights of Man [applause].

We are going to rule not by the peace of guns and bayonets but by a peace of the heart and will [applause].

And for all that, dear fellow countrymen, be sure that we will count not only on our enormous strength and immense riches but on the assistance of numerous foreign countries whose collaboration we will accept if it is offered freely and with no attempt to impose on us an alien culture of no matter what nature [applause].

Source: Robin McKown, *Lumumba: A Biography* (New York: Doubleday & Company, 1969).

Telegram from the Embassy in Belgium to the Department of State, July 19, 1960

The following American diplomatic cable was transmitted only two weeks after Congo's independence and conveys the impressions of the American author on how events there developed and their implications for the future. The cable refers to "Deptel," which is shorthand for department telegram, and the author's identity is not provided.

- Why did Americans conclude that Lumumba's government had to be overthrown?

- Based on what you have learned about the Cold War, what might have been the American "vital interests" the preservation of which warranted a regime change in Kinshasa?

258. While Deptel 147 addressed Leopoldville and problem dealing with Lumumba is Leopoldville's responsibility, Department and Leopoldville may wish consider following Embassy views based on numerous discussions with Belgians. Specific suggestions may be rapidly overtaken by fast-moving developments, but Embassy believes situation calls for urgent measures on various levels if even reasonable degree stability and Western entrée into Congo to be salvaged from present anarchic situation.

1. Whatever circumstances and motivations may have led to present situation, Lumumba has now maneuvered himself into position of opposition to West, resistance to United Nations and increasing dependence on Soviet Union and on Congolese supporters (Kashamura, Gizenga) who are pursuing Soviet's ends. Only prudent, therefore, to plan on basis that Lumumba government threatens our vital interests in Congo and Africa generally. A principal objective of our political and diplomatic action must therefore be to destroy Lumumba government as now constituted, but at the same time we must find or develop another horse to back which would be acceptable in rest of Africa and defensible against Soviet political attack.

Source: Harriest Dashiell Schwar and Stanley Shaloff, eds., *Foreign Relations of the United States, 1958–1960*, vol. XIV (Washington, DC: U.S. Government Printing Office), 330.

Further Reading

Gibbs, David N. *The Political Economy of Third World Intervention: Mines, Money, and U.S. Policy in the Congo Crisis.* Chicago: The University of Chicago Press, 1991.

Gondola, Ch. Didier. *The History of Congo.* Westport, CT: Greenwood Press, 2002.

Hochschild, Adam. *King Leopold's Ghost: A Story of Greed, Terror, and Heroism in Colonial Africa.* New York: Houghton Mifflin, 1998.

Kalb, Madeleine G. *The Congo Cables: The Cold War in Africa—From Eisenhower to Kennedy.* New York: Macmillan 1982.

Nzongola-Ntalaja, Georges. *The Congo from Leopold to Kabila: A People's History.* London: Zed Books, 2002.

Web Resources

Anup Shah, "The Democratic Republic of Congo," GlobalIssues.org, August 21, 2010, www.globalissues.org/article/87/the-democratic-republic-of-congo.

Congo (Kinshasa) Chronology, http://www.worldstatesmen.org/Congo-Kinshasa.html.

Congo War Resource, http://congowarresource.org/.

Democratic Republic of the Congo, Stanford University, http://library.stanford.edu/depts/ssrg/africa/zaire.html.

Democratic Republic of the Congo Page, University of Pennsylvania, www.africa.upenn.edu/Country_Specific/Zaire.html.

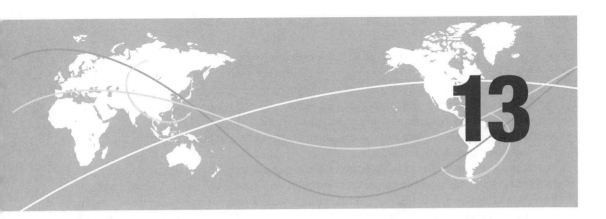

Berlin

A Global Symbol of the Iron Curtain

(1945–1991)

Eliza Ablovatski and Elaine MacKinnon

I<small>N 2009 PEOPLE ALL ACROSS THE GLOBE CELEBRATED THE TWENTIETH ANNIVERSARY</small> of the events of 1989 when the Berlin Wall fell, paving the way to the reunification of Germany and the end of the Cold War. For those of us who now teach, one notable aspect of this anniversary was the shock of realizing that events that were so pivotal to our own intellectual and academic path happened before most of our students now were born! One of this chapter's authors entered college in the fall of 1989 and remembers watching the news about the Berlin Wall in her Russian history class, which paused to track these monumental current events. As a historian of Central Europe and a former resident of Berlin, she often finds it natural to use the shorthand "fall of the Berlin Wall" as a way of talking about post-1989 transitions. Berlin is truly central to international understanding of Cold War history, as well as to the commemorations and histories of the transition taking place throughout Europe with the collapse of communism.

The post–World War II division of Europe into two hostile political, economic, and military blocs or alliances was one of the defining features of the Cold War. And Berlin, the divided former capital of Nazi Germany, seemed more than anywhere else to exemplify this divide. Thousands of miles of borders marked the so-called Iron Curtain from the Baltic Sea in the north to the Balkan Peninsula in the south. Within Berlin itself, a fortified dividing line developed in stages, while the two Germanys were divided by a much longer internal border. Yet the nearly one hundred miles of cement wall erected beginning in August 1961, furnished with guard towers and barbed wire, seemed above all to exemplify the barbarity of this division of Europe, especially since at least a third of its distance ran right through the heart of the city, slicing through residential and commercial districts and cutting the single city in two.

As I sit here at my office computer, I am looking at what connects me to the city of Berlin—a chunk of concrete, grey and crumbly, in a plastic container. I, like perhaps millions of others across the globe, own a piece of this wall. My piece regrettably was not hand-chiseled, at least not by me, nor do I have any certification of authenticity except for the testimony of the student who kindly gave it to me years ago. I have stood on a section of the wall, but not in Berlin; wandering the harbor in Portland, Maine, I came across a memorial to the people of Berlin and climbed up on what is claimed to be a genuine section of the structure. Ironically, in Berlin itself, the idea has been to forget the wall ever existed, and what remains of it has been gathered in a remote sector to be ground into dust. New modern high-rises and shopping emporia have taken its place, yet it lives on elsewhere in the world as a tribute to the triumph of freedom. It is also, however, a graphic reminder of the role of the absurd in Cold War politics and the peculiar status accorded to Berlin by both the United States and the Soviet Union. Perhaps the greatest irony lies in the transformation of this concrete symbol of communist intransigence into a marketable commodity that even the East German regime itself sought to capitalize on in the months before reunification in 1990.

My piece of the wall takes me back to my childhood and my struggles to comprehend exactly what a "cold war" was. The wall helped me to picture what people meant by an "iron curtain." A concrete wall made more sense to me than a curtain made of iron. The wall divided Berlin just as the curtain divided Europe into East and West. But the wall also made me very sympathetic to those who could not climb over it—I understood what it was like to not be able to go somewhere you desperately wanted to be. Yet if true confessions are to be made, I must admit that for a number of years the truly peculiar situation of Berlin, and the reason why the wall existed there, actually eluded me. I just accepted it as a symbol of two worlds that stood opposed to each other without grasping that Berlin, even its western parts, stood 110 miles deep within the territory of East Germany. Somehow I thought of it as being on the border of East Germany and West Germany, not as an enclave within East Germany. I now make it a point when teaching about Berlin and the wall to clarify where it stood, so students can understand the complexities of Berlin's role in the Cold War. Even in my ignorance the wall alone provided a powerful symbol, with its cold, forbidding façade of concrete, barbed wire, tank barriers, and armed guards. Like so many during the Cold War, I viewed the wall not as the East Germans insisted on referring to it, as an "antifascist protective rampart," but as an ugly reminder of a system that had to build walls to keep its unhappy people from breaking free of it, and as metaphor for the seemingly eternal standoff between East and West in the Cold War.

This chapter will take you into Berlin during the period 1945 to 1990 to examine the myriad ways in which the story of this city illuminates the superpower rivalry known as a the Cold War. Of course, one can argue that the killing fields of Cambodia or the demolished villages of Vietnam are equal or better avenues into studying the global reach and impact of the Cold War. But Berlin is the keystone in the arch of the war. It was central to the early emergence of conflict between the former allies—the United States and the

Soviet Union—and it figured prominently in the war's moments of greatest tension (the Cuban Crisis of 1962), as well as during its most relaxed periods (détente from 1969 to 1979). Finally, the dismantling of Berlin's concrete divider known as "the wall" provided both a literal and symbolic end to the Cold War division of Europe. In the two decades since 1989, referring to the "fall of the Berlin Wall" has become a shorthand way of talking about the end of the era of Soviet-controlled state socialist regimes in Eastern Europe. The Berlin Wall as a physical marker, and the breaching of it on November 9, 1989, stand in for political transformation in the whole region. The images of Germans celebrating on top of the Berlin Wall on the night of November 9 seem to embody the largely nonviolent and popular revolutions of 1989, just as images of the massively fortified wall through the heart of Berlin had stood for almost three decades as symbols of a whole system of rule and of the so-called Iron Curtain, even though when Winston Churchill coined that phrase in 1946 neither German state had been created and a wall through Berlin was far from anyone's imagination.

BERLIN AND THE WORLD: *A City Shaped by the Cold War*

Berlin's prominence in Europe and the world was well established long before the Cold War transformed it into a universal symbol of resistance to tyranny. Interestingly, Berlin began as a divided city, consisting of two villages, Berlin and Kölln, on opposite sides of the River Spree. Founded as a fishing and trading settlement, Berlin grew into an international metropolis largely through military prowess and the development of industry. It served first as the capital of the Kingdom of Prussia, and, after 1871, of the newly unified German Empire. By 1914 it was the second-largest city in Europe, with over four million inhabitants, and was a major center of Germany's explosive growth in industrial production, particularly in the chemical and electrical industries. It suffered severely from food shortages during World War I, and in 1918 revolution broke out in its streets, forcing the kaiser to flee. Berlin retained its political prominence, however, as capital of both the Weimar Republic (1918–1933) and then of the Nazi state (1933–1945). It also remained a major international economic, industrial, scientific, and commercial hub, and in the 1920s it was one of the most culturally vibrant cities in Europe.

But in 1945 Berlin lay in ruins, a shell of its former self, with less than half of its pre-war population of 4.5 million, though this was rising due to an influx of refugees. During the final months of World War II, the Allied powers of Britain, the United States, and the Soviet Union closed in on the city, striking at the heart of the Third Reich in hopes of forcing Adolph Hitler into an unconditional surrender. Allied planes bombed relentlessly day and night, and Soviet tanks entered from the east. Hardly a building stood in the city center, and it would take several thousand workers more than two years to fill in all of the bomb craters and trenches. The city's residents hid beneath the rubble, scavenged for food, water, and fuel, and wondered what their fate would be after Hitler committed suicide and the Reich collapsed. For many it was death—starvation and disease took the lives of over ten thousand Berliners in 1946 alone.

But what most Berliners and millions across the globe did not know was that from the ashes and rubble of this horrific war, the most costly in history, yet another conflict was brewing: the Cold War. This conflict would threaten all of them with global nuclear annihilation. Born out of disagreements between the Soviet Union and its allies over the fate of Germany and Soviet-occupied Eastern Europe, the Cold War was also a rivalry for global military, economic, and political domination, fueled by fundamental ideological differences between the capitalist United States and the communist Soviet Union, both of which emerged from World War II as preeminent industrial and military superpowers. Berlin and the fate of Germany, with its central location, resources, and industrial potential, seemed to all as the key to control over postwar Europe, and neither side was willing to cede it to the other.

Initially the victorious Allied powers put agreements into effect dividing Germany into zones of military occupation by the United States, the Soviet Union, Great Britain, and France. A similar division into four occupation zones was made in Austria (which had been incorporated into Nazi Germany in 1938) and in the two capitals, Berlin and Vienna. Each power was responsible for its zone, but Berlin was jointly controlled by all four powers, despite its division. In 1945 all four powers assumed that these divisions were a temporary part of the postwar occupation, but relatively quickly both the international actors, as well as Germans on both sides of the zonal borders, began to take actions that made a unified German future less likely. As relations deteriorated between the United States and the Soviet Union, Berlin took on greater significance, as did the whole of Germany. The United States and its allies France and Britain increasingly favored reconstruction of Germany and its industry, while the Soviet Union demanded reparations and the dismantling of German economic assets. The United States sought to rebuild Germany as a Western ally in part because of the expansion of Soviet control into Eastern Europe and the presence of the Red Army in such countries as Poland, Hungary, and Romania. There was fear in the United States that a dangerous power vacuum existed in Europe and that its war-torn and devastated economies and societies were vulnerable to communist influence. In 1947 it still seemed possible that in France and Italy communists could win elections. This concern fueled the massive US aid program known as the Marshall Plan, which, beginning in 1947, provided over $13 billion in reconstruction funds to Europe. The governments of Great Britain and France supported the US efforts, but they were not in a position to offer much economic or even military assistance, as they themselves struggled to recover from war and from the subsequent erosion of their colonial empires. Thus, by 1947 Berlin was being held up in the United States as an important outpost for stemming communist expansion; it was also becoming in practical terms an invaluable location for surveillance and espionage. In time Berlin would reportedly have more secret agents per acre than any other place in the world. The centrality of Berlin for both superpowers is indicated by the heavy military presence each had in Germany. Both stationed more troops in their respective zones of Germany than in any other sector in Europe. By the end of the Cold War, the United States had over 70 percent of its European-based forces in the western sector of Germany, totaling 250,000 troops according to some estimates, while the Soviet Union kept between 350,000 and 400,000 troops in the east.

Germany's political division did not become a reality, however, until the creation of two states, first the Federal Republic of Germany (FRG, or West Germany), declared in May 1949, and then the German Democratic Republic (GDR, or East Germany), declared in October 1949. (See Map 13.1.) These new states were created following several months of Cold War drama, above all, the Soviet Union's Berlin blockade in 1948–1949 that prevented the United States, Great Britain, and France from supplying West Berlin sectors. The Soviet Union hoped to push its former allies completely out of Berlin in response to the steps being taken to unify their respective zones in Germany under a single currency, a new deutsche mark. When the three allies announced that the new mark would be introduced into Berlin, the Soviet Union declared that rail links between the western zones and the western sectors of Berlin were closed due to "technical difficulties."

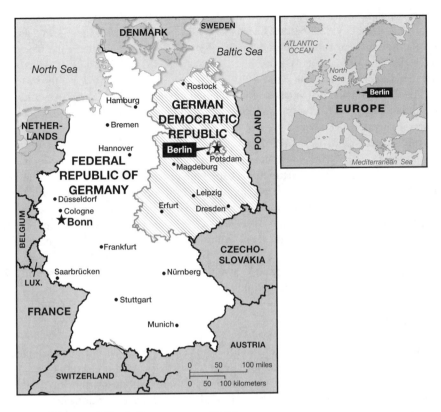

Map 13.1. West and East Germany, ca. 1949

In 1949 the three occupation zones of the French, the British, and the Americans merged to form the Federal Republic of Germany, or West Germany. It covered more than twice the area of the German Democratic Republic, or East Germany, which was formed from the Soviet occupation zone. Note the location of Berlin, deep inside of East Germany and close to Poland, and how this made the city a useful location for conducting Western surveillance and propaganda behind the Iron Curtain.

This was followed by the closing down of all routes for incoming traffic, trucks, and barges, and the Soviet authorities shut off all electricity as well to the western sectors of the city.

But Russian leader Joseph Stalin's move backfired, for it only served to solidify the determination of West Berliners to resist incorporation into the Soviet sphere. The United States responded by organizing the remarkably successful "Berlin Airlift," also known as "Operation Vittles," during which time a nearly constant stream of American and British airplanes carried at least two million tons of food and other goods into West Berlin; the children of West Berlin endearingly referred to the planes as the "candy bombers" or "raisin bombers" because the pilots would drop sweets, particularly chocolate bars, as they landed. At one point late in the airlift a fully supplied plane was landing in West Berlin every sixty-two seconds, each one a beacon of hope to the hungry and cold citizens, much of their city still in ruins from the war. The Berlin blockade became a defining moment in the Cold War, for it not only confirmed but deepened the US commitment to remain in Berlin, which then became a signpost for its capacity and intention to stand up to Soviet expansion, as well as a matter of American prestige. During the blockade Berlin became a divided city, well before the wall was built, as each side set up separate administrative structures that remained intact even after the Soviet Union lifted the blockade in May 1949. The ordeal secured the bond between West Berliners and Americans, and amplified the fears of many in Western Europe that the Soviet Union was a threat to security. This in turn helped to accelerate completion of plans for the North Atlantic Treaty Organization (NATO), which committed the United States militarily to the defense of Western Europe.

While the political division of Germany was not inevitable (after all, Austria was divided and occupied for ten years, yet it emerged a unified country after receiving its independence in 1955), the zones of occupation shaped the postwar rebuilding of the country and particularly shaped the physical space and culture of the city of Berlin. From the postwar occupation through to German reunification in 1990, Berlin was a place of diplomacy, espionage, and ideological showmanship. Some of the iconic postwar architecture of the city in both divisions reflects this political and cultural dueling, such as the Axel Springer Publishing skyscraper in West Germany and the Television Tower (Fernsehturm) and many high-rise apartment buildings in East Germany. Part of the motivation for building these structures was the impression they would make on Berliners across the border.

The Uprising of June 17, 1953

The Berlin loophole continued to provide both tension and relief in the early years of divided Germany. This was particularly true of the mass exodus that followed the Soviet suppression of a workers' uprising in June 1953. Just months after Stalin's death in March of that year, this protest over wages and prices in East Germany erupted, marking the first popular revolt against a state socialist regime in Eastern Europe. It escalated from complaints over unfair production quotas to demands for free elections, and before the regime knew what was happening, there was open opposition in the streets of Berlin and in other industrial regions of the GDR. The East German leadership worried that it could not control the situation alone and sought protection and support at Soviet military headquarters in Berlin. On the afternoon of June 17, the Soviet military appeared with sixteen divisions of soldiers and tanks, clearing the streets without major resistance and arresting thousands of "provocateurs" (despite the massive show of force, only about three dozen protesters and bystanders lost their lives). The East German government and its leader, Walter Ulbricht, survived, but the world had witnessed the first outbreak of popular resistance in the Soviet bloc, as well as the Soviet determination to use military force to keep its satellite nations under communist rule. These June uprisings were followed in the 1950s by similar revolts in Poland, Hungary, and in 1968 in Czechoslovakia, and each time the Soviet Union responded with a military crackdown, establishing a pattern that would last until the fateful year of 1989.

Within East Germany, the Soviet intervention, with its mass arrests and the declaration of a state of emergency, led to the loss of almost four hundred thousand citizens across the internationally controlled Berlin border. While a huge demographic setback, this "release" may have actually aided the regime in its compromises with the skilled workers who remained behind. In fact, many of the specific demands regarding wages and working conditions put forth by the laborers who protested in June 1953 were actually met by the GDR government in a series of economic reforms after it had quashed the uprising.

Berlin as a Focal Point of Superpower Attention

Throughout the 1950s Berlin held practical significance, as well as rhetorical and symbolic value. It remained a divisive issue for the United States and the Soviet Union, as both sides refused to give up their respective occupation rights. As a result, Berliners lived with the constant threat that the Cold War could become hot at any moment. Nowhere else in the world did Western soldiers and tanks confront so directly the forces of the Soviet Red Army. At times the Soviet Union, to prove its legal right to fly Soviet airplanes in the air corridors in and out of Berlin whenever they pleased, would step up harassment of Western aircraft flying to and from Berlin, creating sonic booms in flight zones or indulging in aerial cat and mouse games such as "buzzing" or flying closely behind American and British civilian airliners. Berlin and the fear of Soviet actions against its western sectors figured prominently in the consciousness of American presidents from Harry Truman to John F. Kennedy, especially after the Soviet Union successfully tested its first atomic bomb in 1949. American policymakers remained committed to maintaining the US occupation in Berlin and secured access to the western sectors, but there now was genuine fear that this could provoke nuclear war with the Soviet Union. Detailed military plans had to be worked out for both nuclear and conventional military responses to any change in the status of Berlin.

The decade of the 1950s was marked by a series of Berlin crises, set off in part by failed negotiations between the United States and the Soviet Union over the status of East and West Germany and the fate of Berlin. It became an accepted feature of Cold War international politics to divide countries deemed vital to each side rather than allow them to enter either bloc in unified form—beginning first with Germany, then Korea, and finally Vietnam. Nonetheless, there were repeated efforts in the 1950s to resolve the German question. The Soviet Union was willing at times to support the reunification of Germany, but only as a neutral nation and not as a member of the US-led NATO. The United States would agree to a unified Germany only on the basis of free elections, which the Soviets feared would lead to a government firmly in the Western camp. Furthermore, the United States, France, and Great Britain refused to recognize the legitimacy of the East German state and would not relinquish their zones of occupation in Berlin, which were becoming increasingly valuable as a conduit for espionage and propaganda into the Soviet bloc. In 1955 they decided to allow West Germany to rearm and join the NATO alliance. The Soviet Union, led by Stalin's successor, Nikita Khrushchev, retaliated by recognizing both German states as legitimate and by admitting East Germany into the Warsaw Pact, its newly formed rival military alliance with its Eastern European satellite nations. Khrushchev then spent much of the period from 1956 to 1961 trying to threaten and bluster the Allied forces out of Berlin or to make staying in Berlin the price for recognition of East Germany. He spawned a series of crises by periodically threatening to sign a peace treaty with the GDR and turn the city over to it, which would then force the United States, France, and Britain to sign a treaty with the GDR in order to continue having access to the western sectors of Berlin. Khruschev accomplished little by these threats, which he always allowed to lapse without taking action, except to exacerbate tensions.

For Khrushchev, Berlin thus was the proverbial "bone" perpetually stuck in his throat. The Soviet Union, after all, had been the first to enter Berlin and theoretically could have laid claim to it all. The Soviets were well aware that the city served as a center for infiltration by Western intelligence and that with substantial subsidies from the United States and the Allies, West Berlin was becoming a showcase of Western freedom and capitalist prosperity. The Soviet Union believed that East Germany's survival was inextricably linked with its own credibility and international prestige, and it wanted the GDR to have control over its own capital. Yet Berlin had its own importance for the Soviet Union as well. It conducted spying operations from Berlin, set up listening posts, and sought ways to destabilize the zones controlled by Western forces. In addition, Berlin became a tool for political leverage in the expanding arena of nuclear competition in the Cold War rivalry with the United States.

The successful testing in 1953 of the first Soviet hydrogen bomb and the launching in 1957 of the Soviet *Sputnik I*, the first unmanned satellite in space, prompted NATO and the Americans in 1958 to explore the option of putting nuclear weapons in Germany. There was now a real fear that the Soviets had the technology to develop intercontinental ballistic missiles that could cover a large range of territory. The Soviet Union in turn strongly opposed a nuclear West Germany and sought to use Berlin to force the West to back off from this proposal. The United States, for its part, was not ready to go to war over Berlin and doubted Khrushchev's own willingness to do so, but there were no guarantees or security on either side. The Soviet Union under Khrushchev was seeking to expand its global influence, buoyed by the dissolution of colonial empires that, by the end of the 1950s, were producing new countries seeking allies and models for development. Khrushchev was well aware that Soviet nuclear capacities lagged behind those of the United States, but he hoped that by making threats and bluffing strategically he could make the West think twice before pressing its advantages. The United States under Dwight D. Eisenhower had undergone a massive expansion of its nuclear arsenal and was firmly committed to a Cold War policy of military containment of communist expansion wherever it threatened areas of vital interest. The Korean War had demonstrated the American willingness to go to war to prevent a divided country from being unified under communist auspices. The anxieties over Berlin and the uncertainties of how far each side was willing to go before blinking is highly telling of what the atmosphere was like during the Cold War.

Building a Wall through the City

These uncertainties were exacerbated by the crippling "brain drain" that was flowing through this crack in the Iron Curtain. From the start, the new East German state faced out-migration to West Germany, and it closed the border to West Germany in 1952, except for the huge Berlin loophole. Initially, despite being officially illegal, this out-migration was actually a mixed blessing for the socialist regime. The regime was freed of possible opponents and able to claim the abandoned property of the people who fled the de-Nazification and economic restructuring in the early GDR. It was generally not workers (who had been the protesters in 1953) who "fled the Republic" (as the crime of illegal emigration was called), but mostly intellectual professionals, as well as farmers and other former small business and property owners. Over time, though, this loss of trained professionals made things difficult in East Germany, as issues such as staffing hospitals became very hard, and their "flight" was politically devastating. By 1961 these professionals had been beneficiaries of free education and promotion within the GDR system, yet they still left, nullifying the state's investment in the future. Twenty percent of East Germany's doctors fled the region after 1954. Altogether, between 1949 and 1958, 2.1 million persons left East Germany and sought asylum in West Berlin, and nearly a million more did so between 1958 and the building of the wall. In the first twelve years of its existence, the East German state lost as much as one-sixth of its population.

This "brain drain" is what finally led to the building of the Cold War's most famous landmark. Though it was at the center of international Cold War politics, the Berlin Wall was primarily a local phenomenon, a response to German and particularly Berlin circumstances, although these were determined by Berlin's unique status that involved four-power administration of its borders. One could say that the Berlin Wall was both built and torn down in response to the exodus of the population from East Germany through the border of the divided capital city (actually, East Berlin was the capital of the GDR, but not of the new FRG, which declared its capital to be Bonn in the Rhine region). Due to a faltering economy and his desperation to stop this "brain drain," East German Communist Party leader Walter Ulbricht asked Khrushchev's permission to build a wall to close the open Berlin border. Subsequently, on early Sunday morning, August 13, 1961, the East German army and security forces began fortifying the border in Berlin with barbed wire and temporary blockades. This new barrier went up in a single night, but in reality the building of what came to be known as the Berlin Wall was a more extended process. Five days after initially closing off the border with barbed wire, having met with little reaction from the West, the East Germans began building a structure made of concrete slabs between the Brandenburg Gate and the Potsdamer Platz. The wall was thought to be more intimidating than the original barrier, and the barbed wire had not been able to stem fully the border crossings and escapes. Then in 1962 a second parallel wall was built about one hundred yards behind the first wall to make it even more difficult for people to escape. The empty space between the walls came to be known as "no-man's-land," or the "death strip." Yet by 1964 there was actually less than ten miles of actual wall, and most of this was in the central part of the city; only in 1976 was the final version of the wall completed. It extended in total about ninety-six miles, twenty-seven of which went through the center of the city and cut through 192 streets, thirty-two railway lines, four underground train lines, and several rivers and lakes. (See Map 13.2.) Along with the wall there were over two hundred guard watchtowers, bunkers, and observation posts, staffed by guards armed with rifles, cameras, and binoculars. Officially the wall was claimed to be a necessary protection against Western agitators disrupting the GDR and also to protect the East German economy (ostensibly from West Berliners buying subsidized goods cheaply across the border). Although the wall did successfully stem the "brain drain," nonetheless around five thousand persons in the course of its history managed to escape, many by digging tunnels beneath it. More than three thousand persons were arrested, and approximately 160 to 200 died trying to escape (exact numbers are not known).

Global Echoes: From Tensions in Berlin to the Brink of Nuclear War in the Caribbean

For the West, the wall was not the ideal solution, and it did make a show of opposition to it. Nonetheless it came more as a relief than a catastrophe. The United States had never been comfortable with the idea of going to war over Berlin, and the Berlin Wall removed the fear that the Soviet Union would have to take military action to prop up East Germany. Though a public relations disaster in many respects, the wall did serve its purpose. It stopped the drain of East Germany's population and allowed it to obtain a degree of stability and even normalcy. As John F. Kennedy is reported to have said, "It's not a very nice solution, but a wall is a hell of a lot better than a war."

The United States was not willing to go to war over the closing off of East Berlin as long as it had access to West Berlin, which it did. There was a showdown of sorts after the wall went up, but it was defused in a remarkably brief period. In October 1961 American diplomats refused to show identification to East German guards at checkpoints, and the

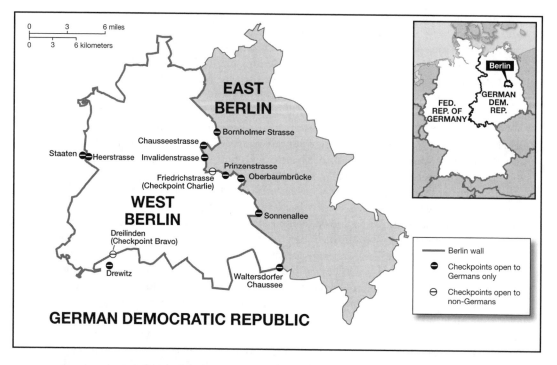

Map 13.2. The Berlin Wall and Its Checkpoints, 1961–1989

The Berlin Wall, the Cold War's most famous landmark, began with barbed wire and concrete barriers built along the twenty-six-mile border between the Russian sector of the city in the east and the British, American, and French zones in the west. The wall grew until it fully enclosed the western sectors, which merged to form West Berlin. People wishing to pass into or out of the city needed to go through checkpoints, a term Allied forces preferred because of the West's nonrecognition of East Germany as a separate state. That nonrecognition continued until 1973, but even after East Germany's entry into the United Nations the term stayed in common use.

Soviet Union responded by bringing tanks to the border. The Americans responded likewise. For sixteen hours, the Cold War witnessed the only time in its history that American and Soviet tanks stared each other down. During these sixteen hours Western armed forces across the globe were on alert, and four US atomic submarines were poised in the North Sea, aiming sixteen warheads at the Soviet Union. But neither side really wanted a fight, and the crisis ended when Khrushchev ordered the Soviet tanks to back off into side streets. Twenty minutes later the United States did the same.

Thus, the wall became an accepted part of the Berlin landscape. For West Berliners their side of the wall became a tourist attraction and the repository of colorful graffiti, providing a stark contrast to the dull grey exterior and forbidding watchtowers on the eastern side. The West Berliners could go right up to the wall and peer through its cracks and play rock music loudly enough to reach the other side. The city boasted new landmarks, particularly the eight checkpoints and border crossings where the US and Soviet zones met. Checkpoint Charlie was located in the heart of Berlin. Checkpoint Bravo was where the autobahn crossed over from East Germany into West Berlin, and Checkpoint Alpha was where the autobahn crossed from West to East Germany. The wall also infused old landmarks with new meaning; the old Brandenburg Gate had managed to survive

World War II without being damaged, and then it became the border between the British zone and the Soviet zone within Berlin. After the wall was erected, traffic between the two zones ceased, and the gate for many became synonymous with the wall and what it meant for Berlin. The gate did not reopen again until December 22, 1989.

For West Berlin, the wall also changed the city's demographics, for the loss of East German labor led to an increase in *gastarbeiter*, or guest workers, primarily from Turkey and later from Yugoslavia. For the people of East Berlin, the wall not only changed the landscape, but it also caused ruptures in their families, neighborhoods, occupations, and life opportunities. It is quite remarkable to think of a modern city being split in two and what that would mean for transportation, mobility, and personal connections. Roads, tram lines, and subway lines had to be shut down; even for those subway lines that stayed running, certain stations where lines crossed from West to East Berlin and back had to be closed and were referred to as "ghost stations." Hundreds of families who lived in the vicinity of the wall found themselves relocated to new high-rise housing developments on the outskirts of the city. East Germans who had worked in West Berlin had to find new jobs. Entire apartment blocks had to be demolished as the wall structure expanded. Some sections of Berlin split by the wall were turned into macabre ghost towns, empty lots with weeds. It is a chilling testimony to the power of the modern state to alter people's lives. East Berliners had their lives most transformed, for it was always easier for foreigners or even West Berliners to move back and forth. For instance, West Berliners were allowed under special agreements to visit relatives in the east during holidays. Practically the only East Germans who could visit West Berlin were those of retirement age, since their potential defection would not affect labor productivity.

Berlin and the Cuban Missile Crisis

Although the wall did serve to alleviate tensions between East and West, there was still one more chapter in the series of Berlin crises that had begun in 1948 with the Berlin Airlift. The city figured prominently in one of the tensest confrontations of the entire Cold War: the Cuban Missile Crisis of October 1962. The world stood at the brink of nuclear catastrophe after the Soviet Union decided to place sixty medium- and intermediate-range ballistic missiles in Cuba, only ninety miles from the US coast. To a certain degree the Cuban crisis was an extension of the Berlin crises, and, in some scholars' views, the culmination of them. Unquestionably, Berlin was on the mind of both Kennedy and Khrushchev, the two leaders during the crisis. Khrushchev's frustration over the failure to resolve the Western presence in Berlin and his desire to gain leverage there contributed to his motives for placing nuclear missiles in Cuba. Throughout the summer of 1962 he publicly berated the West for its continued occupation of Berlin and for its refusal to sign a peace treaty with East Germany. Khrushchev hoped that missiles at the back door of the United States might push it to be more flexible in its German and Berlin policies, while also redressing the nuclear imbalance. The United States had placed more than one hundred nuclear missiles in Italy and Turkey, and Khrushchev wanted Americans to know how it felt to have similar weapons in such close proximity to them.

For his part, Kennedy felt constrained throughout the crisis by the fear that the Soviet Union could retaliate for any show of force the United States might make against Cuba by moving against West Berlin. He also knew that allowing the missiles to remain in Cuba would inevitably strengthen the Soviet position in Berlin, which he was already concerned about, and on September 8, just days before the crisis broke, Kennedy had asked for more reserve troops to be sent to Berlin. In his speech to the nation on October 22 about the missile crisis, Kennedy made it clear that the United States was prepared to step in to protect West Berlin, and he indeed made plans at that time for a counterblockade of the city and for a military response against Cuba if the Soviets acted in Berlin. Kennedy's firm and forceful response, in which he announced a naval quarantine and prepared a carefully calibrated strategy for an escalated military response consisting first of airstrikes and then invasion of Cuba, was perhaps unexpected for Khrushchev. He had hoped that Kennedy would not even find out about the missiles until they were already in place, and he did not seem to have planned on Kennedy being willing to threaten military force.

To a certain extent, the peaceful outcome of this crisis, which saw the Soviets agree to remove the missiles placed in Cuba in return for the pledge of the United States not to invade Cuba, contributed to the waning of tensions over Berlin as well. Kennedy's clear intention to escalate the military response may have convinced Khrushchev not to test the United States further over Berlin. He still made impulsive threats in private conversations about what the Soviets could do in Berlin if provoked, but in the end the Soviet Union accepted the wall as the ultimate resolution for the survival of the East German state.

Thus, the building of the Berlin Wall and the removal of the missiles from Cuba marked an end to the ongoing Berlin crises, and to a certain extent the centrality of Berlin in Cold War power politics lessened. The people of Berlin learned to live with the wall, and it served as a powerful propaganda tool for Western leaders.

Berlin's "Politics of the East" Aids the West

Though no longer a flashpoint, Berlin remained a powerful symbol of the two opposing worldviews, which became increasingly apparent when one flew above the city and could see the contrasts in the two sectors. East Berliners continued to capture the attention of Western audiences with spectacular attempts at escape; the American television network NBC even agreed in 1962 to finance an escape in exchange for exclusive filming rights to the entire operation. Forty-one persons, primarily university students in West Berlin, joined in building the tunnel and, in addition to furnishing money for the tunnel's construction, NBC provided radios for the builders to communicate with each other. Diplomats from Asian and African countries based in Berlin were also known for helping smuggle out escapees, as they could travel through checkpoints without having their cars searched. There were sensational spy swaps as well, including the exchange of the only Soviet spy ever tried and found guilty in the United States, Rudolf Able, and American U-2 pilot Francis Gary Powers, who was shot down in May 1960 deep inside Soviet territory while photographing Soviet nuclear installations.

Berlin was also a key arena for processes that became part of what has been called the era of détente, the stage in the Cold War (1969–1979) that saw a relaxation of tensions between the United States and the Soviet Union, highlighted by the historic signing in 1972 of the world's first arms control limitation treaty, SALT I. In Europe détente took the form of *ostpolitik*, which means literally the "politics of the East"; it entailed West Germany pursuing a more flexible and pragmatic policy toward the Soviet Union and the Eastern bloc of Soviet satellite nations, including East Germany. It was spearheaded by the man who had served for many years as the mayor of West Berlin, Willy Brandt. In 1966 Brandt became foreign minister of West Germany, and then in 1969 he became chancellor. While serving as mayor in 1961–1962, Brandt realized that the wall was a reality that Germans would have to adjust to, for clearly the West was not going to take military means to remove it. So he began looking for ways to live with that reality and carried this sensibility with him when he became the West German foreign minister. Brandt was the first to establish diplomatic relations with Eastern European nations, hitherto nonexistent because the latter recognized East Germany, and then he opened talks with the Soviet Union that led to the 1971 Berlin Agreement guaranteeing the independence of West Berlin, which was signed by all four occupying powers. One year later West Germany signed the Basic Treaty, which granted recognition to East Germany and gave each Germany "permanent representation" in the other's capital.

Ostpolitik also included landmark exchanges and trade relations that allowed massive numbers of West German visitors to travel to East Germany, and along with them went highly prized Western consumer goods and staples, including coffee, jeans, and rock albums by the Rolling Stones and the Beatles. This development may have done more to undermine the foundations of communist rule in Eastern Europe than any of the costly missiles each superpower aimed at each other. *Ostpolitik* allowed greater interaction between East and West and increased the awareness of East Berliners, as well as of others within the Soviet bloc, of the glaring disparity between the opportunities and conveniences offered by the rival systems. It then proved harder and harder to suppress the expectations of those behind the Iron Curtain who were tired of waiting for communism to deliver on its promises to achieve higher living standards than in the West.

The Fall of the Wall and the End of the Cold War

To truly understand the momentous developments that led to the end of the Cold War in 1990–1991, one cannot focus solely on Berlin and the fall of the wall. The impetus for change came from Mikhail Gorbachev, the Soviet leader who came to power in 1985 and subsequently pursued unprecedented policies of reform known as *perestroika* (restructuring) and *glasnost* (openness). In the arena of foreign policy he stunned the world by declaring that Soviet troops would no longer intervene militarily to prop up Eastern European regimes. This announcement spurred momentous change in the Eastern bloc, including Poland's first multiparty elections in 1989 and the June victory of labor leader Lech Walesa and the revived trade union party Solidarity. The East German state, led by Erich Honecker, tried to ignore all calls for change, including ones sent directly from Gorbachev, but events elsewhere in Eastern Europe intervened to accelerate the tides of history. The disarming of the border between Hungary and Austria in the summer of 1989 led to thousands of East German tourists being allowed to cross into West Germany without having to scale or dig under a wall. Thousands more GDR citizens camped out in the West German embassies and legations, in East Berlin, in Warsaw, and particularly in Prague. On September 30 the GDR regime consented to let these émigrés travel across GDR territory to West Germany in trains from Prague (now remembered as the "freedom train"). Protests arose in Leipzig and then spread across the GDR, growing in size until by the end of October hundreds of thousands were demonstrating for the right to travel freely and for reform. The GDR's fortieth anniversary celebration on October 7 saw crowds cheering the visiting Gorbachev but admonishing their own leaders for their failure to liberalize. Ten days later, reformers within the GDR's ruling Socialist Unity Party, or SED, ousted Honecker, but it was too late to stem the storm about to engulf them.

Famously, the Berlin Wall's "fall" on November 9 was an accident, a fateful breakdown in communication. The new head of the GDR, Egon Krenz, gave Günther Schabowski, the Communist Party's media spokesman, new liberal travel regulations to announce at a press conference, and in some confusion Schabowski declared them effective immediately, even though that had not been the leadership's intention. East Germans began to mass on the borders to cross. Without clear orders, the Berlin Wall border guards lifted the barriers and allowed the crowds across, although it was not until December that West Germans were allowed free entry in the other direction. Almost from the start of these events, the wall itself had begun disintegrating; it was chipped apart for souvenirs and broken through to create new crossings. Yet the events in Berlin that evening should not necessarily be seen as the much-vaunted "end of the Cold War." When the Berlin Wall fell, the Cold War did not immediately cease to exist. In the minds of people across the world, however, it did not really matter much anymore, because the wall was gone. For much of the world, the wall *was* the Cold War, in cold, hard cement.

GLOBAL ENCOUNTERS AND CONNECTIONS:
Berlin as a Cold War Symbol and Microcosm

The symbolic and physical demolition of the wall was followed globally by similar retrenchments of support for Cold War regimes and a relaxation of competition and militarism. Some do not date the end of the Cold War until the dissolution of the Soviet Union, a process begun by the 1991 August coup in Moscow and finalized by the Christmas Day resignation of Soviet president Mikhail Gorbachev. But the fall of the wall was a significant catalyst, for it signified that the Soviet Union was no longer going to hold its empire together by force. Without this force, there was little to bind it, whether this meant the countries of Eastern Europe or its own constituent republics.

Without the Berlin Wall, the Eastern bloc, and the Soviet Union, the Cold War as the world had known it lost its meaning. In 1990 the two divided Germanys reunited under a democratic and capitalist framework. The former Soviet republics became independent countries following their own paths, though they did not always move toward either market capitalism or democracy. Elements of the Cold War have reappeared with the resurgence of Russia as a formidable geopolitical power due to its oil and gas revenues, but it is not the same global battle of rival ideologies and different economic models of development. The United States now faces not one single rival, but instead more directly threatening multiple "enemies" in the form of international terrorism, economic instability, and a range of marketplace competitors from the European Union to the newly emerging economies of nations such as Brazil, India, and China.

Berlin today is ablaze with change, full of energy for its new challenges, but it is also grappling with problems left over from the Cold War division of the city. The search for a new German identity has not been as easy as many envisioned in the heady days of celebration on the remnants of the crumbling wall. The city's dilemmas are mirrored across the country, as East Germans have struggled with assimilation and the unequal economic prospects and opportunities afforded by unification. While West Germany was becoming increasingly multicultural in its demographics due to an influx of foreign guest workers, East Germany remained more isolated, and this has produced tensions and xenophobia in certain regions of the former GDR.

The Cold War transformed the city of Berlin from the administrative, cultural, economic, and political capital of the Third Reich into a battleground between East and West, a place where the entire world watched the Cold War play itself out before their eyes. The people of West Berlin took on mythological status; the city became not just an urban space but a metaphorical community for those pledged to defend the free world against tyranny. Today Berlin strives to replace the myth with reality and put the past behind it, following as before the informal slogan that hung above the Breitscheidtplatz, "Berlin remains Berlin, no matter what!" (*Berlin bleibt doch Berlin*).

ENCOUNTERS AS TOLD: PRIMARY SOURCES

The following two sources provide differing perspectives on the meaning and legacy of the post–World War II division of Europe and of Germany. They reinforce the centrality, both physically and metaphorically, of Berlin and particularly the Berlin Wall in the Cold War. As you read them, consider whether their different historical contexts might account for their contrasting assessments of communism and its legacy.

Remarks at the Rudolph Wilde Platz, by John F. Kennedy

The following are excerpts from the speech delivered by US president John F. Kennedy at the Rudolph Wilde Platz in West Berlin, in front of the Berlin Wall, on June 26, 1963. Much was improvised, including his famous "Ich bin ein Berliner," stemming, some believe, from his emotional response to seeing the actual wall in front of him.

- What, according to Kennedy, did the wall represent?

- What differences does it epitomize to him between communism and Western democracy?

- How does Kennedy use the wall in waging a rhetorical Cold War?

- What can one conclude from this about the significance of Berlin for Western propaganda?

Two thousand years ago the proudest boast was "civis Romanus sum." Today, in the world of freedom, the proudest boast is "Ich bin ein Berliner."

I appreciate my interpreter translating my German!

There are many people in the world who really don't understand, or say they don't, what is the great issue between the free world and the Communist world. Let them come to Berlin. There are some who say that communism is the wave of the future. Let them come to Berlin. And there are some who say in Europe and elsewhere we can work with the Communists. Let them come to Berlin. And there are even a few who say that it is true that communism is an evil system, but it permits us to make economic progress. Lass' sie nach Berlin kommen. Let them come to Berlin.

Freedom has many difficulties and democracy is not perfect, but we have never had to put a wall up to keep our people in, to prevent them from leaving us. I want to say, on behalf of my countrymen, who live many miles away on the other side of the Atlantic, who are far distant from you, that they take the greatest pride that they have been able to share with you, even from a distance, the story of the last 18 years. I know of no town, no city, that has been besieged for 18 years that still lives with the vitality and the force, and the hope and the determination of the city of West Berlin. While the wall is the most obvious and vivid demonstration of the failures of the Communist system, for all the world to see, we take no satisfaction in it, for it is, as your Mayor has said, an offense not only against history but an offense against humanity, separating families, dividing husbands and wives and brothers and sisters, and dividing a people who wish to be joined together. . . .

Freedom is indivisible, and when one man is enslaved, all are not free. When all are free, then we can look forward to that day when this city will be joined as one and this country and this great Continent of Europe in a peaceful and hopeful globe. When that day finally comes, as it will, the people of West Berlin can take sober satisfaction in the fact that they were in the front lines for almost two decades.

All free men, wherever they may live, are citizens of Berlin, and, therefore, as a free man, I take pride in the words "Ich bin ein Berliner."

Source: John F. Kennedy, "Remarks at the Rudolph Wilde Platz, Berlin," June 26, 1963, John F. Kennedy Presidential Library and Museum, www.jfklibrary.org/Asset-Viewer/oEX2uqSQGEGIdTYgd_JL_Q.aspx.

"East Germans Lost Much in 1989," by Bruni de la Motte

The following article was published in the online version of the British newspaper *The Guardian* by a woman who grew up in East Germany. The article contains her reflections upon the impact of the fall of the Berlin Wall. While the fall was captured in photographs of joyous celebrations, the aftermath was not met with the same sense of jubilation by all East Germans.

- How does the author describe the impact of the fall of the Berlin Wall on the people of East Germany?

- What elements of East German life does she describe as being positive? What was negative in her view?

- What might account for the tone underlying her discussion of German unification and East Germany's legacy?

- This article generated a lively discussion among respondents, many of whom disagreed with her. Why do you think this was the case? What might be the reasons given by those critical of her depiction of life in East Germany?

On 9 November 1989 when the Berlin Wall came down I realised German unification would soon follow, which it did a year later. This meant the end of the German Democratic Republic (GDR). . . . Of course, unification brought with it the freedom to travel the world and, for some, more material wealth, but it also brought social breakdown, widespread unemployment, blacklisting, a crass materialism and an "elbow society" as well as a demonisation of the country I lived in and helped shape. Despite the advantages, for many it was more a disaster than a celebratory event. . . .

Little is known here about what happened to the GDR economy when the wall fell. Once the border was open the government decided to set up a trusteeship to ensure that "publicly owned enterprises" (the majority of businesses) would be transferred to the citizens who'd created the wealth. However, a few months before unification, the then newly elected conservative government handed over the trusteeship to west German appointees, many representing big business interests. The idea of "publicly owned" assets being transferred to citizens was quietly dropped. Instead all assets were privatised at breakneck speed. More then [sic] 85% were bought by west Germans and many were closed soon after. In the countryside 1.7 million hectares of agricultural and forest land were sold off and 80% of agricultural workers lost their job. . . .

As a result of the purging of academia, research and scientific establishments in a process of political vetting, more than a million individuals with degrees lost their jobs. This constituted about 50% of that group, creating in east Germany the highest percentage of professional unemployment in the world; all university chancellors and directors of state enterprises as well as 75,000 teachers lost their jobs and many were blacklisted. . . .

Since the demise of the GDR, many have come to recognise and regret that the genuine "social achievements" they enjoyed were dismantled: social and gender equality, full employment and lack of existential fears, as well as subsidised rents, public transport, culture and sports facilities.

Source: Bruni de la Motte, "East Germans Lost Much in 1989," *The Guardian*, November 8, 2009, www.guardian.co.uk/commentisfree/2009/nov/08/1989-berlin-wall.

Further Reading

Cherny, Andrei. *Candy Bombers: The Untold Story of the Berlin Airlift and America's Finest Hour.* New York: G. P. Putnam's Sons, 2008

Funder, Anna. *Stasiland: Stories from Behind the Berlin Wall.* London: Granta Books, 2004.

Harrison, Hope. *Driving the Soviets up the Wall: Soviet-East German Relations, 1953–1961.* Princeton Studies in International History and Politics. (Princeton: Princeton University Press, 2005).

Ladd, Brian. *The Ghosts of Berlin: Confronting German History in the Urban Landscape.* Chicago: University of Chicago Press, 1998.

Major, Patrick. *Behind the Berlin Wall: East Germany and the Frontiers of Power.* Oxford: Oxford University Press, 2011.

Meyer, Michael. *The Year that Changed the World: The Untold Story Behind the Fall of the Berlin Wall.* New York: Scribner, 2009.

Nelson, Walter Henry. *The Berliners: Their Saga and Their City.* New York: David McKay Company, Inc., 1969.

Postcards from Checkpoint Charlie: Images of the Berlin Wall. Introduction by Andrew Roberts. Bodleian Library, University of Oxford, 2008. Collected from The John Frazer Collection of Propaganda Postcards, John Johnson Collection of Printed Ephemera in the Bodleian Library.

Rose, Brian. *The Lost Border: The Landscape of the Iron Curtain.* Princeton: Princeton Architectural Press, 2004.

Schick, Jack M. *The Berlin Crisis, 1958–1962.* Philadelphia: University of Philadelphia Press, 1971.

Smith, Jr., Arthur L. *Kidnap City: Cold War Berlin.* Westport, CT: Greenwood Press, 2002

Taylor, Frederick. *The Berlin Wall: A World Divided, 1961–1989.* New York: Harper Collins Publishers, 2006.

Web Resources

The Berlin Airlift Online Archive, Harry S. Truman Presidential Library, www.trumanlibrary.org/whistlestop/study_collections/berlin_airlift/large/.

Berlin Wall Guide (with interactive tour), *The Guardian*, www.guardian.co.uk/travel/interactive/2009/oct/23/berlin-wall-history-guide.

Chronicle of the Berlin Wall, www.chronik-der-mauer.de/index.php/de/Start/Index/id/652147.

"The Cold War in Berlin," John Fitzgerald Kennedy Presidential Library, www.jfklibrary.org/JFK/JFK-in-History/The-Cold-War-in-Berlin.aspx.

The Cold War International History Project Digital Archive, Woodrow Wilson International
Center for Scholars, www.wilsoncenter.org/digital-archive. Click on "Germany in the
Cold War"; "East German Uprising"; "End of the Cold War."

The Cold War Museum, Berlin Wall Exhibits,
www.coldwar.org/museum/berlin_wall_exhibit.asp.

Time Video: "The Iconic Photo of the Fall of the Berlin Wall,"
www.time.com/time/video/player/0,32068,49315435001_1936561,00.html.

Spiegel Online International, "A Photographer Remembers: Forbidden Photos of Everyday
Life in East Germany," www.spiegel.de/international/germany/0,1518,707570,00.html.

The Wall inside the City, Berlin.de, www.berlin.de/mauer/verlauf/index/index.en.php.

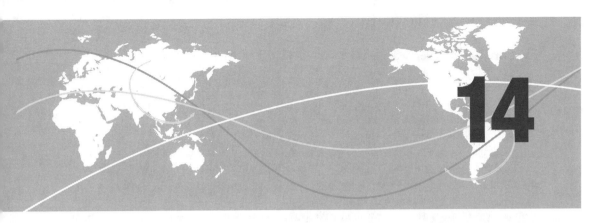

New York

Opportunity and Struggle in a Global City

(1911–2011)

GREGORY SMITHSIMON

AMERICANS HAVE LONG HELD NEGATIVE VIEWS ABOUT CITIES. FOR MANY, New York City has epitomized everything supposedly wrong with urban areas: hostile, impersonal, poverty stricken, overpriced, profligate, crowded, and dirty. Yet other images of New York challenge those ideas. The city is punctuated by the high-rises of international corporate headquarters and filled with neighborhoods that have nurtured hip-hop, jazz, punk rock, abstract expressionist painting, and beat writers. Other images challenge the city's stereotype as impersonal, such as intimate immigrant neighborhoods, talkative cab drivers, and shop owners who greet their regular customers. When people see beyond the city's famous landmarks, they are reminded that for many, New York is not impersonal; it is home.

Therefore, I was surprised to find that even the urban studies majors at a college in New York City where I taught believed it was a perilous, cold-hearted place. The excitement of New York had drawn them from around the world, but they were sure New Yorkers were heartless and would mug you for a dollar. Have a heart attack on the subway platform and they'll just step over you to get to their train. This hadn't been my experience—when my father-in-law collapsed in the subway, strangers carried him to his apartment. Whenever there was a car accident at an intersection, a crowd rushed in to offer help. To test my students' image of the city, I bought each of them a wallet. We filled them with a few dollars, a subway card, old credit cards, and family photos. The students fanned out across the city in pairs. They took turns, one student pretending to drop their wallet while walking down the street, the other recording what happened. They were each supposed to do this ten times, and their largest concern before beginning was how they would be able to get a passing grade when their wallet was stolen on the first try. To the students' surprise, 85 percent of all dropped wallets were returned. Thirteen percent were not seen by anyone. Only 2 percent were taken. In some cases, returning the wallet was a group effort. One team described how "a middle-aged white woman, who first noticed the wallet, called out, 'That lady dropped her wallet!' which caused another bystander to bend down and pick up the wallet, which was then passed off to two African American girls who ran ahead to return the wallet. This combined effort of four people is an unexpected but surprisingly pleasing result." New York, it turned out, is a pretty good place to lose a wallet.

Having grown up in the suburbs, I had imagined New York like my students did, as a riotous hub of excitement, possibility, and danger. Turn-of-the-century jazz musicians may have called it "the Big Apple" in contrast to the smaller venues they played while on tour, but my father maligned the city as "the big bullet" due to its reputation for crime, violence, and disorder. New York showed contradictory sides at every opportunity. It is the place to go for aspiring artists, writers, activists, innovators—but how do they pay the rent? It is the center of culture in America, but so much of it is not attractive to look at. The monotony, loneliness, expense, and waste of having to drive everywhere in the suburbs had exhausted me. In New York one can take the train to things the rest of the world only gets to visit on vacation. There are writers, publishers, magazines, politics, and art galleries. Movie stars walking down the street. New York City boasts so many historic landmarks that the commute to work for my summer job took me from the *Seinfeld* diner via subway past Central Park, Times Square, and Madison Square Garden, down to Wall Street, the New York Stock Exchange, and almost in sight of the Brooklyn Bridge and the Statue of Liberty. But with everything going on, it wasn't always clear there was room for everyone—one had to be tough and hold their ground or risk being pushed out of the city altogether.

The confusion regarding New York comes in large part from its dual aspects. The people are helpful but the economic and social structures are harsh. It is polarized between rich and poor. It has diverse and integrated public spaces but racially segregated residential neighborhoods. Today, the dual city is also a global city. Global cities are central nodes in stock trading, bond selling, and other financial transactions of global capitalism. They are centers of immigration, culture, and cultural synthesis. The dual roles of the global city paradoxically give New York incredible financial resources and unique cultural diversity alongside striking levels of poverty and ongoing social conflict.

This chapter examines New York's duality as a global city in several areas. First, globalization provides a powerful economic engine to the city, but one that has caused considerable damage and inequality. Second, for a hundred years that economic dynamism has been fueled by the labor of immigrants to New York. Generations of new arrivals have been simultaneously welcomed and exploited. Finally, New York's racial and ethnic diversity makes the city a model of how a heterogeneous community can live together, but it is also a site of ongoing discrimination.

NEW YORK AND THE WORLD: Immigration and Industry

New York is the largest city in the United States. Initially comprised of the island of Manhattan, four additional boroughs (the Bronx, Queens, Brooklyn, and Staten Island) were added to the city in 1898. Today, the city is home to 8.3 million people, more than live in the next two largest cities in the United States—Los Angeles, California, and Chicago, Illinois—combined. In terms of the population inside the legal limits of the city, New York doesn't rank in the top ten among cities globally. But measured by its sprawling metropolitan area (which includes a larger urban region of twenty million people), New York is among the five largest urban areas in the world—smaller than the Tokyo, Japan, metro area, but comparable to Mumbai, India; Seoul, South Korea; and Mexico City, Mexico (the largest city in North America). New York has been a center of industry and trade since its inception, when in 1614 the Dutch founded New Amsterdam where the Hudson River meets New York Harbor. The Dutch traded for furs, particularly beaver, with the Mahicans and later Mohawk Indians. The importance of trade did not diminish over time. Three hundred years later, in the 1930s, half of all international goods traded with the United States passed through the Port of New York.

New York's significance has always been as a trade city, and its position as such has long relied on its location at the base of the Hudson River and the edge of the Atlantic Ocean. Well positioned to access both European and American markets, New York grew as a banking and trading center. When the Erie Canal was completed in 1825, it provided the final link in a water route between New York and Chicago. Grain, beef, and industrial products from America's massive Midwestern heartland could be cheaply shipped from Chicago to the seaports of New York and on to the rest of the world. New York banks not only financed the construction of the canal, they also funded much of Chicago's reconstruction after the great fire of 1871.

Immigrants in the Industrial City

New York's most economically profitable eras have been during periods of great immigration. The explosive growth of the industrial era between the 1880s and 1924 required the labor of immigrants. These immigrants mostly came from Ireland, Russia, and Italy, but they also arrived from the Caribbean and Northern Europe. New York had the *pull* of industrial jobs, but it also played a global role in the forces that *pushed* immigrants from their home country. At the turn of the last century, peasants in areas as far away as Eastern Europe could not compete with the low-cost grain being grown in the American Midwest, shipped from Chicago to New York, and sold in Europe at prices below what it cost European farmers to grow their own. When they could no longer make a living farming, many peasants emigrated.

Industries in New York during the nineteenth and early twentieth centuries tended to specialize in customized products, small batches, or quick turnaround. Unlike spread-out, single-story, mass-production factories, New York industries operated in "loft" buildings that stacked four to six stories of manufacturers on top of each other. While the scale of each business was small, collectively, industry in New York was anything but. New York's two largest industries at the time, garments and printing, dominated their sectors nationally. At the start of the century, 70 percent of women's clothes and 40 percent of men's clothes were made in New York. Although New York also housed factories for everything from sugar refining to piano production, light industries outnumbered the "heavy" industries, such as steel, shipbuilding, and auto manufacturing, which were the heart of other northeastern US cities. In addition to industrial production, communication, transportation, and banking remained influential sectors.

The growth of New York's garment industry demonstrates the scale of the city's industry and its intimate connection to immigrant workers. This industry boomed with the huge demand for uniforms during the Civil War. (Prior to the 1860s, most Americans made their own clothes.) New York's size, supply of labor, and transportation networks positioned it to dominate the new garment industry. In the first two decades of the twentieth century, when immigrants were coming through New York's Ellis Island in the largest numbers, the US garment industry was growing at two or three times the rate of an already thriving American economy. Two-thirds of the nation's garment industry was located in New York, where it employed particularly large numbers of Jewish immigrant women, many of whom had worked in the garment trade in their native Russia. They sewed everywhere from cramped apartments to factories staffed with hundreds of workers.

Conditions in the garment industry were ripe for severe exploitation. Since they were competing with countless other small shops in the same area, owners cut prices as low as possible and then worked their employees to the bone to extract profits. A shop could employ a few dozen to a few hundred workers in several specialized (and gender-segregated) roles. Initially, sewing machine operators were most often the men who owned the garment shop, but later women began running the machines. Finishers were most often teenaged or young women who sewed details onto the garment. Pressers, who operated the heavy irons that pressed the clothes, were often older men. Many factories were hot and poorly ventilated. Fabric fibers filled the air, and heaps of cloth and trimmings nearly as tall as the seamstresses made fire a constant hazard. Owners often cut corners and underpaid wages. During busy seasons, employees worked seven days a week, fifty to seventy hours a week. During slow periods, they could find no work at all. The low cost of opening a garment factory, and the large number of jobs it generated, made clothing a key industry for both immigrant business owners and immigrant workers.

Mary Domsky-Abrams was one of the thousands of immigrant garment workers in New York. Domsky-Abrams lived on Rutgers Street, which was in the Russian Jewish neighborhood of the Lower East Side. Less than a year after she arrived in the United States, she was working as a sewing machine operator making women's shirts at the Triangle Shirtwaist Factory. Workers there made only four to six dollars a week and faced poor treatment and unsafe conditions typical for this time period. The floor had only one exit so that a guard could check each worker's purse as they left; the owner believed the women brought purses to steal finished shirts. Domsky-Abrams's machine was right next to the front door, which was kept locked. The bosses never spoke to the workers, who interacted only with the manager.

The Triangle Shirtwaist Factory was on the top floors of a ten-story loft building. Just before closing time on Saturday, March 25, 1911, a fire broke out on the eighth floor. It spread rapidly through the room, which was piled high with fabric, scraps, and clothing. Desperate workers tried to flee, but locked doors blocked their way. The fire escape quickly collapsed. Some workers tried to escape on the elevator, but the heat soon warped the elevators tracks and rendered it unusable. Law students from the adjoining New York University building helped some fifty workers across the rooftop of the factory to theirs, but most were trapped. In little more than fifteen minutes, 146 people were killed. The victims were mainly immigrant women, many from Russian Jewish families. Mary Domsky-Abrams survived.

Garment workers had gone on a citywide strike a year before the fire seeking union recognition and improved conditions, but they had been defeated by the stubborn resistance (and the violent thugs) led by Max Blanck and Isaac Harris, the very men who owned the Triangle factory. Blanck and Harris were acquitted of responsibility for the fire, the inadequate fire escapes, and the locked factory doors. The fire catalyzed the growth of garment unions, but pressure to institute workplace safety regulations was stymied by business owners who said that government should not regulate private industry. Frances Perkins, a progressive New York activist, witnessed the Triangle fire. Eventually, she and others pushed the state to institute fire codes and workplace regulations. When she was named US secretary of labor under President Franklin Delano Roosevelt almost two decades later, reformers were able to introduce similar regulations, based on New York's progressive innovations, nationwide.

Conditions for the city's industrial workers also improved with unionization. In addition to negotiating for higher wages, unions endorsed politicians who improved workplace regulations and promoted a strong social safety net—affordable housing, free public education, and support for those who couldn't work. Such policies reduced the extreme income inequality that characterized the early period of industrialization and brought greater security to working New Yorkers.

While garment factory conditions improved markedly in the United States with unionization and regulation, by the 1970s manufacturers had moved their operations to countries where labor regulations were not well enforced, and labor unions faced violent reactions from owners and police. Fires that were disturbingly similar to the one in the Triangle Shirtwaist Factory continued to occur one hundred years later. In December 2010, twenty-six workers were killed and over one hundred injured in the Ha-Meem factory fire in Bangladesh. The factory made pants for US companies. In echoes of the Triangle fire, the blaze began on the ninth floor and quickly spread to the tenth, and witnesses said four of the seven exits were locked. Workers couldn't make it down the crowded stairways. The heat and flames drove all but three of those who died to jump from the windows. Incredibly, while the Triangle workers earned fourteen cents per hour (about $3.20 in today's dollars), one hundred years later the Bangladeshi workers at Ha-Meem were earning only twenty-eight cents per hour. The global economy has reintroduced the extreme exploitation that characterized the garment industry in New York in 1911.

By the time unionization and safety regulations were well established, the turn-of-the-century wave of immigration had ended. Anti-immigrant sentiment had grown in the United States, culminating in the passage of a series of bills that virtually halted immigration in 1924. Ellis Island grew empty. In the decades that followed, New York began a long period of decline relative to the rest of the United States.

The Ebb and Flow of New York City: Domestic Migration

Although international migration to the United States came to a virtual halt, internal migration—by African Americans from the South—continued at a rapid pace. In the early twentieth century, New York, like most northern cities, was whiter than most American suburbs are today; as late as 1930, less than 5 percent of New Yorkers were black. By that time, however, large numbers of African Americans had begun taking trains from the rural South in the movement known as the Great Migration. African Americans who arrived in the city at that time were confronted with racial intolerance. Their arrival prompted some cultural exchange across racial boundaries in music, literature, fine arts, and dance. It also had an impact on politics, including the formation of the National Association for the Advancement of Colored People (NAACP) and other civil rights groups. As a center of global media, New York broadcast these modern elements of black culture and American racial prejudices to the rest of the world.

Prior to the Great Migration, African Americans in New York lived in small communities that were comparatively mixed. The early twentieth century saw a nationwide wave of anti-black riots, however, including several in New York City. Fear of further violence forced African Americans to move into larger, more segregated neighborhoods, creating extensive urban, black ghettos for the first time. By 1930, 70 percent of residents in Harlem were African American. Artists and intellectuals associated with the Harlem Renaissance of that period, such as poet Langston Hughes, musician Duke Ellington, and nationalist Marcus Garvey, became global symbols not just of thriving black culture, but of US segregation and American culture generally.

Black-white segregation was distinctive in several ways. Neighborhoods in New York City that were thought of as Irish, Italian, Scandinavian, Russian, or German were actually shared by several ethnic groups. Most Italians didn't live in Little Italy, most Irish didn't live in Hell's Kitchen, and most Russians didn't live in the famous Lower East Side. This was not true for African Americans. Most lived in segregated neighborhoods, and those neighborhoods were routinely more than 95 percent black. Furthermore, while the children of immigrants easily moved out of enclaves when they became adults, high levels of black segregation persisted through the twentieth century and into the twenty-first with little change.

The Great Depression of the 1930s was particularly difficult for African Americans. In contrast, during World War II, there was virtually unlimited demand for workers (and soldiers). But work remained segregated, housing was deteriorating and crowded, and consumer goods were rationed. Through wartime programs African American could gain training in skilled trades, but they still had difficulty finding jobs in skilled positions. The Brooklyn Navy Yard ran twenty-four hours a day, building naval vessels and shipping 25 percent of all US materiel the military used in Europe. However, although the yard employed seventy thousand people, less than 6 percent of them were African American. During this time, blacks made modest progress by getting the federal government to encourage the hiring of African American workers in shipbuilding and other strategic industries. Often, African Americans were relegated to difficult, dirty jobs far below their skill level.

Industry after the War

At the end of World War II, New York was a highly unionized, highly skilled city. In 1947 it had more manufacturing jobs than Philadelphia, Pennsylvania; Detroit, Michigan; Boston, Massachusetts, and Los Angeles combined. More than a third of those in manufacturing made garments, 10 percent were in printing, and another 10 percent worked making food and beverages. In 1950 the major garment union had over two hundred thousand members in New York City. Unions gained improved wages and health care benefits for their members and reduced working hours. Larger unions even built large apartment complexes to provide modern, spacious housing with conveniences such as hot and cold running water for workers and their families. The city pitched in by becoming a leader in building affordable housing. In contrast to the desperation of immigrant workers in the 1920s, their descendants enjoyed relative security and prosperity.

The gains made by labor unions in the decades after the Triangle fire (both in working conditions and wages) significantly improved working-class life in New York. But those benefits were not equally shared by African Americans and a growing Puerto Rican community. In 1959 African Americans' wages were 25 percent less than the city's overall average; Puerto Ricans averaged 37 percent less than the city as a whole. African Americans remained locked out of many industrial and public sector jobs. Large numbers of African Americans worked in the hotel and service sector, though rarely in positions in which they interacted with customers. Blacks and Puerto Ricans also worked in large numbers in the garment industry, but they were often given the worst-paid jobs.

African Americans and Puerto Ricans arriving in New York sought the same kinds of industrial jobs immigrants before them had found. Particularly during the full-employment years of World War II, they joined the industrial workers in northern cities. But both groups faced unyielding discrimination and racism. White residents began relocating to the suburbs and the "Sunbelt" of the southwestern United States when African Americans moved into their neighborhoods. Just as critically, factories relocated as well. The loss of industry in urban areas was underway.

Immigrants in the Global City

By the 1970s, the US economy was facing a protracted crisis. Unemployment and inflation were high, and profits were low. To regain those lost profits, businesses attacked the unions that had succeeded in guaranteeing higher wages. Hundreds of thousands of garment industry jobs left New York, first moving to the southern United States, where they could pay lower wages because state laws made it more difficult for workers to unionize. They later moved even further away to Central America, the Caribbean, and eventually Asia—particularly seeking out countries where dictatorships fought against unionization and kept wages even lower.

Garment jobs that stayed in New York were increasingly nonunion. These workers—who in the 1970s were often women from Puerto Rico, Latin America, and later China—soon experienced conditions much like those of their Jewish predecessors. Wages fell and hours grew longer. By the 1990s, the US Department of Labor concluded that half of all garment factories in the United States met their definition of a "sweatshop," in which there were multiple serious violations of labor or safety regulations.

Cities other than New York were hit just as hard by deindustrialization. Pittsburgh, Pennsylvania, so defined by its steel plants that the city's football team was called the Steelers, lost most of its smokestacks. Auto factories began closing in Detroit, sending the "Motor City" into a tailspin. Chicago's famous meatpacking plants (from which the Chicago Bulls basketball team took its name) were replaced by operations in rural areas closer to cattle ranches. Cities such as Philadelphia and Baltimore, Maryland, lost shipyards and steel, automobile, and other factories. Cities in other industrialized nations, such as those in Europe, also lost heavy industry. England lost industrial, coal mining, shipbuilding, and shipping jobs. Like New York, London replaced docks with office buildings and high-income housing, seeking to replace those blue-collar sectors with financial and managerial sectors in the globalizing economy.

Since jobs were leaving the city, so did people. New York's decline in tax revenue in 1975 pushed the city government near bankruptcy. The 1975 "fiscal crisis" marked a rude shift in the organization of the city's economy. To restore the city's finances, the state selected a group of bankers to restructure the city's budget. They cut into city workers' wages and social programs, raised subway fares, and reduced funding for everything

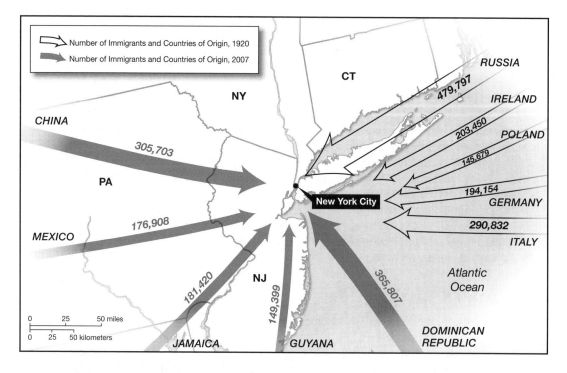

Map 14.1. Top-Five Countries of Origin for Immigrants to New York City, 1920 and 2007

Immigration connected New York primarily to Europe in 1920. By 2007, immigrants came from around the world, including Asia, the Caribbean, and South America. Countries that sent large numbers of immigrants one hundred years ago remain connected to New York through immigration. (For example, in 2007, 80,500 people moved to New York from Russia; 67,287 came from Ireland.) New York has grown from 5,620,048 people in 1920 to 8,308,147 people in 2007. Immigration to New York is particularly diverse compared to other US cities; across these decades, no one country has contributed more than a small minority of total immigration.

from parks to the public university. Instead of a blue-collar city with a strong social safety net, the leaders of New York's financial community sought to restructure it as a capital of international finance. The financial sector, which had always been important in New York, grew considerably. The city became dominated by FIRE (finance, insurance, and real estate). By 1997 one in six jobs in New York was in one of the FIRE industries. New York's economy now depended on rapid, profitable manipulation of investments and the management of large corporations instead of the creation of goods. By 2010 a quarter of the value of all corporate stock in the world was traded on the New York Stock Exchange. New York came to have less in common with other deindustrialized cities and more in common with a network of "global cities" such as London, England; Tokyo, Japan; Los Angeles; Paris, France; and Hong Kong, China. Spaced around the world, these cities allowed complicated financial transactions to go on twenty-four hours a day as the sun set on one global city and rose in the next.

New York's role as a global city was met with renewed growth in population. When Congress closed the nation to immigrants in 1924, one of the few opponents to this was Emanuel Celler, a congressman of Jewish and Catholic parents who grew up in the immigrant neighborhoods of Brooklyn. Celler campaigned for forty years to lift the immigration restrictions (which were racially discriminatory). In 1965, in response to an increased need for highly skilled technical workers, the Hart-Celler Act reopened the United States to immigrants. The new law allowed for five categories of immigrants: those with in-demand professional skills (such as scientists and engineers), people with family members already in the country, political refugees, wealthy business investors, and a small number of people who won "green card lotteries" in countries from which few people come to the United States. (Note that even now, people without advanced degrees or family connections have virtually no way to move to the United States legally, unlike in the earlier industrial era.) After four decades of decline, New York became a primary destination for immigrants once again.

Today, 37 percent of New Yorkers are foreign-born, almost as high a percentage as in the days of the Triangle fire. Immigrants in the city today are more diverse than one hundred years ago, and more diverse than in other cities. Whereas more than 70 percent of immigrants in Los Angeles speak Spanish and 45 percent are from Mexico, in New York the largest nationality—immigrants from the Caribbean nation of the Dominican Republic—make up only 10 percent of all immigrants. None of the next largest groups—from China, Russia, Jamaica, India, Colombia, Mexico, and Italy—make up even 5 percent of New York's total immigrant community. New York therefore displays a remarkable cultural mix, which can be seen in examples such as a hospital that serves food that is both Chinese *and* kosher (to cater to both Chinese and Orthodox Jewish patients) and the 138 languages spoken in Queens, the nation's most diverse county. (See Map 14.1.)

United States immigration preferences for technically skilled workers means that many immigrants come to work in more highly paid occupations, which often means they have access to higher education and higher household earnings. New York has a higher proportion of immigrants with technical visas than other parts of the country. At the same time, New York is also home to immigrants from China, Mexico, and elsewhere that do not arrive with technical skills. Such workers face similar options to immigrants from one hundred years ago, often sewing at machines that look almost identical to those used in the era of the Triangle Shirtwaist Factory.

The split trajectory of Chinese immigrants reflects the divergent prospects of immigrants as a whole in New York: While significant numbers come for professional jobs in banking, the sciences, or engineering, working-class immigrants work long hours in restaurants, stores, and factories to get by. The changes after the 1975 financial crisis shrank the ranks and wages of the middle class and stable working class. This, coupled with the financial industry's supersized salaries and bonuses, caused income inequality in New York to return to historic highs. After accounting for inflation, wages have fallen for US workers since the 1970s, while income for the smaller upper-income groups has risen significantly. The bifurcation of immigrant experiences, like those of the highly skilled and the working-class Chinese immigrants, reflects increasing polarization of wages in the United States since the fiscal crises of the 1970s.

Race and Inequality

Multiplying the diverging prospects for upper- and lower-income immigrants are the American patterns of racial discrimination imposed on immigrants. Just as there is great diversity among immigrants in New York, there is considerable diversity within the city's racial groups, too. Over half of black New Yorkers are Caribbean or Caribbean American, and many others are recent immigrants from Africa. (Many of the city's best known hip-hop artists come from the city's Caribbean communities, including early pioneers like DJ Kool Herc, Afrika Bambaataa, and Grandmaster Flash, as well as Notorious B.I.G., Foxy Brown, Nicki Minaj, and Wyclef Jean.) New York's Latino community is equally diverse. In many cities, Latinos are immigrants and most come from Mexico. In New York, members of the largest group of Latinos are not immigrants at all: Puerto Ricans make up a third of Latino New York. Since Puerto Rico is part of the United States, Puerto Ricans are US citizens from birth. Among other things, this means they can vote, which allows broader electoral participation in Puerto Rican communities. In addition, Puerto Ricans have been coming to New York since the nineteenth century, thus they have a more established community. New York has had daily Spanish-language radio for nearly fifty years. Among immigrant Latinos, the largest group are Dominican. Immigrants' racial diversity is exemplified by black Latinos (particularly from countries such as the Dominican Republic, Cuba, and Puerto Rico), white Latinos (from the same countries and others), and Latinos who often describe themselves as neither black nor white. The considerable differences among New York Latinos in terms of race, nationality, citizenship, and class shatter the idea of a single community. In fact, while the census calls this group "Hispanic," and people in other regions prefer Latino or Chicano, New Yorkers rarely use any of these terms, identifying themselves by nation, not ethnicity (as Puerto Ricans, Dominicans, Mexicans, etc.), reflecting differences among these groups rather than commonalities.

Diversity does not mean integration or equality, however. While riding the subway presents an image of New York as very diverse, those trains collect passengers coming from very racially segregated neighborhoods. Those segregated neighborhoods are often the basis of dangerous inequality. Amadou Diallo was a twenty-three-year-old West African immigrant living in the Bronx. He grew up and studied in Liberia, Togo, Bangkok, Singapore, and London. By 1999 Diallo had been in the United States for little over two years and was working as a street vendor. On February 4, 1999, he was shot to death in the doorway of his apartment building by four police officers. Diallo's murder triggered widespread outrage. In the ten years after the shooting, New York police shot to death a black or Latino man at the rate of approximately one per month.

Immigrant groups that had previously avoided the type of racial profiling that plays a role in the disproportionate risk black and Latino men face in interactions with the police saw that relationship change after the terrorist attacks on New York's World Trade Center on September 11, 2001. After September 11, the United States initiated the National Security Entry Exit Registration System (NSEERS). The program tracked men from twenty-four predominantly Muslim nations in the United States. Nearly eighty-three thousand men complied with the requirement to register and be interviewed by the federal government. While none of the men interrogated turned out to have connections with terrorists, more than fourteen thousand were identified as being in violation of their visas and were deported. Multiple accounts described New Yorkers who arrived at immigration offices and were stunned when they were handcuffed, interrogated for up to twenty-four hours without food or water, and deported for technical violations such as information that had not been updated on their immigration papers or work permits that had not been fully processed before they had begun jobs. Some signed documents they could not understand that consented to their deportation. Family members were either abandoned in New York or had to return to their home countries as well. Other families rushed to leave voluntarily rather than face interrogation under NSEERS. Businesses in neighborhoods with large Muslim population closed or were hurriedly sold. New York's sizeable Muslim communities were significantly affected by these dislocations.

In both dramatic and everyday ways, immigrants' lives in New York are shaped by policies of discrimination and profiling. Black immigrants have often described being unprepared for the type of race-based discrimination they experience upon arrival. Other groups who seek to avoid being identified by racial stereotypes have found their identity in the United States is shaped by national and international forces beyond their control.

GLOBAL ENCOUNTERS AND CONNECTIONS:
New York in a Global Hierarchy

Both locally and in the international economy, New York promises dynamic opportunities coupled with dangerous conditions. For the past one hundred years, New York's position in the global economy has made it a destination for immigrants even though it has established punishing conditions for many new arrivals. Beyond its borders, New York has influenced the economy nationally and internationally.

The city is at once thriving and impoverished; a success story and a persistent crisis. The city regained the population lost in the era of the 1975 fiscal crisis, but it has not returned to the levels of broad-based prosperity it enjoyed before that period. The gap between rich and poor is greater in Manhattan than anywhere else in the United States: for every dollar earned by the richest fifth of New Yorkers, the poorest 20 percent earned only two cents. Persistent poverty and unemployment were exacerbated by the 2008 recession and concentrated among disadvantaged racial groups. The financial sector remained in New York after September 11, but this industry, on which so much of New York relies, is notoriously volatile.

On the international stage, New York has a similarly dual image. The city's concentration of global media companies allows it to shape its global image in a favorable light, as a center of glamour, culture, and fashion. At the same time, New York's fashion industry has spurred a century of deadly factory fires both in the United States and abroad as companies strive to produce fashionable attire at the cheapest cost.

In the financial sector, New York's investment banks play a disproportionate role in economies in the rest of the world. The recession that affected much of the world beginning in 2008 was heavily influenced by unregulated trading of mortgage-backed securities on Wall Street, which encouraged the inflation and subsequent crash of real estate prices. Two years later, the New York–based investment bank Goldman Sachs was implicated in concealing the extent of Greek debt during that country's 2010 fiscal crisis. Goldman and New York's Citigroup were major creditors in the Mexican peso crisis of 1995. In that case, the terms of repayment (negotiated in large part by the United States) were so severe that they altered food prices and had measurable effects on the diets of everyday Mexican people. In these ways, New York's financial sector has considerable influence in the funding, organization, and consequences of global capitalism.

As in other global cities, New York's opportunities remain evident, but its shortcomings are just as real. The city has exercised a striking, dynamic power in the international movement of people, money, culture, and goods. That power, however, has been shaped by inequality and discrimination, so that the beneficiaries and targets of New York's economic ambition have always fared very differently. At each stage, New Yorkers have sought to rectify structural inequalities: tens of thousands of garment workers organized into unions, New York African Americans became leading civil rights and black power advocates, and immigrants organized against ethnic profiling. Throughout this period, the extent to which people from all over the world who have come to New York are able to refashion the city has determined how equitably or unevenly its prosperity is spread.

The industrial revolution made New York immensely productive but brought great risks as well. The first document provides a firsthand account of the worst industrial fire in US history. While the economic disparities in New York can be great, the second excerpt, a journalist's firsthand experiences on September 11, 2001, highlight that this city of often segregated diversity can come together in a united front.

"Eyewitness at Triangle," by William G. Shepherd

Newspaper reporter William Shepherd happened to witness the terrible fire at the Triangle Shirtwaist Factory on March 25, 1911. His graphic account relays the horror of the bystanders. Also watching in the crowd was Frances Perkins, a young labor reformer. Galvanized by what she saw, Perkins first worked in New York State to improve workplace safety, fire codes, and inspections. As secretary of labor under President Franklin Delano Roosevelt, she continued to reform working conditions, instituting the forty-hour workweek and requirements for overtime pay.

- The fire took place in a city crowded with pedestrians. How did the city shape the tragedy and people's recollection of it?

- For decades after the Triangle fire, new US safety regulations prevented fires such as this one. But in the global economy production has moved to less regulated factories abroad, and such fires have returned. What strategies would be most effective at making workplaces safer in the current era of globalization?

- William G. Shepherd, the reporter, concludes his account by linking a garment workers' strike the previous year to the fire. How does he see the two linked?

I saw every feature of the tragedy visible from outside the building. . . . I learned a new sound—a more horrible sound than description can picture. It was the thud of a speeding living body on a stone sidewalk.

Thud-dead, thud-dead, thud-dead, thud-dead . . .

The first two thud-deads shocked me. I looked up—saw there were scores of girls at the windows. The flames from the floors below were beating in their faces. . . .

I even watched one girl falling. Waving her arms, trying to keep her body upright until the very instant she struck the sidewalk, she was trying to balance herself. Then came the thud—then a silent unmoving pile of clothing and twisted, broken limbs. . . .

As I reached the scene of the fire, a cloud of smoke hung over the building. . . . I looked up to the seventh floor. There was a living picture in

each window—four screaming heads of girls waving their arms.

"Call the firemen," they screamed—scores of them. "Get a ladder," cried others. They were all as alive and whole and sound as were we who stood on the sidewalk. I couldn't help thinking of that. We cried to them not to jump. We heard the siren of a fire engine in the distance. The other sirens sounded from several directions.

"Here they come," we yelled. "Don't jump; stay there."

One girl climbed onto the window sash. Those behind her tried to hold her back. Then she dropped into space. I didn't notice whether those above watched her drop because I had turned away. Then came that first thud. I looked up, another girl was climbing onto the window sill; others were crowding behind her. She dropped. I watched her fall, and again the dreadful sound. Two windows away two girls were climbing onto the sill; they were fighting each other and crowding for air. Behind them I saw many screaming heads. They fell almost together, but I heard two distinct thuds. Then the flames burst out through the windows on the floor below them, and curled up into their faces.

The firemen began to raise a ladder. Others took out a life net and, while they were rushing to the sidewalk with it, two more girls shot down. The firemen held it under them; the bodies broke it; the grotesque simile of a dog jumping through a hoop struck me. Before they could move the net another girl's body flashed through it. The thuds were just as loud, it seemed, as if there had been no net there. It seemed to me that the thuds were so loud that they might have been heard all over the city.

I had counted ten. Then my dulled senses began to work automatically. I noticed things that it had not occurred to me before to notice. Little details that the first shock had blinded me to. I looked up to see whether those above watched those who fell. I noticed that they did; they watched them every inch of the way down and probably heard the roaring thuds that we heard.

As I looked up I saw a love affair in the midst of all the horror. A young man helped a girl to the window sill. Then he held her out, deliberately away from the building, and let her drop. . . . He held out a second girl the same way and let her drop. Then he held out a third girl. . . . They were as unresisting as if he were helping them onto a streetcar instead of into eternity.

Then came the love amid the flames. He brought another girl to the window. Those of us who were looking saw her put her arms around him and kiss him. Then he held her out into space and dropped her. But quick as a flash he was on the window sill himself. His coat fluttered upward—the air filled his trouser legs. I could see that he wore tan shoes and hose. His hat remained on his head. . . .

We found out later that, in the room in which he stood, many girls were being burned to death by the flames and were screaming in an inferno of flame and heat. He chose the easiest way and was brave enough to even help the girl he loved to a quicker death, after she had given him a goodbye kiss.

The firemen raised the longest ladder. It reached only to the sixth floor. I saw the last girl jump at it and miss it. And then the faces disappeared from the window. But now the crowd was enormous, though all this had occurred in less than seven minutes, the start of the fire and the thuds and deaths. . . .

The floods of water from the firemen's hose that ran into the gutter were actually stained red with blood. I looked upon the heap of dead bodies and I remembered these girls were the shirtwaist makers. I remembered their great strike of last year in which these same girls had demanded more sanitary conditions and more safety precautions in the shops. These dead bodies were the answer.

Source: William G. Shepherd, "Witness Watches Helplessly As Fire Victims Leap To Their Death," United Press International, March 25, 1911.

"Shaken Lower Manhattan Neighbors Find Each Other after September 11 Disaster; Vow to Stay Together and Rebuild the Community," by Robert Simko

Battery Park City is an upper-income neighborhood directly across from the World Trade Center. When the towers collapsed, debris and ash cascaded into residents' living rooms. People fled the area, some jumping on boats to cross the Hudson River to New Jersey. Many could not return for months. The publisher of the community paper, *The Battery Park City Broadsheet,* happened to be outside that morning and photographed the South Tower as the second plane crashed into it. The paper's editor was on the streets throughout the following days to provide this firsthand account of how September 11 looked to people who lived in the shadow of the World Trade Center, and how the tragedy removed barriers from the city's diverse population as residents helped one another get through the day.

- How does the response of New Yorkers to September 11 compare to the reaction of bystanders to the Triangle fire? How does it compare to Hollywood depictions of disasters?

- The Triangle fire was a result of the city's position in the global economy, and it reshaped the city's economy in the decades that followed. What is your sense of the long-term effect of September 11, 2001?

- This account of September 11 is intensely local. To the extent that the article aptly captures residents' priorities on September 11, how would you expect the community to connect this event to the world beyond their neighborhood?

8 A.M., TUESDAY MORNING, PRIMARY DAY SEPTEMBER 11.

It's the familiar rushed jumble of breakfast, dressing, plans for the afternoon, making two lunches, tucking them into backpacks. Waiting for the elevator, Lucy describes a bad dream involving explosions and fire. Fifteen minutes later, Theo and Mom head off for school by bicycle, dodging last-minute campaigners along the way. It's a beautiful, sunny morning, and the world is full of friendly hellos and smiles. And suddenly we are fleeing smoke and destruction, shaking, crying. And where is the children's father?!

After facing unspeakable terror on September 11 when two planes hit the World Trade Center and caused their fiery collapse, the residents of lower Manhattan are coming together, determined to rebuild their community. Robert Simko, Broadsheet publisher, eventually checked in unscathed, at least physically, but some neighbors are not accounted for. What follows is a range of voices recounting experiences during the week of September 11 through 18.

TUESDAY, SEPTEMBER 11

8:48 a.m.—Flying south over lower Manhattan with a terrible roar, a Boeing 767 slams into the north tower of the World Trade Center. "I was standing in front of P.S. 234, greeting all the voters and parents and just feeling the energy of the first day of kindergarten—and I heard this groaning whine of a jet and looked up to see it overhead so close as though you could almost touch it," says Cass Collins. "It sailed dead-on into the tower, and it was clear to me in that instant that it was deliberate. And then I saw this inverted V-shaped scar on the tower begin to glow inside."

8:55 a.m.—BPC attorney Les Jacobowitz sees people engulfed in flames on the sidewalk at the base of the World Trade Center. As construction workers help them, Mr. Jacobowitz runs to the intersection of West and Vesey Streets to direct traffic away from the disaster site. . . .

9:03 a.m.—Flying over New York Harbor and southern Battery Park City, a second Boeing 767 hits the south tower. Eric Nevin is watching from his apartment at 71 Broadway. "The south tower is framed in my window . . . and as I stared at it, the second plane appeared and impossibly smashed into it, creating a horrible fireball explosion. . . ."

9:59 a.m.—The first tower collapses. "I still have trouble believing, understanding," recalls Mr. Nevin. "The south tower issued a sickening rumble like that of an avalanche, and my eyes took in the beginning of the collapse, the impossible accordion-like surrender of this tower-mountain that had always seemed among the most permanent of human-made structures. . . .

"Running uptown maybe a half block from our building, I 'knew' a third plane was about to crash into the towers. Wrong," remembers Kathleen Bachand. "The noise was the roar from the first tower crumbling and the ground going out from under us. Everyone was screaming to get down. We were covered by debris and choking. I was holding onto Joe when the billow of gray smoke came over us and went to pitch black. I couldn't see him and I was holding him. When it started lifting just enough to see through the gray we started running again. . . ."

11 a.m.—"I'm running with my baby near the Museum of Jewish Heritage and a man opens his car door and calls to me," says Dean Lubnick. "I say, 'Take my baby. I have to find my wife.' He says, 'No, your baby needs you. I'll find your wife.'" The hero, David Chase, catering manager of the Ritz-Carlton, finds Mr. Lubnick's wife, Lee, and leads her back to her husband and baby Rebekah. . . .

WEDNESDAY, SEPTEMBER 12

7 a.m.—Eerily quiet except for a wail of sirens. The air downtown is smoky. The barricades have been moved from Franklin Street to Chambers Street. Sixty men stride down Hudson Street wearing hardhats.

Journalists from all over the world have arrived and set up camp. At her apartment in Gateway Plaza, Georgie Meinhofer, an elderly woman who lives alone, begins to make breakfast for a few neighbors who have stayed. When the knock comes on her door to evacuate, she invites the officers in for some pierogis. . . .

SATURDAY, SEPTEMBER 15

Residents of lower Manhattan stream into a basketball court at the corner of Canal and Thompson Streets, drawn to a meeting called by downtown leaders and publicized by word of mouth and the Internet.

Approximately 500 people gather, most seeing each other for the first time since Tuesday. Tears and hugs abound.

10:15 a.m.—Bob Townley, executive director of Manhattan Youth, calls the meeting to order: "The lower Manhattan community stands ready to assist in the rescue effort of our neighbors, co-workers, fathers, mothers, brothers, and sisters. No matter what it takes. We stand ready to assist those who have lost their family members. As a community, we stand ready to rebuild commerce, businesses, schools, parks, and homes. We stand ready to help our new homeless and jobless.

"We stand ready to return to normal. Gain access to our homes. Open our schools. Socialize our youth. Open our Little Leagues, recreation programs, and care for our seniors. Our children are scared. We understand. We tell them to be brave. We will help them thrive. We will not leave. We will rebuild our community."

Source: Robert Simko, "Shaken Lower Manhattan Neighbors Find Each Other After September 11 Disaster; Vow to Stay Together and Rebuild the Community," *The Battery Park City Broadsheet*, September 22, 2001.

Further Reading

Abu-Lughod, Janet L. *New York, Chicago, Los Angeles: America's Global Cities.* Minneapolis: University of Minnesota Press, 1999.

Bloom, Nicholas Dagen. *Public Housing that Worked: New York in the Twentieth Century.* Philadelphia: University of Pennsylvania Press, 2008.

Fitch, Robert. *The Assassination of New York.* New York: Verso, 1996.

Freeman, Joshua. *Working-Class New York: Life and Labor since World War II.* New York: Free Press, 2000.

Freeman, Lance. *There Goes the 'Hood: Views of Gentrification from the Ground Up.* Philadelphia: Temple University Press, 2006.

Halle, David, ed. *New York and Los Angeles: Politics, Society, and Culture: A Comparative View.* Chicago: University of Chicago Press, 2003.

Lehrer, Warren, and Judith Sloan. *Crossing the Blvd: Strangers, Neighbors, Aliens in a New America.* New York: Norton, 2003.

Sites, William. *Remaking New York: Primitive Globalization and the Politics of Urban Community.* Minneapolis: University of Minnesota Press, 2003.

Web Resources

New York: A Documentary Film Online, PBS, www.pbs.org/wnet/newyork/.

New York City Historical Maps, http://gis.nyc.gov/doitt/nycitymap/.

New York City Historical Photographs, Centennial Classroom, www.nyc.gov/html/nyc100/html/classroom/photos/index.html.

New York City Historical Society: Slavery in New York, www.slaveryinnewyork.org/history.htm.

New York City Timeline, http://www.newyorkcitytimeline.com/.

The Triangle Factory Fire archival documents, www.ilr.cornell.edu/trianglefire/.

Bibliographic Note

In addition to the works included in the Further Reading section, the following sources provide information and analysis of particular relevance to the topics discussed in the chapter: Richard Harris, "Industry and Residence: The Decentralization of New York City, 1900–1940," *Journal of Historical Geography* 19, no 2 (1993): 169–190; Douglas Massey and Nancy Denton, *American Apartheid: Segregation and the Making of the Underclass* (Cambridge: Harvard University Press, 1993); Lorraine Minnite, "Outside the Circle: The Impact of Post-9/11 Responses on Immigrant Communities in New York," in *Contentious City: The Politics of Recovery in New York* City, ed. John Mollenkopf (New York: Sage, 2005), 165–204; Andy Newman, "With Hospital Bed, You Get Eggroll, and It's Kosher," *New York Times*, February 2, 2003; Sam Roberts, "In Manhattan, Poor Make 2¢ for Each Dollar to the Rich," *New York Times*, September 4, 2005; Stephen Steinberg, *Ethnic Myth: Race, Ethnicity, and Class in America* (Boston: Beacon, 1989); David Von Drehle, *Triangle: The Fire that Changed America* (New York: Atlantic Monthly Press, 2003); Elijah Wald, *How the Beatles Destroyed Rock n Roll: An Alternative History of American Popular Music* (New York: Oxford University Press, 2009).

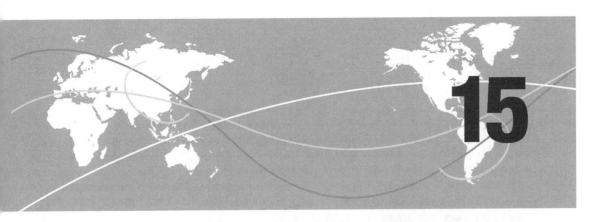

15

Dubai

Global Gateway in the Desert

(1820–2010)

NEEMA NOORI

UBAI WAS THE SITE OF MY FIRST ACADEMIC JOB. AFTER COMPLETING MY graduate training in sociology, I was hired by the Department of International Studies at the American University of Sharjah. Sharjah, located only six miles (ten kilometers) from Dubai, is the third largest of the seven city-states that make up the United Arab Emirates (UAE). Because of Dubai's emergence as the regional center for trade, finance, and tourism, not to mention smuggling and human trafficking, it was an opportune place and time to teach and conduct research on the subject of globalization.

As I think about my three years in the UAE, two memories help capture Dubai's many contradictions, as well as its dizzying pace of transformation from that of a remote British outpost to what urban historian Mike Davis refers to as one of the world capitals of the twenty-first century: the beauty and deceptive tranquility of the Strait of Hormuz and the bustling, often chaotic atmosphere of Dubai's shopping districts, malls, and highways.

It is 2005 and the first winter in Dubai for my family and me. We are driving north toward the Musandam peninsula, a sliver of landmass that stretches across the Strait of Hormuz at the mouth of the Persian Gulf, only thirty-four miles (fifty-five kilometers) from the Iranian mainland. Strangely, Musandam, though part of Oman, is enclosed entirely by the UAE. The British are responsible for this classic example of imperial gerrymandering. The scenery is spectacular. Sheer cliffs loom precariously over the sea. The narrow two-lane road we are driving on clings to the unforgiving cliff wall on my right. The water below is so clear that one can make out the silhouettes of large fish. With so much natural beauty to see, it is hard to stay focused on the road. Far removed from the brisk pace of life in Dubai, this is a deceptively serene place. The Strait of Hormuz, only a handful of kilometers away, marks the chokepoint for the global economy. Twenty-five percent of the world's oil is transported through these waters, making it one of the most geopolitically important places on Earth.

Hidden from view here is the large-scale smuggling operation that keeps Iran supplied with cigarettes, alcohol, consumer electronics, and goods essential to the running of the Iranian economy. Smugglers with boats of all sizes brazenly ply these waters. Because of long-standing cultural ties and kinship networks that straddle the Persian Gulf and pre-date the modern nation-states of Iran, UAE, and Oman, the smuggling operations are protected and facilitated by strong family ties on both shores. Fortunately for the smugglers, despite the UAE and Oman's close relationship with the United States, neither country has done much to stop the flow of goods across the Persian Gulf.

We are here for the water as well, but not as an avenue to barter in the black market economy. At our destination along the shore we board a *dhow* that will take us to Telegraph Island, a well-known snorkeling site that formerly housed a communication center built in 1864 that linked telegraph cables between India and the United Kingdom. These majestic vessels with triangular sails were used for centuries to ferry commercial goods between East Africa, the Persian Gulf, and South Asia and are now powered by motor engines. Decked out traditionally to appeal to tourists, our *dhow* has a large Persian carpet in its center. Desolate and seemingly of little historical value, Telegraph Island conveys a sense of remoteness. As I swim closer to the shore, I observe the outline of the original station and a battered cement staircase leading up from the shore to the surface of the island. All that remains of the original building site are the fading remnants of a series of stone walls. Nothing here conveys the strategic importance of this place to the British Empire.

My second memory is very different from the one of the quiet yet industrious waters of the Strait of Hormuz. It is the fall of 2007—my last year in the UAE. I step out of a cab. Though it is 8 pm and the sky is dark, with its oppressive heat and humidity Dubai feels like a sauna. Due to road construction delays, what should have been a forty-five-minute drive has turned into a ninety-minute slog. The roads are overcrowded, and the city itself is a vast construction site as Dubai is creating a new city center anchored by what will soon be the tallest building in the world. I am late for my meeting with Salim, an Afghan student of mine who will soon travel to New York to begin his graduate studies in public administration.

Resembling a Hollywood movie set, Dubai has an artificial feel. I am headed to the original downtown, one of the few parts of the city that does not have this quality. Densely populated, with a diverse mixture of building styles that date back to the 1970s and 1980s, this is one of the few parts of the city with a vibrant street life. Dubai's street life has increasingly shifted to the rarefied corridors of its expansive shopping malls, where Western corporate stores such as H&M, the Body Shop, and Chili's compete for space in cavernous halls that bear the scent of Chanel and Dior. Sanitized, dehumidified, and air conditioned, even the air suggests artifice. Though very little of the architecture in this part of the city could be characterized as traditional, the concentration and diversity of buildings and businesses convey an authenticity missing from other parts of the city. The businesses and restaurants located here cater predominantly to the working-class and non-Western tourists who flock to Dubai. I doubt that this area, bustling with activity, will ever be displaced as the commercial heart of the city.

As I make my way north in the direction of the gold market, the sidewalk becomes more crowded. To the left are the familiar Persian carpet stores that line this side of the street. Shimmering silk carpets trap my gaze. Not for long, however, as the blaring horns from the street capture my attention. I turn left, away from the traffic, and begin to make out bits and pieces of conversation. Bags in their hands, a middle-aged Russian couple excitedly exits the store in front of me. I pause to let them by and notice the advertisements in the windows. Cyrillic characters announce a half-price sale on fine leather goods and fur coats. None of the signs here are in English or Arabic. Of course, who would need a fur coat in this part of the world? Farther down, I hear other languages being spoken: Persian, Urdu, English, and Arabic. On my left, a door opens and I hear a wisp of a familiar song. A closer look reveals album covers from Los Angeles of the latest Iranian pop stars: due to bans on pop music, Iran's music industry has relocated to L.A.

As I venture further into the bazaar, I struggle against the crowds pressing against me. Shops selling everything from Italian chandeliers to sporting goods compete for space along the narrow alleys. Since it is a Thursday, many people have come to take advantage of their time off to do their shopping prior to the start of the weekend. In 2006 the weekend was altered from Thursday-Friday to Friday-Saturday, bringing the UAE in closer alignment with the Westernized global standard. The mostly male throng of shoppers is now so dense that car traffic has ceased. Aside from the women employed in the services sector as nannies, maids, office workers, flight attendants, and sex workers, most of Dubai's expat labor force consists of men. I could be in Karachi or Mumbai, anywhere but Dubai. This cosmopolitan city, from its Hollywood-ready skyscrapers to its bustling downtown, is truly international. Its geographic location has long set Dubai at a crossroads for travel and trade, and in the twenty-first century it sits at the forefront of globalization. Two keys to Dubai's economic success are maintaining access to a cheap immigrant labor force and disciplining its migrant labor force—the multitudes of young men bustling around me in Dubai's old downtown. Though the political leadership deserves some credit, much of Dubai's success today is due to the exploitative labor policies that provide the UAE with an unremitting flow of inexpensive labor power.

This chapter will provide a brief history of Dubai's rise from British colonial outpost to a center of global commerce. It will assess competing explanations for Dubai's rise and fall. The Dubai story provides a useful and timely case study to examine issues that lie at the heart of current debates on globalization. To some, Dubai is a success story to be replicated across the Middle East. Western policymakers have even advocated for the adoption of elements of Dubai's flexible labor market. For others, Dubai represents a dystopian future to be avoided.

DUBAI AND THE WORLD: *Coveted and Dependent Commercial Hub*

Dubai's birth and subsequent survival is due to the sustained intervention of great powers such as the United Kingdom and the United States. In the late 1600s, Great Britain supplanted the Portuguese as the dominant colonial presence in the Persian Gulf. The Portuguese built numerous fortresses throughout the Persian Gulf, including one in Musandam and another on the opposing side of the Strait of Hormuz in Iran. In so doing, the Portuguese left a larger and longer-lasting material footprint than did the British. In 1820, to put an end to piracy and to create safer shipping lanes to India, British naval forces imposed a blockade on Ras Al Khaimah, a city-state that is currently part of the UAE. After a brief naval siege, the British forced the existing tribal leaders in what is now the UAE to sign a peace treaty. Traditionally, in Arabic a tribal leader was referred to as the sheikh. In the Persian Gulf today, the heads of state are generally referred to as sheikhs.

British Colonialism and the Rise of a Vital Port

With the arrival of the Portuguese and the British, the region was drawn into a system of global trade governed by Western powers. Prior to the sixteenth century, ports along the Persian Gulf were integrated into regional trade networks linking commercial nodes along the Indian subcontinent with mercantile hubs along the east coast of Africa. Diasporas from a wide swath of Eurasia and Africa settled in these ports and helped coordinate trade across vast distances.

The treaty signed in 1820 granted safe passage to British ships but did nothing to stop the signatories from attacking one another. The tribes governing the Arabian Peninsula at the time were politically fragmented, and incorporation into the empire only served to deepen existing divisions. In 1853 the British brought the sheikhs back to the table to sign the Perpetual Maritime Truce, which called for an end to all fighting at sea. Up until independence in 1971, the states comprising the United Arab Emirates were referred to as the Trucial States. The Trucial States signed an additional agreement with the British in 1892 that barred diplomatic activity with foreign powers. Prior British approval was a precondition for any discussion with outside powers. Britain was concerned with maintaining a secure corridor between the Persian Gulf and India, its prized colonial possession in South Asia. Because British occupation of the region predated the discovery of oil, colonial agents demonstrated little interest in adjudicating territorial conflicts or determining the degree of authority exercised by local sheikhs. Aside from its geopolitical significance, the British were largely indifferent to the region. Interestingly, from 1873 to 1946, the British government of India, rather than the British Foreign Office in London, assumed responsibility for the Trucial States. This reinforced South Asia's longstanding social and economic links to the region; a legacy of British imperialism that is reflected in the region's continued reliance on Indian labor, both intellectual and physical. After Indian independence in 1947, the Foreign Office in London reasserted control of the day-to-day administration of the Trucial States and other imperial interests in the Persian Gulf.

Significantly, in brokering these agreements the British signed independent treaties with each sheikh. This practice solidified the power of the leading tribal families and ensured that those families would continue to maintain their dominant positions. Most of these families, such as the Maktoum family of Dubai, are still in power. Moreover, signing individual treaties created a political environment that inhibited cooperation and fostered conflict between the newly formalized tribal territorial units. These early imperial interventions helped create the political framework that led to the modern nation-states of the UAE, Kuwait, Qatar, Bahrain, and Oman. As this early history of the region demonstrates, the UAE, along with the other countries that constitute the Gulf Cooperation Council (GCC), did not emerge organically. Indeed, to this day, they owe their security to foreign powers.

Despite overseeing Dubai's foreign affairs and laying claim to its mineral resources, British colonial officers did not intervene in the domestic affairs of the city-state. The Maktoum family was given full control over Dubai's port, one of only a handful of natural deepwater ports in the Persian Gulf. In 1922, following the first discovery of oil in 1908, Dubai's ruler signed an agreement to grant oil concessions solely to companies appointed by the British government.

Dubai's emergence as an entrepôt, a duty-free port used as a waypoint for transshipment, occurred in 1887, when Iran reasserted control over Bandar Lengeh, a port in southern Iran. The customs regulations imposed by the new sovereign power displaced many of the existing merchants. Maktoum bin Hashar, Dubai's ruler at the time, invited these Arab and Persian merchants to relocate to Dubai, which benefited immensely from their extensive social networks and mercantile expertise. Conventional historiography cites this as the pivotal moment in shaping Dubai's evolution into a global entrepôt.

Sheikh Rashid, the grandson of Maktoum bin Hashar, ruled from 1958 to 1990. Sheikh Rashid continued his grandfather's legacy and invested heavily in improving Dubai's commercial infrastructure. He built an international airport, established an independent airline, constructed the world's largest commercial port in 1976, and promoted the development of a nascent banking industry. According to Persian Gulf historian Rosemarie Said Zahlan in her 1998 *The Making of the Modern Gulf States*, Sheikh Rashid, himself a leading businessman, "administered Dubai as a large corporation."

The Making of a Corporate City-State

When Britain withdrew from the Persian Gulf in 1971, the Trucial States were politically decentralized, resembling more a confederation of loosely allied political units than a centralized federal state. (See Map 15.1.) Between 1971 and the present, Abu Dhabi, due mostly to its superior oil wealth, emerged as the capital of the UAE. Though the ruling family of Abu Dhabi has sought to further centralize power, the city-states that make up the UAE continue to experience substantial autonomy; the UAE is now free to formulate its own foreign policy and to determine the usage of its natural resources. Nevertheless, the United States has supplanted the United Kingdom as the dominant external power in the region, operating air and naval bases in Iraq, Bahrain, Qatar, and Kuwait. It has also negotiated agreements with the UAE and Oman, allowing the United States access to military bases in both countries.

The Iranian Revolution of 1978, followed by the Iran-Iraq War (1980–1988), disrupted trade flows across the Persian Gulf. However, both the revolution and the war served Dubai's economic interests, as thousands of wealthy Iranians moved their assets offshore for protection. The conflict also generated other opportunities for financial gain. After Iranian militants occupied the US embassy and held those inside hostage, US president Jimmy Carter's administration froze all Iranian assets held in the United States. In 1984 the United States imposed further economic sanctions, prohibiting US weapons sales to Iran. Economic sanctions against Iran continue to be in effect, but the economic blockade has not deterred smugglers from the UAE, which reaps rewards by continuing to conduct trade with Iran. The sanctions create lucrative business opportunities for those willing to make the four- to six-hour trip to Iran across the Strait of Hormuz and from other points along the UAE coastline. The UAE has long benefited from the activities of smugglers. In the 1960s and 1970s, when India placed a ban on importing gold, Emirati smugglers supplied Indian jewelry merchants.

Dubai's early reliance on trade, both licit and illicit; its ability to profit from regional insecurity; and its dependence on imperial power for protection are factors that are remarkably consistent with Dubai's current status, even as it sits poised to become a global capital. The costs of Dubai's success, however, are not borne equally. Citizens of Dubai, who constitute an increasingly small proportion of the total population of their city due to the large number of expatriates also residing there, have traded political rights for economic rights. Though they cannot vote or run for office, numerous financial perks mute concerns over their political and cultural marginalization. The large and growing migrant workforce, on the other hand, including sex workers, finds itself subject to a coercive disciplinary regime that has little concern for economic exploitation and

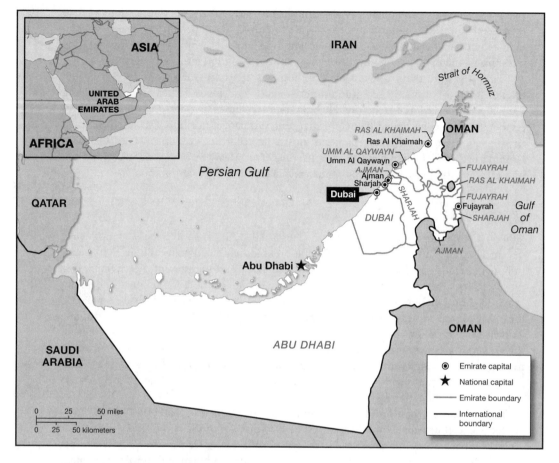

Map 15.1. United Arab Emirates

More a confederation of loosely allied states than a unified nation, the seven emirates that constitute the United Arab Emirates, including Dubai, are largely an artifact of British imperialism. Neighboring Iran's proximity to Dubai facilitates the smuggling activities that undermine US sanctions against that country.

other human rights abuses. Indeed, Dubai is widely acknowledged to be the human trafficking capital of the region. The government's dominant objectives vis-à-vis this migrant labor force is to maintain access to cheap labor, to prevent the emergence of an organized labor movement, and to defend Dubai's carefully cultivated international brand.

Brand Dubai

Many oil-dependent states in the Middle East have suffered what social scientists call the mineral resource curse. Virtually all of the oil-rich nations in the region have authoritarian regimes with limited political and economic rights. Though blessed with an abundance of oil, countries such as Libya, Iraq, Kuwait, Saudi Arabia, and Iran have not successfully used their resources to promote long-term development projects to diversify their economies. These countries remain highly dependent on oil revenues. Political scientists

Lisa Anderson and Giaccomo Luciani have argued that these authoritarian regimes use their oil wealth to purchase the loyalty of their citizens. Since oil revenues lessen the need to rely on taxes for government expenditures, oil-wealthy states in the region remain insulated from public pressure. Rather than use oil profits to invest in infrastructure or human capital development, the bulk of the revenue is used to stifle opposition to the state. As such, many of these regimes suffer from oversized bureaucracies; indeed, most members of the upper and middle classes work for the government.

Though Dubai shares many of these characteristics, including an authoritarian government, it has successfully developed an economy that is no longer reliant on oil revenues. Unlike many of its neighbors in the Persian Gulf, Dubai has limited oil resources. At current production levels, its supply of oil is expected to run out by 2025. Beginning in the 1980s, Dubai made a concerted effort to transform itself into the shopping capital of the region. At first, it targeted tourists from the region itself. Compared to Saudi Arabia and post-revolutionary Iran, Dubai's cosmopolitanism offers a welcome respite from the strict moral codes enforced in both Iran and Saudi Arabia, Dubai's largest and wealthiest neighbors.

After the collapse of the Soviet Union in 1992, Dubai benefited enormously from tourists hailing from Russia and other former Soviet republics. Lured to Dubai because of its proximity, lax visa regulations, cheap prices, and reputation as a shopping paradise, customers from throughout the former Soviet Union flocked to Dubai. Most of these early customers, many traveling on chartered flights, used their time in Dubai to purchase luxury goods for resale in their home countries. Since 2000 Dubai has successfully broadened its tourist appeal to Europe and North America.

The current ruler of Dubai, Sheikh Mohammed bin Rashid Al Maktoum, or "Sheikh Mo," as he is referred to by Western expats in Dubai, has invested heavily in the construction of architectural landmarks since becoming the crown prince and de facto ruler in 1995. This investment was a calculated strategy to compensate for Dubai's inherent lack of natural or man-made landmarks worthy of capturing global attention. Due also to its inhospitable climate—daytime temperatures in the summer can reach 45 degrees Celsius (113 degrees Fahrenheit)—Dubai is an unlikely tourist destination, particularly for shopping. The numerous indoor shopping malls built during Sheikh Mohammed's tenure helped address this problem.

Mohammed Maktoum publicly refers to himself as the first CEO head of state. In doing so, he shares the same governing philosophy as his father, Sheikh Rashid. In the 1950s, Dubai's population was thirty thousand. Today it is nearly five hundred times larger, with a population of 1.7 million. Dubai's GDP per capita rose from $19,000 in 2000 to $33,500 in 2007. Its rate of economic growth has been nothing short of spectacular. In 2007, one year before the onset of the global financial crisis, Dubai was at the peak of an unprecedented economic boom. Sheikh Mohammed had embarked on the construction of the world's largest airport, aquarium, indoor ski park, shopping mall, and the world's tallest building. More controversial were a series of colossal man-made islands built off the cost of the UAE, which are thought to add approximately 752 kilometers of beachfront property to Dubai.

Between 2000 and 2005, Dubai enjoyed a world-record economic growth rate of 13.4 percent. By 2007 this remote former British colonial outpost had emerged as the financial capital of the Middle East and was poised to become a global financial center. Dubai's flagship air carrier, Emirates Airlines (now the sixth-largest airline in the world), had just completed multibillion-dollar purchases from Airbus and Boeing. Through a series of acquisitions, Dubai Ports World (DPW), a government-backed port operations company, had become the world's fourth-largest ports operator, with branches in forty-one different countries. Emaar, a government-backed real estate company, had begun developing real estate projects in Tunisia, Morocco, India, and Saudi Arabia: gated communities whose design was perfected in Dubai itself. Emaar's gated communities in Dubai were used to showcase and advertise the luxurious lifestyle and living arrangements that it hoped to develop in surrounding regions.

In successfully crafting and publicizing the Dubai brand around the globe, Mohammed Maktoum created a template for urban design and governance that others have sought to emulate. From Astana, the new capital of Kazakhstan, to newly emerging gated communities in North Africa, Dubai's influence is apparent. This is in part what makes Dubai a global capital. The Dubai model of governance, which banned organized labor, levied no taxes, and embraced free markets under the leadership of an enlightened despot, was the object of international envy. Advocates of the Dubai model have argued that democracy is an impediment to a free market and perhaps obsolete. Political analysts have gone so far as to proclaim that in a globalized world, power would recede from large territorial states such as the United States in favor of cities. Theorists of globalization such as Manuel Castells predict a global network of cities whose economic, political, and social connections to each other would supersede the degree to which they were locally embedded in national economies.

Much of the literature extolling the virtues of the Dubai model and written in praise of the administrative genius of Mohammed Maktoum and his forbears, however, neglects mentioning the role of great powers such as the United States and United Kingdom in guaranteeing the region's security. More tragic is the literature's virtual silence on Dubai's legacy of human rights abuses in the form of human trafficking and labor exploitation that underpin much of its economic success.

The Kefala System

Through 2001, thanks in part to Dubai's careful crafting of its international brand, press coverage of the city-state had been largely positive. Dubai was touted as a paragon of economic success that other developing nations should use as a model. Western press coverage of Dubai shifted after the September 11 terrorist attacks. Dubai was excoriated in the Western press for not doing enough to prevent Al-Qaeda and other illicit transnational organizations from using the UAE's banking services for unlawful financial transactions. It has also faced growing criticism for its labor practices.

Dubai's construction boom of the past decade, though financed by high oil prices and speculative real estate investment, was mostly dependent on massive flows of cheap labor from South Asia. Prior to the global recession, only 10 percent of Dubai's population of 1.7 million consisted of UAE citizens. The remainder of the population was—and continues to be—made up of migrant workers, predominantly from India, Pakistan, Bangladesh, the Philippines, and Iran. This large, multinational, expatriate workforce lacks basic rights. Those employed in the construction industry work under particularly harsh conditions, are paid little, and can face deportation for contesting the terms of their contracts. In addition to widespread labor abuses, international human rights organizations are critical of the Dubai government's complicity in the city's evolution into a regional center for human trafficking.

One of the central themes of this chapter concerns the similarities between the current phase of globalization and the one that existed at the beginning of the twentieth century. Curiously, though moving goods and transmitting information has never been easier or comparatively cheaper, in an international system comprised of fully developed nation-states with secure borders, the movement of people has never been harder. Ironically, more people are on the move than at any time since the early 1900s. With the proliferation of guest worker programs, export processing zones, and alternative mechanisms for controlling migratory streams, these flows take place under very different conditions than the previous episode of globalization. Dubai's system of managing labor flows illustrates this point.

Cheap imported labor is managed by the *kefala* system, a coercive regime designed to regulate short-term labor contracts and manage the flow of migrant workers. It is in place throughout the Persian Gulf states of Kuwait, Qatar, the UAE, Bahrain, Oman, and Saudi Arabia. Similar to eighteenth-century forms of indentured servitude practiced in the British Empire, all workers brought in from the outside must be sponsored by a citizen of the UAE. One's work contract is tied directly to the sponsor. Though renewable, work permits are issued only for a three-year period. And, once a work permit is issued, employees cannot change jobs unless they leave the country and reapply for a visa from abroad.

Despite their low wages and dangerous working conditions, Persian Gulf countries like the UAE have not faced significant labor shortages. This is due to two factors: poverty in the nations that supply labor and the unethical tactics employed by regional recruitment agencies. Poverty ensures a continuous supply of labor, while the unscrupulous practices of recruitment agents result in such high levels of debt that migrant laborers cannot afford to leave. Most construction workers are hired through local recruitment agencies that charge high fees to finance visa and travel expenses to the UAE. According to a Human Rights Watch report issued in 2006, construction workers pay on average $2,000 to $3,000 in fees to labor recruitment agencies. Though these fees are illegal, the government does little to enforce the bans. Most laborers begin working in Dubai with large debts that they must repay; many spend the first two years of their employment servicing debt. During this period they are unable to send remittances home to their families. To add to their financial insecurity and to prevent them from quitting, construction companies confiscate passports and withhold wages for the first two months of employment. According to UAE labor laws, the employer takes full economic and legal responsibility for the employee. As such, employers have the legal right to confiscate and hold an employee's passport. Because sponsorship is a virtual birthright, the *kefala* system has made it possible for middle-class Emirati households to afford multiple maids, nannies, and gardeners. And UAE citizens are not the only ones to benefit from the ready availability of affordable domestic support. High-wage expats, members of Dubai's white-collar migrant workforce, similarly take advantage of the affordability of maids and nannies, citing these services as one of the perks of life in Dubai.

In its 2006 report, Human Rights Watch criticized government authorities both at the federal level and in Dubai for not doing enough to monitor working conditions across the UAE. According to the report, the UAE government deploys 140 inspectors to monitor the working conditions of more than 240,000 businesses employing over 2.5 million migrant workers throughout the country. The federal laws offering protections for migrant workers are rarely enforced, including the law requiring a minimum wage. According to the report, the average construction worker in Dubai earns only $140 a month.

Due to the heat, working conditions are brutal, with average summer temperatures often exceeding 102 degrees Fahrenheit and an average rate of humidity that is above 80 percent. Because safeguards are minimal and enforcement is lax, construction work sites are dangerous and worker deaths are not unusual. The suicide rate among migrant workers is also high. Faced with high debts and an inability to remit money to their families, the plight of construction workers is desperate.

Long commutes to and from work, often in buses that lack air conditioning, add to an already grueling workday that is over eleven hours long on average. Construction workers in Dubai are bused in from segregated labor camps located on the city's periphery. The accommodations for workers are primitive, with eight to twelve men per room, sharing communal restrooms and kitchens. Recent Western-based media reports describe unsanitary conditions that include exposed pools of raw sewage at the labor camps.

Though maids may live in more luxurious settings, they work in the least regulated economic sphere: the household. Working alone and far removed from friends and family members, maids are vulnerable to abuse. Because boundaries between employee and family member are often blurred, nannies and maids are often forced to work long days with few breaks. Ironically, their adoption as members of the family often exposes them to greater degrees of exploitation. Importantly, these observations about household work are universally applicable. The plight of domestic workers in Dubai, however, is made worse by both the coercive effects of the *kefala* system, the state's weak regulatory apparatus, and the employer's authority to confiscate employee passports.

Even though prostitution serves as a key, yet unacknowledged, component of the tourist industry, sex workers are the most vulnerable of Dubai's migrant workforce. Victims of sex trafficking tell similar stories of being falsely recruited to Dubai to work as sales clerks or waitresses. Upon arrival, their passports are confiscated and they are coerced into prostitution. Though many are trafficked into Dubai, some, it is important to note, come to Dubai and work of their own free will. Due to prostitution's illegality, sex workers face multiple threats, from abusive clients and pimps to a police force that has historically targeted the victims of trafficking rather than the traffickers. As an illustration of this contradiction, in response to claims that the Dubai government was indifferent to the problem of human trafficking, over 4,300 prostitutes were rounded up and deported in 2006. Official reports of the sweep noticeably did not emphasize the arrest of pimps or traffickers.

Emirati citizens benefit from the *kefala* system in a number of ways. In addition to offering an affordable source of household support, the existing labor regime allows Emirati entrepreneurs to profit from their ability to sponsor employees for foreign business owners who are dependent on local partners for access to workers. Hence, the system itself offers Emirati citizens a source of revenue. However, because of its wage-dampening effects, the *kefala* system has made it difficult for Emirati citizens to find work in the private sector. Because low-wage migrant workers are not allowed to change jobs without the permission of their employers, salaries are kept artificially low. Therefore, like most oil-wealthy countries in the region, the government is both the largest and most attractive job source for citizens.

Citizenship is also one of the casualties of the *kefala* system; becoming a citizen is out of the question for most migrant workers and their families. Even children born and raised in Dubai by migrant parents are denied citizenship rights. Marriage to an Emirati citizen also does not guarantee that the spouse will obtain citizenship rights. Foreign women who marry Emirati men have an easier route to citizenship. Importantly, the children of these unions have full access to citizenship. Foreign men who marry Emirati women, on the other hand, are barred from citizenship. Their children are also typically denied citizenship. This example of gender bias points toward a more serious problem of gender inequality in the UAE. Due to patriarchal government policies and a male-dominated political system, women continue to face institutional discrimination. For example, women can travel outside of the country only with the permission of their husbands or fathers. Nonetheless, it is important to note that Emirati women now constitute the majority of college students in the country, a trend that bodes well for women's empowerment in the future.

GLOBAL ENCOUNTERS AND CONNECTIONS:
Crosscurrents of Finance, Trade, and Terrorism

Dubai's economic growth has in large part benefited from regional insecurity. As mentioned earlier, the Iranian Revolution of 1978 and the subsequent Iran-Iraq War served as boons to Dubai's economy. Unsettled by the revolution and the war and motivated by a desire to protect their assets, oil-rich Iranian businessmen transferred their wealth to Dubai. In 1979, following the Iranian takeover of the American embassy and the seizure of sixty-six members of the embassy staff, the United States imposed an economic embargo on Iran. Dubai consequently became the main trade portal to Iran and smuggling once again flourished. Amid the growing fear that Iran's nuclear energy program could have a more sinister military application, US presidents George W. Bush and Barack Obama have strengthened sanctions that were first imposed in 1970.

Throughout this period, trade between Iran and Dubai has remained robust. On December 13, 2010, the executive director of UAE customs was quoted by the Web site PressTV as saying that "despite sanctions, Iran tops Dubai's economic partners list." According to him, the volume of trade between Tehran and Dubai exceeded $13 billion in 2009. The true amount is certainly much higher. The $13 billion figure represents only legal commerce. It does not account for the illicit trade. Despite these economic ties, however, official relations between the UAE and Iran remain tense.

A diverse array of transnational criminal and terrorist organizations, such as the Russian mafia, Al-Qaeda, and D-Company, have relied on Dubai's financial institutions, ports, and lucrative real estate markets to move, launder, and conceal their assets, financial and otherwise. Up through the global financial crisis of 2008, Dubai's heated real estate market allowed investors to purchase office space, homes, and apartments for resale at a significant profit. As such, real estate served as a convenient instrument for money laundering. Many of these properties changed hands repeatedly without ever being occupied. Given Dubai's historic ties to illegal economic practices, such as smuggling, and the degree to which Dubai's banks are linked to and are a part of the globe's financial circuitry, it is not surprising that the UAE is so deeply enmeshed in illicit forms of globalization.

Due to the long-standing existence of illicit economic enterprises, such as the current smuggling activity with Iran and previous operations such as the use of Dubai as a base from which to transport gold into India in the 1970s, local banks and financial institutions in Dubai have had to devise clandestine strategies for making payments and transferring capital. Apart from the hidden techniques adopted by its national banks to transfer capital, informal mechanisms for moving money have developed parallel to those used by formal banks. One such system used extensively throughout the Persian Gulf and South Asia, called the *hawala* system, enables individuals to transfer funds through proxies. Though used extensively by migrant workers to remit money home cheaply to their families, it is also an important tool for facilitating illicit financial transactions. To send money abroad using the *hawala* system, the customer commissions a *hawala* broker, known as a *hawaladar*, who then contacts a colleague at the site where the money is to be sent. For a small transaction fee, the *hawaladar* on the other end will disperse funds to the appropriate person.

What makes this social-network-based financial system unusual is that it is conducted entirely on the basis of trust. At the time of the transaction, no money is physically transferred between the individual who sends the money and the person who receives the payment. The brokers involved in the transactions make independent arrangements to settle debts at a later date. Because these transactions take place outside of conventional financial institutions, government agencies cannot regulate the transactions and no taxes are paid. Dubai's reliance on *hawala* networks and its innovative development of Islamic banking institutions are important factors in explaining its economic success. It is commonly referred to as the regional *hawala* capital.

Because *hawala* operates largely outside the domain of formal banking structures or the purview of government bureaucracies, organizations such as Al-Qaeda have successfully used the *hawala* system to hide money, make payments, and to safely move large sums of money to support their activities. Although attempts have been made to impose tighter regulations designed to staunch the flow of illicit funding through Dubai's banks, American government officials remain critical of these efforts, arguing that they do not go far enough to restrict funds going to terrorist groups. The 2010 WikiLeaks release of American diplomatic memos suggests that though the United States remains strongly aligned with the UAE, it continues to distrust the rulers' efforts to block terrorist entrepreneurs from using local financial institutions.

In 2003 the UAE began requiring *hawala* brokers to register with its Central Bank. To legally engage in *hawala* exchange, applicants must now pass a test that assesses their knowledge of money laundering and terrorism financing laws. Once they have registered, brokers are required to maintain records of transactions and to report suspicious activities. However, the registration requirement is not widely enforced, nor is there a legally defined penalty for operating a *hawala* service. Due to the ubiquity of *hawala* and the crucial role it plays in allowing migrant workers to send money home, banning it is impractical.

Dubai's willingness to harbor international criminal networks predates the rise of Al-Qaeda. Dawood Ibrahim, head of South Asia's largest and most powerful transnational criminal organization, D-Company, planned the 1993 Mumbai bombings, which killed 250 people, from his home in Dubai. Ibrahim earned his wealth from running a sophisticated gold smuggling operation out of Dubai, where he lived from 1984 until 1993. Dubai later ignored the Indian government's extradition request and Ibrahim was able to escape to Pakistan.

Just as Dubai's size, sophistication, location, transportation infrastructure, and the discretion of its governing authorities make it appealing to smugglers, drug traffickers, and human traffickers, it also appeals to the US military. The UAE has served as a logistics hub for American military interventions in Afghanistan and Iraq, and Dubai has been dubbed the "busiest commercial terminal in the world" for America's Middle East wars. Halliburton, a multinational corporation that originally specialized in oil and gas operations but now also provides military services, moved its international headquarters to Dubai in 2007. The company garnered millions of dollars worth of contracts for the US military in Iraq and Afghanistan.

Global Financial Crisis

The 2008 global financial crisis took a particularly heavy toll on Dubai. Given the degree to which Dubai was dependent on globalization in the form of trade, investment, and tourism, this was not surprising. Construction on some of the UAE's most well-known projects stalled. Were it not for the intervention of Abu Dhabi, Dubai would have defaulted on its debt obligations. To compensate for Abu Dhabi's support, Dubai changed the name of the tallest tower in the world from Burj Dubai to Burj Khalifa, after Sheikh Khalifa, the current ruler of Abu Dhabi. For the first time in years, rates of immigration

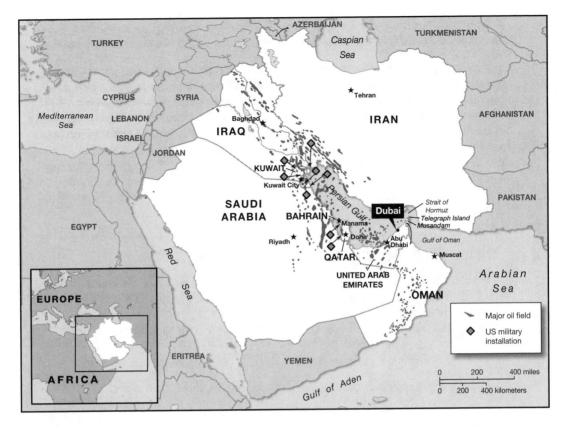

Map 15.2. The Persian Gulf

Twenty-five percent of the world's oil—approximately seventeen million barrels per day—transits through the Strait of Hormuz. With 55 percent of the world's proven oil reserves, the Persian Gulf, including the United Arab Emirates, is arguably the world's most geopolitically important region. Given the region's strategic value, it is not surprising that the United States maintains such a heavy military presence in the Persian Gulf.

stalled as large numbers of migrant workers sought opportunities elsewhere. Today, office building and residential real estate vacancy rates across Dubai remain high.

Though by 2011 Dubai had begun to recover, other oil-rich city-states in the region now compete with the UAE for regional primacy. Qatar recently won an international competition to host the World Cup in 2022. Abu Dhabi has begun construction on its own set of iconic landmarks. New York University, along with the Louvre and Guggenheim art museums, are all in the process of opening branches in Abu Dhabi. With the largest sovereign wealth fund in the world at over $600 billion and the seventh-largest oil reserves, Abu Dhabi is positioned for further growth. Because America's continued presence in the region serves as a crucial guarantor of regional security, Persian Gulf states such as Saudi Arabia, Kuwait, Bahrain, Qatar, and the UAE will continue to reap the rewards that flow from their geographic location. (See Map 15.2.) And, importantly, the coercive labor practices that dominate the region ensure continued flows of cheap labor. The global financial crisis of 2008, however, highlights the degree to which the city-states of the Gulf are more sensitive than most to realignments of global power and changes in transitional flows of capital.

In a country that has a quiescent press and lacks voting rights, opposition parties, and labor unions, the only organizations reporting on and advocating for human rights issues belong to global civil society. Though international nongovernmental organizations (IN-GOs) such as Human Rights Watch have vocally criticized Dubai, their activism demonstrates the strengths and weaknesses of a global civil society. Theorists of globalization have argued that the rising power of nongovernmental organizations such as Human Rights Watch diminishes the autonomy and sovereignty of nation-states. Some have even argued that global civil society can fulfill the functions of a domestic civil society. Dubai's experience suggests that these views exaggerate the influence of INGOs and their ability to promote human rights.

Human Rights Watch Letter to UAE Minister of Labor

Human Rights Watch (HRW), an international nongovernmental organization, published a series of scathing reports on human rights abuses in Dubai. The US government echoed these concerns. The text below contains excerpts from a Human Rights Watch letter written to the UAE minister of labor. This letter was written prior to the issuance of the HRW's formal report. The letter poses questions that concern labor rights and government oversight of the UAE's construction industry.

- What are the target audiences for this letter and the subsequent report?

- How do organizations such as HRW hope to improve human rights in undemocratic countries such as the UAE that lack labor unions, a free press, and a vibrant civil society?

- The letter asks for clarification on the number of worksite inspectors in the country. What does the dearth of inspectors suggest about the government's commitment to regulating labor standards?

- Given what you know about labor conditions in Dubai, what additional question would pose to the minister of labor?

- Based upon the issues raised in this letter, would you say that migrant workers in the United States enjoy stronger workplace protections? How do the social and political contexts for migrant work in the UAE differ from those of the United States?

July 14, 2006

His Excellency Dr. Ali Abdulla Al Kaabi
Minister of Labor
Ministry of Labor,
Dubai, United Arab Emirates

Your Excellency,

Human Rights Watch is preparing a report regarding the conditions of migrant workers in the United Arab Emirates (UAE). We recently conducted a fact-finding mission in the UAE. Our goal is to include the views and testimonies of the people who work in the UAE, their employers, and the UAE government, with respect to the policies and conditions governing migrant work there. . . .

We would appreciate your comments on the following issues by July 31st, 2006; if we receive your comments by then, we will certainly reflect them in our upcoming publication. . . .

According to our research, the Ministry of Labor currently employs eighty inspectors to oversee the labor practices of the 246,420 companies that employ migrant workers. Is this figure correct? How many companies have these inspectors inspected in the past two years? Are the findings of their inspections made public, and if so, can we obtain copies of their findings for the past three years? Does the Ministry of Labor have any plans to increase the number of inspectors? . . .

In August 2005, local media in the UAE published reports that the number of migrant workers working in the construction sector who died in 2004 exceeded 800. The official government figure for the number of workplace deaths in 2004 is thirty-four. How do you explain the discrepancy between the government's statistics and the reported figures? In particular, are the companies operating in "Free Zones" required to report to the government incidents of death and injury at their work-sites? How do you gather statistics on the number of laborers injured or killed on construction sites? What kind of provisions for medical care, social security benefits, and transfer of remains are made available, if any?

According to the UAE labor law, all companies are obligated to report death and injuries at workplace to the Ministry of Labor. According to the Ministry of Labor officials, quoted in the media, only six companies filed reports of death and injury in 2005. What is the government doing to make sure that companies report instances of death and injury?

On September 23, 2005, hundreds of workers for the Al Hamed Development and Construction of Abu Dhabi publicly protested that their employer had not paid them their salary for the past four months. Your office immediately ordered Al Hamed Development and Con-

struction to pay the workers their full unpaid wages. As of April 3, 2006, when we interviewed workers at Al Hamed Development and Construction, they told us that they were paid only two months of back-wages. The Al Hamed workers said that as of April 3, 2006, they are owed three months of wages. Please provide us any information regarding any actions your government has taken to resolve this matter. How is the government holding Al Hamed Company accountable for its persistent violation of workers rights?

In the course of our research, we have come across many cases of workers who have been abandoned by their employers. In these cases, the employers held back paying wages to their workers for many months and then fled the country. Under UAE law, all companies must have a business partner who is a UAE national. However, our research indicates that the UAE nationals are not being held accountable in these cases. Can you provide us with information regarding the identity and number of UAE nationals found guilty of violating UAE labor laws, particularly in cases of bankrupt construction companies?

We would like to ask your response to the particular case of East Coast & Hamriah Company. On April 13, 2005, the Sharjah Federal Court of the First Instance has issued verdicts that the company owes 23 of its workers various dues. However, because the Lebanese owner of the company has fled, the authorities have told the workers there is no way they can recover their lost wages and that the company's UAE partner is not liable. Could you please respond why in this case the UAE partner is not being held liable? Please see copies of court rulings in the case of three out of the 23 workers attached to this letter. . . .

According to Article 63 of the UAE labor law, the Ministry of Labor is required to put in place a minimum wage. Why has the Ministry never fulfilled its legal obligation? What is the government currently doing to fulfill this legal requirement?

Please do not hesitate to include any other materials, statistics, and government actions regarding the conditions of migrant workers in the UAE that you think might be relevant. Thank you in advance for your time in addressing this urgent matter.

Sincerely,

Hadi Ghaemi
Researcher
Middle East and North Africa Division
Human Rights Watch

Source: "Building Towers, Cheating Workers: Appendix 1: Human Rights Watch Letter to UAE Minister of Labor," July 14, 2006, www.hrw.org/en/node/11123/section/10.

Further Reading

Ali, Syed. *Dubai: Gilded Cage*. New Haven: Yale University Press, 2010.
Davis, Mike. "Fear and Money in Dubai." *New Left Review* 41 (2006): 46–68.
Hvidt, Martin. "The Dubai Model: An Outline of Key Development-Process Elements in Dubai." *International Journal of Middle East Studies* 41 (2009): 397–418.
Zahlan, Rosemari Said. *The Making of the Modern Gulf States*. Reading, England: Ithaca Press, 2002.

Web Resources

"Conditions of Dubai's Immigrant Workers Highlighted," BBC News video, January 20, 2011, www.bbc.co.uk/news/world-middle-east-12246979.
Dubai History, www.dubai-architecture.info/HIST-DUBAI.htm.
Economic development of the UAE, UAE Interact, www.uaeinteract.com/news/default.asp?ID=11.

Bibliographic Note

In addition to the works included in the Further Reading section, the following sources provide information and analysis of particular relevance to the topics discussed in the chapter: Ashfaq Ahmed, "Expats Make Up 99% of Private Sector Staff in UAE," Gulfnews.com, April 7, 2008, http://gulfnews.com/news/gulf/uae/employment/expats-make-up-99-of-private-sector-staff-in-uae-1.96744 (accessed December 10, 2011); Syed Ali, *Dubai: Gilded Cage*, (New Haven: Yale University Press, 2010); Ben Anderson, "Dubai: From Riches to Rags," *BBC Panorama*, April 6, 2009, http://news.bbc.co.uk/panorama/low/front_page/newsid_7981000/7981320.stm (accessed December 10, 2011); "Building Towers, Cheating Workers: Exploitation of Migrant Construction Workers in the United Arab Emirates," Human Rights Watch, November 11, 2006, www.hrw.org/en/reports/2006/11/11/building-towers-cheating-workers (accessed December 10, 2011); Manuel Castells, *The Rise of the Network Society*, (Malden, MA: Blackwell Publishers, Inc., 1996); Pratap Chatterjee, "Ports of Profit: Dubai Does Brisk War Business," *Corpwatch*, February 25, 2006, www.corpwatch.org/article.php?id=13322 (accessed December 10, 2011); "Emiratis in Private Sector Make 0.3 Percent of Workforce," Gulfnews.com, June 24, 2009, http://gulfnews.com/news/gulf/uae/employment/emiratis-in-private-sector-make-0-3-percent-of-workforce-1.28862 (accessed December 10, 2011); Gregor McClenaghan and Suha Maayeh, "Hawala Money Transfers Defy Regulation Efforts," *The National*, August 26, 2008, www.thenational.ae/news/uae-news/hawala-money-transfers-defy-regulation-efforts (accessed December 10, 2011); "Site Worker Death Toll Exceeds 800," *Construction Week* 83 (August 6–19 2005); "Tehran Ranks Dubai's 2nd Trade Partner," PressTV, December 13,

2010, www.presstv.ir/detail/155255.html (accessed December 10, 2011); "UAE Authorities Deport Thousands of Sex Workers," *Gulf Times*, March 16, 2007, www.gulftimes.com/site/topics/printArticle.asp?cu_no=2&item_no=138407&version=1&template_id=37&parent_id=17 (accessed May 2, 2011); Kevin Whitelaw, "Dubai Rides the Oil Boom, *U.S. News and World Report*, June 5, 2008, www.usnews.com/news/world/articles/2008/06/05/dubai-rides-the-oil-boom (accessed December 10, 2011).

Index